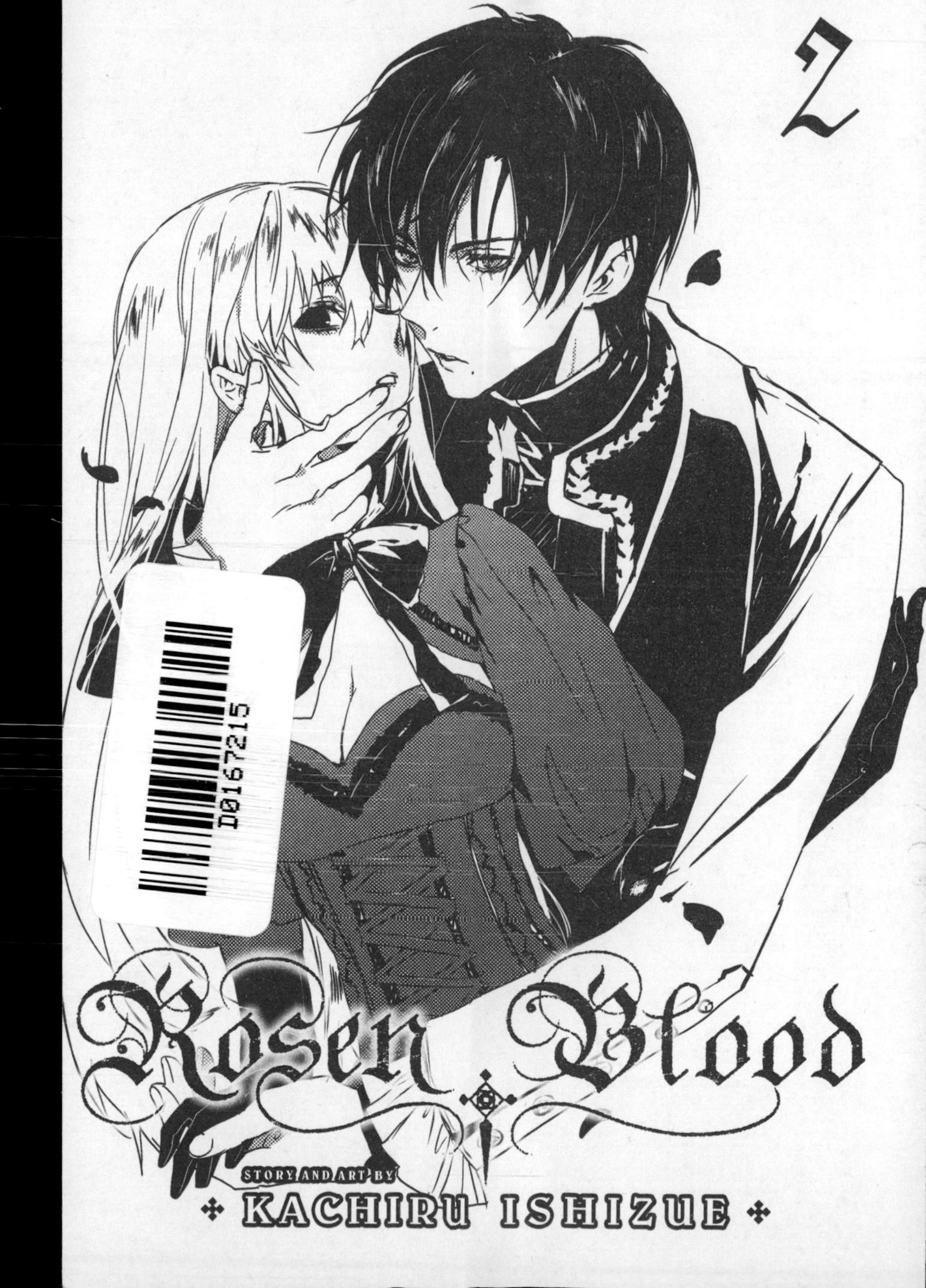

2

Rosen Blood

STORY AND ART BY

KACHIRU ISHIZUE

Characters

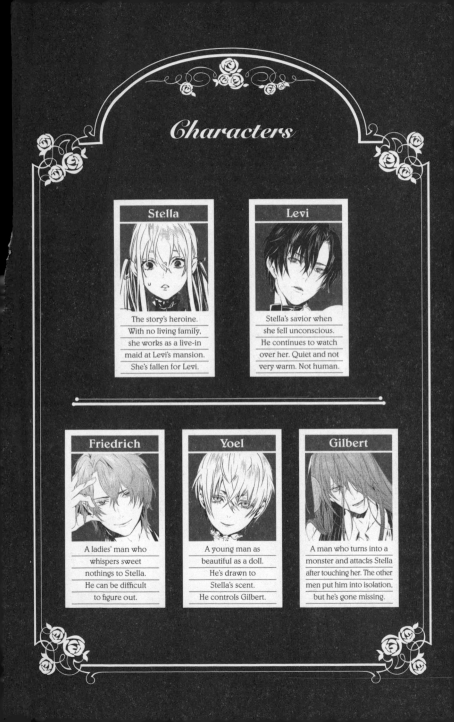

Stella

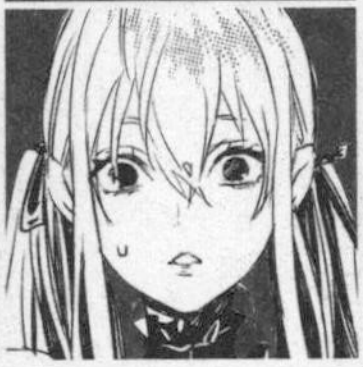

The story's heroine. With no living family, she works as a live-in maid at Levi's mansion. She's fallen for Levi.

Levi

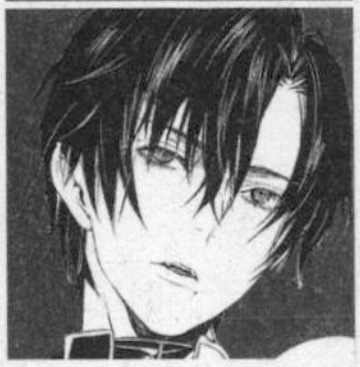

Stella's savior when she fell unconscious. He continues to watch over her. Quiet and not very warm. Not human.

Friedrich

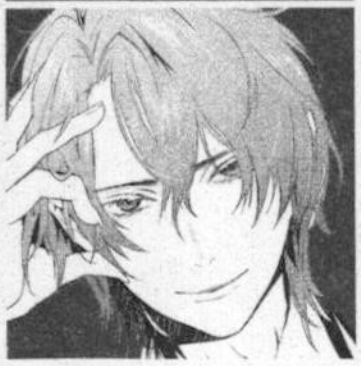

A ladies' man who whispers sweet nothings to Stella. He can be difficult to figure out.

Yoel

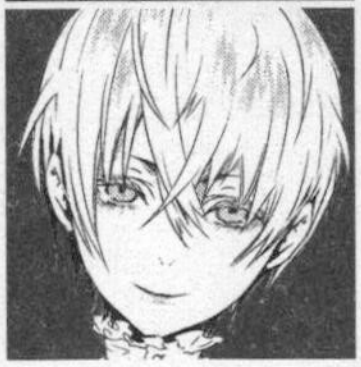

A young man as beautiful as a doll. He's drawn to Stella's scent. He controls Gilbert.

Gilbert

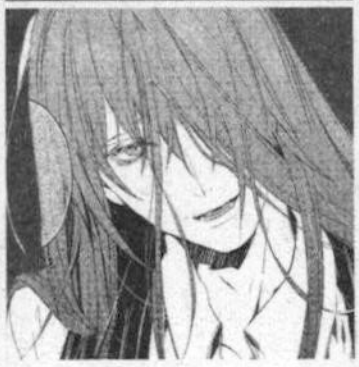

A man who turns into a monster and attacks Stella after touching her. The other men put him into isolation, but he's gone missing.

Story

A young girl named Stella begins working at an isolated mansion that's home to four strange but beautiful men: Levi, Friedrich, Yoel, and Gilbert. Stella keeps finding herself in horrifying situations, and Gilbert nearly assaults her. Still, she slowly learns to get along with the residents…and discovers the truth about their nonhuman nature and their need to consume crystallized humans. What will become of Stella as she proposes to feed these men with her own bodily fluids?

I WILL...
...BECOME YOUR FOOD SOURCE.

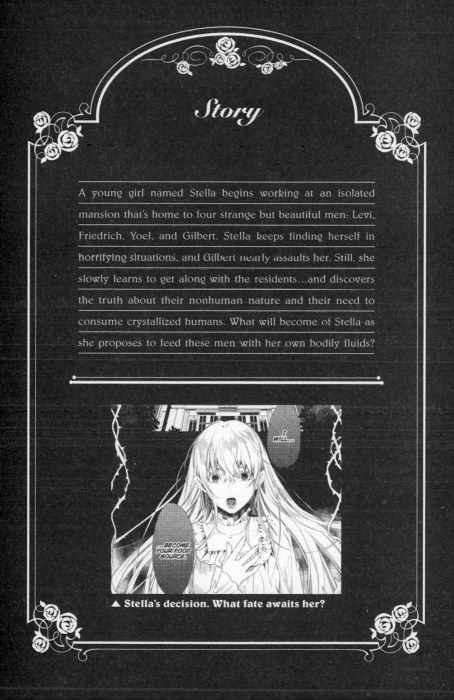

▲ **Stella's decision. What fate awaits her?**

Contents

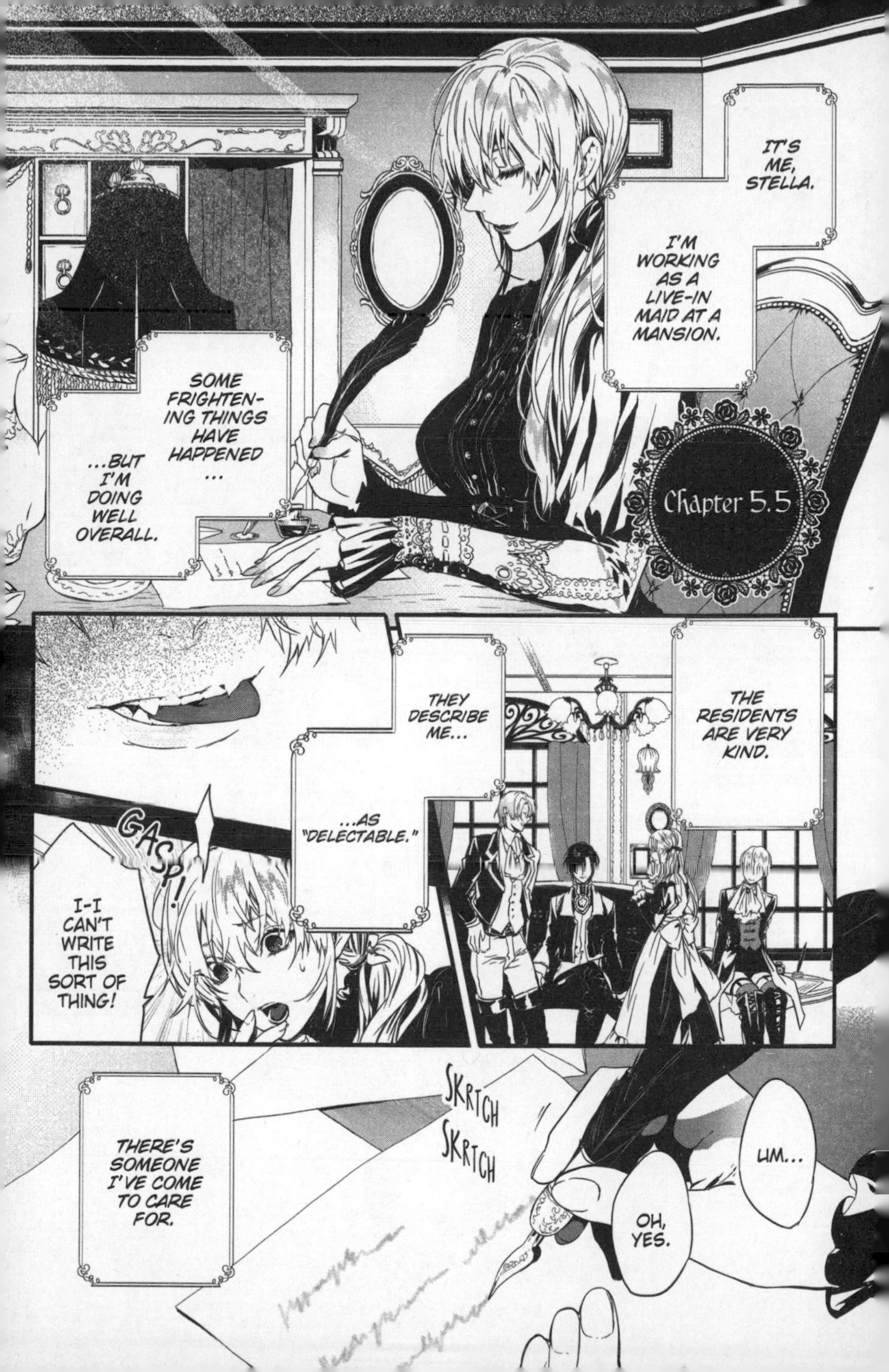
IT'S ME, STELLA.
I'M WORKING AS A LIVE-IN MAID AT A MANSION.
Chapter 5.5
SOME FRIGHTENING THINGS HAVE HAPPENED...
...BUT I'M DOING WELL OVERALL.
THE RESIDENTS ARE VERY KIND.
THEY DESCRIBE ME...
...AS "DELECTABLE."
GASP!
I-I CAN'T WRITE THIS SORT OF THING!
UM...
OH, YES.
SKRTCH
SKRTCH
THERE'S SOMEONE I'VE COME TO CARE FOR.

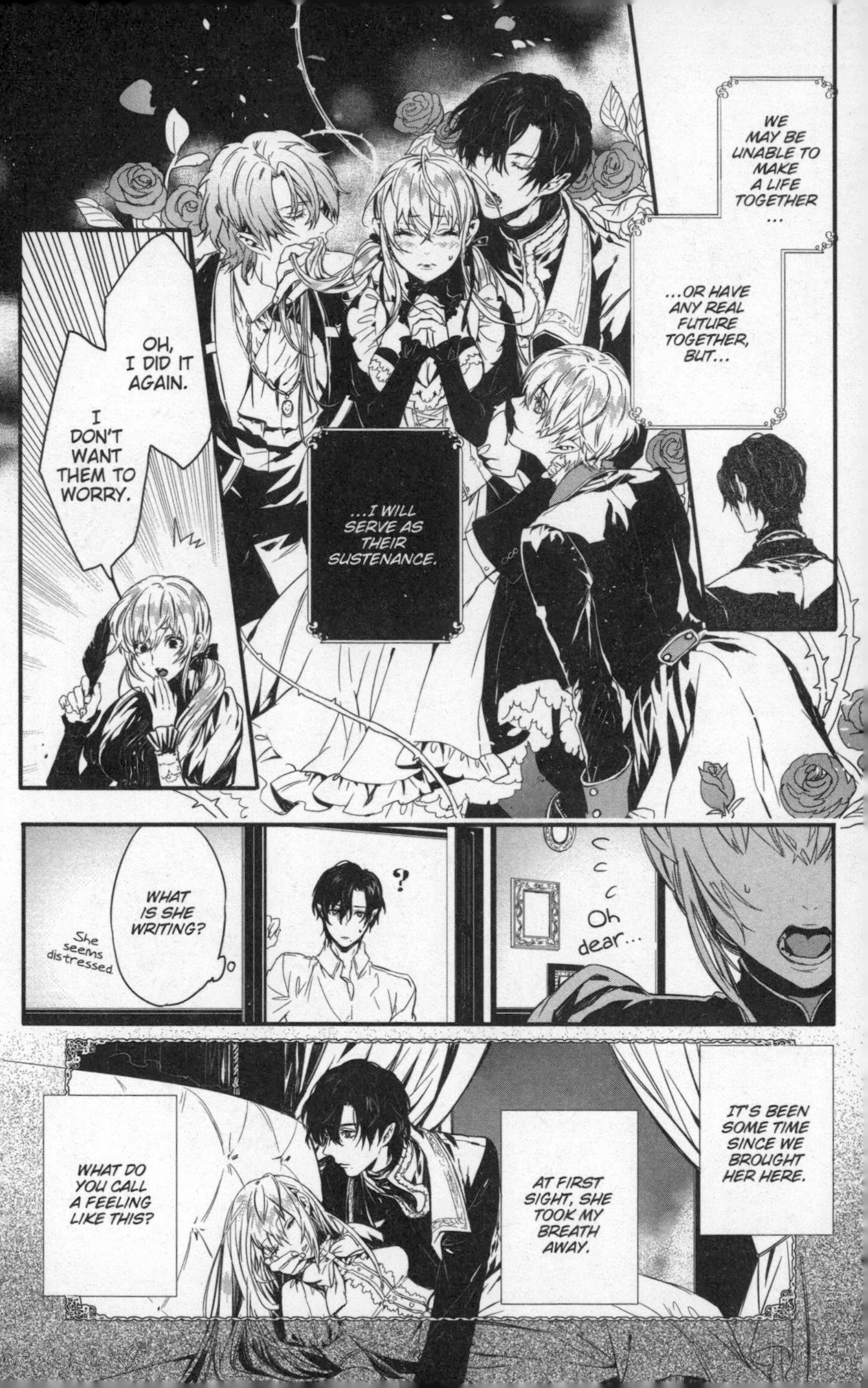
WE MAY BE UNABLE TO MAKE A LIFE TOGETHER ...
...OR HAVE ANY REAL FUTURE TOGETHER, BUT...
...I WILL SERVE AS THEIR SUSTENANCE.
OH, I DID IT AGAIN.
I DON'T WANT THEM TO WORRY.
Oh dear...
?
WHAT IS SHE WRITING?
She seems distressed.
IT'S BEEN SOME TIME SINCE WE BROUGHT HER HERE.
AT FIRST SIGHT, SHE TOOK MY BREATH AWAY.
WHAT DO YOU CALL A FEELING LIKE THIS?

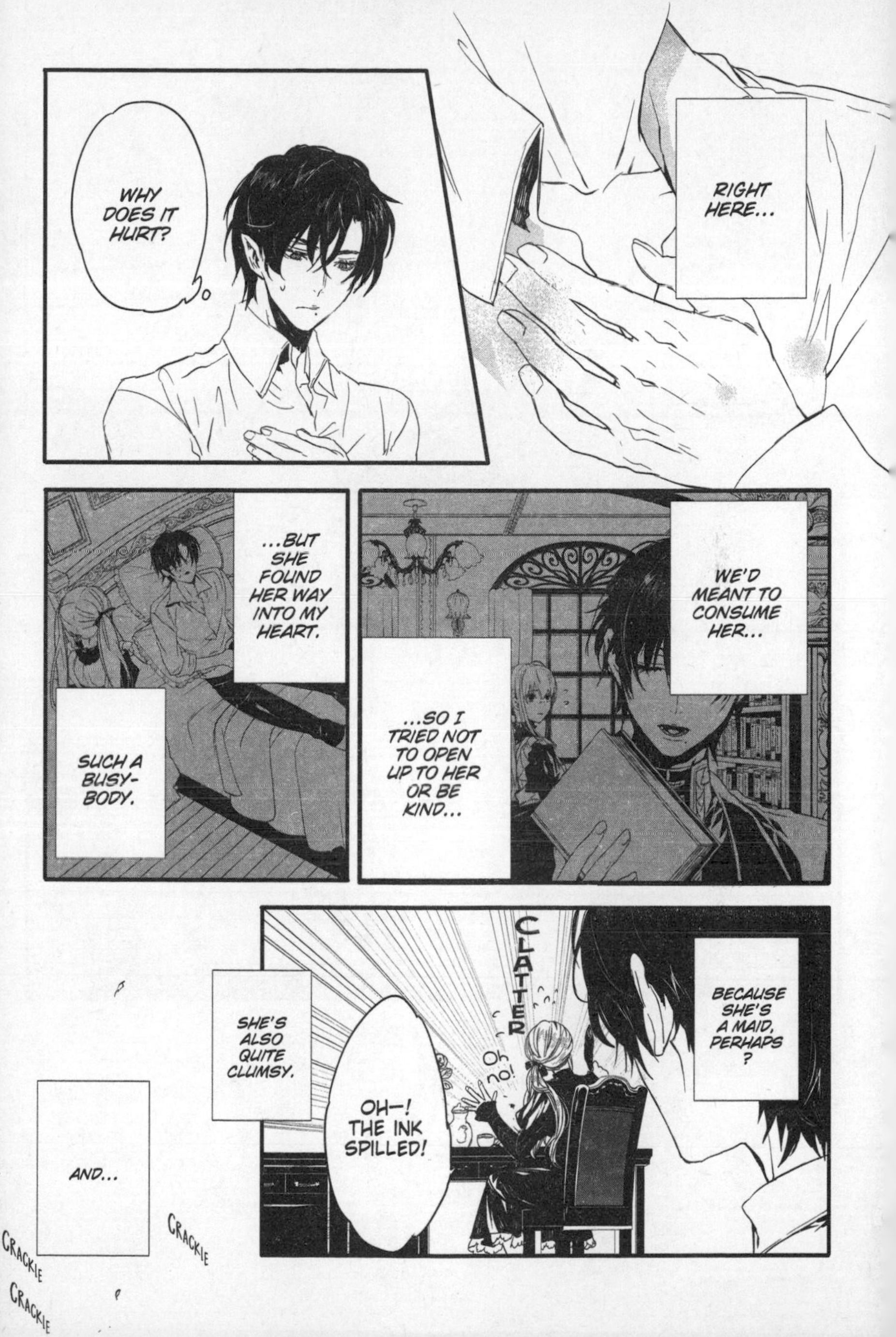
RIGHT HERE...
WHY DOES IT HURT?
WE'D MEANT TO CONSUME HER...
...SO I TRIED NOT TO OPEN UP TO HER OR BE KIND...
...BUT SHE FOUND HER WAY INTO MY HEART.
SUCH A BUSY-BODY.
BECAUSE SHE'S A MAID, PERHAPS?
CLATTER
Oh no!
OH—! THE INK SPILLED!
SHE'S ALSO QUITE CLUMSY.
AND...
CRACKLE
CRACKLE
CRACKLE

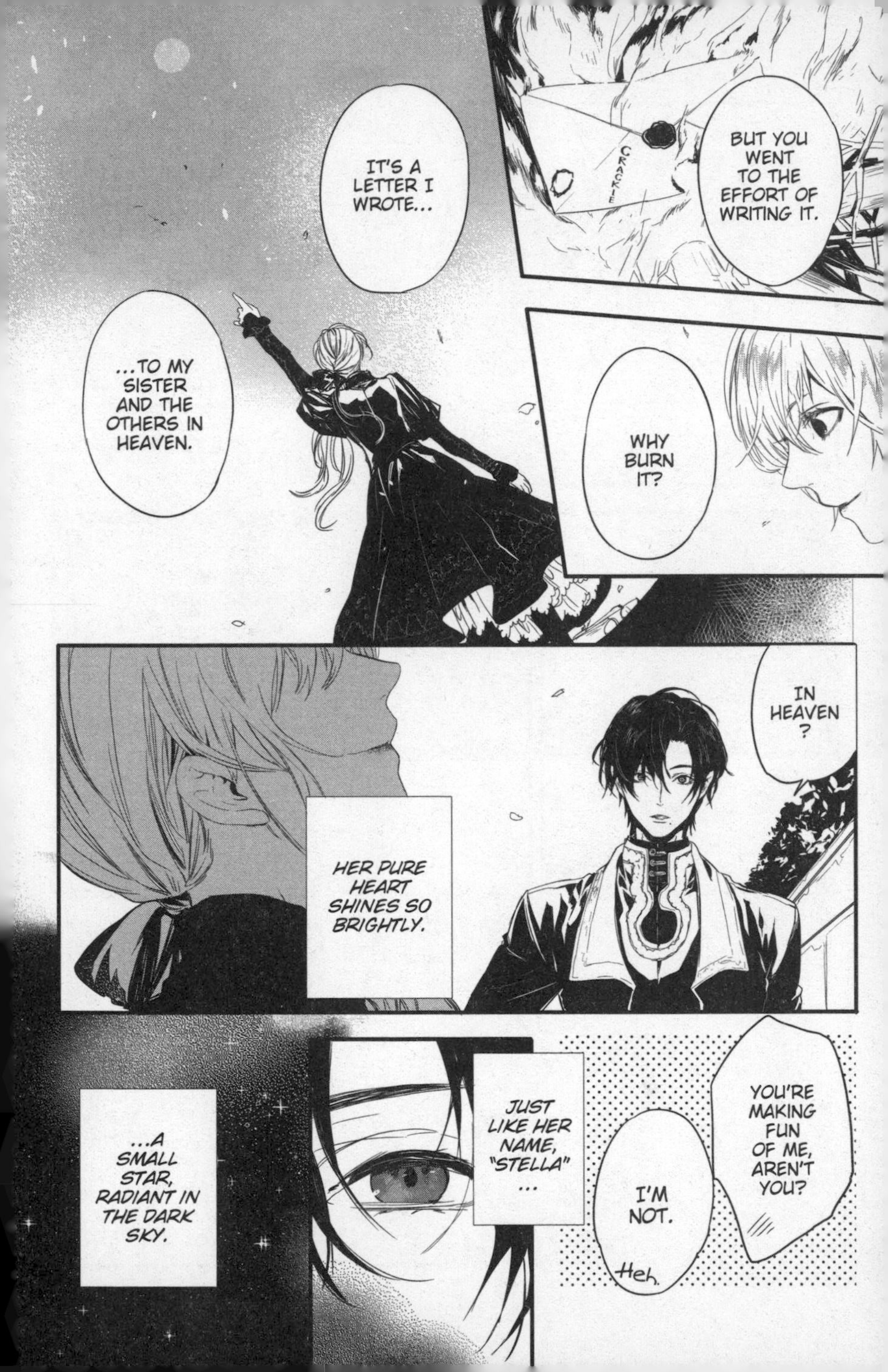
BUT YOU WENT TO THE EFFORT OF WRITING IT.
CRACKLE
WHY BURN IT?
IT'S A LETTER I WROTE...
...TO MY SISTER AND THE OTHERS IN HEAVEN.
IN HEAVEN?
HER PURE HEART SHINES SO BRIGHTLY.
YOU'RE MAKING FUN OF ME, AREN'T YOU?
I'M NOT.
Heh.
JUST LIKE HER NAME, "STELLA"...
...A SMALL STAR, RADIANT IN THE DARK SKY.

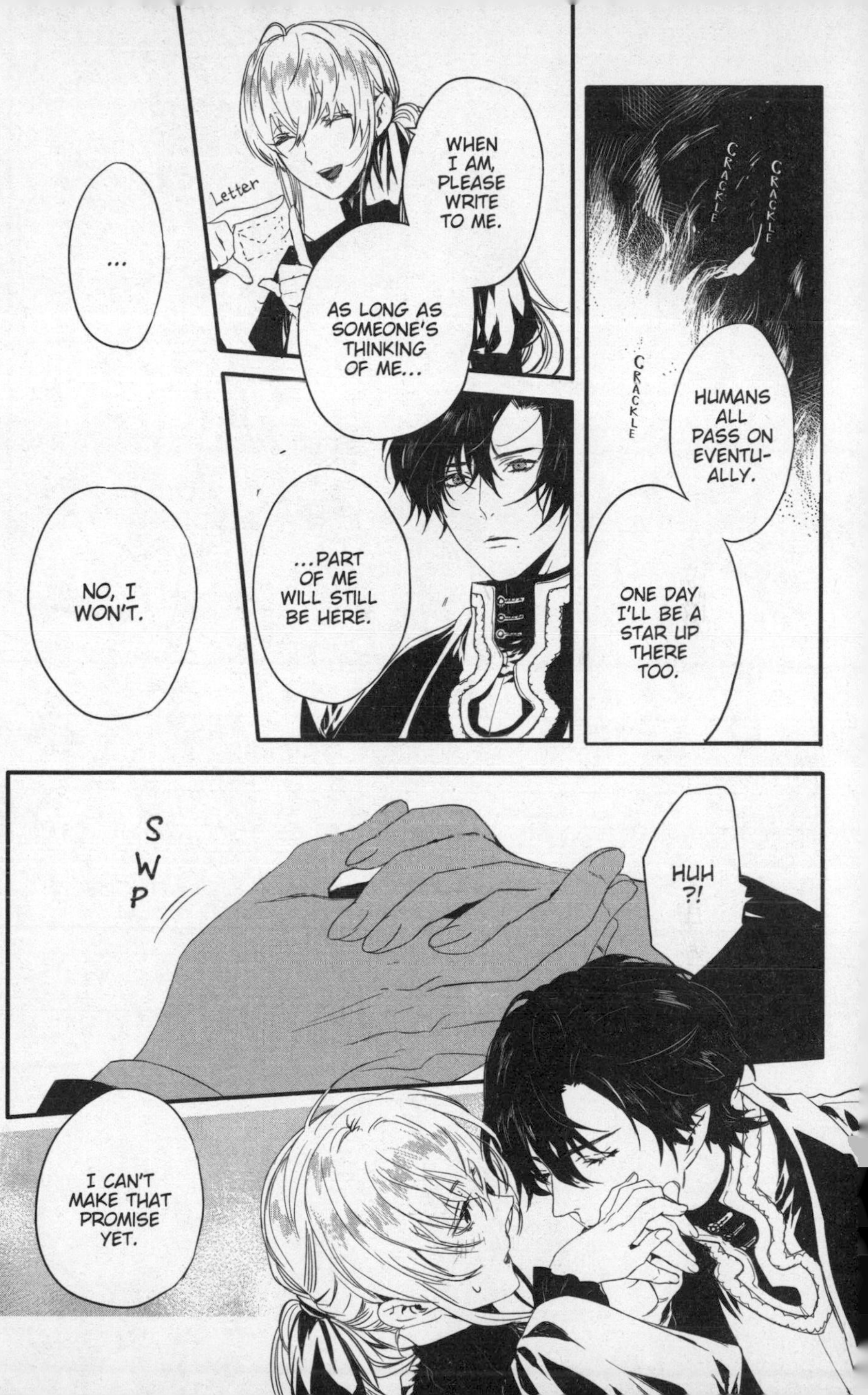
CRACKLE CRACKLE
CRACKLE
HUMANS ALL PASS ON EVENTUALLY.
ONE DAY I'LL BE A STAR UP THERE TOO.
WHEN I AM, PLEASE WRITE TO ME.
Letter
AS LONG AS SOMEONE'S THINKING OF ME...
...PART OF ME WILL STILL BE HERE.
...
NO, I WON'T.
HUH ?!
SWP
I CAN'T MAKE THAT PROMISE YET.

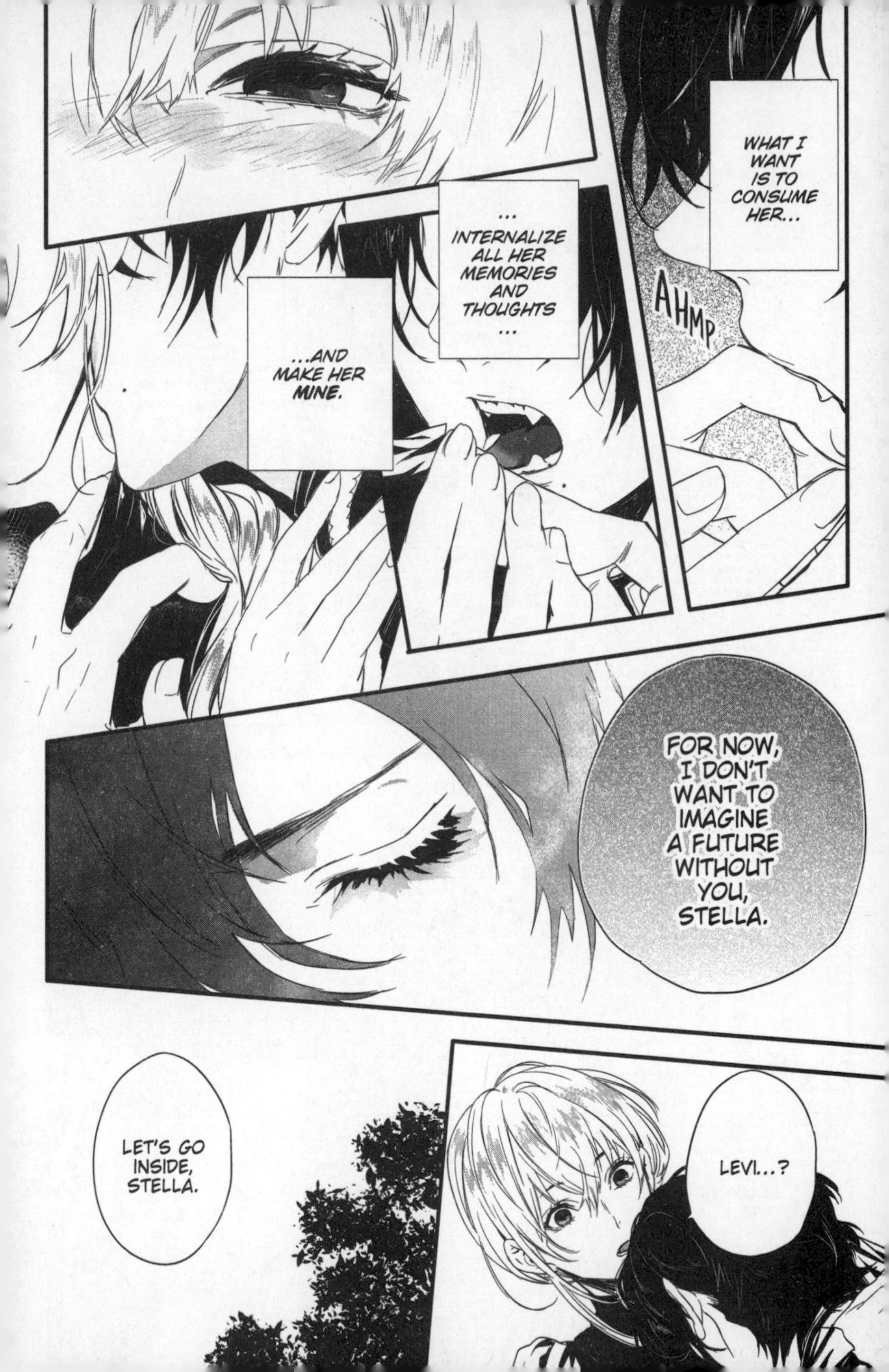
WHAT I WANT IS TO CONSUME HER...
AHMP
... INTERNALIZE ALL HER MEMORIES AND THOUGHTS ...
...AND MAKE HER MINE.
FOR NOW, I DON'T WANT TO IMAGINE A FUTURE WITHOUT YOU, STELLA.
LEVI...?
LET'S GO INSIDE, STELLA.

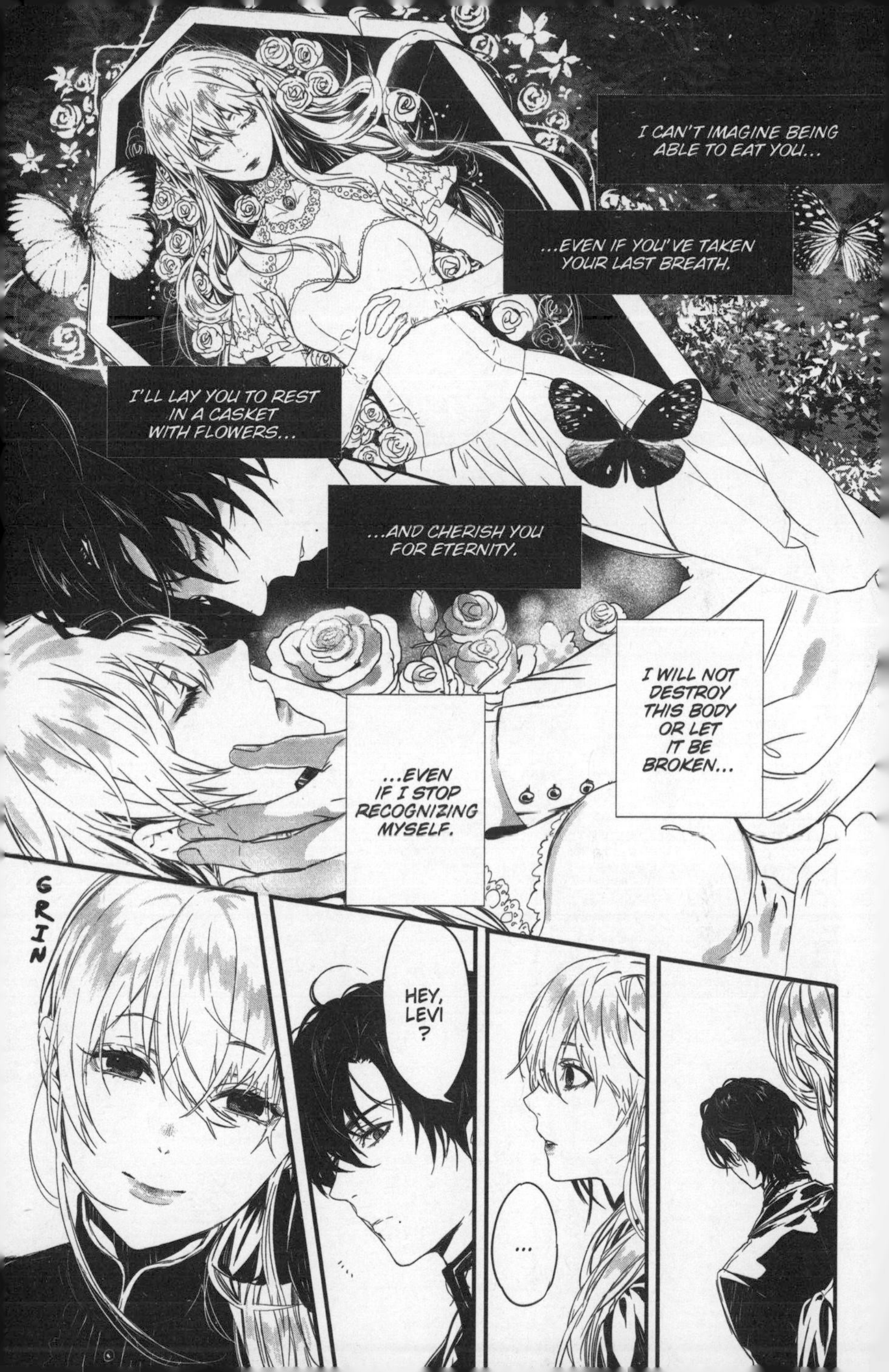
I CAN'T IMAGINE BEING ABLE TO EAT YOU...
...EVEN IF YOU'VE TAKEN YOUR LAST BREATH.
I'LL LAY YOU TO REST IN A CASKET WITH FLOWERS...
...AND CHERISH YOU FOR ETERNITY.
I WILL NOT DESTROY THIS BODY OR LET IT BE BROKEN...
...EVEN IF I STOP RECOGNIZING MYSELF.
...
HEY, LEVI?
GRIN

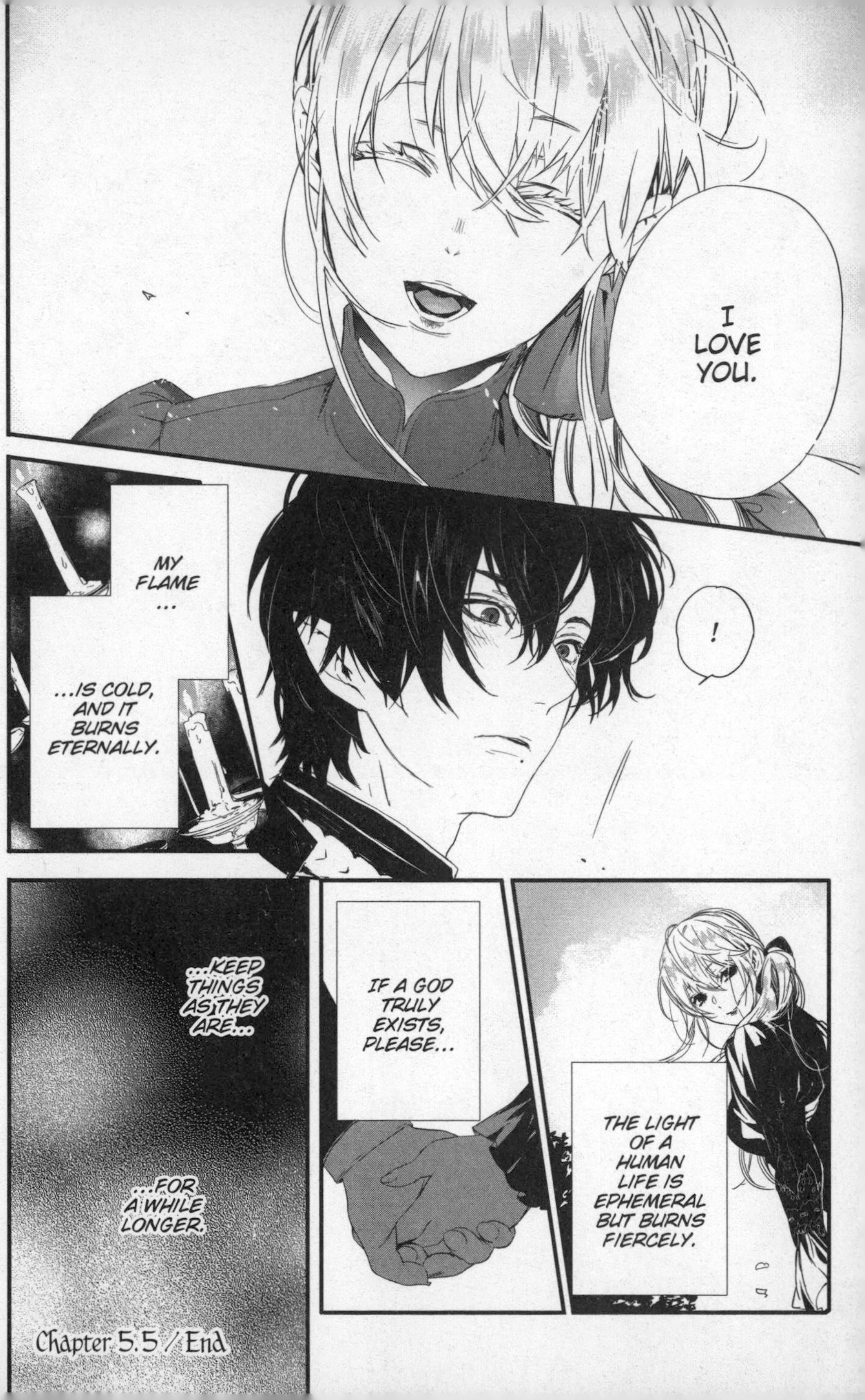
I LOVE YOU.
!
MY FLAME...
...IS COLD, AND IT BURNS ETERNALLY.
THE LIGHT OF A HUMAN LIFE IS EPHEMERAL BUT BURNS FIERCELY.
IF A GOD TRULY EXISTS, PLEASE...
...KEEP THINGS AS THEY ARE...
...FOR A WHILE LONGER.
Chapter 5.5 / End

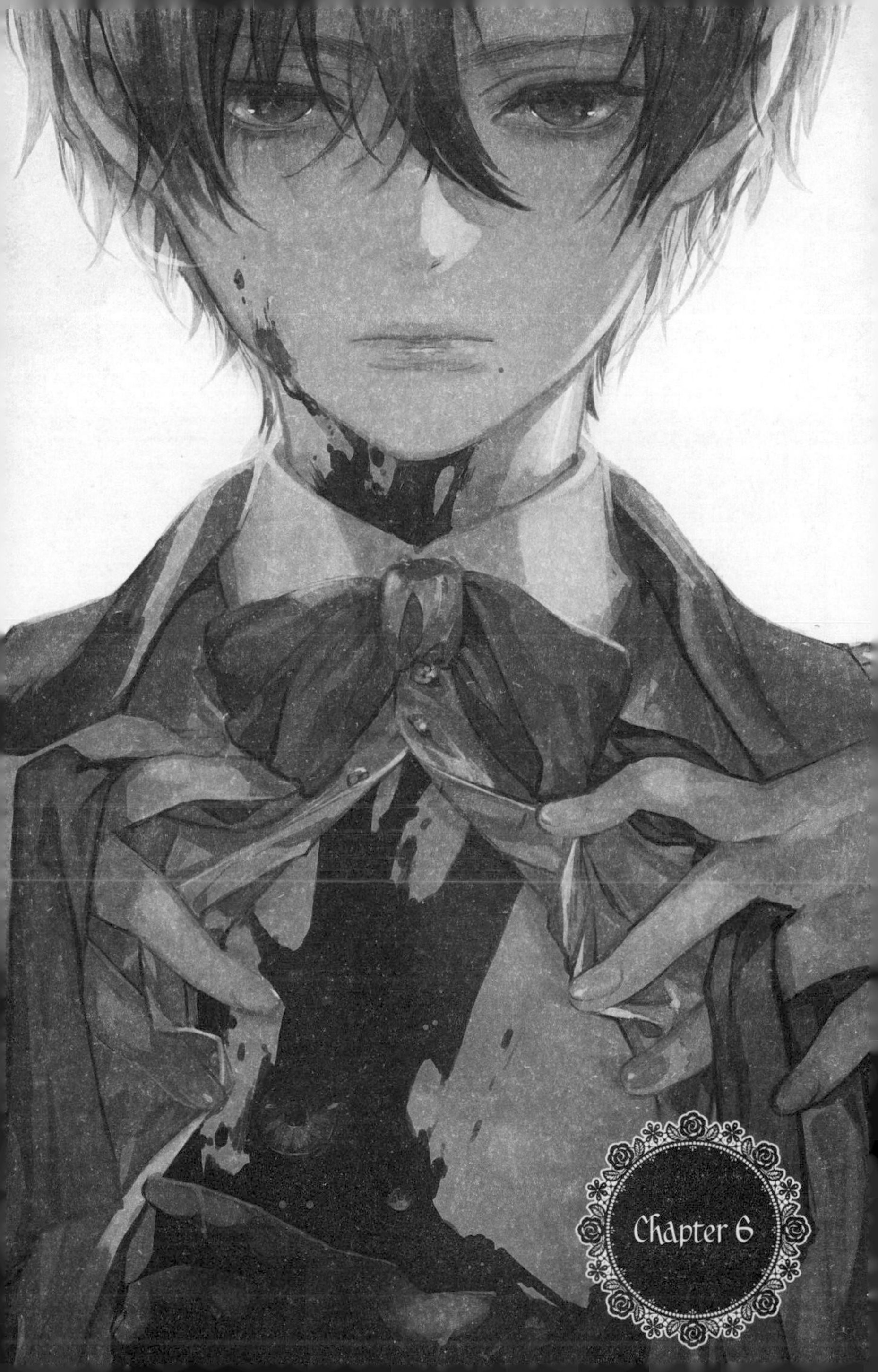
Chapter 6

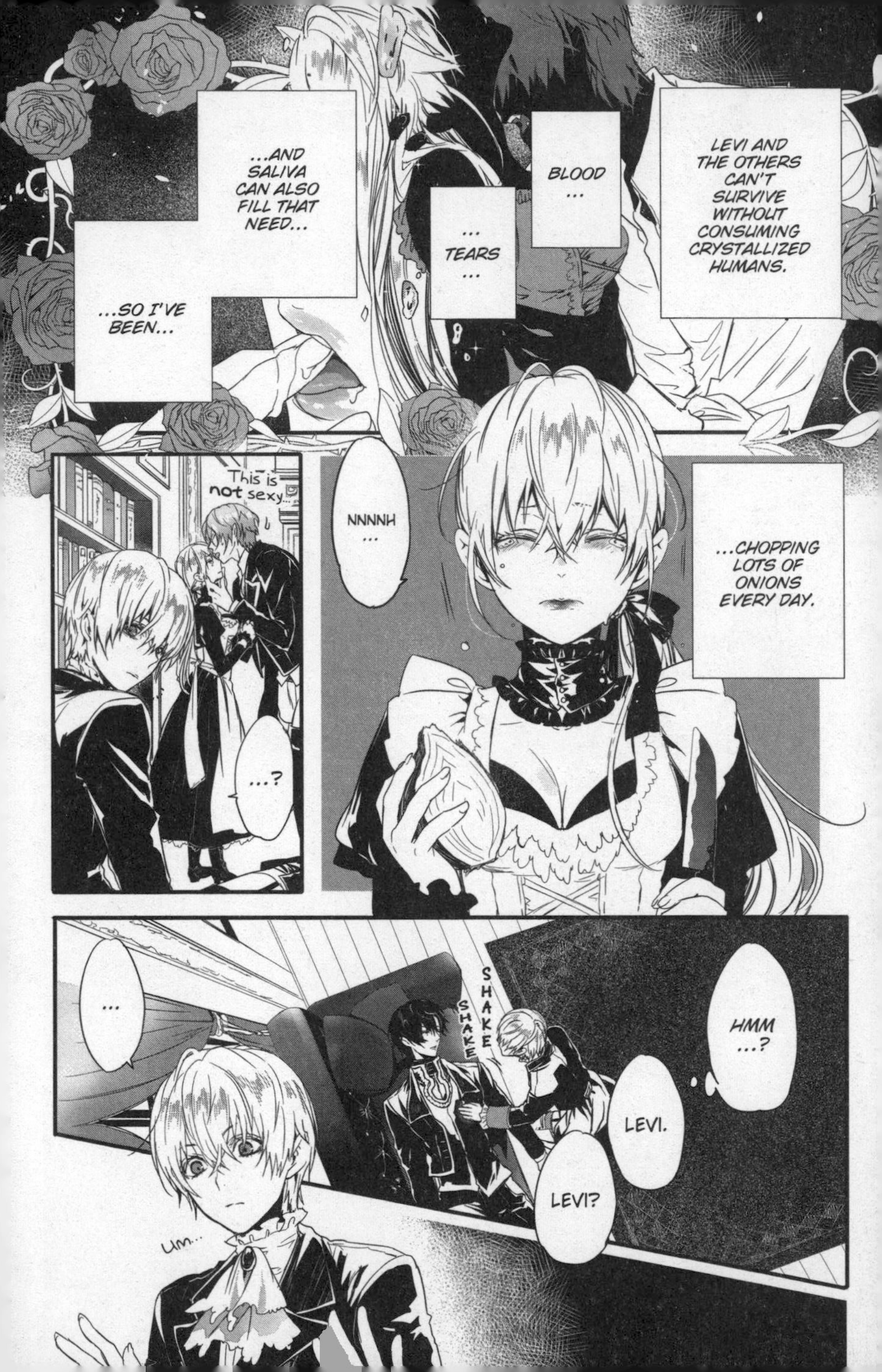
LEVI AND THE OTHERS CAN'T SURVIVE WITHOUT CONSUMING CRYSTALLIZED HUMANS.
BLOOD...
...TEARS...
...AND SALIVA CAN ALSO FILL THAT NEED...
...SO I'VE BEEN...
...CHOPPING LOTS OF ONIONS EVERY DAY.
NNNNH...
This is not sexy...
...?
HMM...?
LEVI.
LEVI?
SHAKE
SHAKE
...
Um...

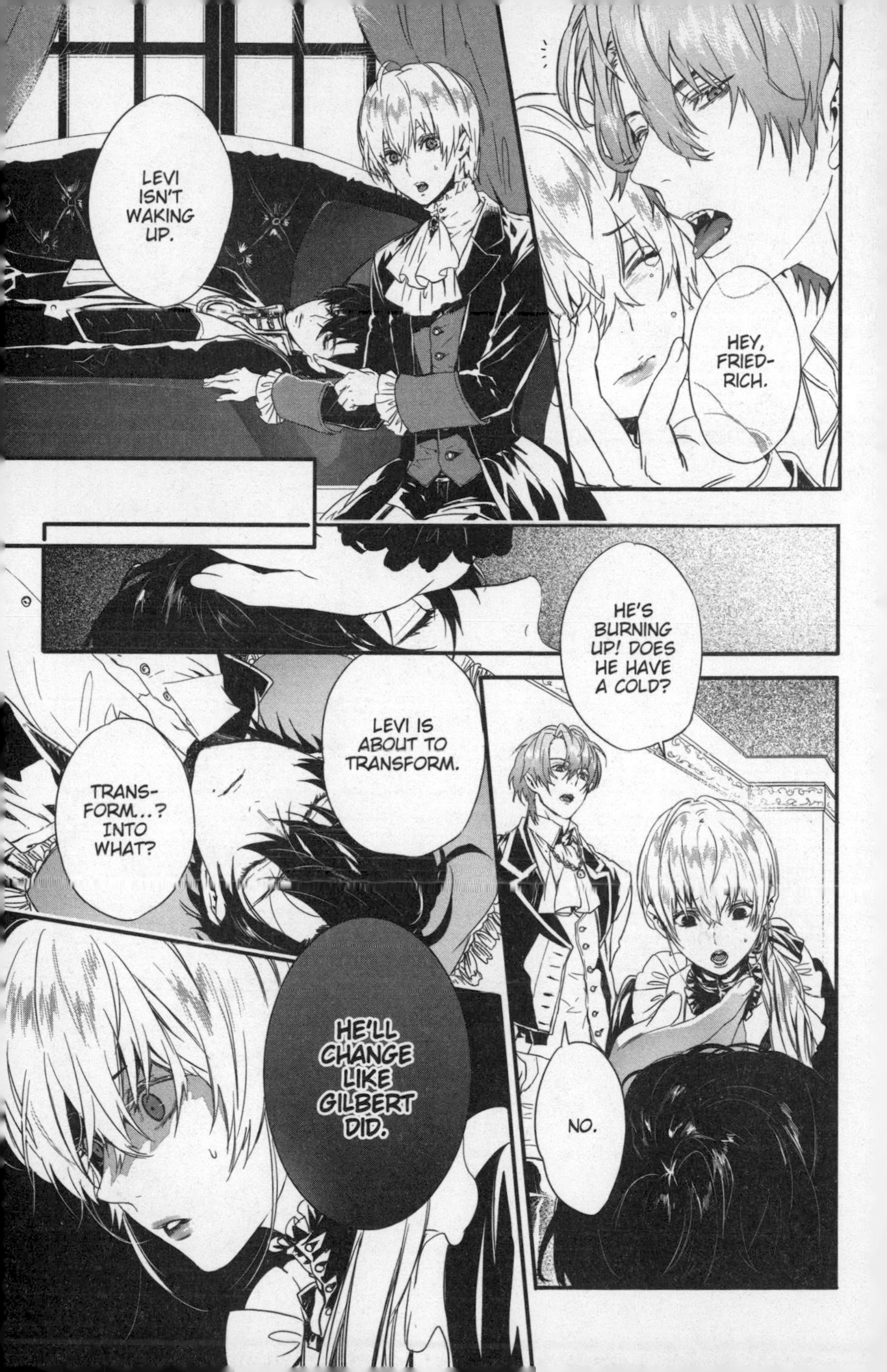
HEY, FRIED-RICH.
LEVI ISN'T WAKING UP.
HE'S BURNING UP! DOES HE HAVE A COLD?
NO.
LEVI IS ABOUT TO TRANSFORM.
TRANS-FORM...? INTO WHAT?
HE'LL CHANGE LIKE GILBERT DID.

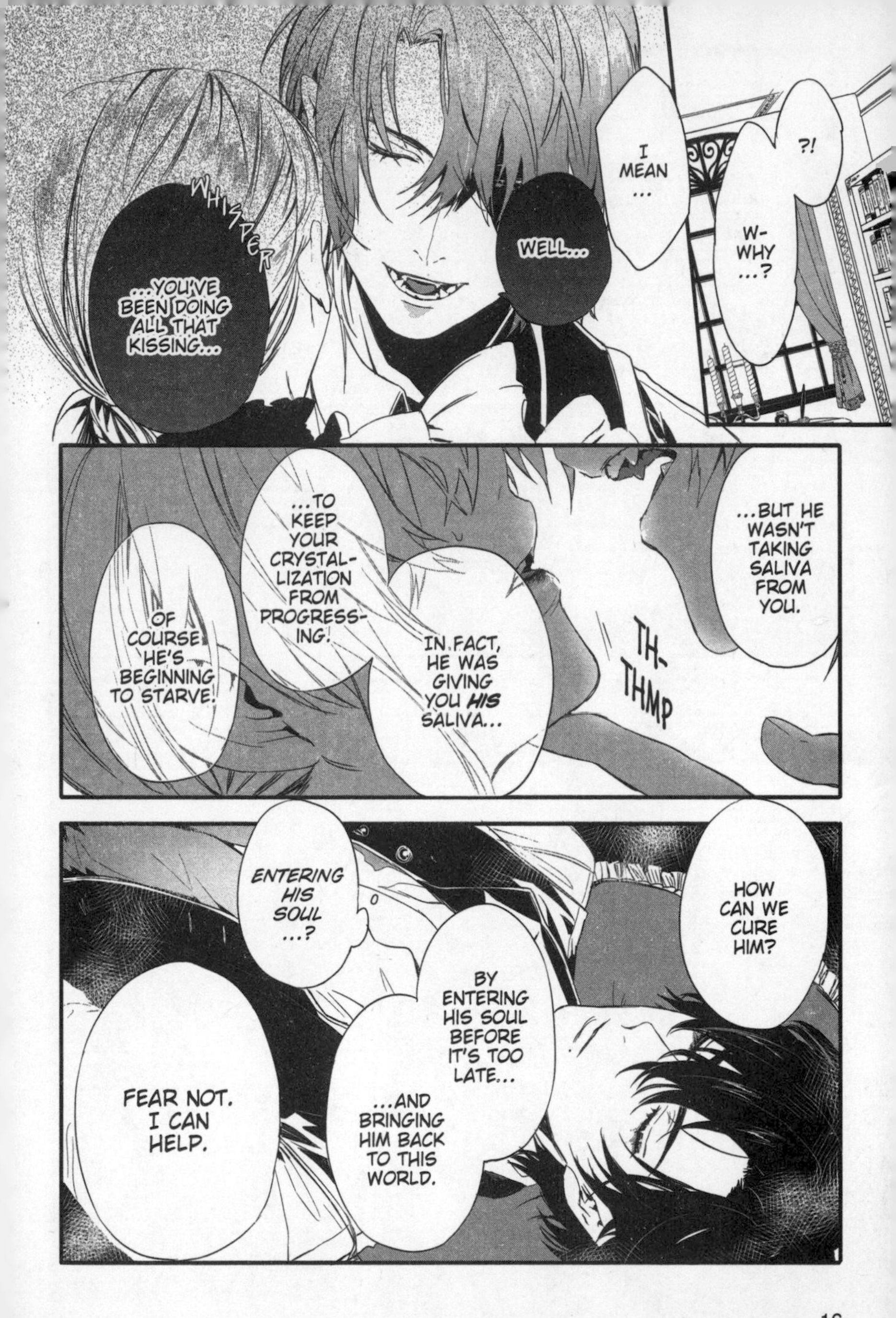
?!
W-WHY...?
I MEAN...
WELL...
WHISPER
...YOU'VE BEEN DOING ALL THAT KISSING...
...BUT HE WASN'T TAKING SALIVA FROM YOU.
TH-THMP
IN FACT, HE WAS GIVING YOU *HIS* SALIVA...
...TO KEEP YOUR CRYSTALLIZATION FROM PROGRESSING.
OF COURSE HE'S BEGINNING TO STARVE.
HOW CAN WE CURE HIM?
BY ENTERING HIS SOUL BEFORE IT'S TOO LATE...
...AND BRINGING HIM BACK TO THIS WORLD.
ENTERING HIS SOUL...?
FEAR NOT. I CAN HELP.

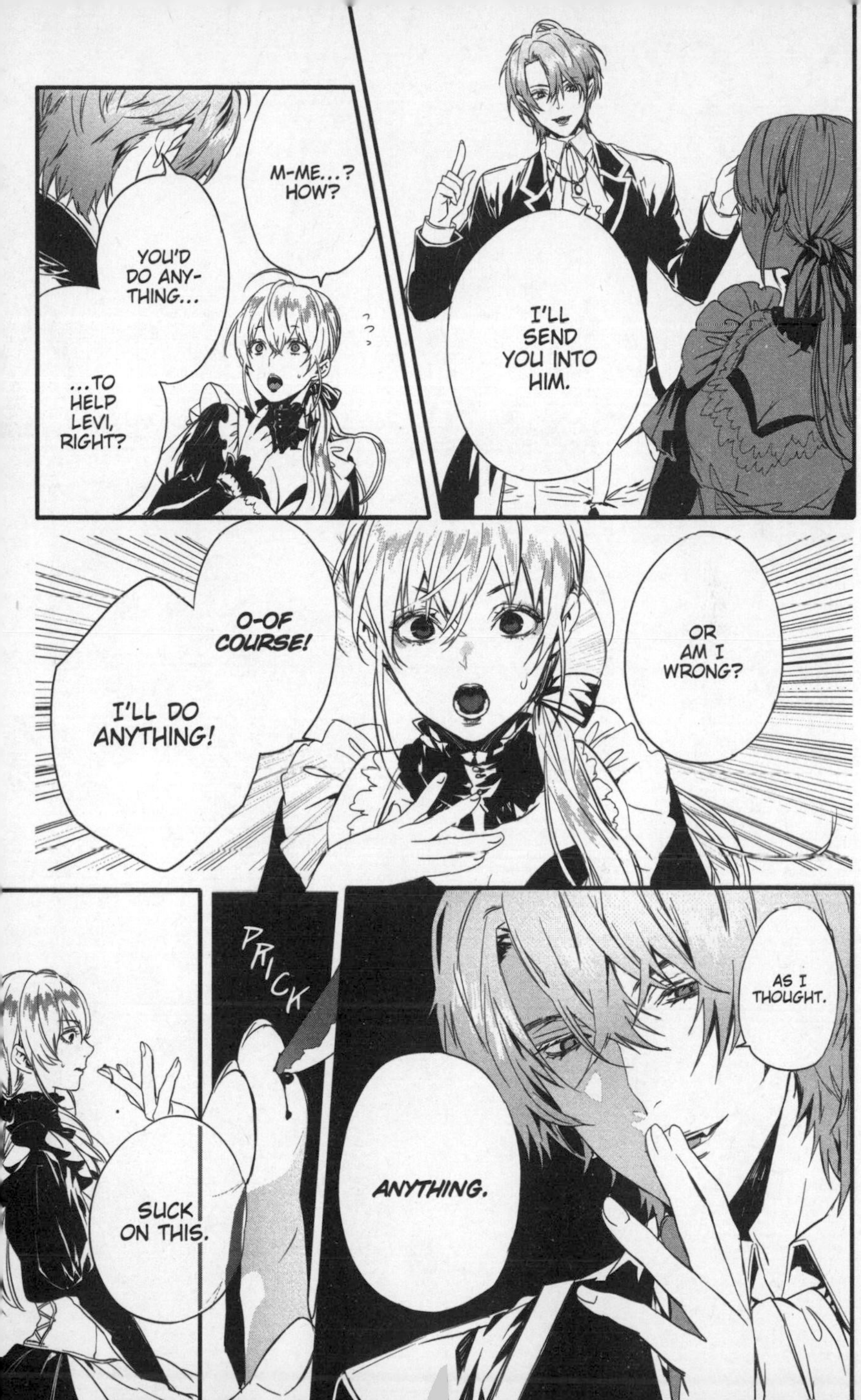
I'LL SEND YOU INTO HIM.
M-ME...? HOW?
YOU'D DO ANY-THING...
...TO HELP LEVI, RIGHT?
OR AM I WRONG?
O-OF COURSE!
I'LL DO ANYTHING!
AS I THOUGHT.
ANYTHING.
PRICK
SUCK ON THIS.

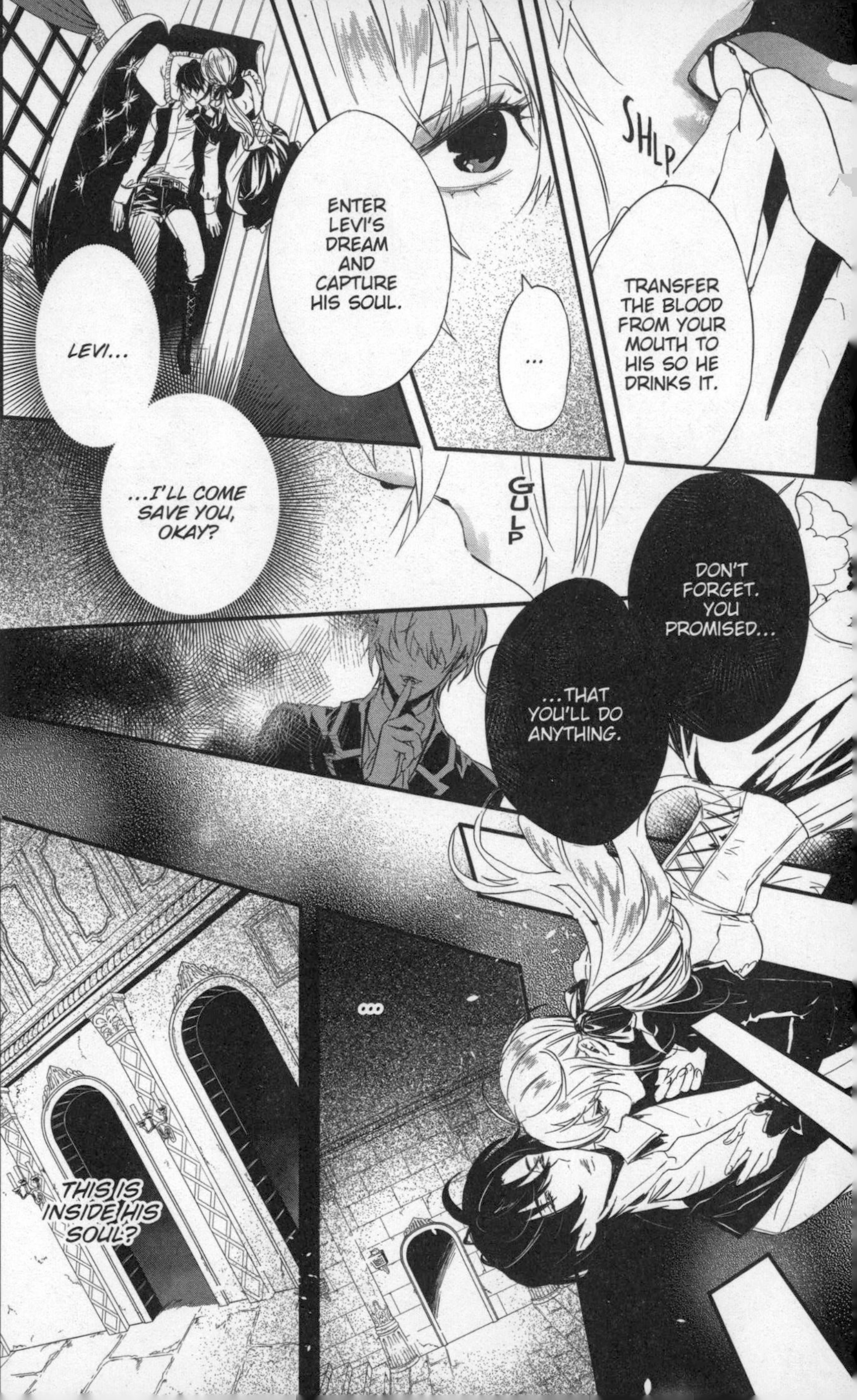
SHLP
TRANSFER THE BLOOD FROM YOUR MOUTH TO HIS SO HE DRINKS IT.
ENTER LEVI'S DREAM AND CAPTURE HIS SOUL.
...
LEVI...
...I'LL COME SAVE YOU, OKAY?
GULP
DON'T FORGET. YOU PROMISED...
...THAT YOU'LL DO ANYTHING.
THIS IS INSIDE HIS SOUL?

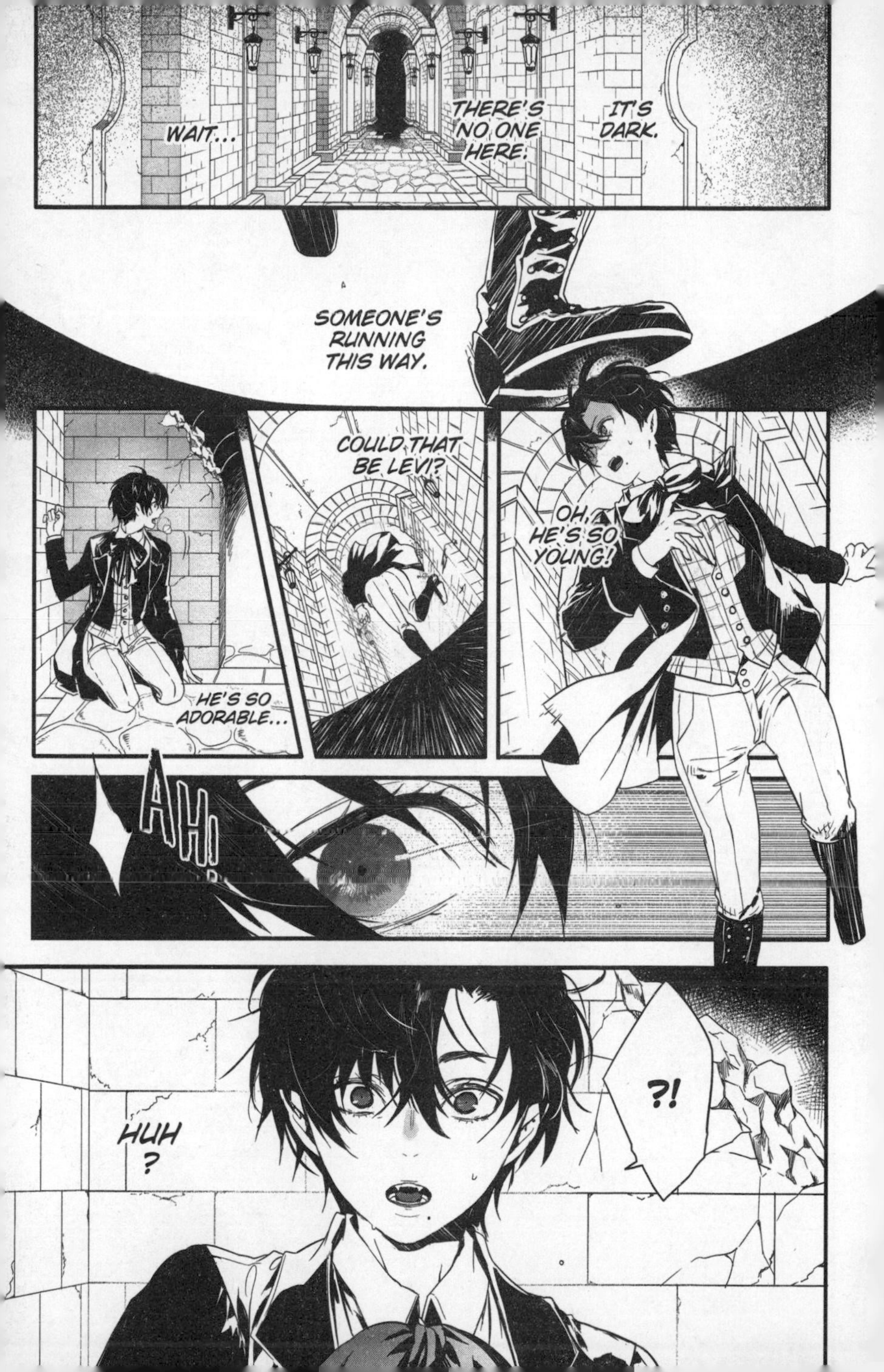
IT'S DARK.
THERE'S NO ONE HERE.
WAIT...
SOMEONE'S RUNNING THIS WAY.
OH, HE'S SO YOUNG!
COULD THAT BE LEVI?
HE'S SO ADORABLE...
AH!
?!
HUH ?

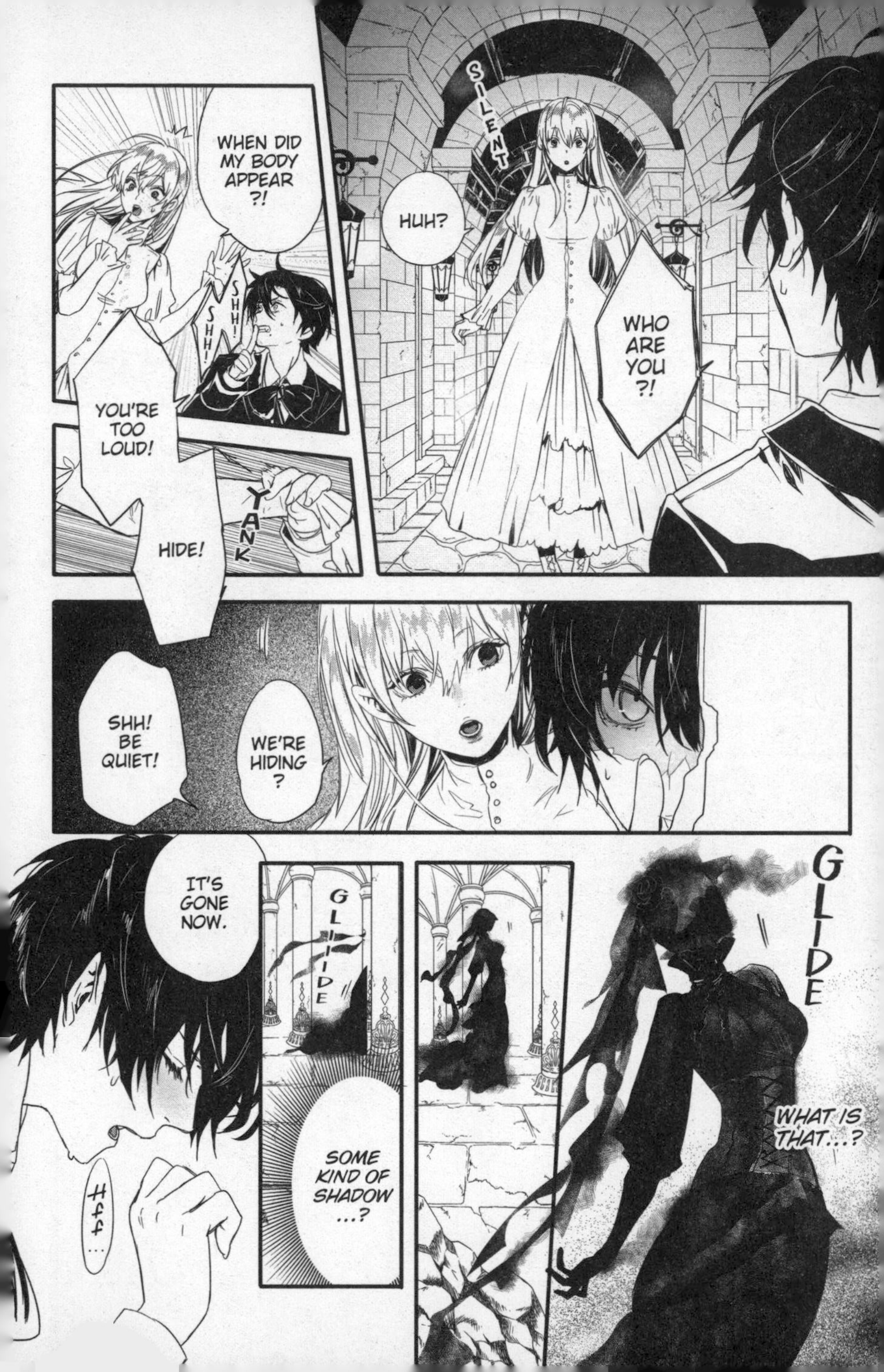
SILENT
WHO ARE YOU?!
HUH?
WHEN DID MY BODY APPEAR?!
SHH! SHH!
YOU'RE TOO LOUD!
YANK
HIDE!
WE'RE HIDING?
SHH! BE QUIET!
GLIDE
WHAT IS THAT...?
GLIIIDE
SOME KIND OF SHADOW...?
IT'S GONE NOW.
Hff...

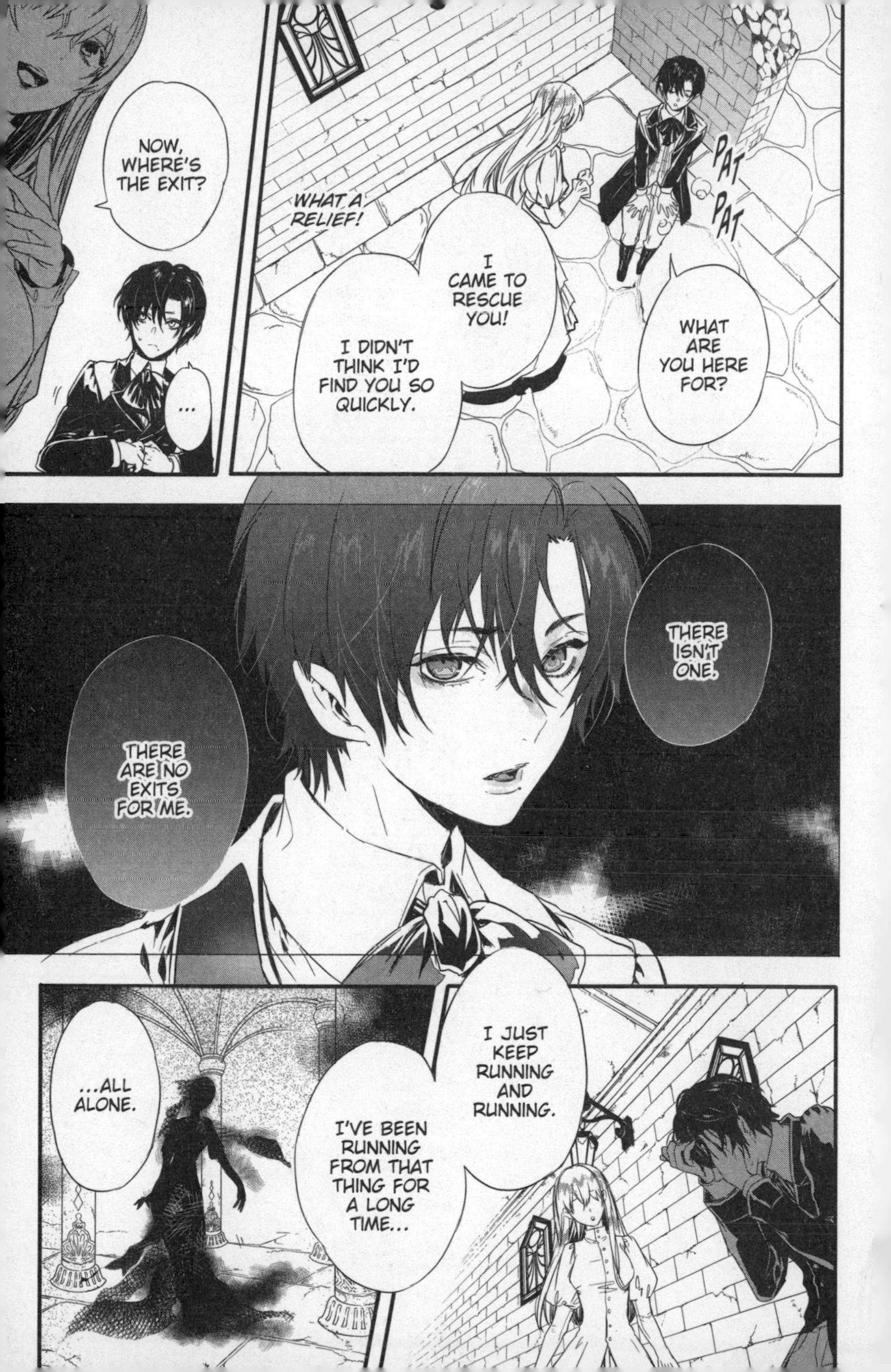
PAT PAT
WHAT ARE YOU HERE FOR?
I CAME TO RESCUE YOU!
WHAT A RELIEF!
I DIDN'T THINK I'D FIND YOU SO QUICKLY.
NOW, WHERE'S THE EXIT?
...
THERE ISN'T ONE.
THERE ARE NO EXITS FOR ME.
I JUST KEEP RUNNING AND RUNNING.
I'VE BEEN RUNNING FROM THAT THING FOR A LONG TIME...
...ALL ALONE.

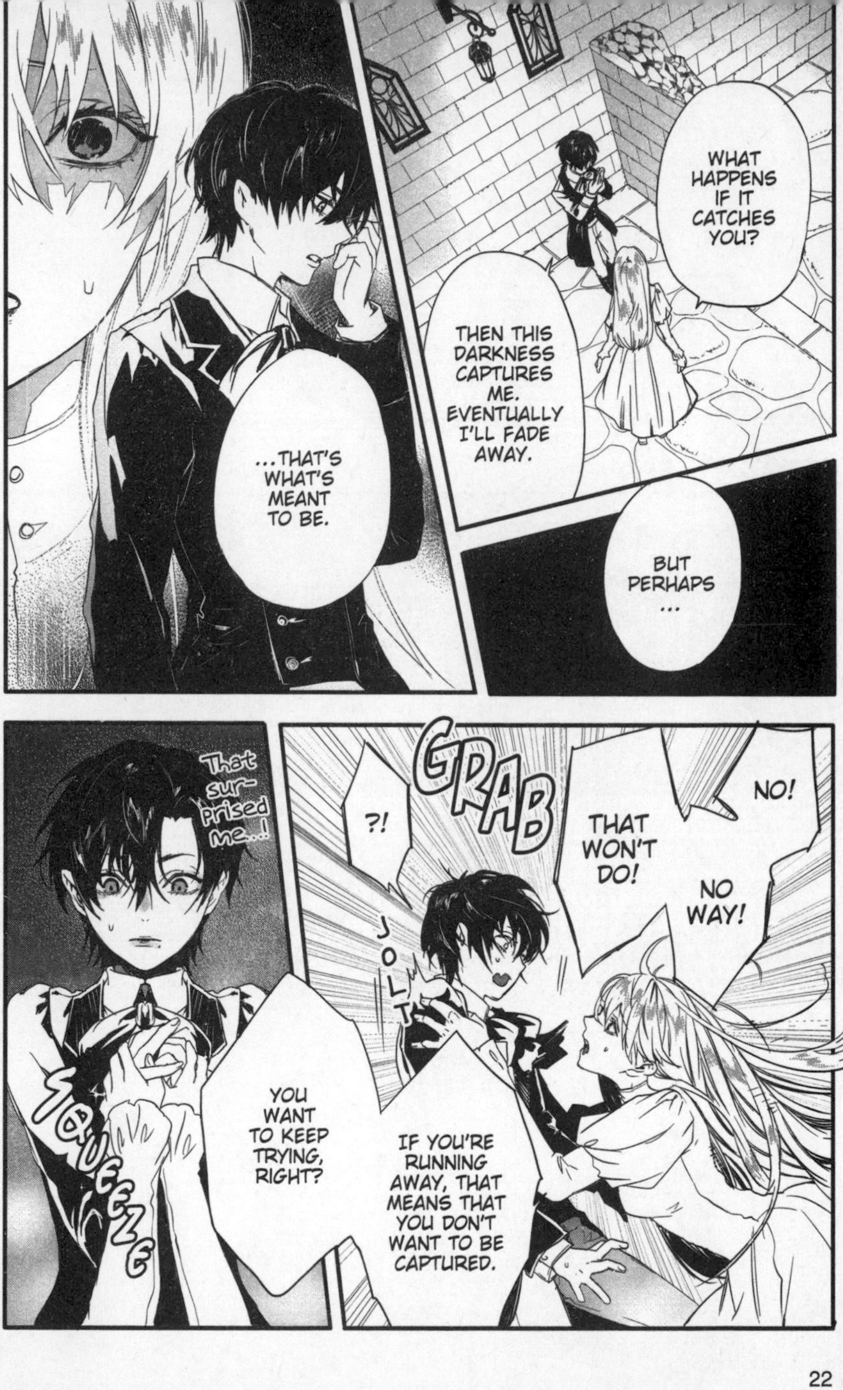
WHAT HAPPENS IF IT CATCHES YOU?
THEN THIS DARKNESS CAPTURES ME. EVENTUALLY I'LL FADE AWAY.
BUT PERHAPS ...
...THAT'S WHAT'S MEANT TO BE.
NO!
NO WAY!
THAT WON'T DO!
GRAB
?!
JOLT
IF YOU'RE RUNNING AWAY, THAT MEANS THAT YOU DON'T WANT TO BE CAPTURED.
YOU WANT TO KEEP TRYING, RIGHT?
That surprised me...!
SQUEEZE

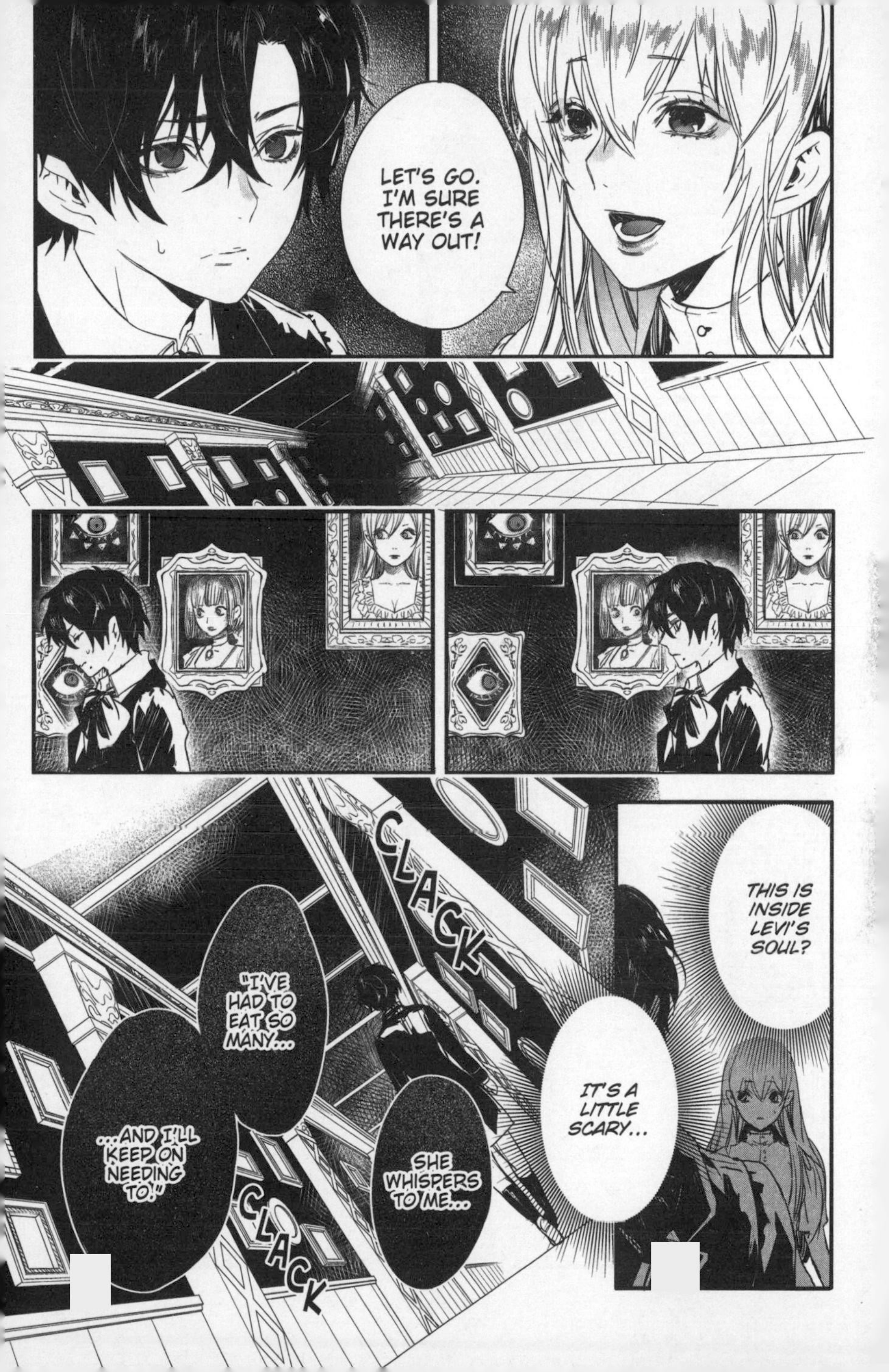
LET'S GO. I'M SURE THERE'S A WAY OUT!
THIS IS INSIDE LEVI'S SOUL?
IT'S A LITTLE SCARY...
CLACK
"I'VE HAD TO EAT SO MANY...
...AND I'LL KEEP ON NEEDING TO."
SHE WHISPERS TO ME...
CLACK

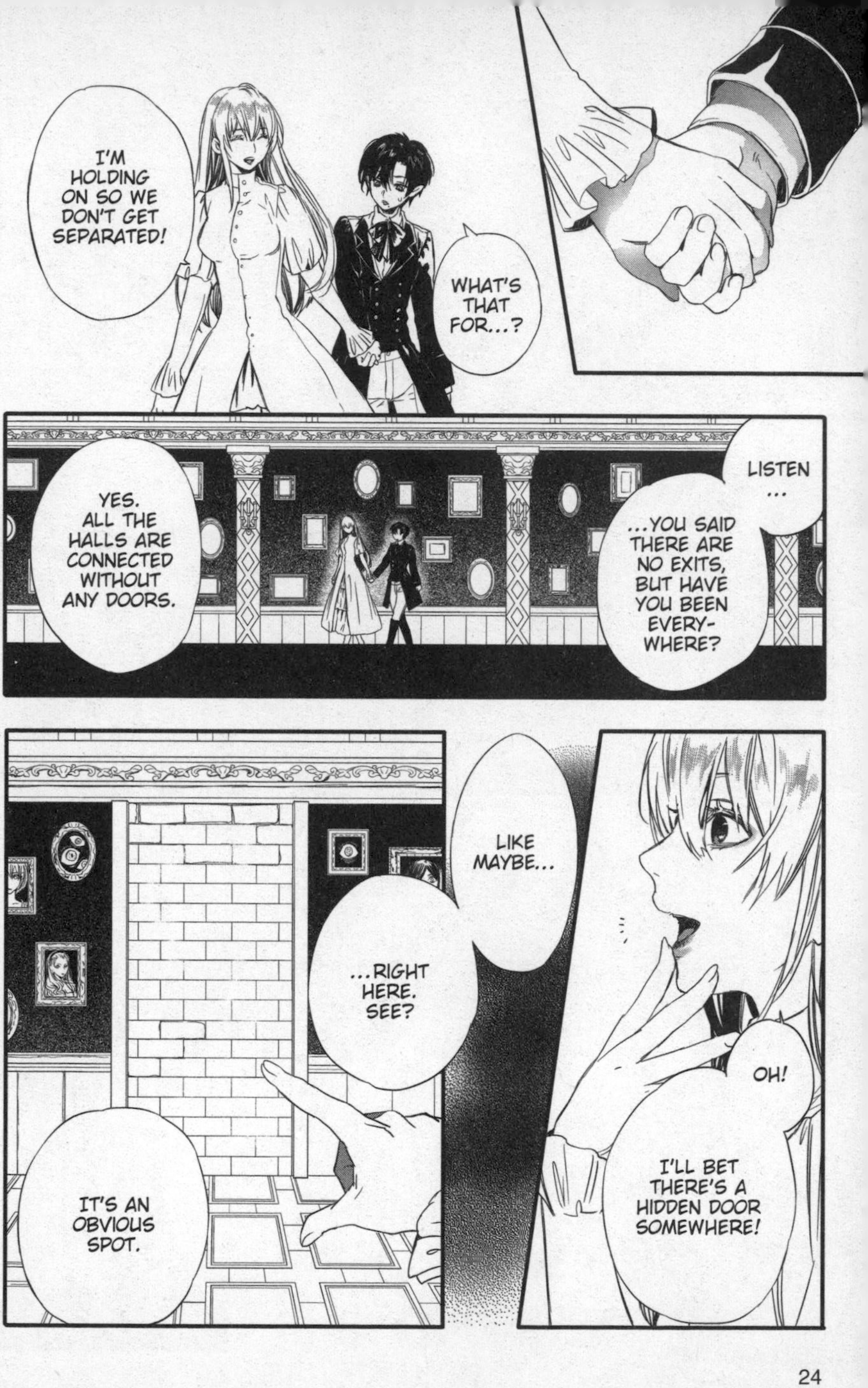
WHAT'S THAT FOR...?
I'M HOLDING ON SO WE DON'T GET SEPARATED!
LISTEN...
...YOU SAID THERE ARE NO EXITS, BUT HAVE YOU BEEN EVERY-WHERE?
YES. ALL THE HALLS ARE CONNECTED WITHOUT ANY DOORS.
OH!
I'LL BET THERE'S A HIDDEN DOOR SOMEWHERE!
LIKE MAYBE...
...RIGHT HERE. SEE?
IT'S AN OBVIOUS SPOT.

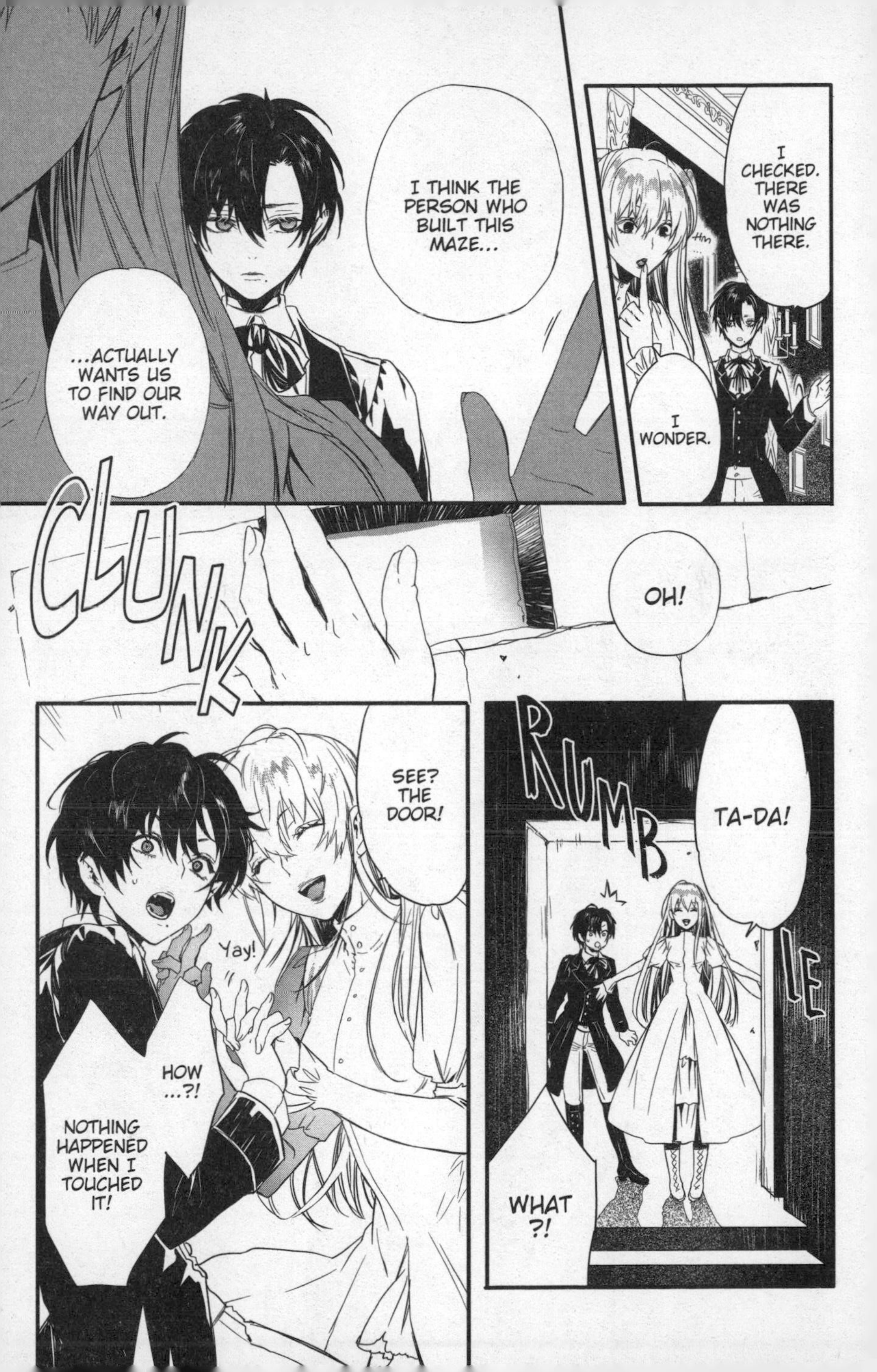

I CHECKED. THERE WAS NOTHING THERE.
Hm...
I WONDER.
I THINK THE PERSON WHO BUILT THIS MAZE...
...ACTUALLY WANTS US TO FIND OUR WAY OUT.
CLUNK
OH!
RUMBLE
TA-DA!
WHAT?!
SEE? THE DOOR!
Yay!
HOW...?!
NOTHING HAPPENED WHEN I TOUCHED IT!

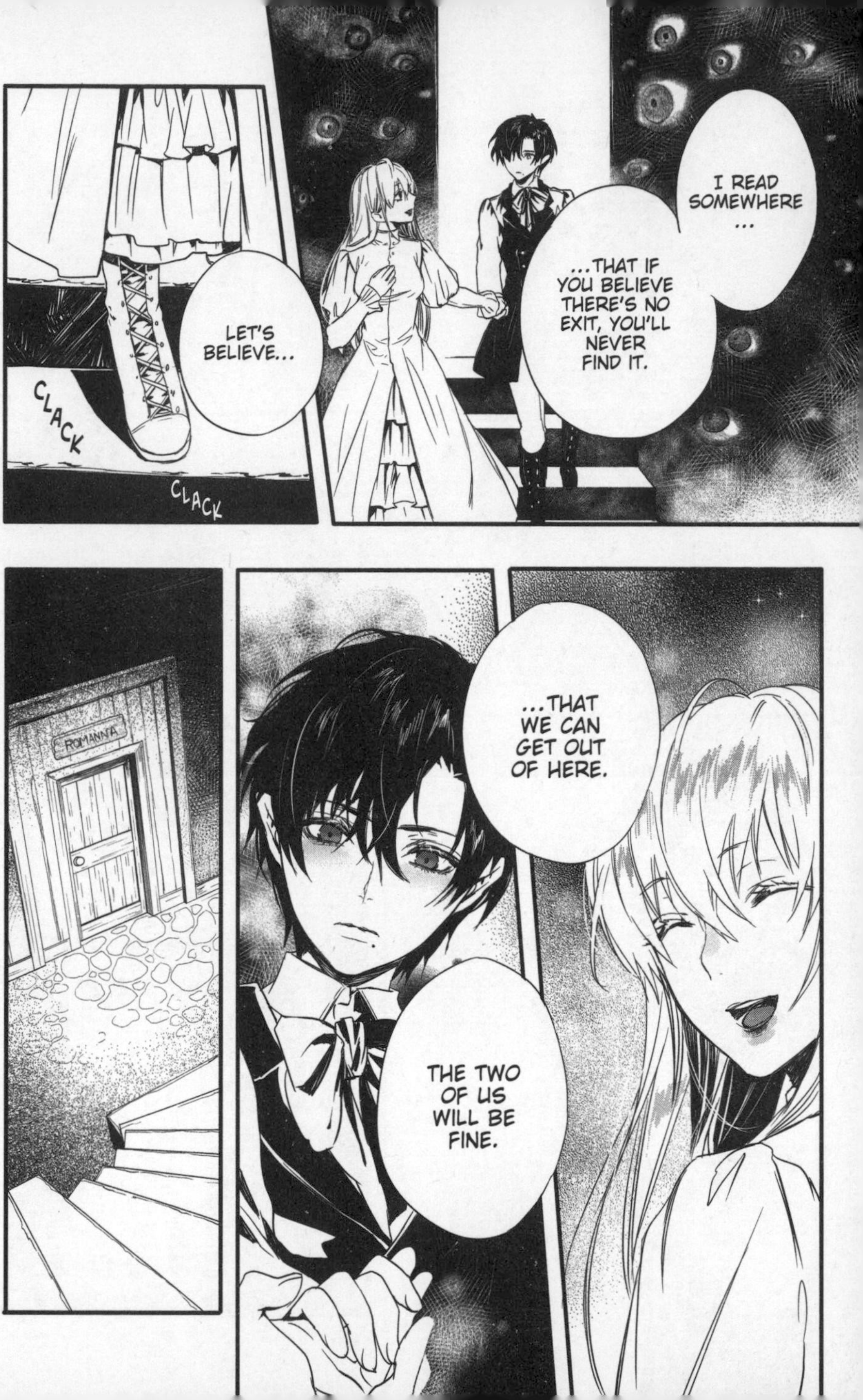
I READ SOMEWHERE ...
...THAT IF YOU BELIEVE THERE'S NO EXIT, YOU'LL NEVER FIND IT.
LET'S BELIEVE...
CLACK
CLACK
...THAT WE CAN GET OUT OF HERE.
THE TWO OF US WILL BE FINE.
ROMANNA

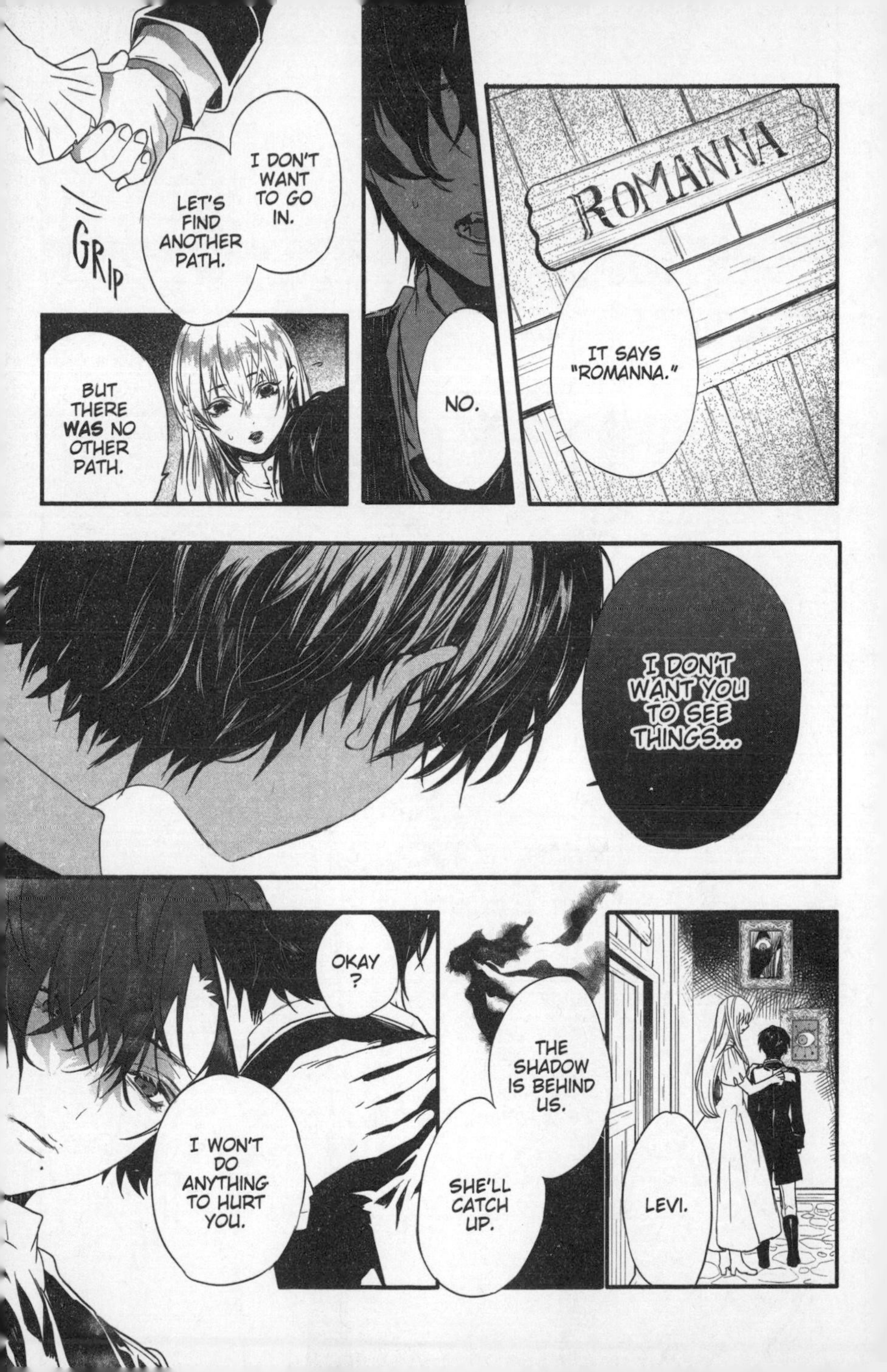
ROMANNA
IT SAYS "ROMANNA."
NO.
GRIP
I DON'T WANT TO GO IN.
LET'S FIND ANOTHER PATH.
BUT THERE WAS NO OTHER PATH.
I DON'T WANT YOU TO SEE THINGS...
LEVI.
THE SHADOW IS BEHIND US.
SHE'LL CATCH UP.
OKAY?
I WON'T DO ANYTHING TO HURT YOU.

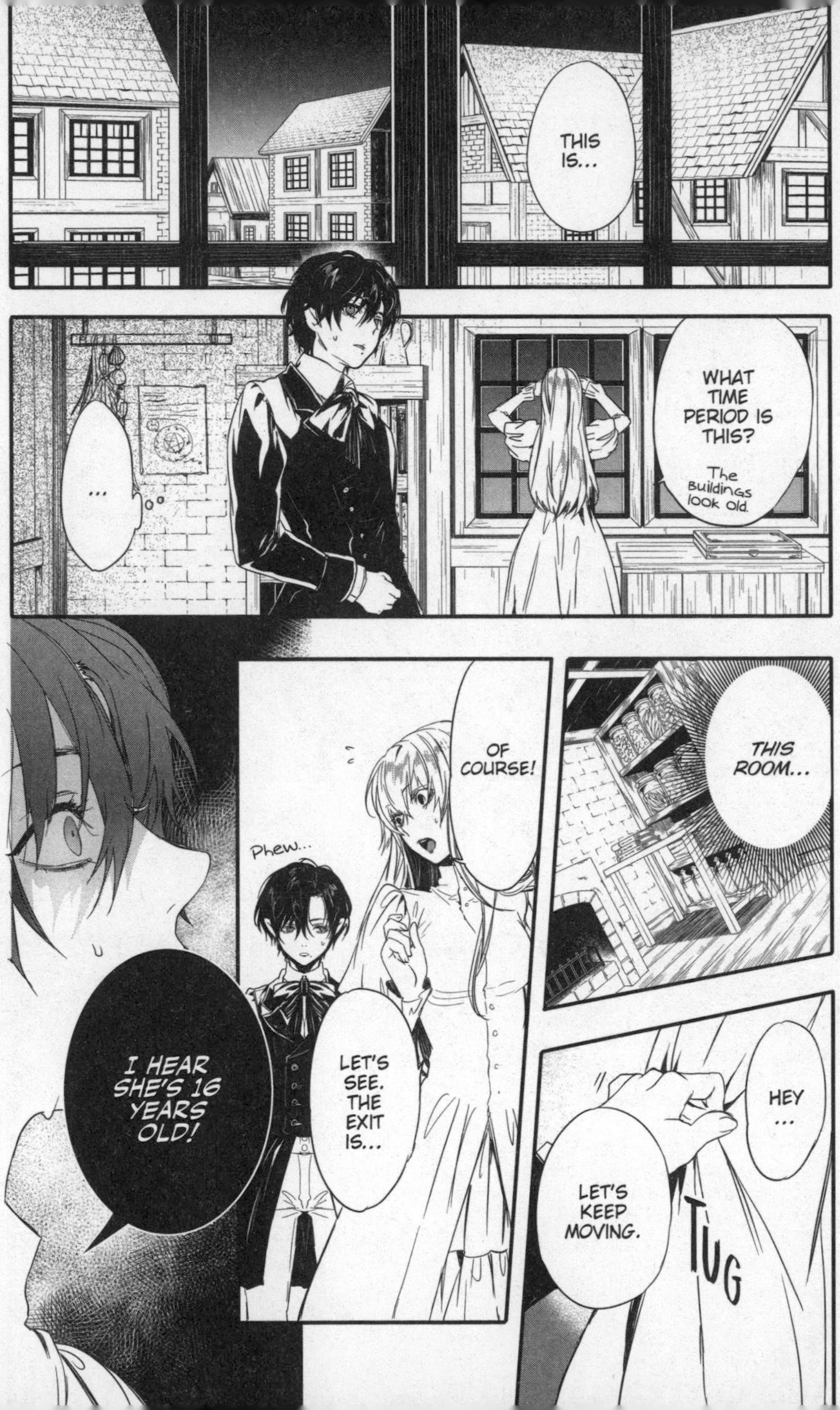
THIS IS...
WHAT TIME PERIOD IS THIS?
The buildings look old.
...
THIS ROOM...
HEY ...
LET'S KEEP MOVING.
TUG
OF COURSE!
Phew...
LET'S SEE. THE EXIT IS...
I HEAR SHE'S 16 YEARS OLD!

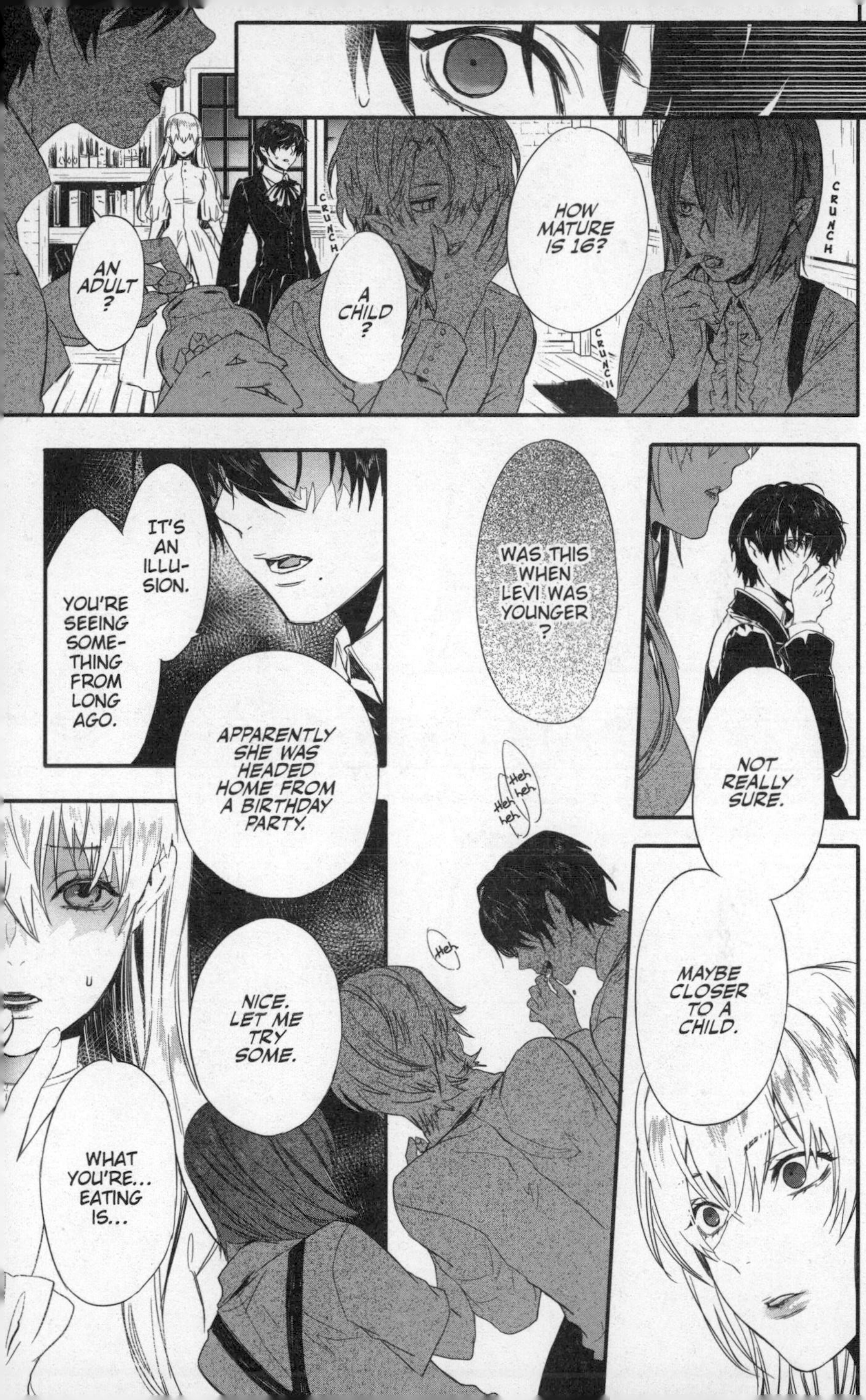
CRUNCH
HOW MATURE IS 16?
CRUNCH
A CHILD?
CRUNCH
AN ADULT?
WAS THIS WHEN LEVI WAS YOUNGER?
NOT REALLY SURE.
IT'S AN ILLUSION.
YOU'RE SEEING SOMETHING FROM LONG AGO.
MAYBE CLOSER TO A CHILD.
Heh heh
Heh heh
APPARENTLY SHE WAS HEADED HOME FROM A BIRTHDAY PARTY.
Heh
NICE. LET ME TRY SOME.
WHAT YOU'RE... EATING IS...

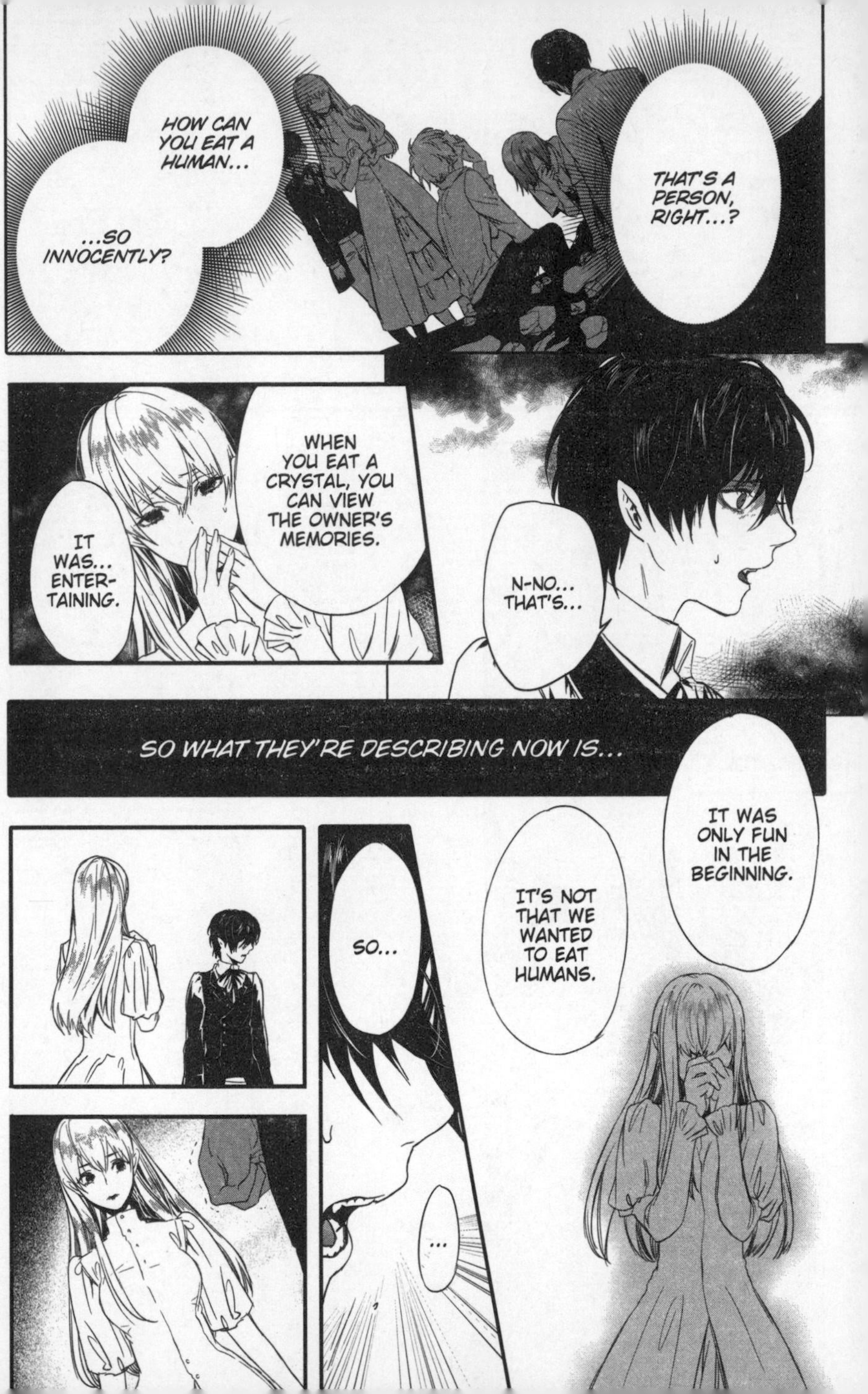
THAT'S A PERSON, RIGHT...?
HOW CAN YOU EAT A HUMAN...
...SO INNOCENTLY?
N-NO... THAT'S...
WHEN YOU EAT A CRYSTAL, YOU CAN VIEW THE OWNER'S MEMORIES.
IT WAS... ENTERTAINING.
SO WHAT THEY'RE DESCRIBING NOW IS...
IT WAS ONLY FUN IN THE BEGINNING.
IT'S NOT THAT WE WANTED TO EAT HUMANS.
SO...
...

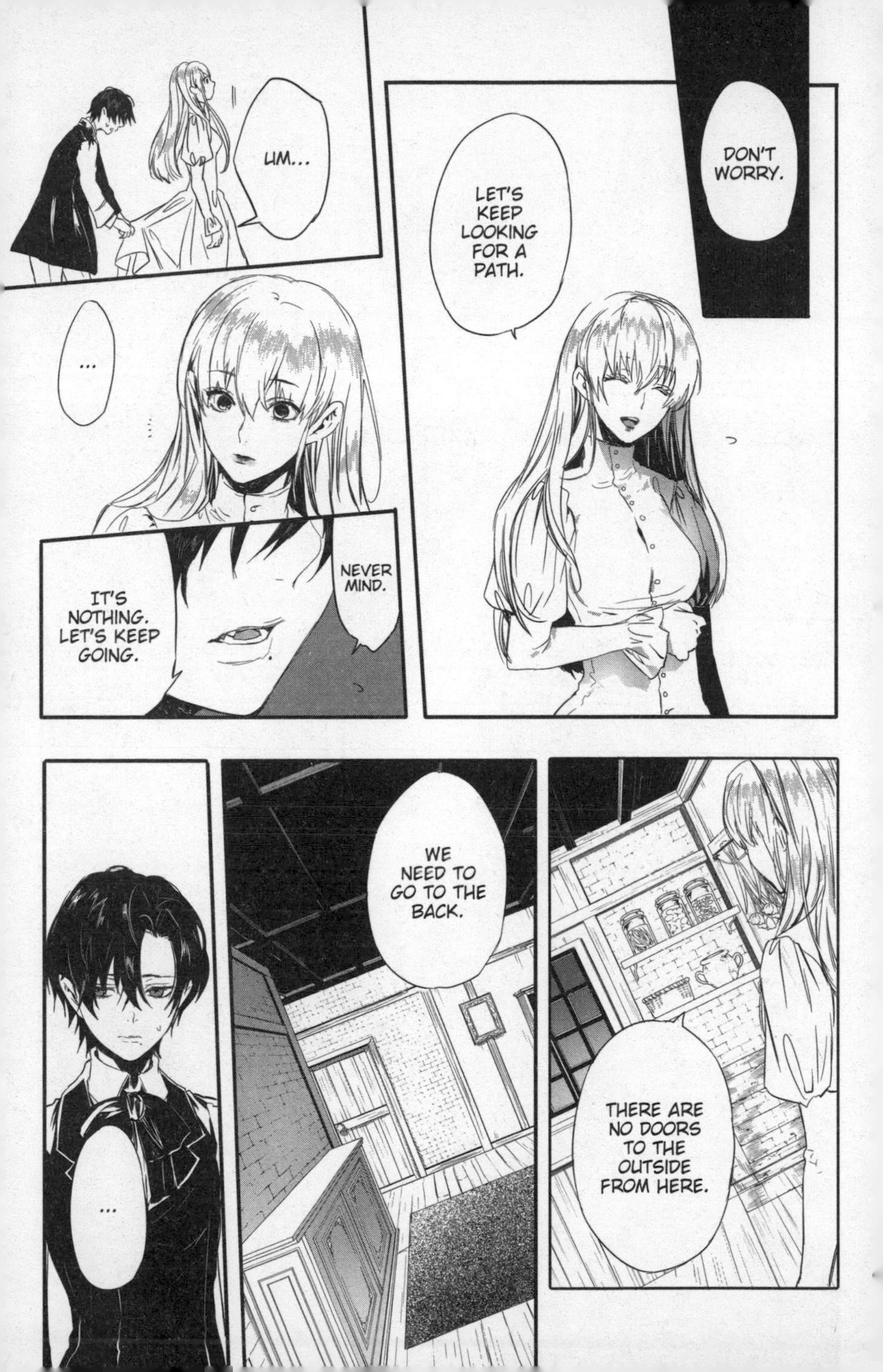
DON'T WORRY.
LET'S KEEP LOOKING FOR A PATH.
UM...
...
NEVER MIND.
IT'S NOTHING. LET'S KEEP GOING.
THERE ARE NO DOORS TO THE OUTSIDE FROM HERE.
WE NEED TO GO TO THE BACK.
...

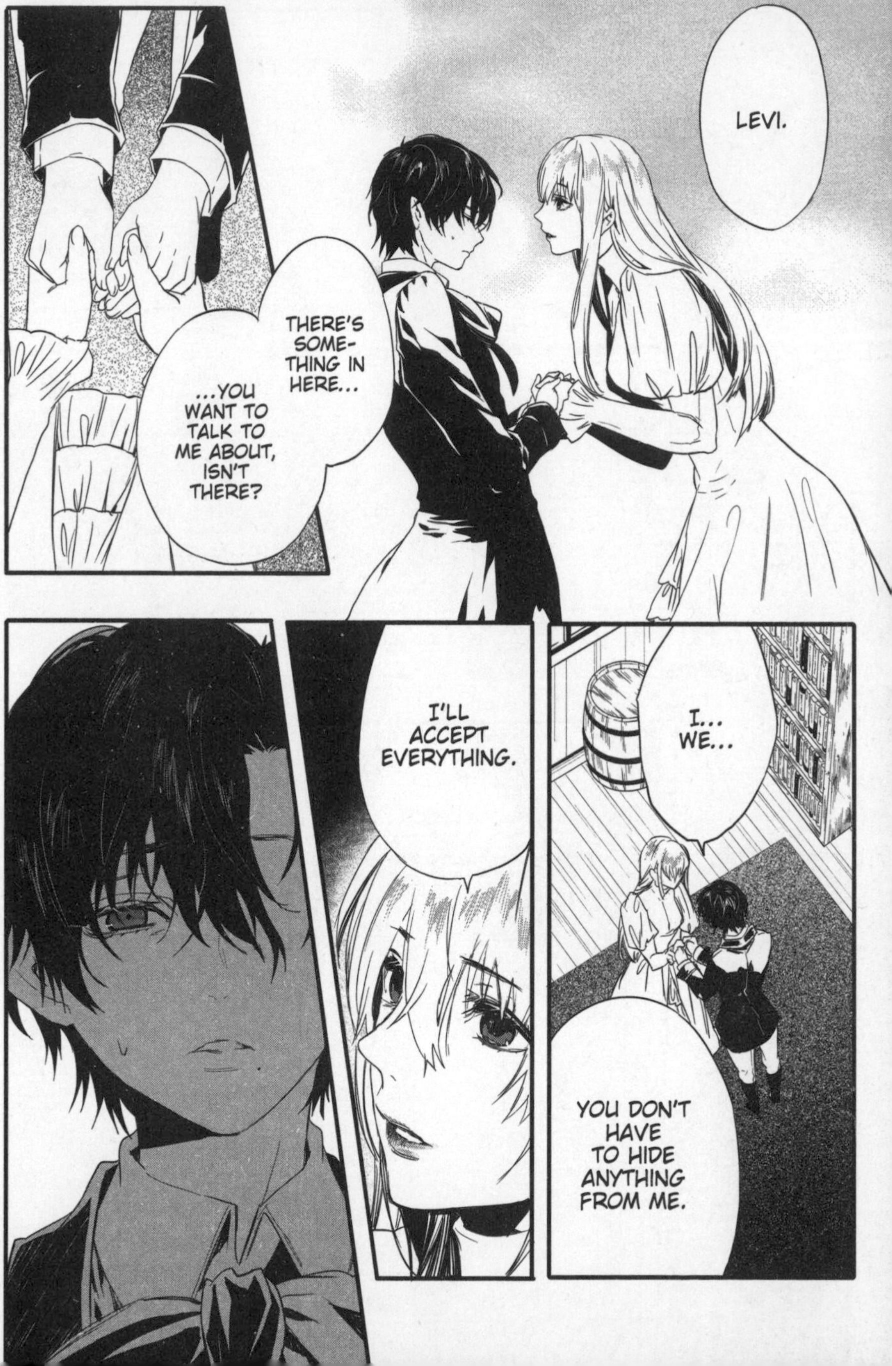
LEVI.
THERE'S SOME-THING IN HERE...
...YOU WANT TO TALK TO ME ABOUT, ISN'T THERE?
I... WE...
YOU DON'T HAVE TO HIDE ANYTHING FROM ME.
I'LL ACCEPT EVERYTHING.

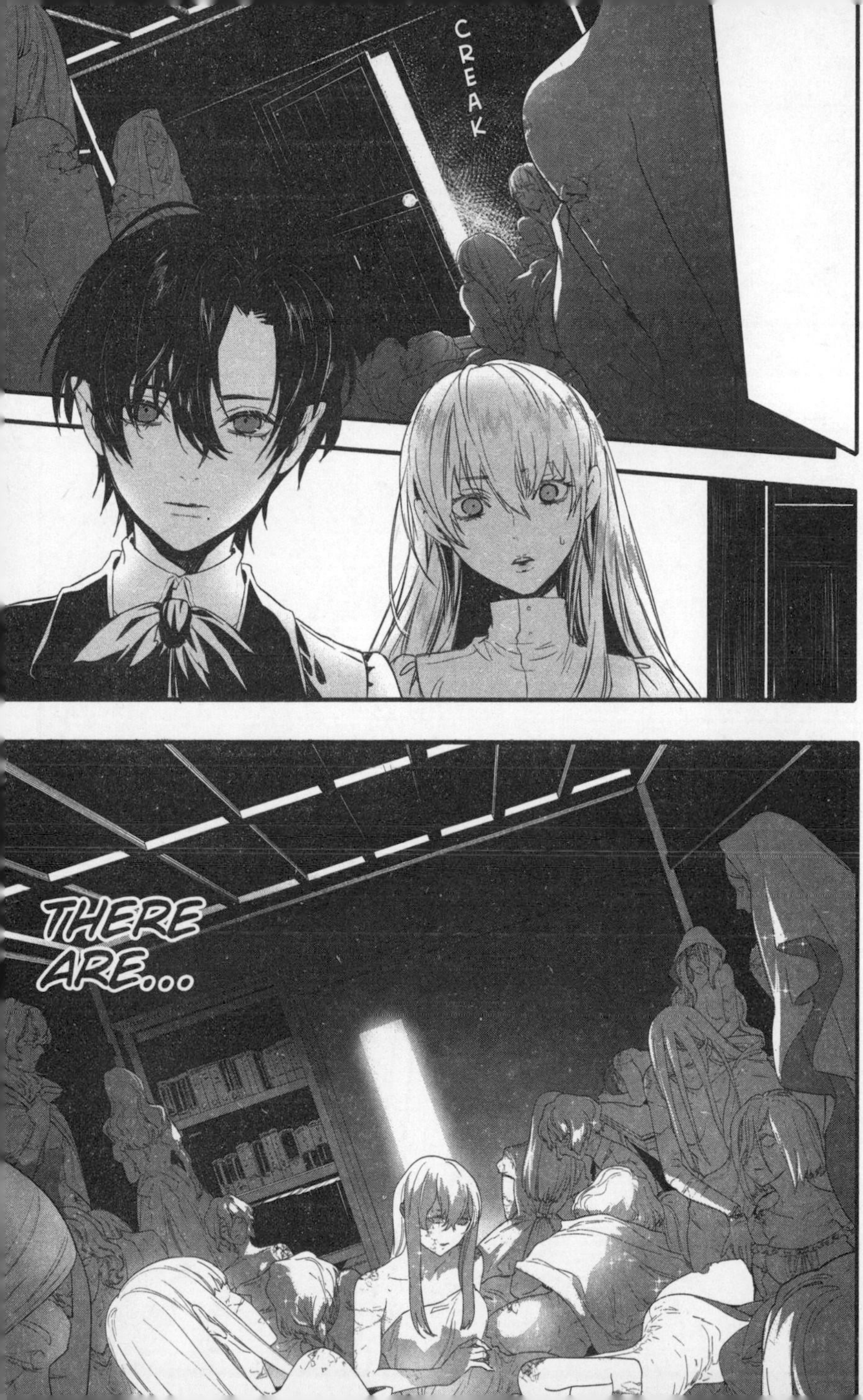
CREAK
THERE ARE...

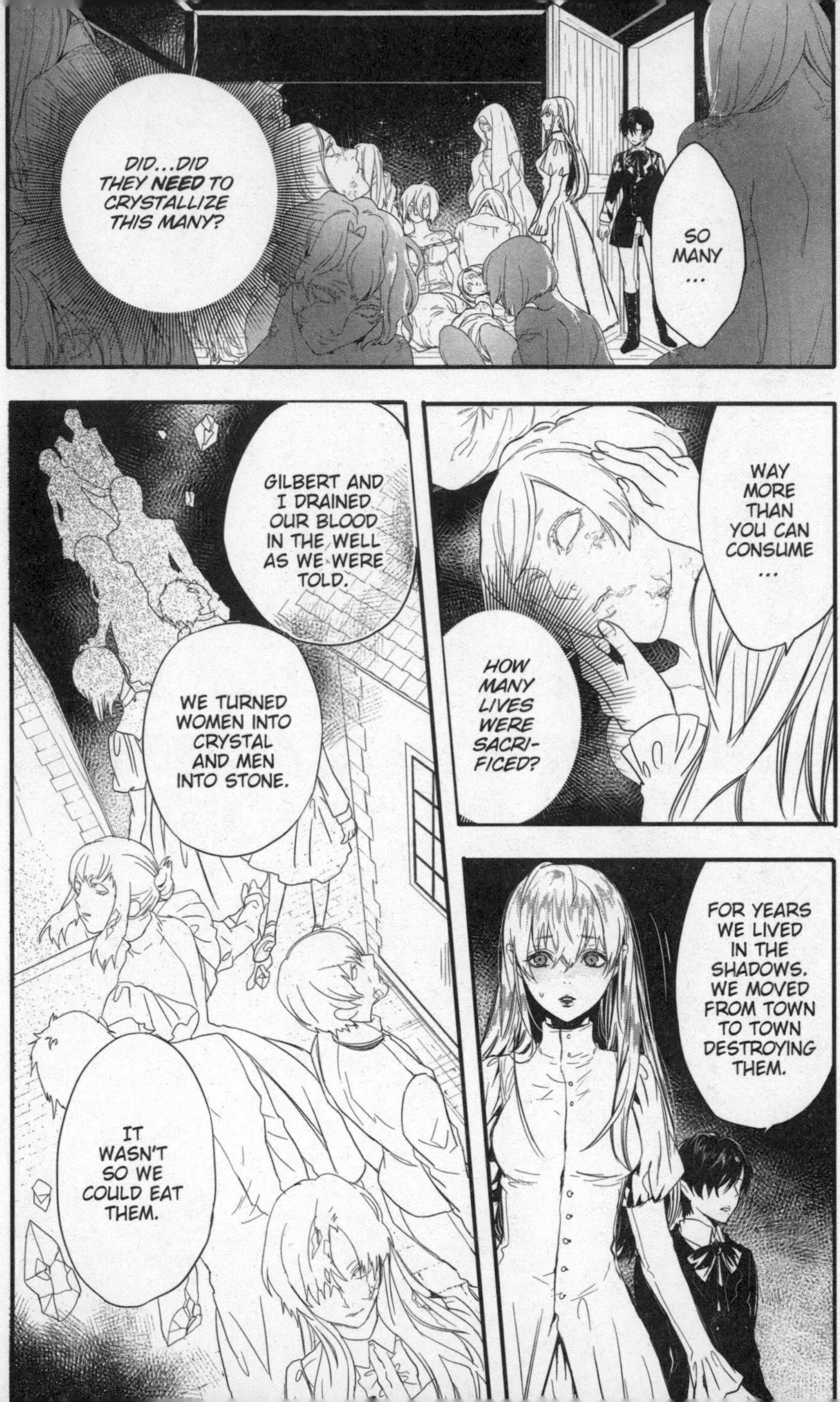
SO MANY ...
DID...DID THEY NEED TO CRYSTALLIZE THIS MANY?
WAY MORE THAN YOU CAN CONSUME ...
HOW MANY LIVES WERE SACRI-FICED?
FOR YEARS WE LIVED IN THE SHADOWS. WE MOVED FROM TOWN TO TOWN DESTROYING THEM.
GILBERT AND I DRAINED OUR BLOOD IN THE WELL AS WE WERE TOLD.
WE TURNED WOMEN INTO CRYSTAL AND MEN INTO STONE.
IT WASN'T SO WE COULD EAT THEM.

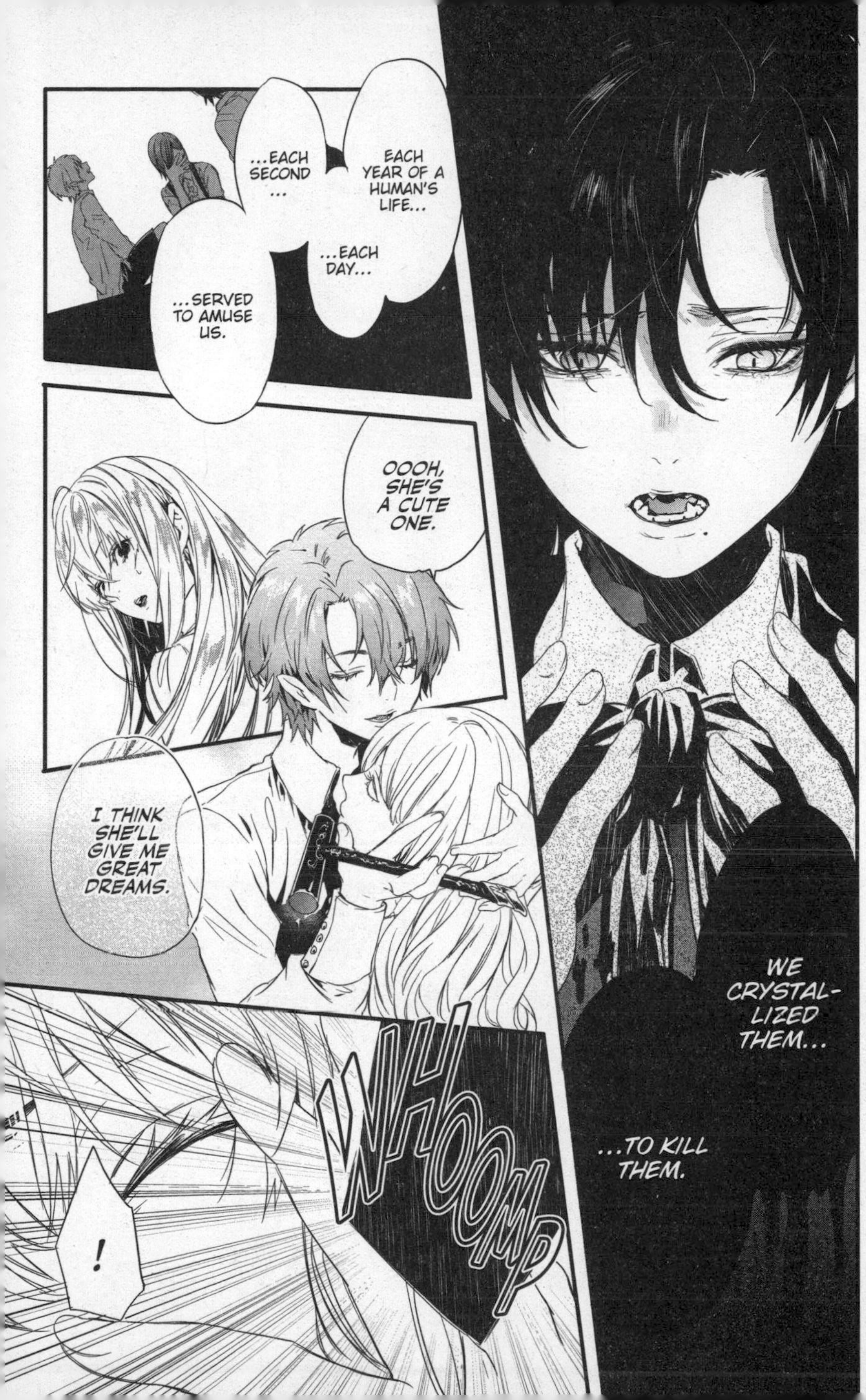
WE CRYSTAL-LIZED THEM...
...TO KILL THEM.
EACH YEAR OF A HUMAN'S LIFE...
...EACH SECOND...
...EACH DAY...
...SERVED TO AMUSE US.
OOOH, SHE'S A CUTE ONE.
I THINK SHE'LL GIVE ME GREAT DREAMS.
WHOOMP
!

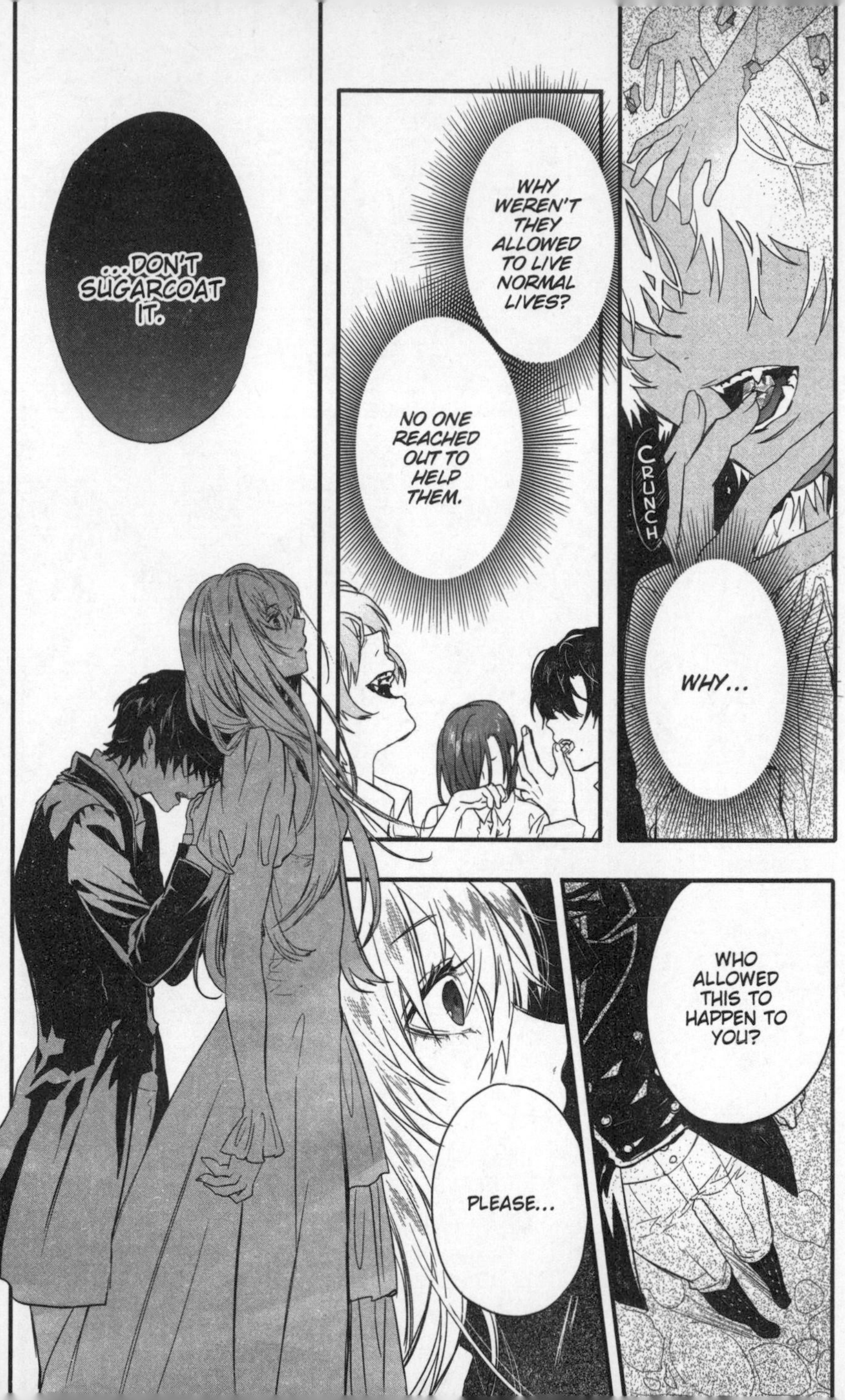
CRUNCH
WHY...
WHY WEREN'T THEY ALLOWED TO LIVE NORMAL LIVES?
NO ONE REACHED OUT TO HELP THEM.
WHO ALLOWED THIS TO HAPPEN TO YOU?
PLEASE...
...DON'T SUGARCOAT IT.

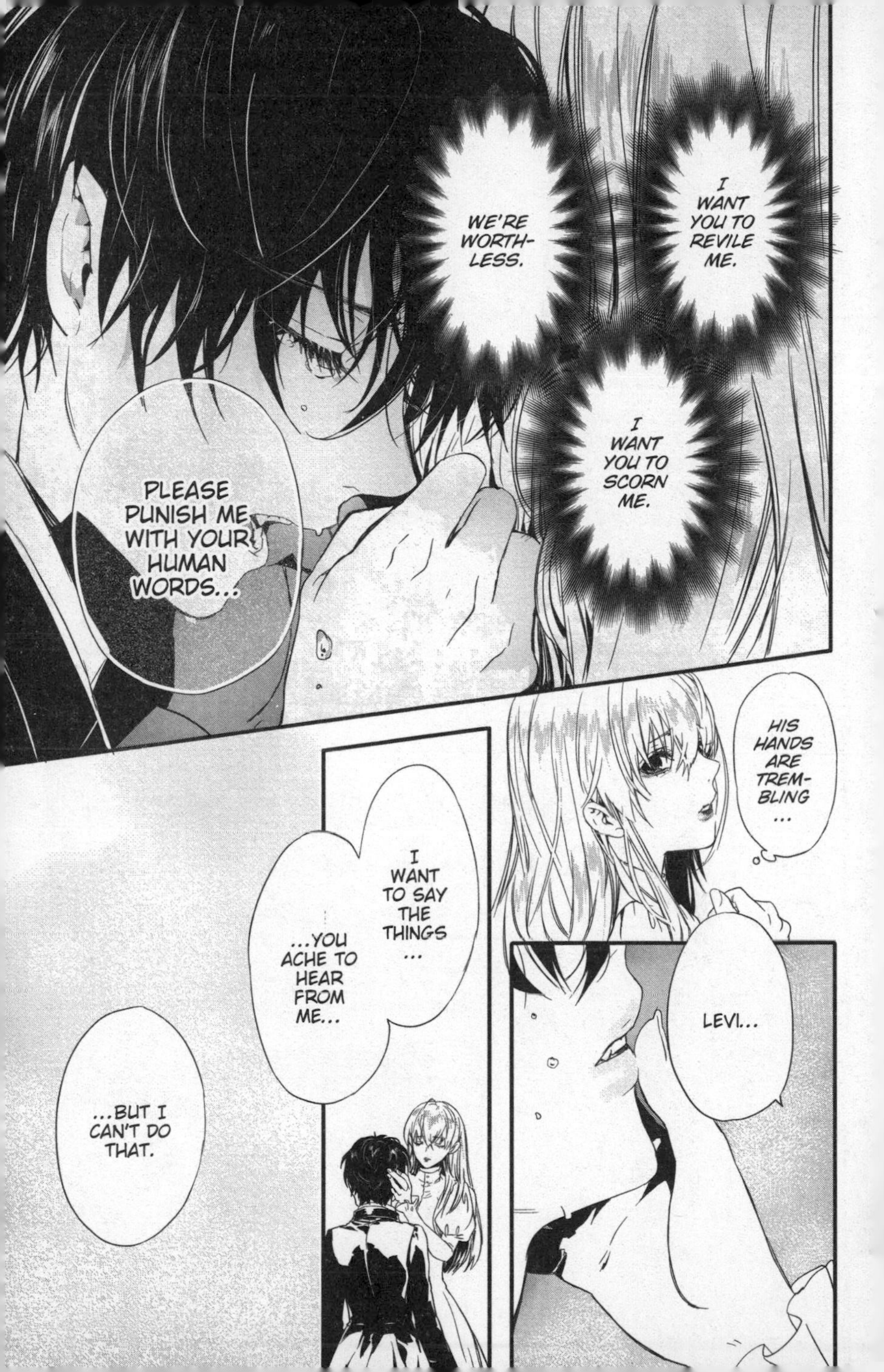
I WANT YOU TO REVILE ME.
WE'RE WORTH-LESS.
I WANT YOU TO SCORN ME.
PLEASE PUNISH ME WITH YOUR HUMAN WORDS...
HIS HANDS ARE TREM-BLING...
LEVI...
I WANT TO SAY THE THINGS...
...YOU ACHE TO HEAR FROM ME...
...BUT I CAN'T DO THAT.

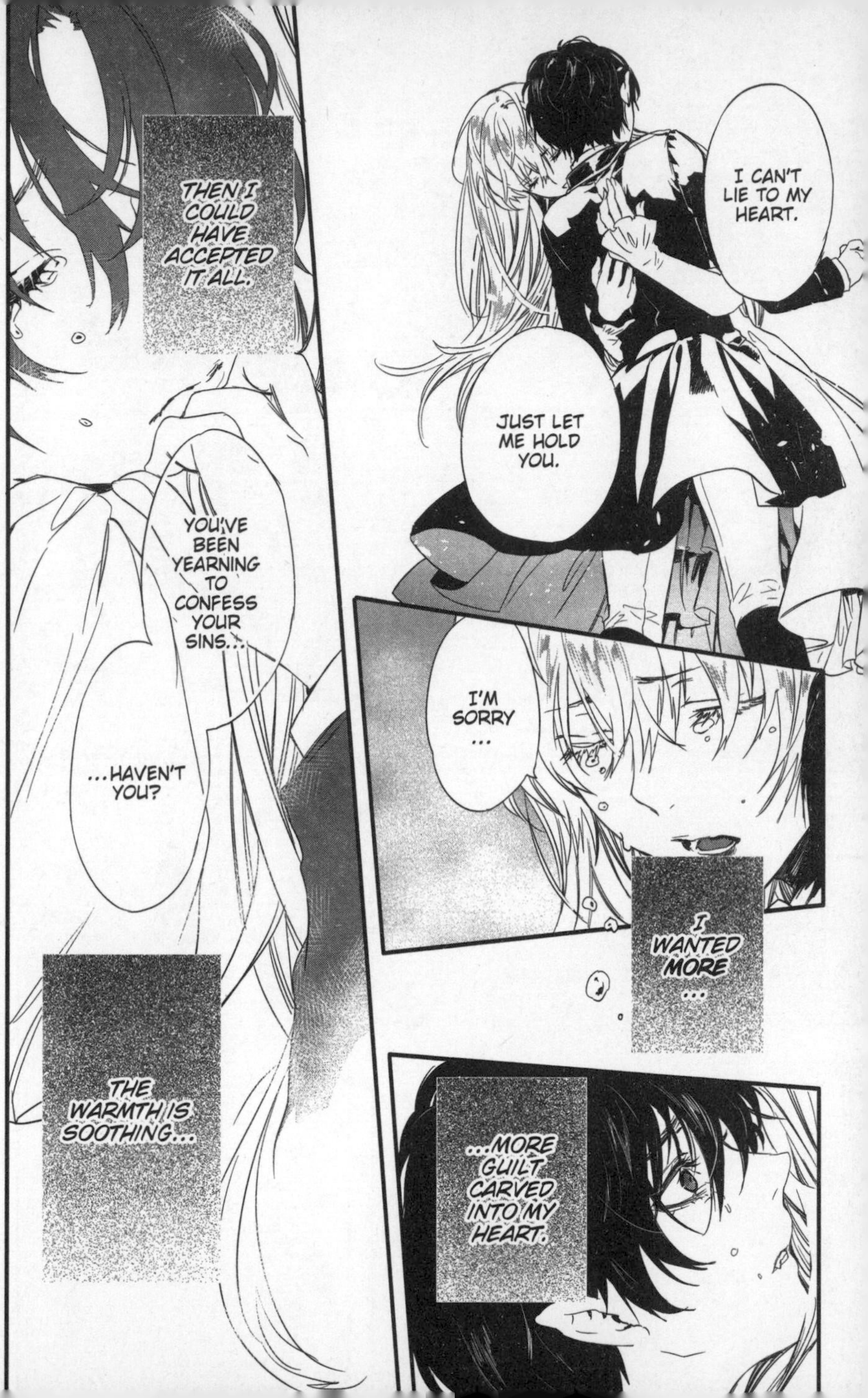
I CAN'T LIE TO MY HEART.
JUST LET ME HOLD YOU.
I'M SORRY...
I WANTED MORE...
...MORE GUILT CARVED INTO MY HEART.
THEN I COULD HAVE ACCEPTED IT ALL.
YOU'VE BEEN YEARNING TO CONFESS YOUR SINS...
...HAVEN'T YOU?
THE WARMTH IS SOOTHING...

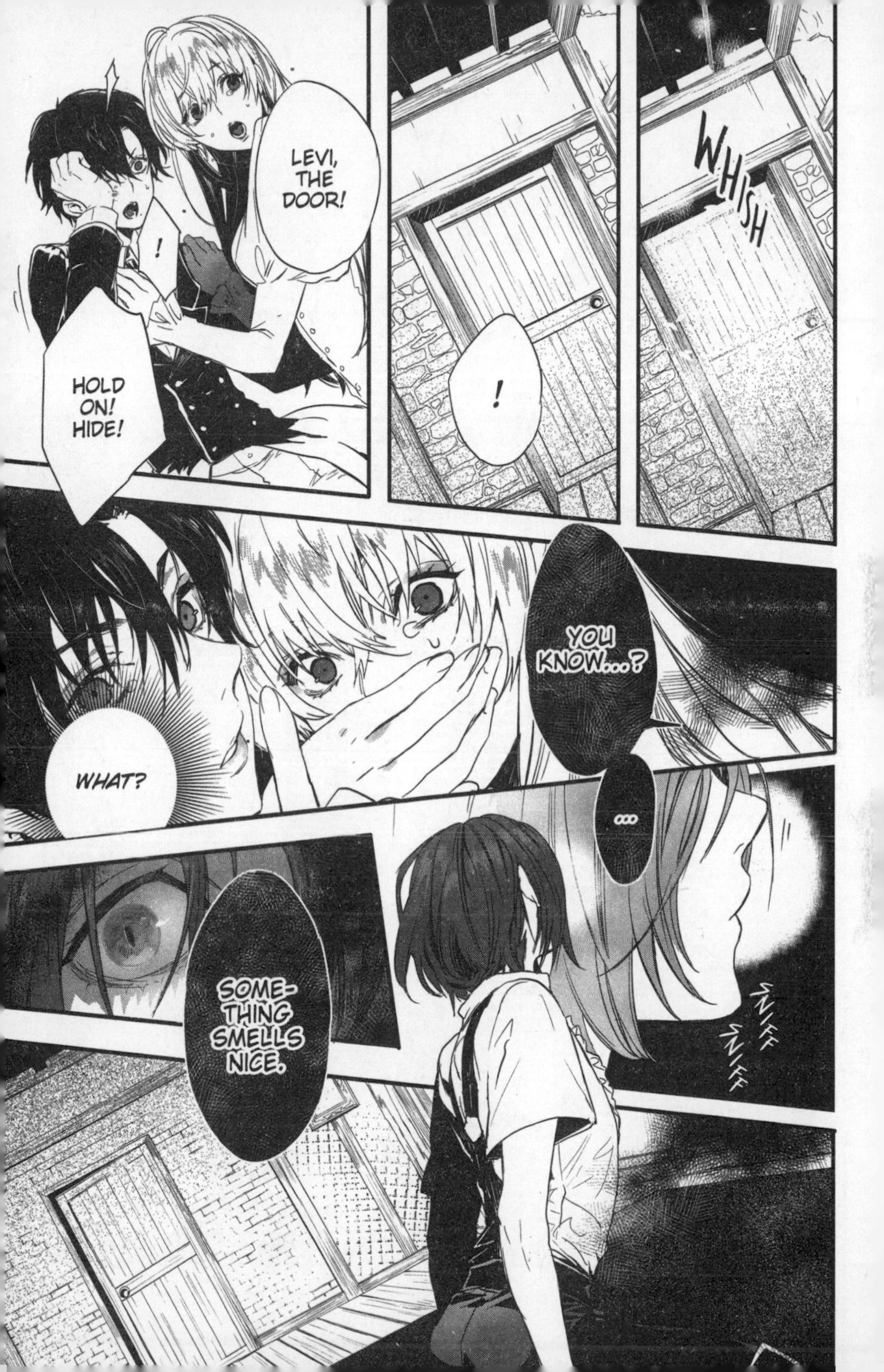
WHISH
!
LEVI, THE DOOR!
!
HOLD ON! HIDE!
YOU KNOW...?
WHAT?
...
SNIFF SNIFF
SOME-THING SMELLS NICE.

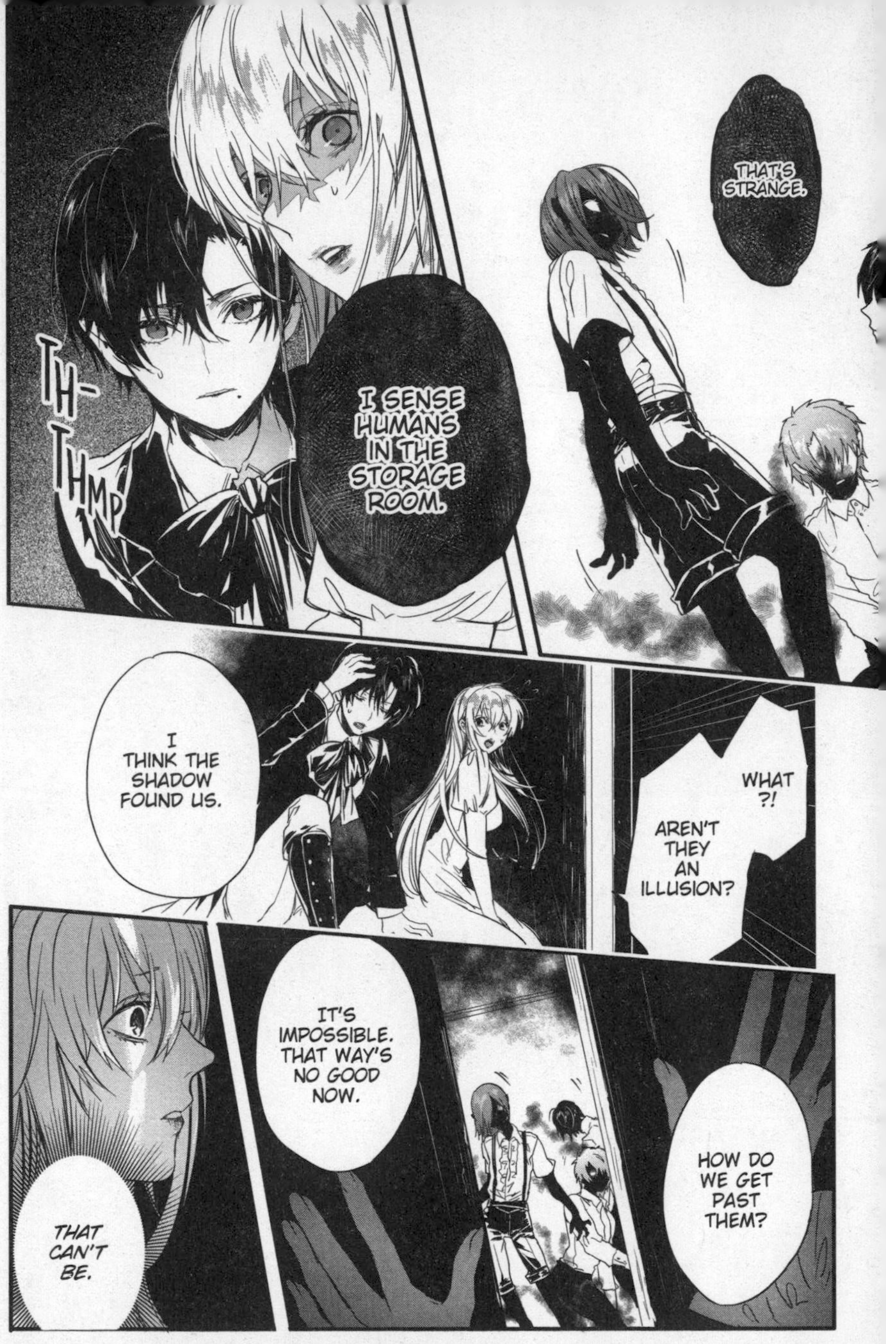
THAT'S STRANGE.
I SENSE HUMANS IN THE STORAGE ROOM.
TH-THMP
WHAT ?!
AREN'T THEY AN ILLUSION?
I THINK THE SHADOW FOUND US.
HOW DO WE GET PAST THEM?
IT'S IMPOSSIBLE. THAT WAY'S NO GOOD NOW.
THAT CAN'T BE.

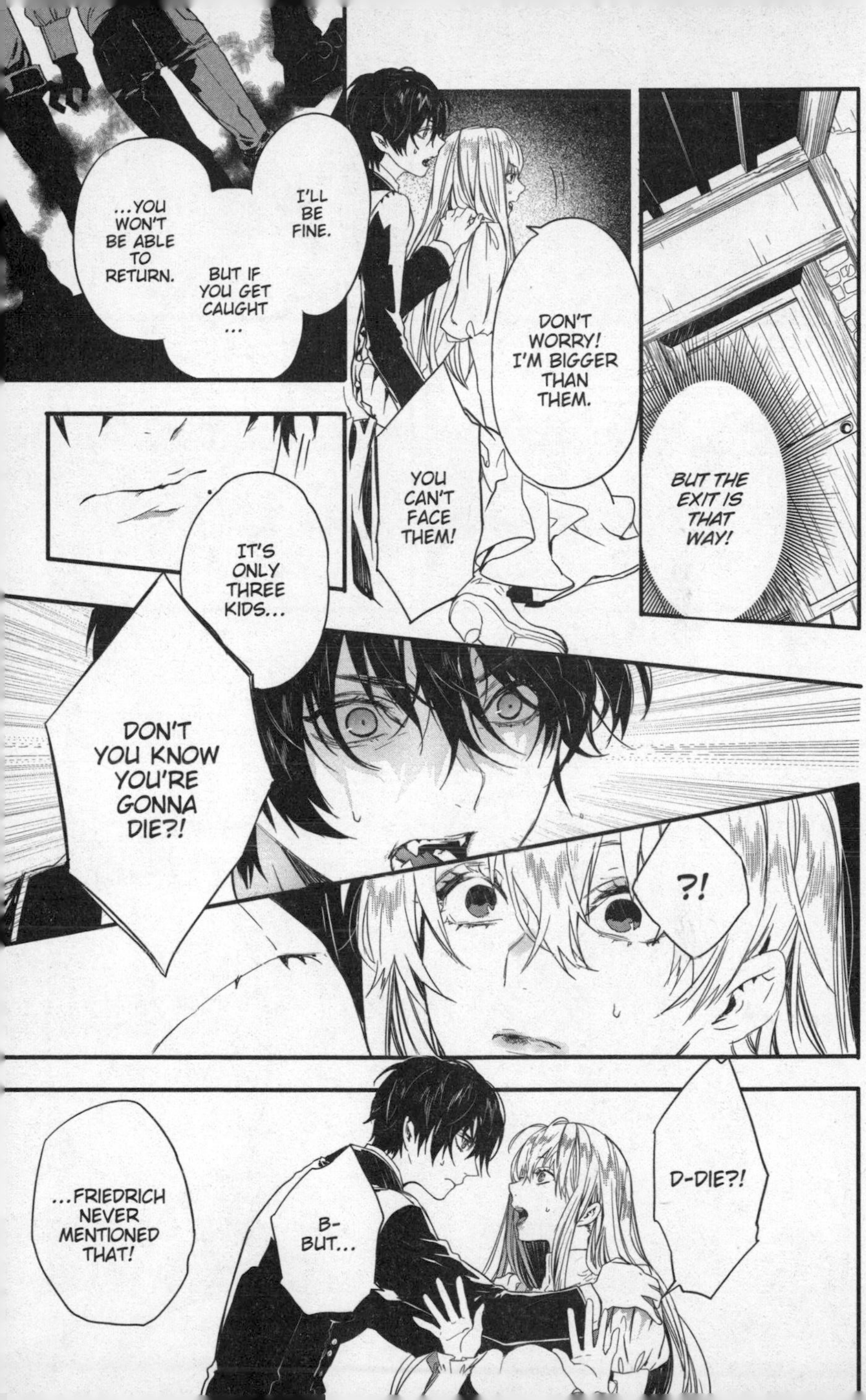
BUT THE EXIT IS THAT WAY!
DON'T WORRY! I'M BIGGER THAN THEM.
YOU CAN'T FACE THEM!
I'LL BE FINE.
BUT IF YOU GET CAUGHT ...
...YOU WON'T BE ABLE TO RETURN.
IT'S ONLY THREE KIDS...
DON'T YOU KNOW YOU'RE GONNA DIE?!
?!
D-DIE?!
B-BUT...
...FRIEDRICH NEVER MENTIONED THAT!

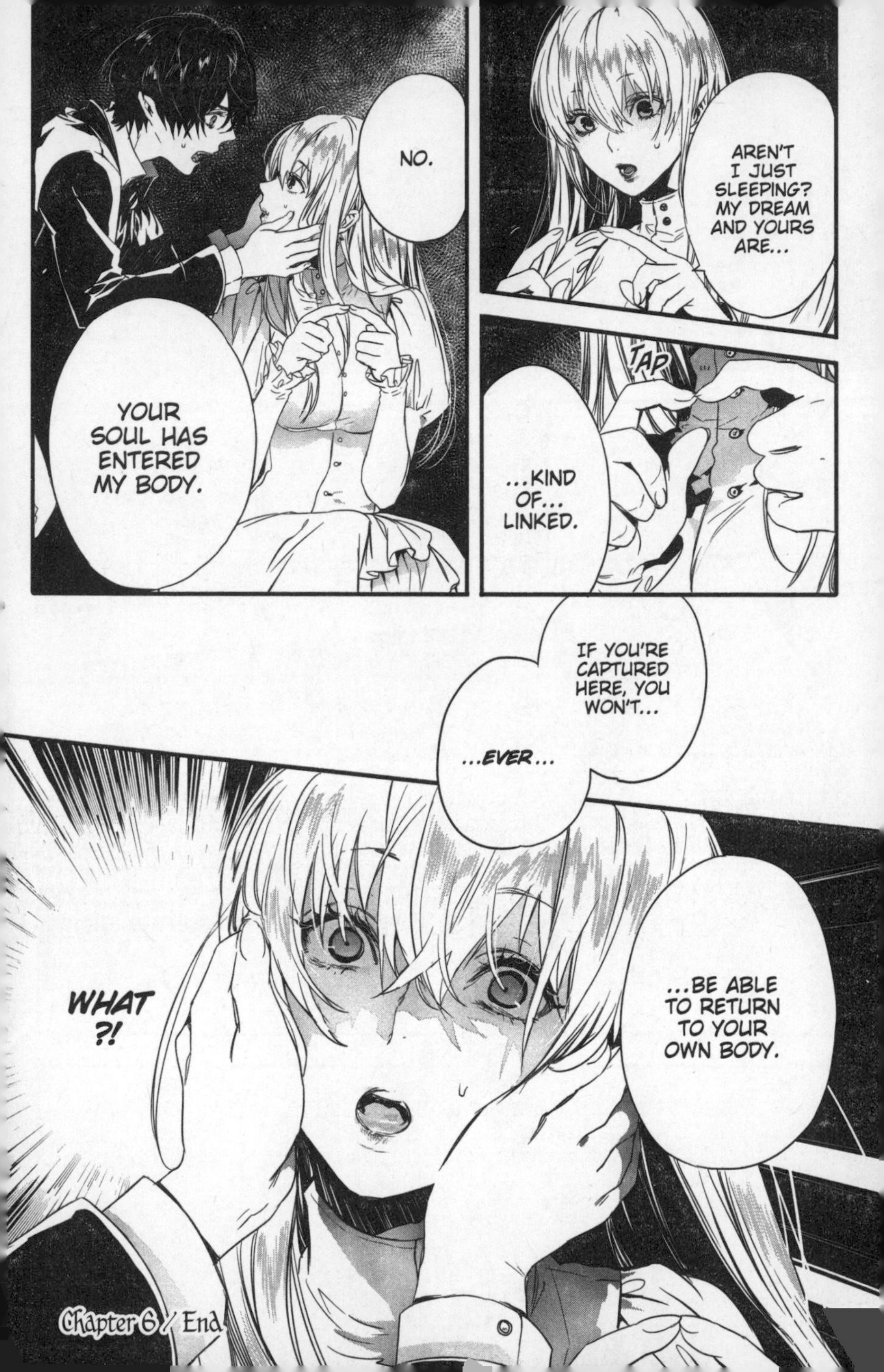
AREN'T I JUST SLEEPING? MY DREAM AND YOURS ARE...
TAP
...KIND OF... LINKED.
NO.
YOUR SOUL HAS ENTERED MY BODY.
IF YOU'RE CAPTURED HERE, YOU WON'T...
...EVER...
...BE ABLE TO RETURN TO YOUR OWN BODY.
WHAT?!
Chapter 6 / End

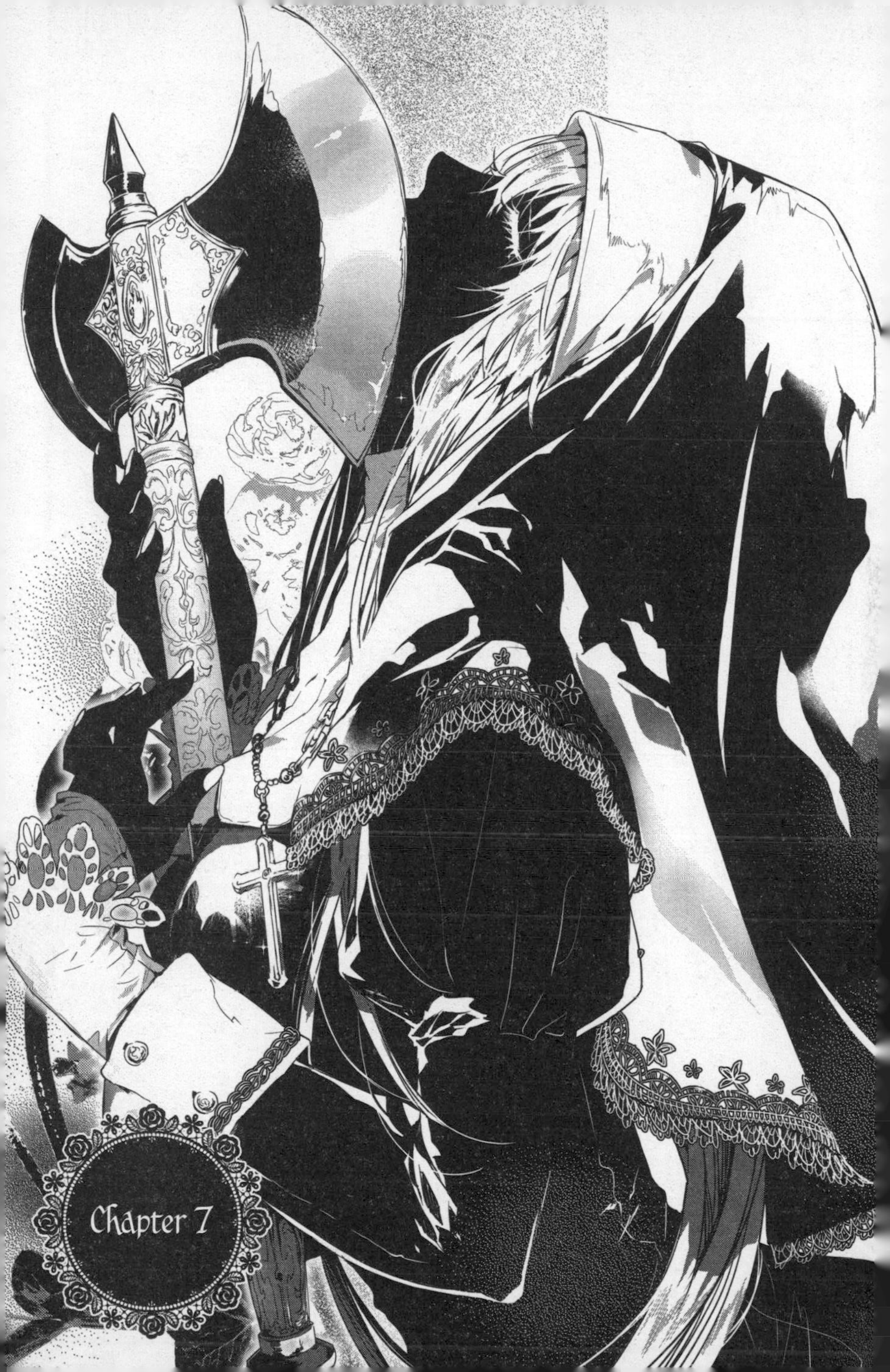
Chapter 7

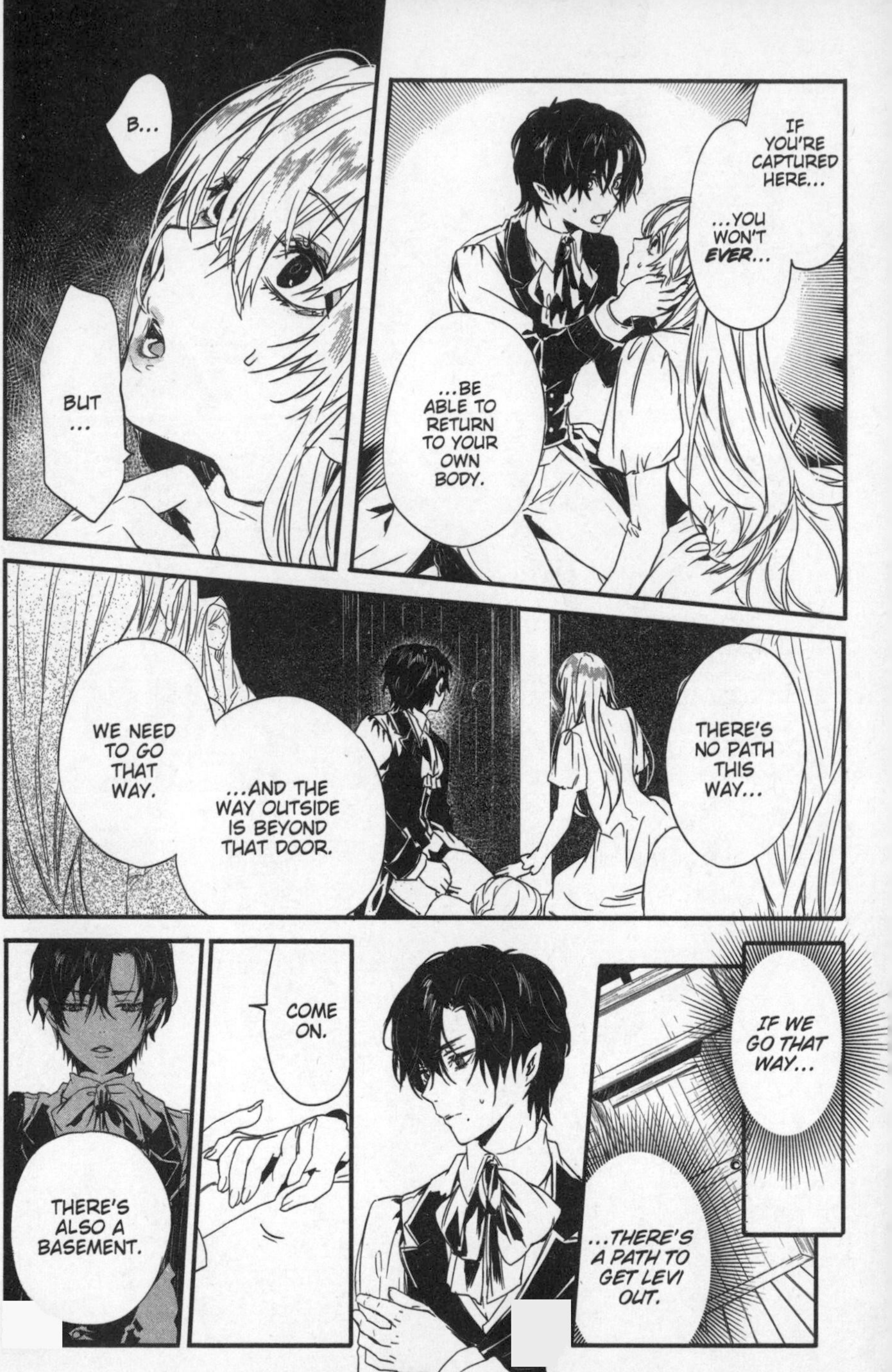
IF YOU'RE CAPTURED HERE...
...YOU WON'T *EVER*...
...BE ABLE TO RETURN TO YOUR OWN BODY.
B...
BUT ...
THERE'S NO PATH THIS WAY...
WE NEED TO GO THAT WAY.
...AND THE WAY OUTSIDE IS BEYOND THAT DOOR.
IF WE GO THAT WAY...
...THERE'S A PATH TO GET LEVI OUT.
COME ON.
THERE'S ALSO A BASEMENT.

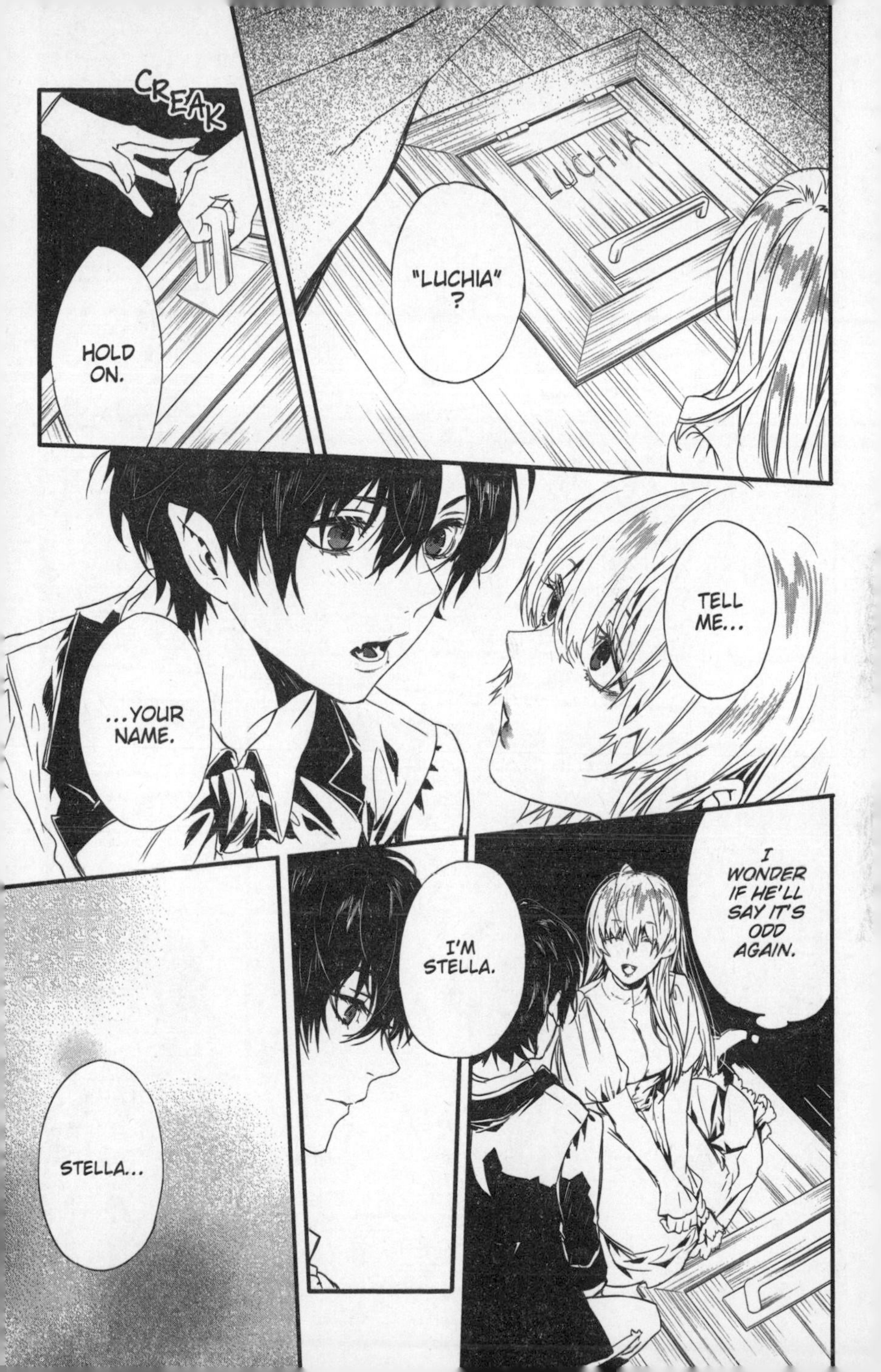
LUCHIA
"LUCHIA"
?
CREAK
HOLD ON.
TELL ME...
...YOUR NAME.
I WONDER IF HE'LL SAY IT'S ODD AGAIN.
I'M STELLA.
STELLA...

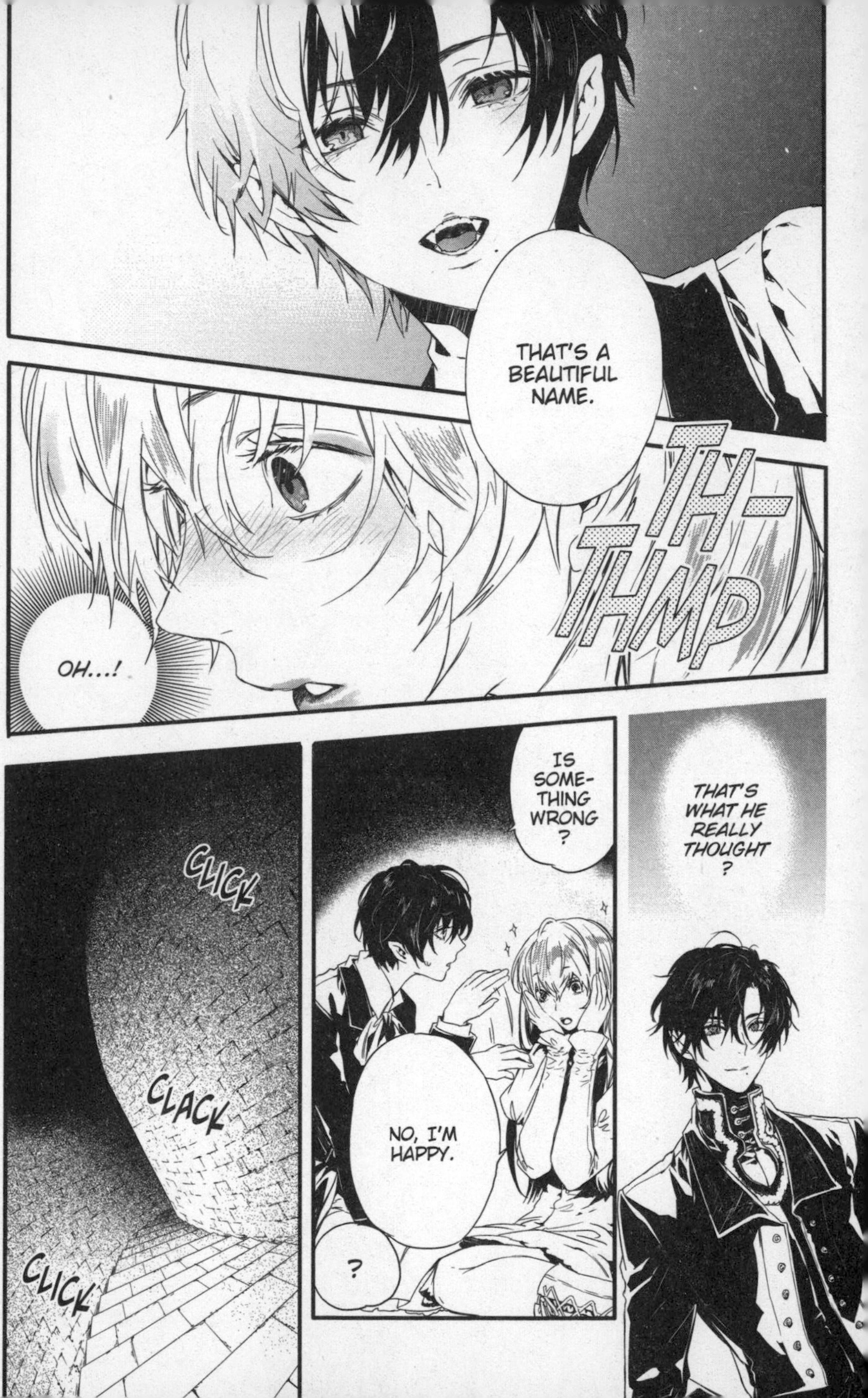
THAT'S A BEAUTIFUL NAME.
TH-THMP
OH...!
THAT'S WHAT HE REALLY THOUGHT?
IS SOME-THING WRONG?
NO, I'M HAPPY.
?
CLICK
CLACK
CLICK

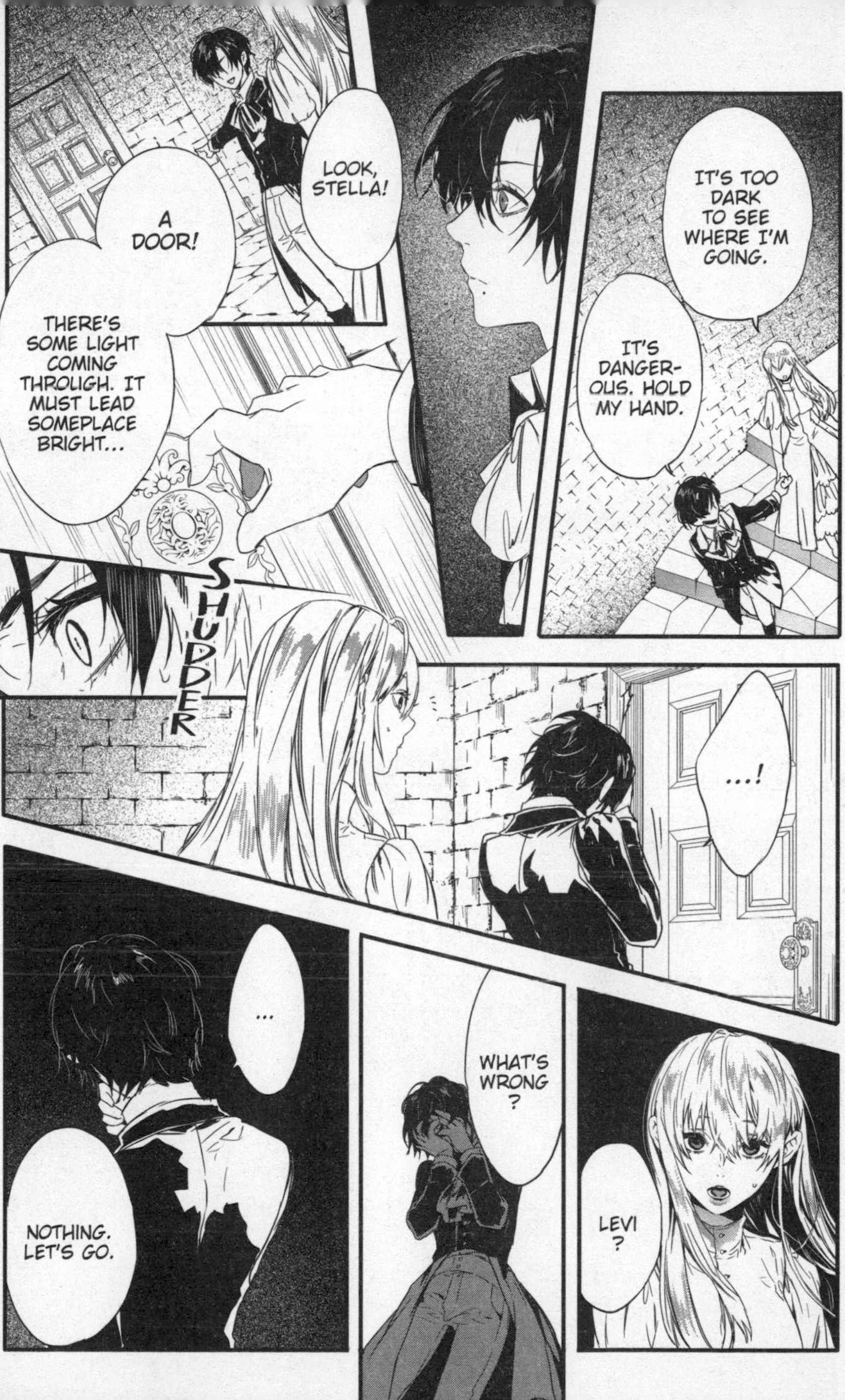
IT'S TOO DARK TO SEE WHERE I'M GOING.
IT'S DANGER-OUS. HOLD MY HAND.
LOOK, STELLA!
A DOOR!
THERE'S SOME LIGHT COMING THROUGH. IT MUST LEAD SOMEPLACE BRIGHT...
SHUDDER
...!
LEVI?
WHAT'S WRONG?
...
NOTHING. LET'S GO.

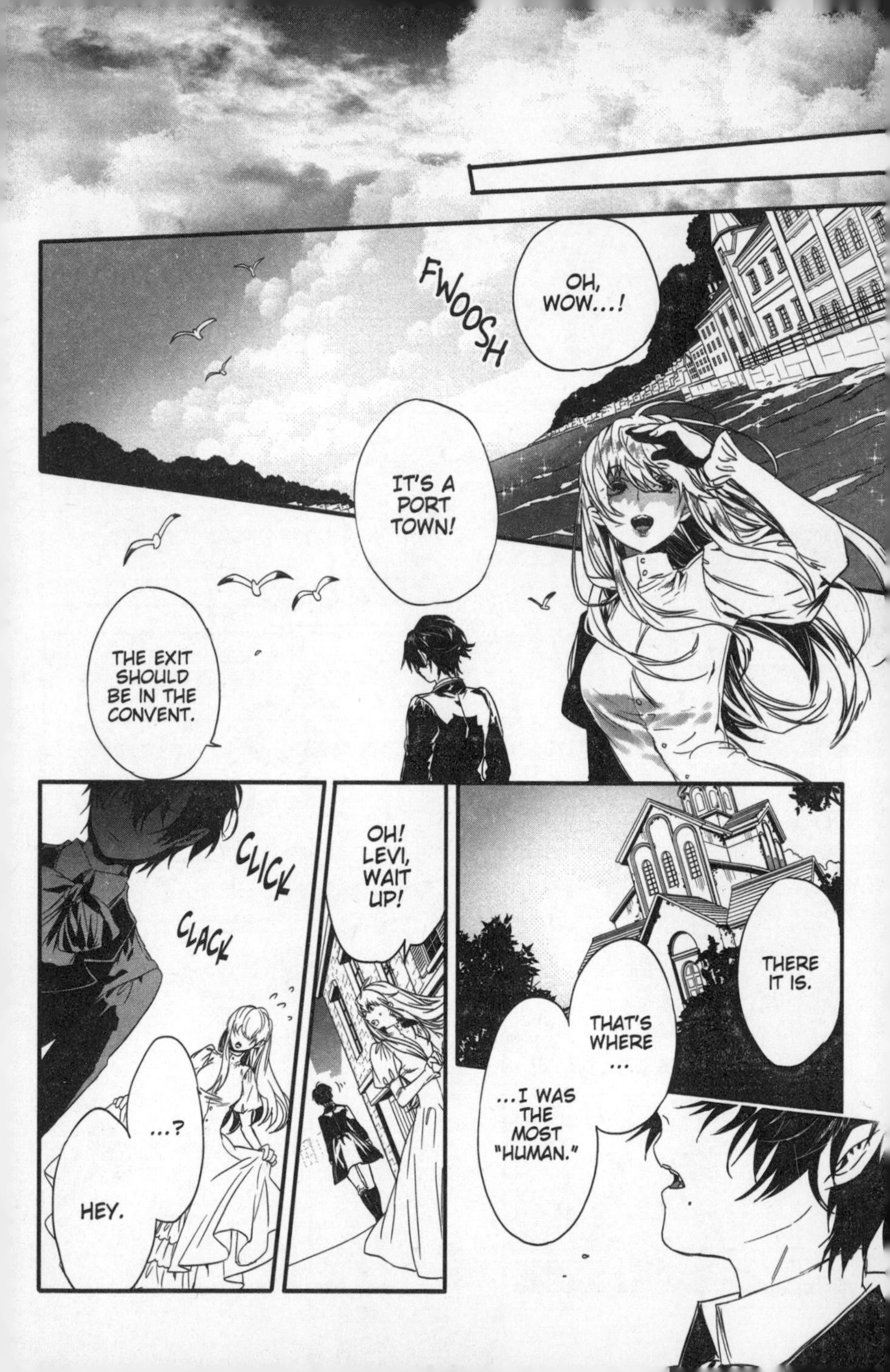
FWOOSH
OH, WOW...!
IT'S A PORT TOWN!
THE EXIT SHOULD BE IN THE CONVENT.
THERE IT IS.
THAT'S WHERE ...
...I WAS THE MOST "HUMAN."
OH! LEVI, WAIT UP!
CLICK
CLACK
...?
HEY.

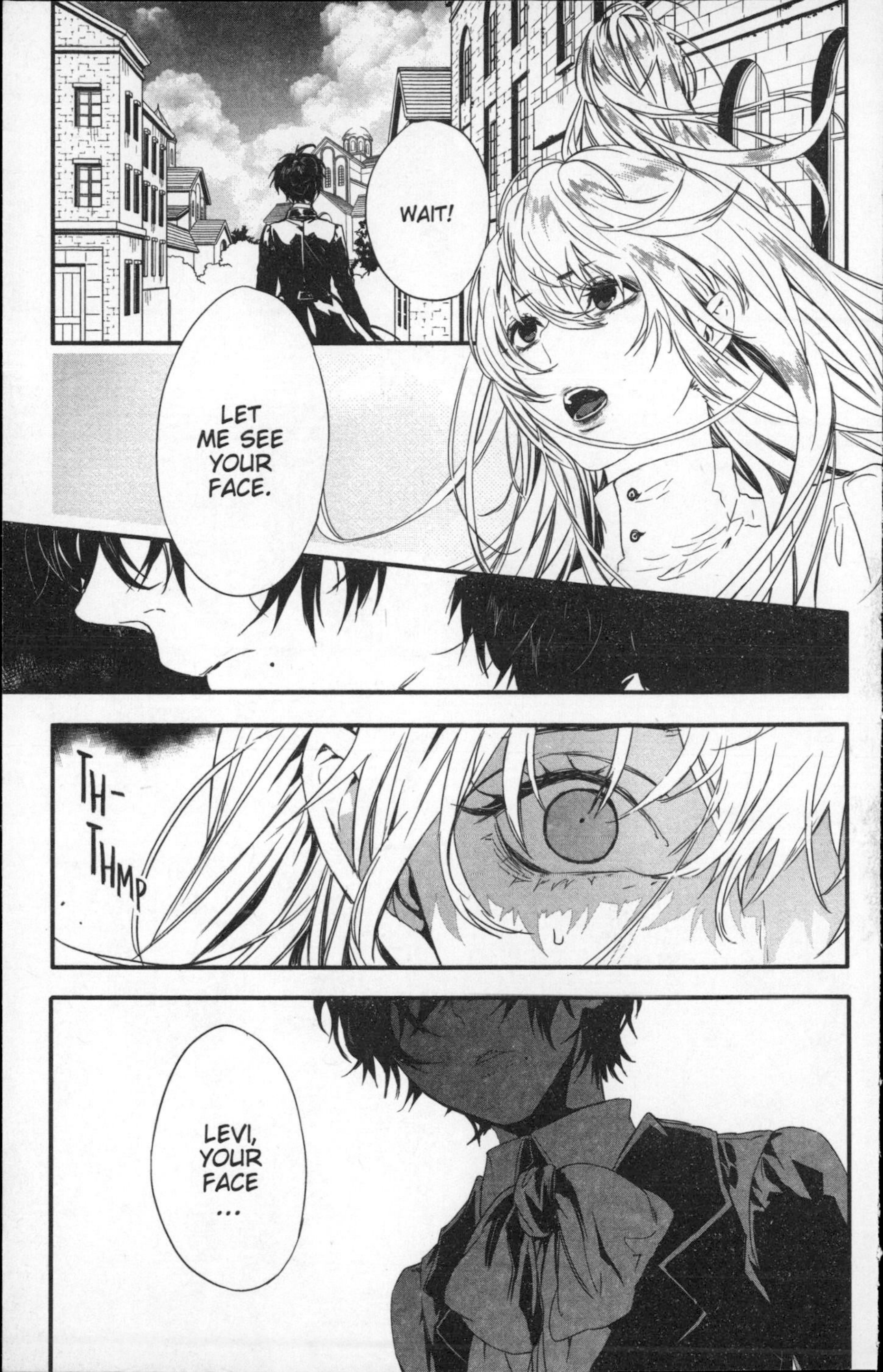
WAIT!
LET ME SEE YOUR FACE.
TH-THMP
LEVI, YOUR FACE ...

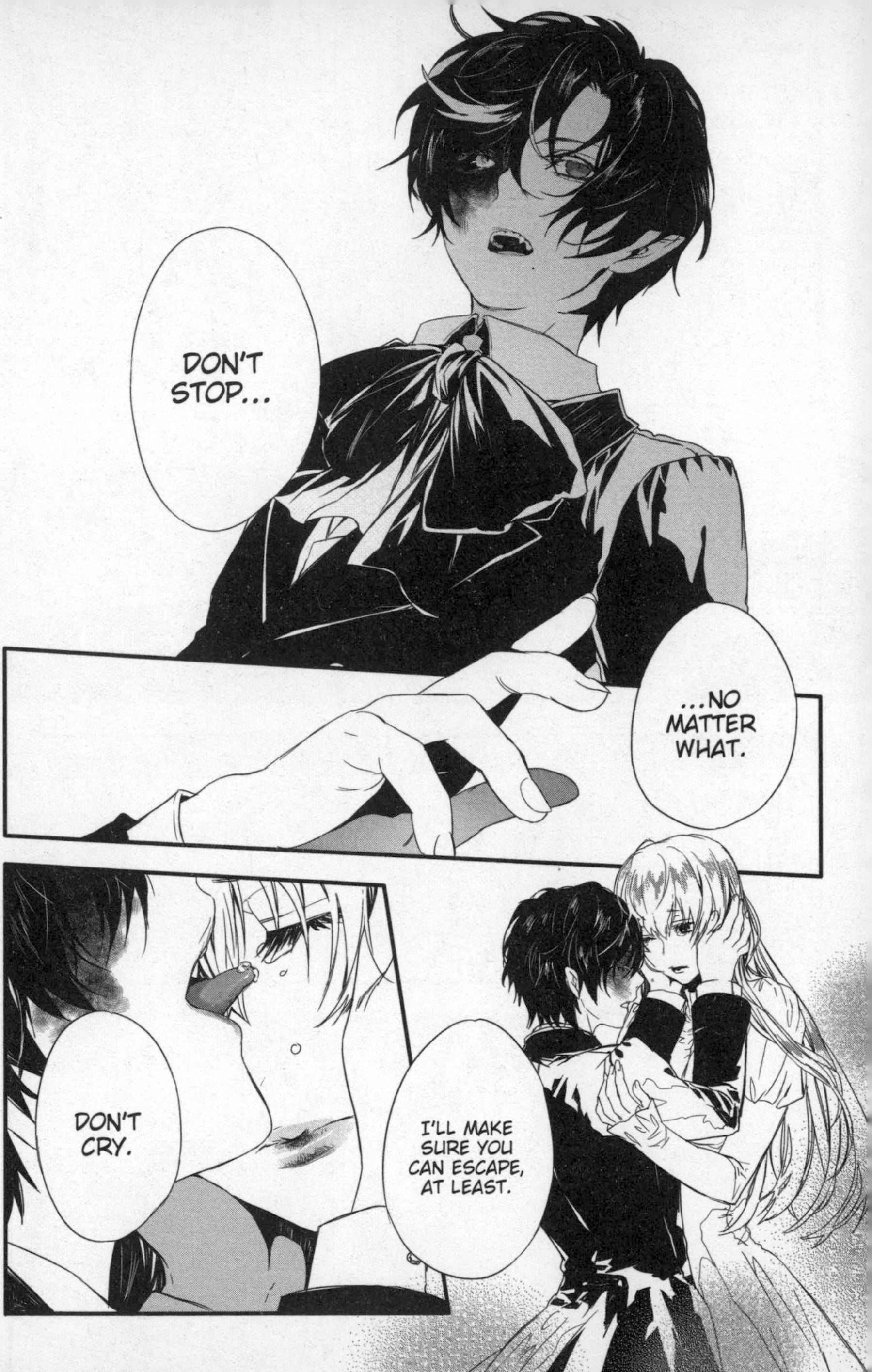
DON'T STOP...
...NO MATTER WHAT.
I'LL MAKE SURE YOU CAN ESCAPE, AT LEAST.
DON'T CRY.

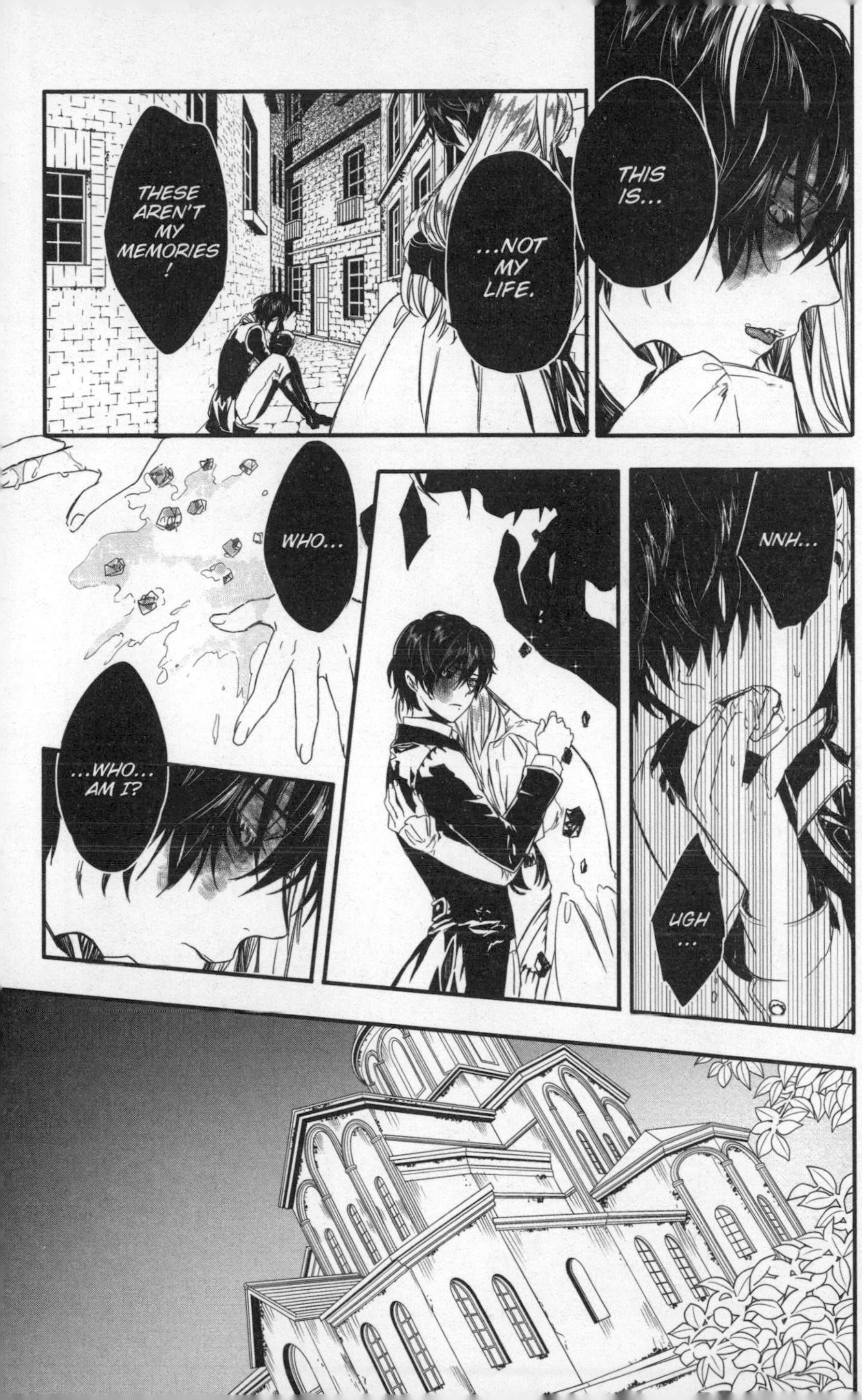
THIS IS...
...NOT MY LIFE.
THESE AREN'T MY MEMORIES!
NNH...
UGH...
WHO...
...WHO... AM I?

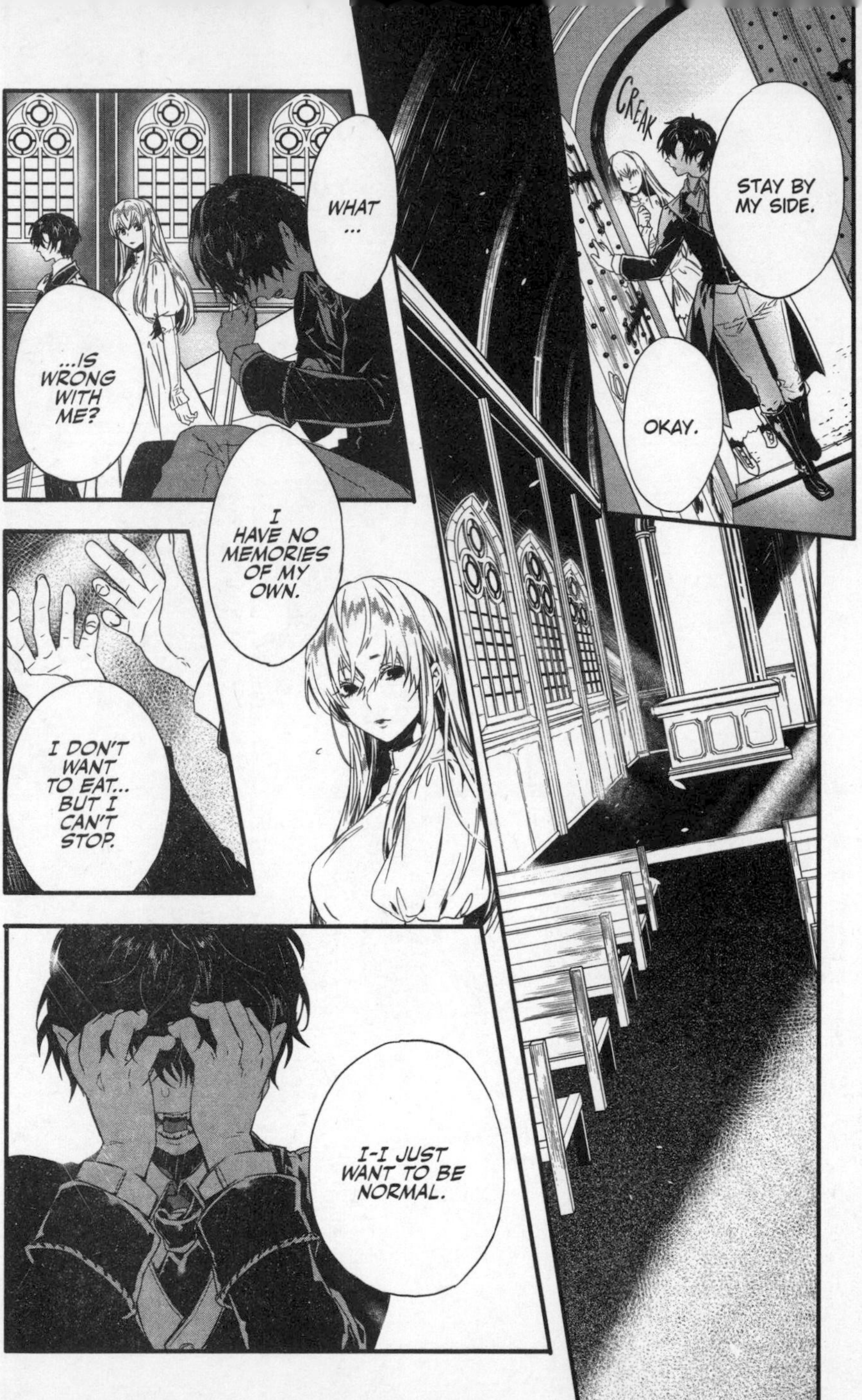
CREAK
STAY BY MY SIDE.
OKAY.
I HAVE NO MEMORIES OF MY OWN.
WHAT ...
...IS WRONG WITH ME?
I DON'T WANT TO EAT... BUT I CAN'T STOP.
I-I JUST WANT TO BE NORMAL.

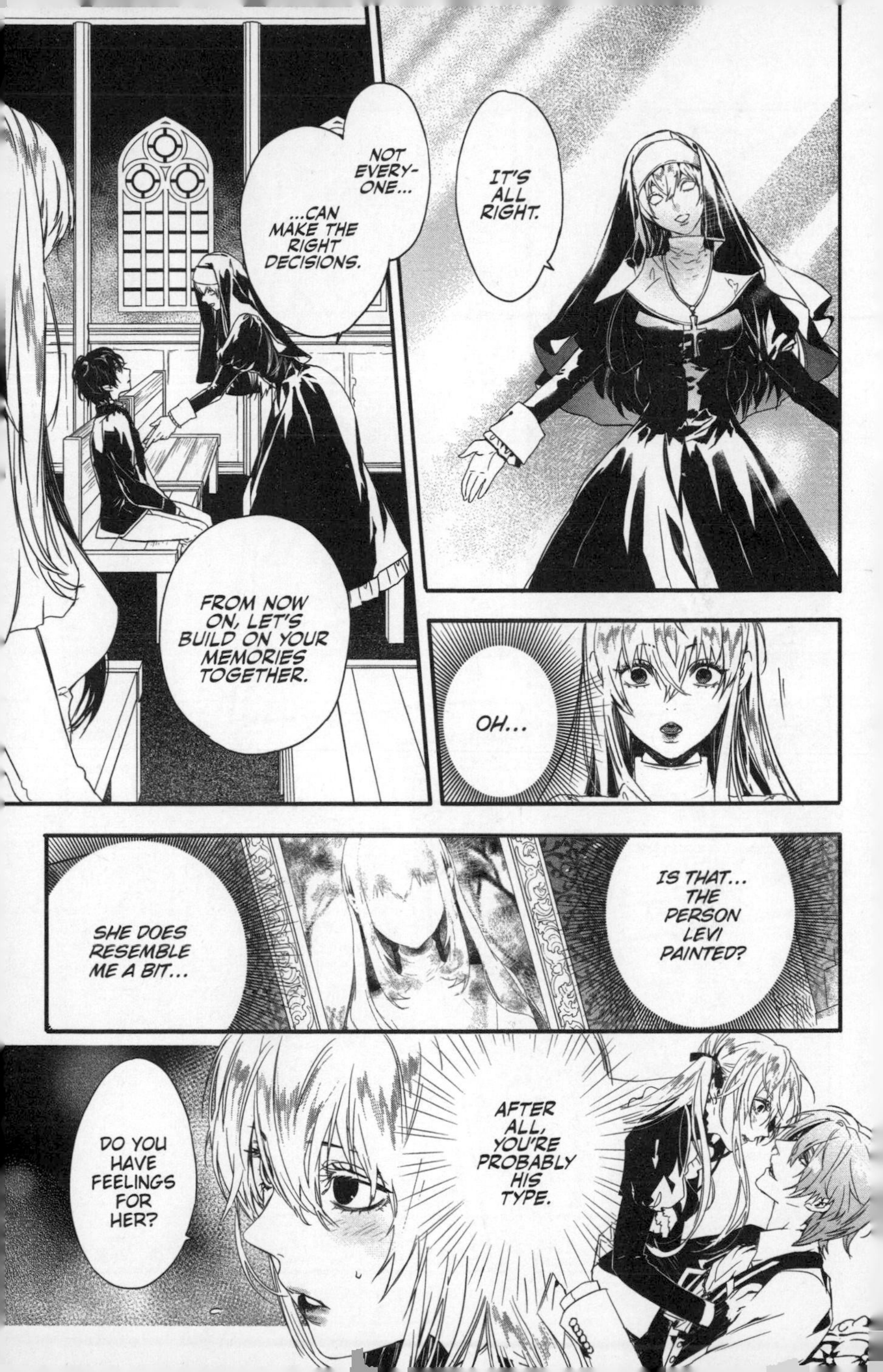
IT'S ALL RIGHT.
NOT EVERY-ONE...
...CAN MAKE THE RIGHT DECISIONS.
FROM NOW ON, LET'S BUILD ON YOUR MEMORIES TOGETHER.
OH...
IS THAT... THE PERSON LEVI PAINTED?
SHE DOES RESEMBLE ME A BIT...
AFTER ALL, YOU'RE PROBABLY HIS TYPE.
DO YOU HAVE FEELINGS FOR HER?

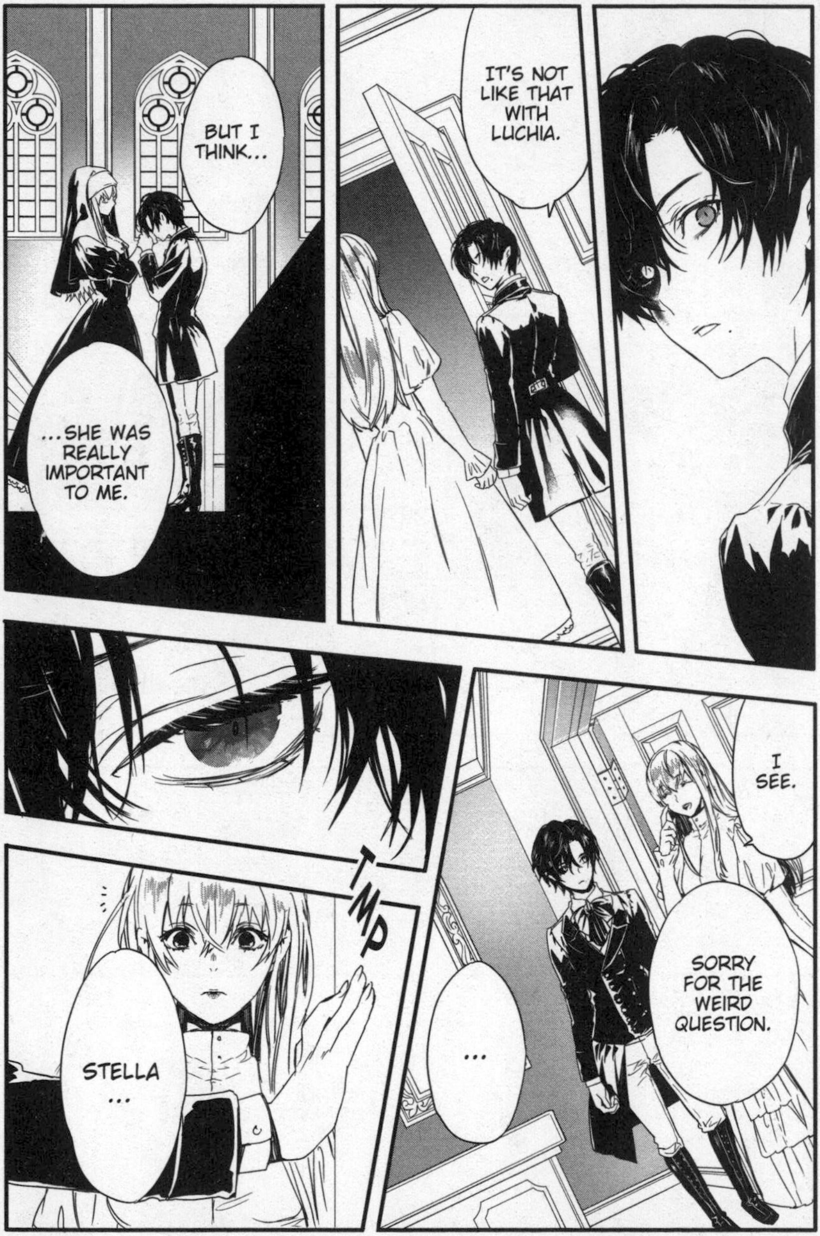

IT'S NOT LIKE THAT WITH LUCHIA.
BUT I THINK...
...SHE WAS REALLY IMPORTANT TO ME.
I SEE.
SORRY FOR THE WEIRD QUESTION.
...
TMP
STELLA ...

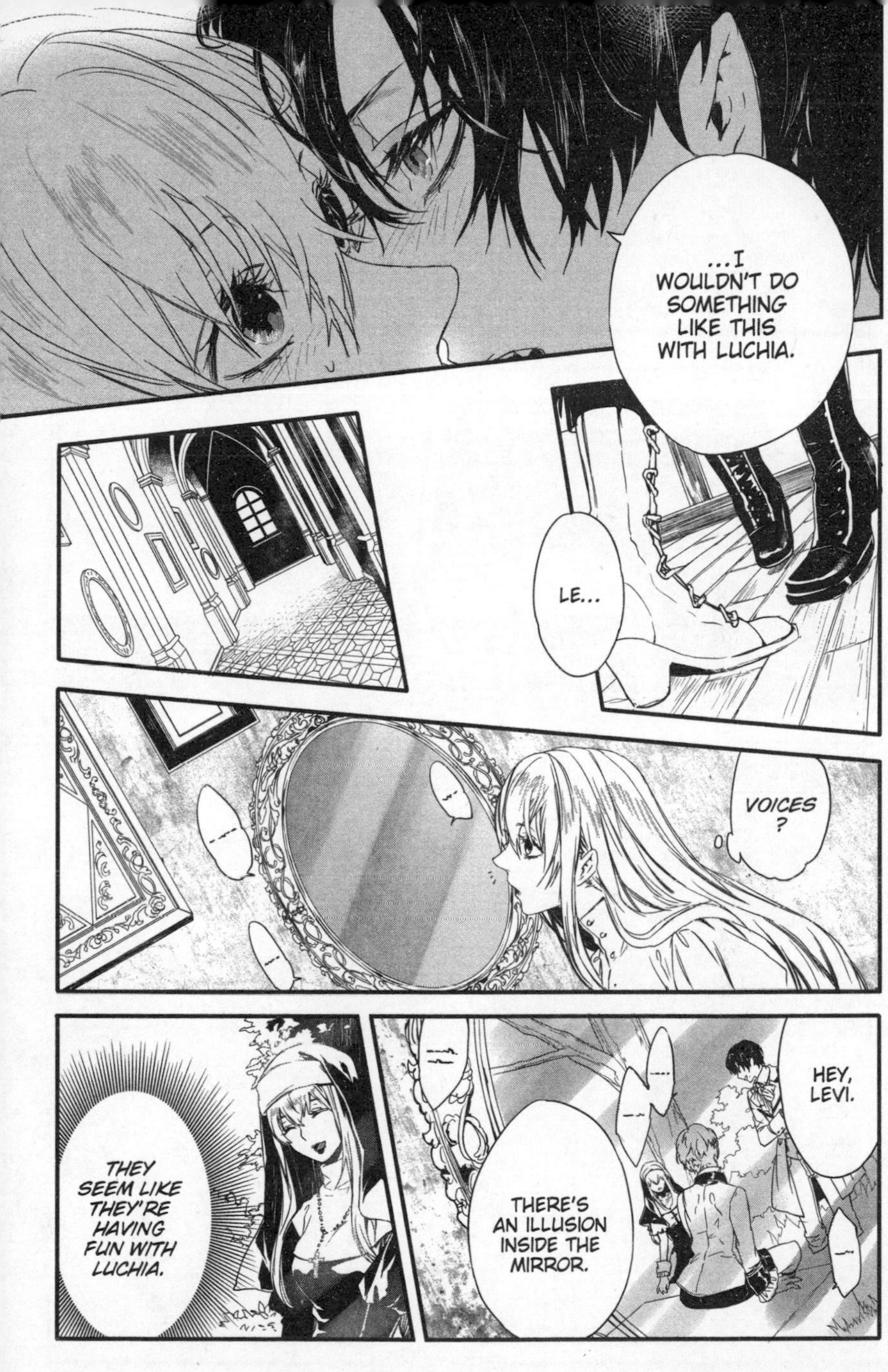
...I WOULDN'T DO SOMETHING LIKE THIS WITH LUCHIA.
LE...
VOICES?
HEY, LEVI.
THERE'S AN ILLUSION INSIDE THE MIRROR.
THEY SEEM LIKE THEY'RE HAVING FUN WITH LUCHIA.

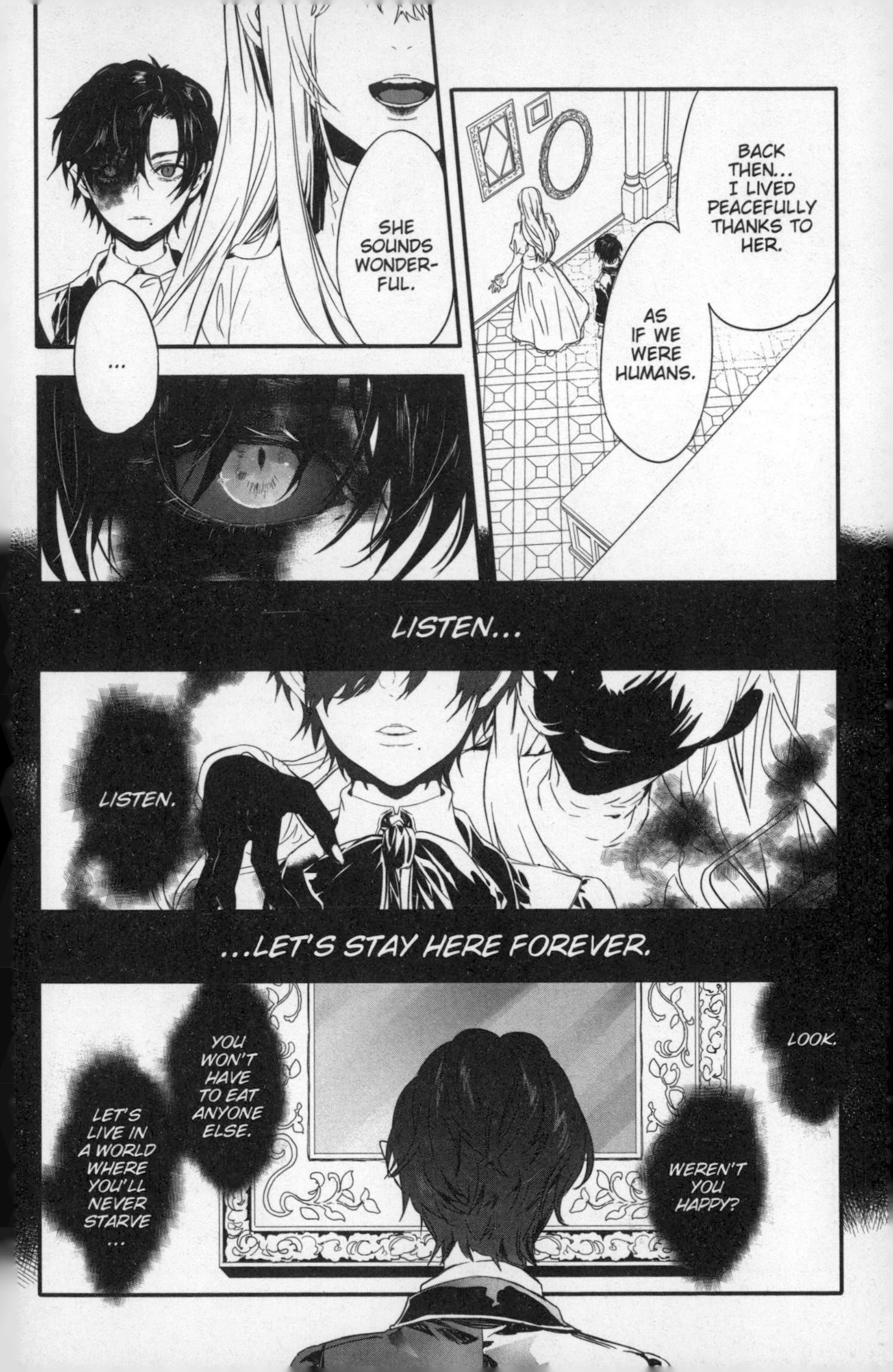
BACK THEN... I LIVED PEACEFULLY THANKS TO HER.
AS IF WE WERE HUMANS.
SHE SOUNDS WONDER-FUL.
...
LISTEN...
LISTEN.
...LET'S STAY HERE FOREVER.
LOOK.
WEREN'T YOU HAPPY?
YOU WON'T HAVE TO EAT ANYONE ELSE.
LET'S LIVE IN A WORLD WHERE YOU'LL NEVER STARVE...

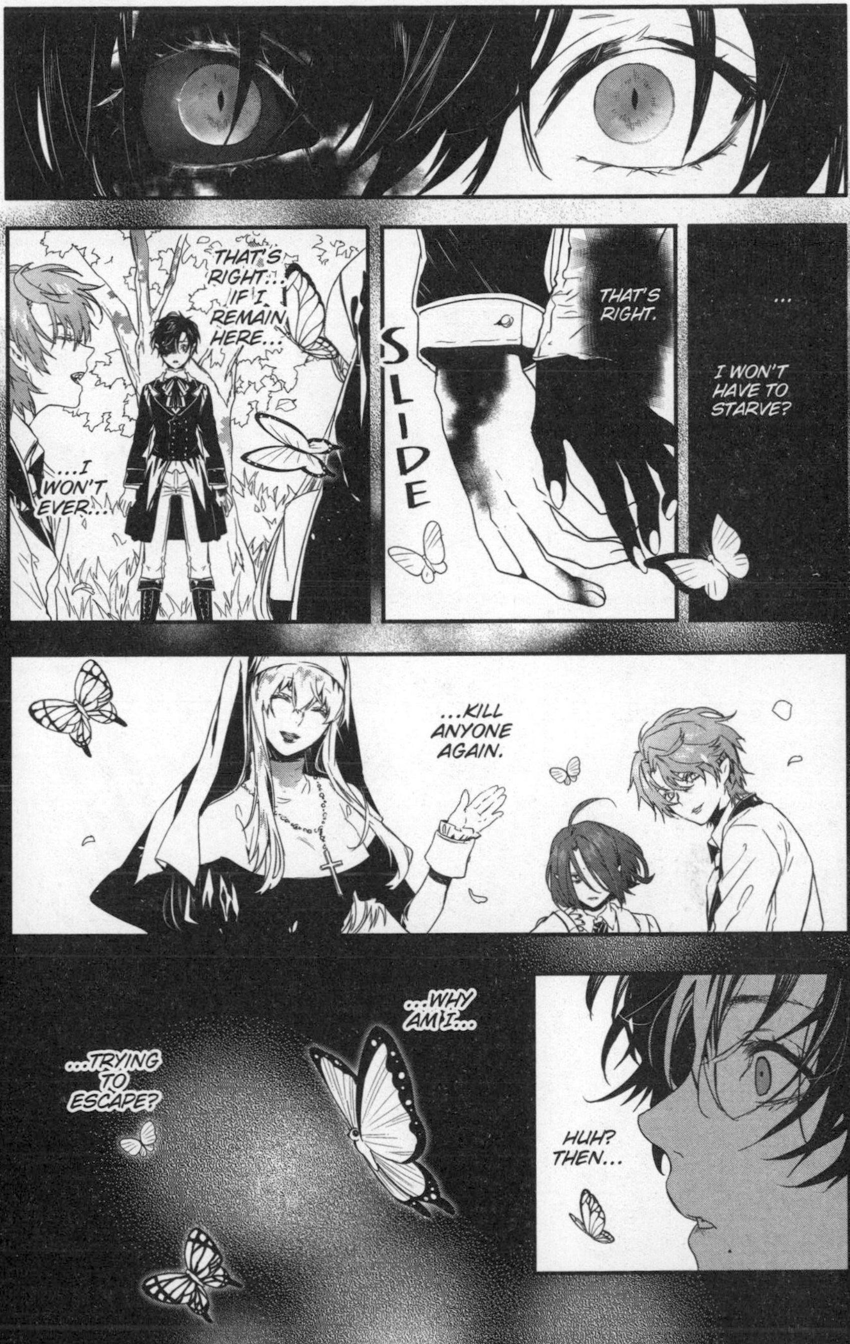
...
I WON'T HAVE TO STARVE?
THAT'S RIGHT.
SLIDE
THAT'S RIGHT... IF I REMAIN HERE...
...I WON'T EVER...
...KILL ANYONE AGAIN.
HUH? THEN...
...WHY AM I...
...TRYING TO ESCAPE?

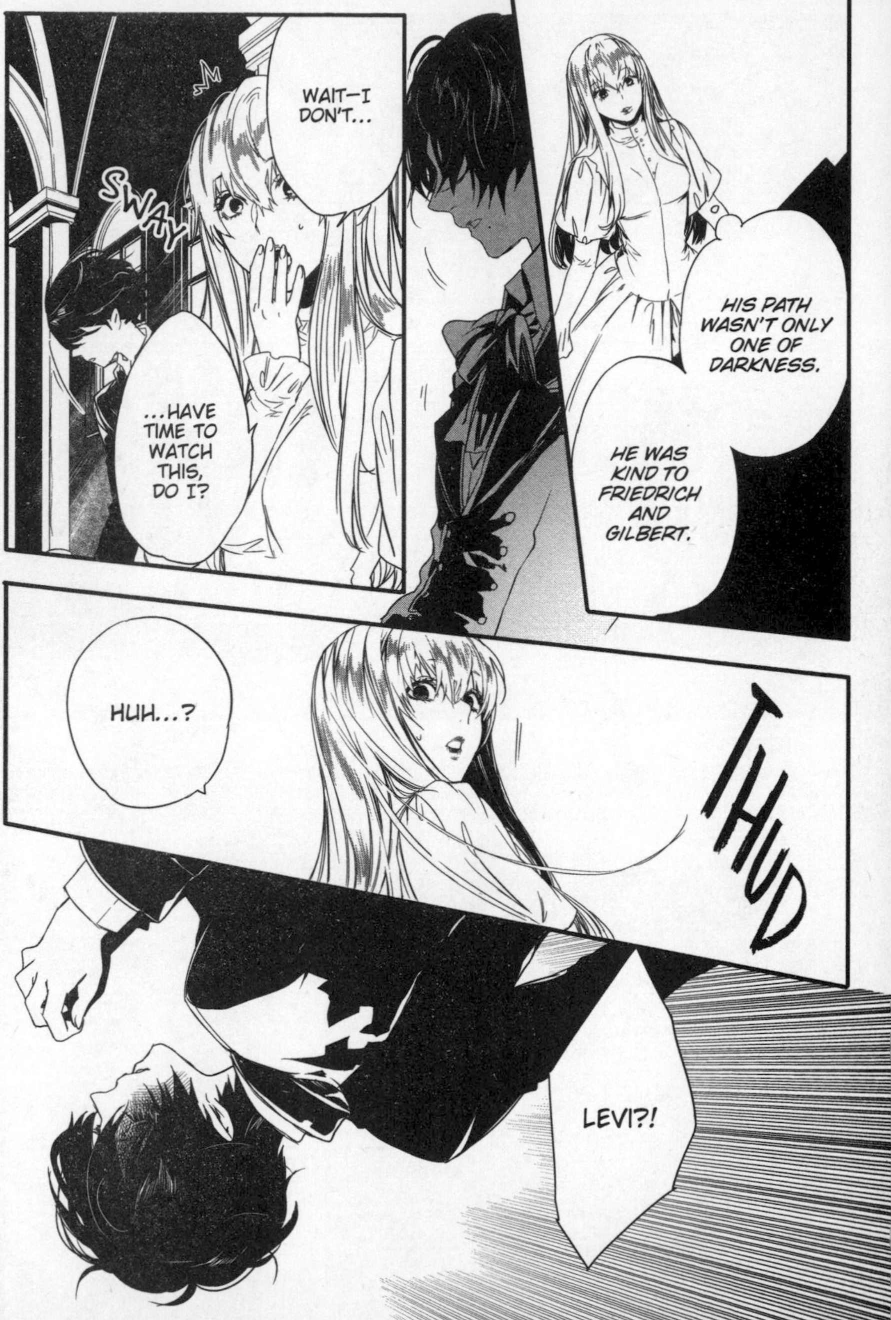
HIS PATH WASN'T ONLY ONE OF DARKNESS.
HE WAS KIND TO FRIEDRICH AND GILBERT.
SWAY
WAIT—I DON'T...
...HAVE TIME TO WATCH THIS, DO I?
THUD
HUH...?
LEVI?!

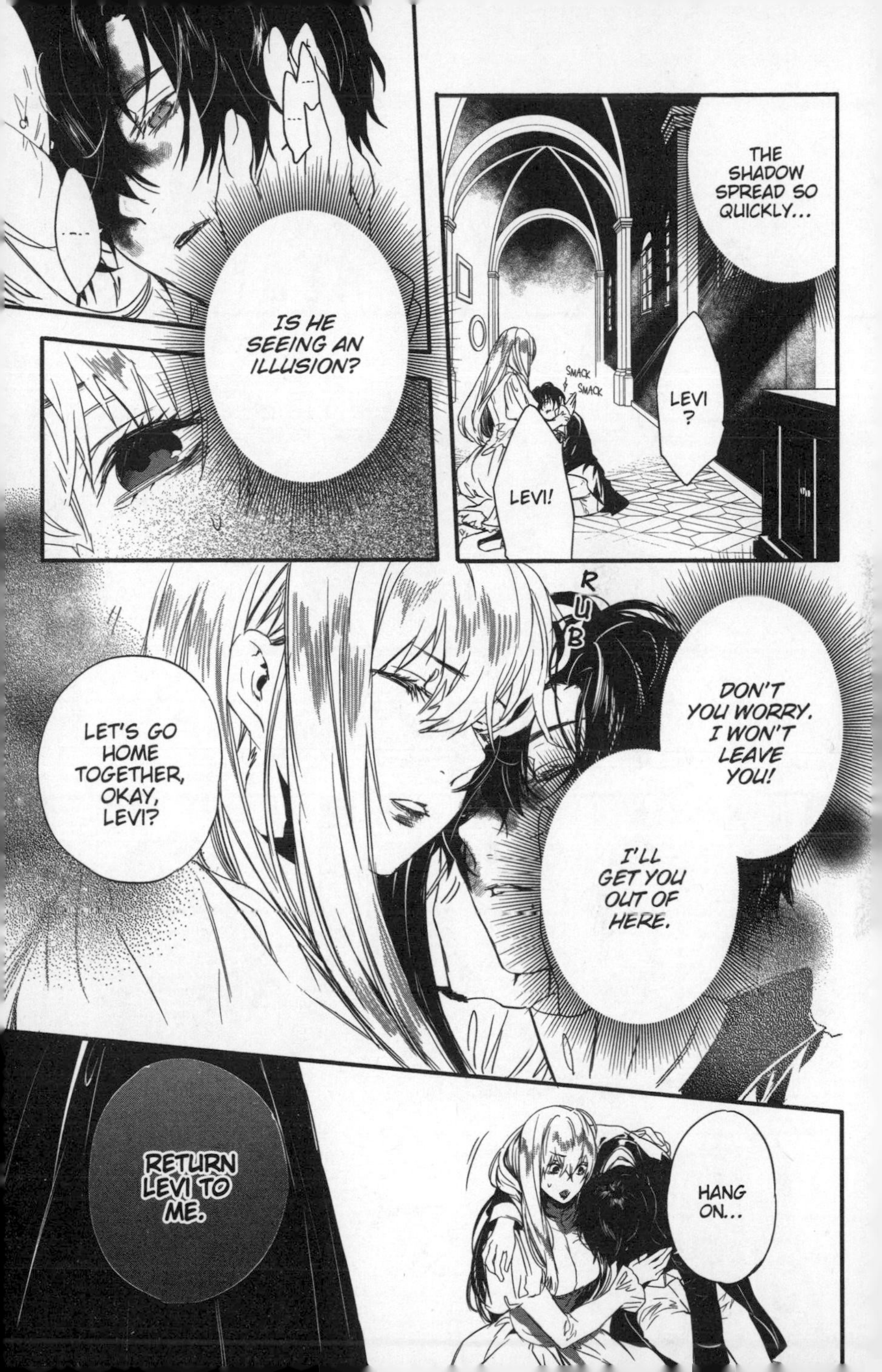
THE SHADOW SPREAD SO QUICKLY...
LEVI?
SMACK SMACK
LEVI!
IS HE SEEING AN ILLUSION?
RUB
DON'T YOU WORRY. I WON'T LEAVE YOU!
I'LL GET YOU OUT OF HERE.
LET'S GO HOME TOGETHER, OKAY, LEVI?
HANG ON...
RETURN LEVI TO ME.

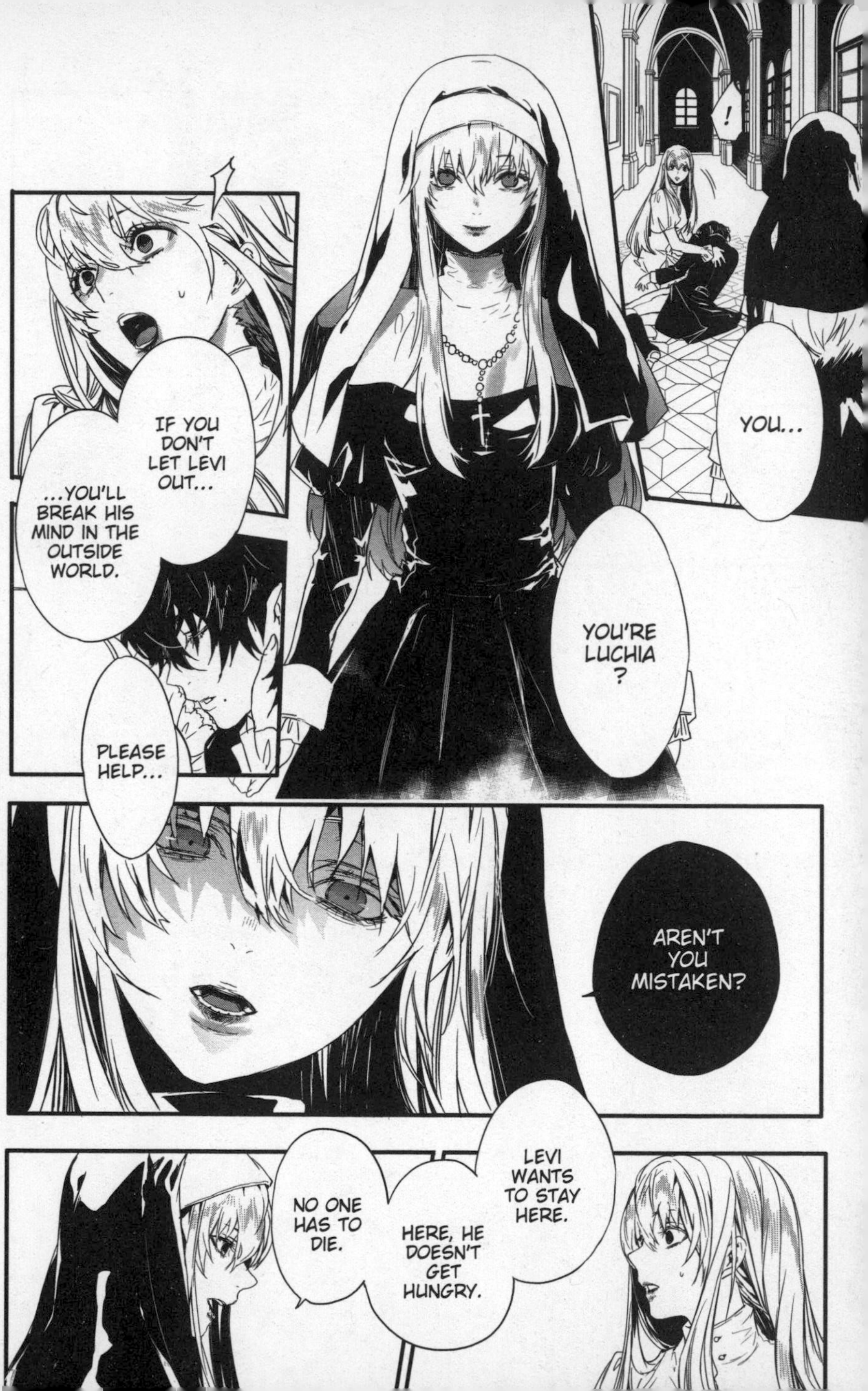
!
YOU...
YOU'RE LUCHIA?
IF YOU DON'T LET LEVI OUT...
...YOU'LL BREAK HIS MIND IN THE OUTSIDE WORLD.
PLEASE HELP...
AREN'T YOU MISTAKEN?
LEVI WANTS TO STAY HERE.
HERE, HE DOESN'T GET HUNGRY.
NO ONE HAS TO DIE.

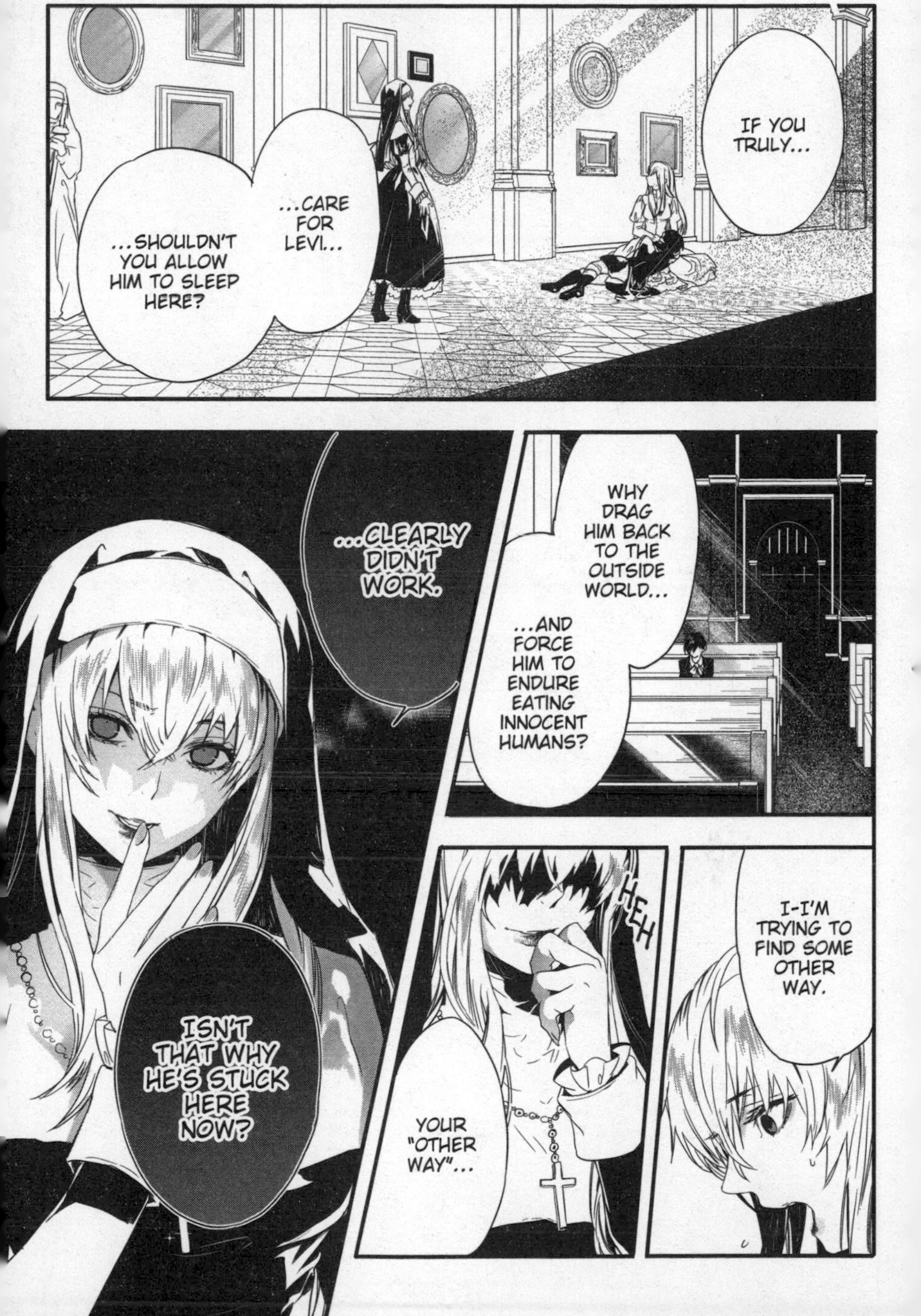
IF YOU TRULY...
...CARE FOR LEVI...
...SHOULDN'T YOU ALLOW HIM TO SLEEP HERE?
WHY DRAG HIM BACK TO THE OUTSIDE WORLD...
...AND FORCE HIM TO ENDURE EATING INNOCENT HUMANS?
I-I'M TRYING TO FIND SOME OTHER WAY.
HEH
YOUR "OTHER WAY"...
...CLEARLY DIDN'T WORK.
ISN'T THAT WHY HE'S STUCK HERE NOW?

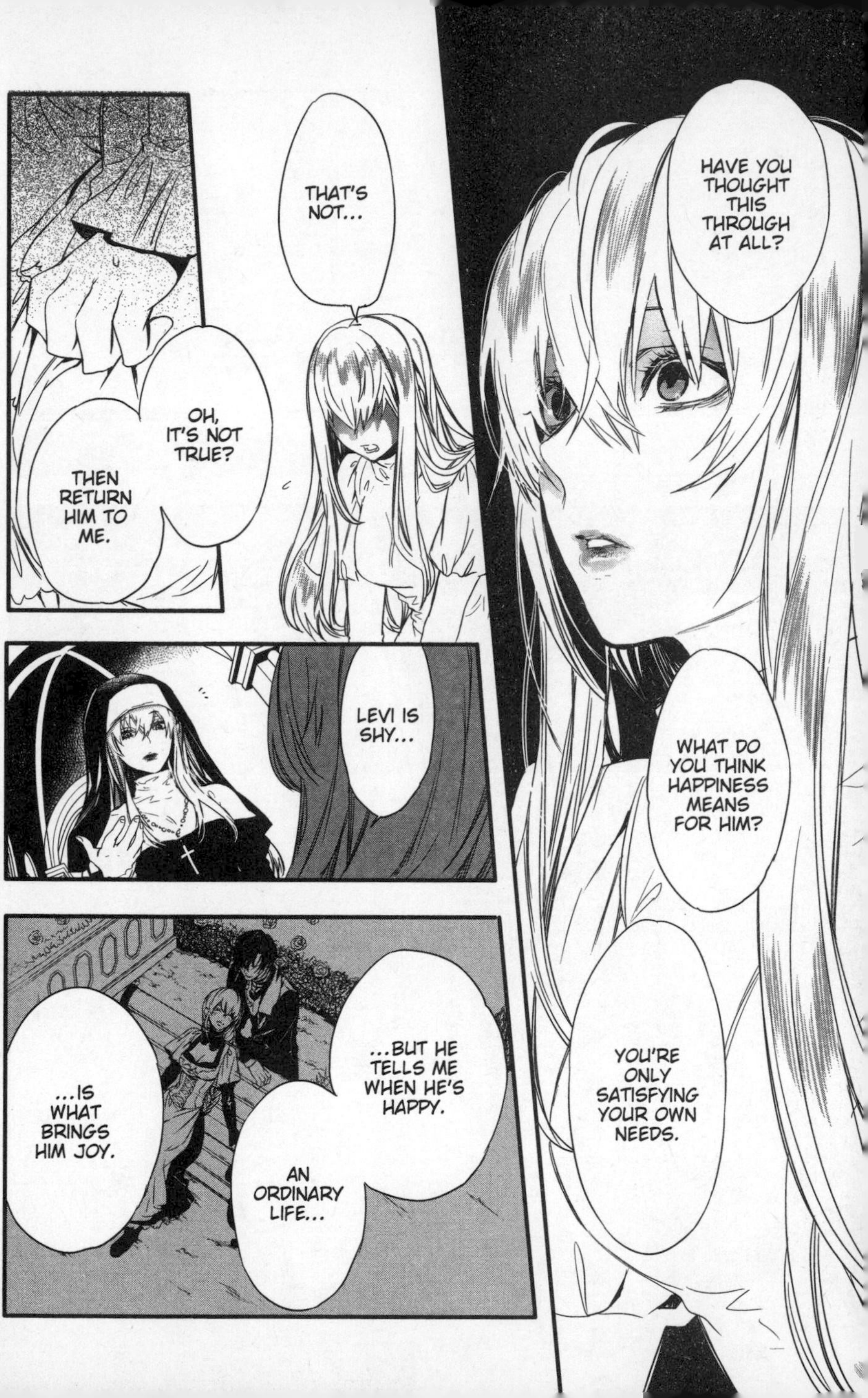
HAVE YOU THOUGHT THIS THROUGH AT ALL?
WHAT DO YOU THINK HAPPINESS MEANS FOR HIM?
YOU'RE ONLY SATISFYING YOUR OWN NEEDS.
THAT'S NOT...
OH, IT'S NOT TRUE?
THEN RETURN HIM TO ME.
LEVI IS SHY...
...BUT HE TELLS ME WHEN HE'S HAPPY.
AN ORDINARY LIFE...
...IS WHAT BRINGS HIM JOY.

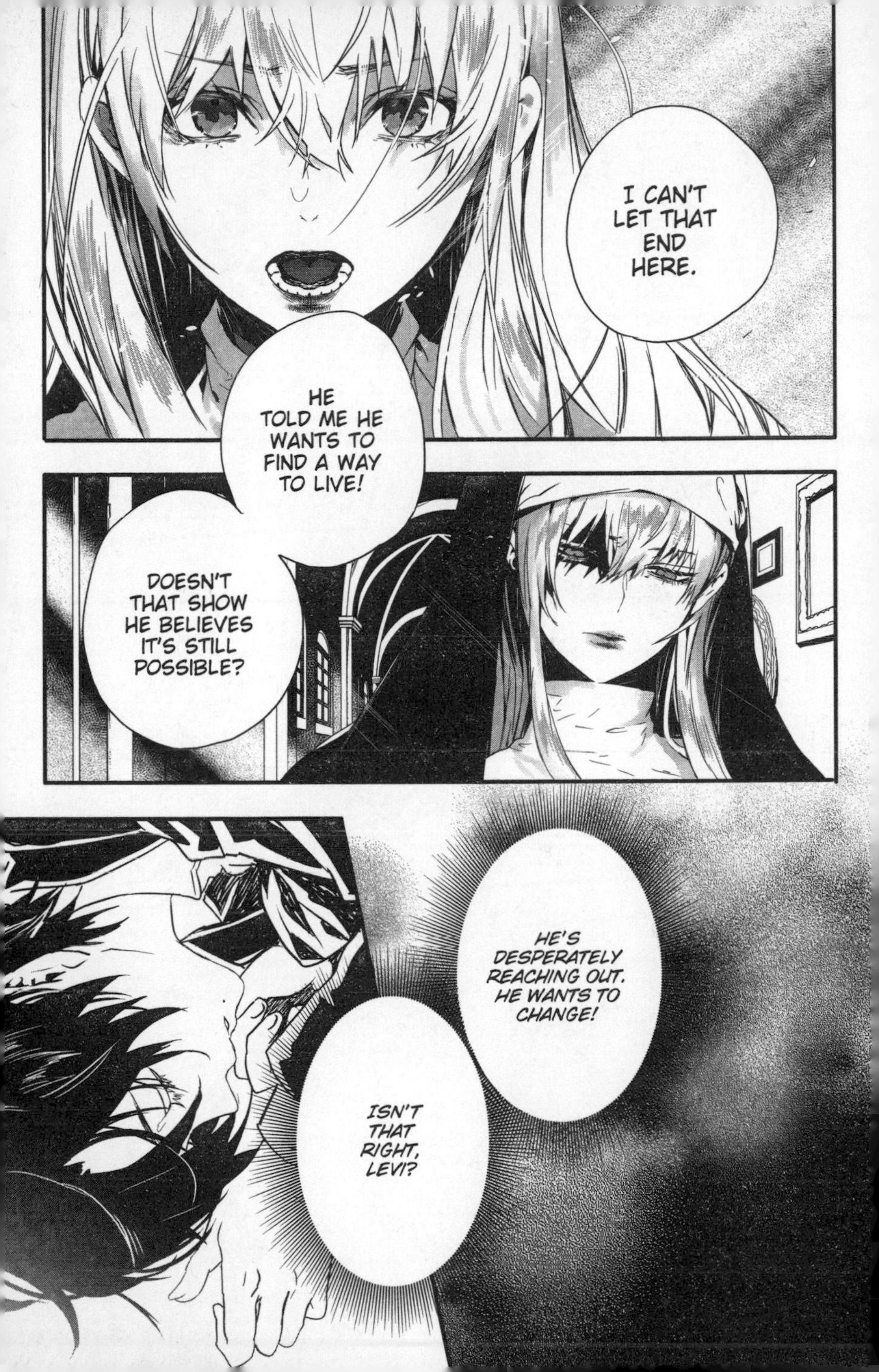
I CAN'T LET THAT END HERE.
HE TOLD ME HE WANTS TO FIND A WAY TO LIVE!
DOESN'T THAT SHOW HE BELIEVES IT'S STILL POSSIBLE?
HE'S DESPERATELY REACHING OUT. HE WANTS TO CHANGE!
ISN'T THAT RIGHT, LEVI?

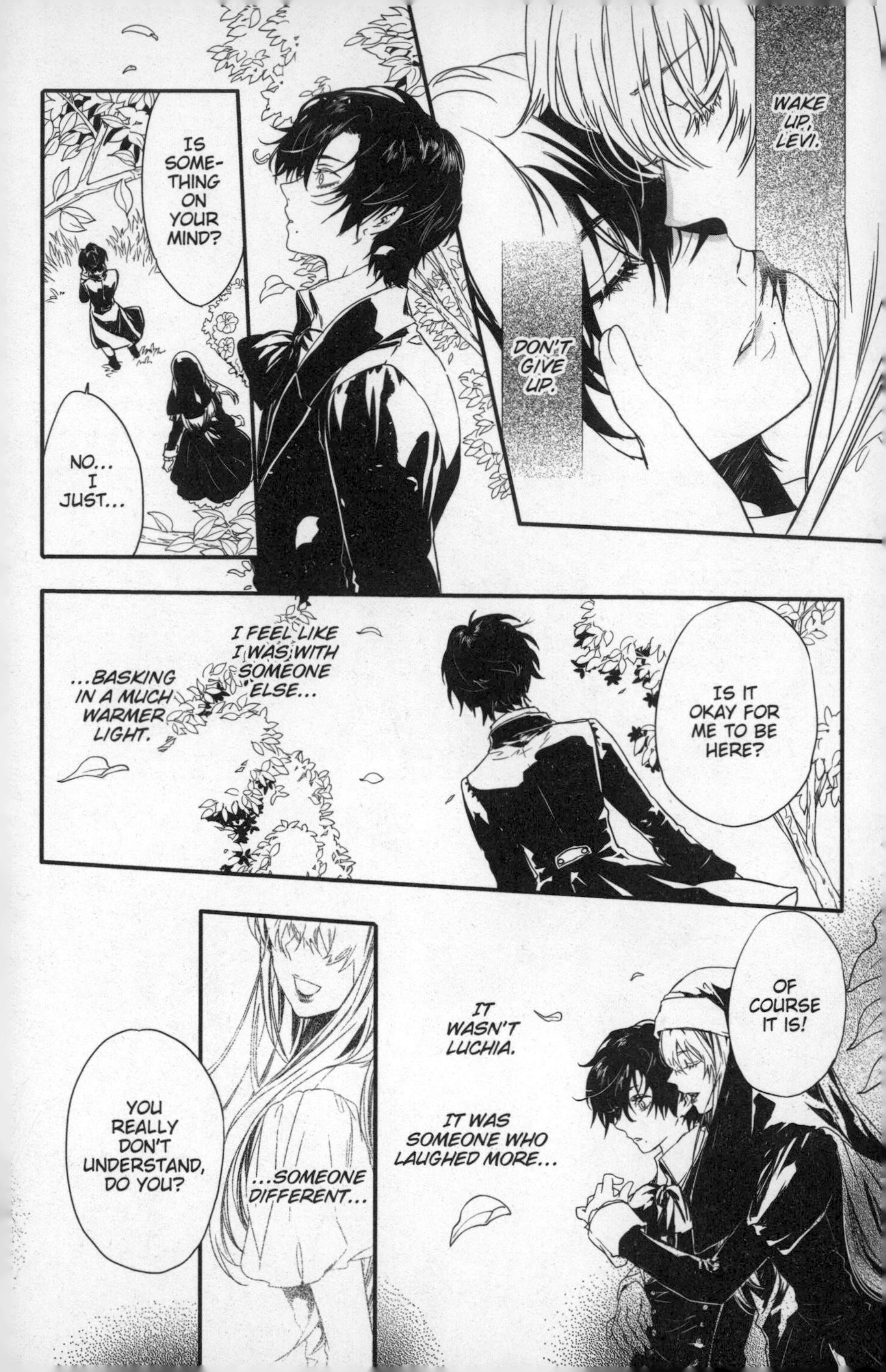
WAKE UP, LEVI.
DON'T GIVE UP.
IS SOMETHING ON YOUR MIND?
NO... I JUST...
IS IT OKAY FOR ME TO BE HERE?
I FEEL LIKE I WAS WITH SOMEONE ELSE...
...BASKING IN A MUCH WARMER LIGHT.
OF COURSE IT IS!
IT WASN'T LUCHIA.
IT WAS SOMEONE WHO LAUGHED MORE...
...SOMEONE DIFFERENT...
YOU REALLY DON'T UNDERSTAND, DO YOU?

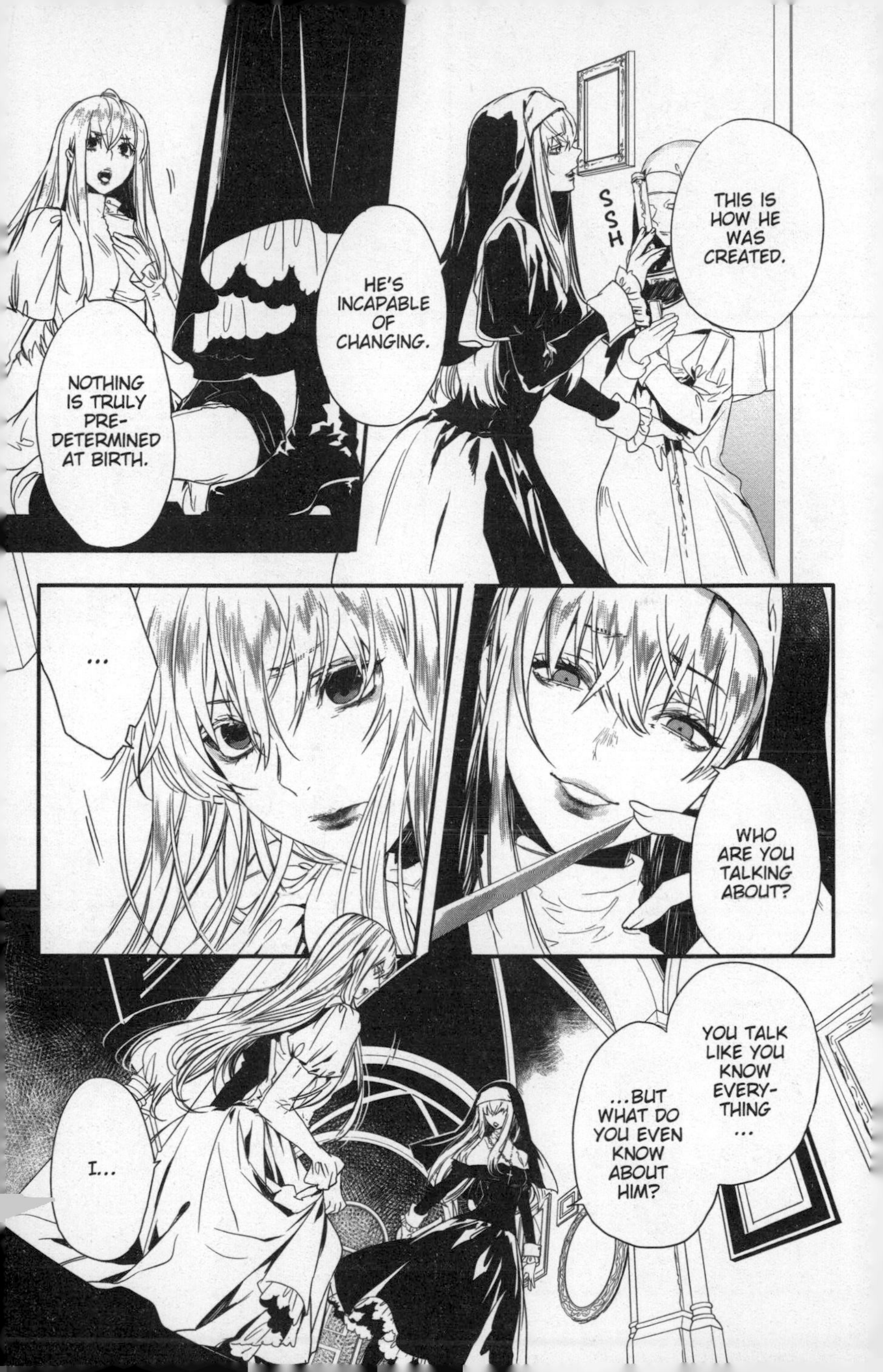
THIS IS HOW HE WAS CREATED.
SSH
HE'S INCAPABLE OF CHANGING.
NOTHING IS TRULY PRE-DETERMINED AT BIRTH.
WHO ARE YOU TALKING ABOUT?
...
YOU TALK LIKE YOU KNOW EVERY-THING ...
...BUT WHAT DO YOU EVEN KNOW ABOUT HIM?
I...

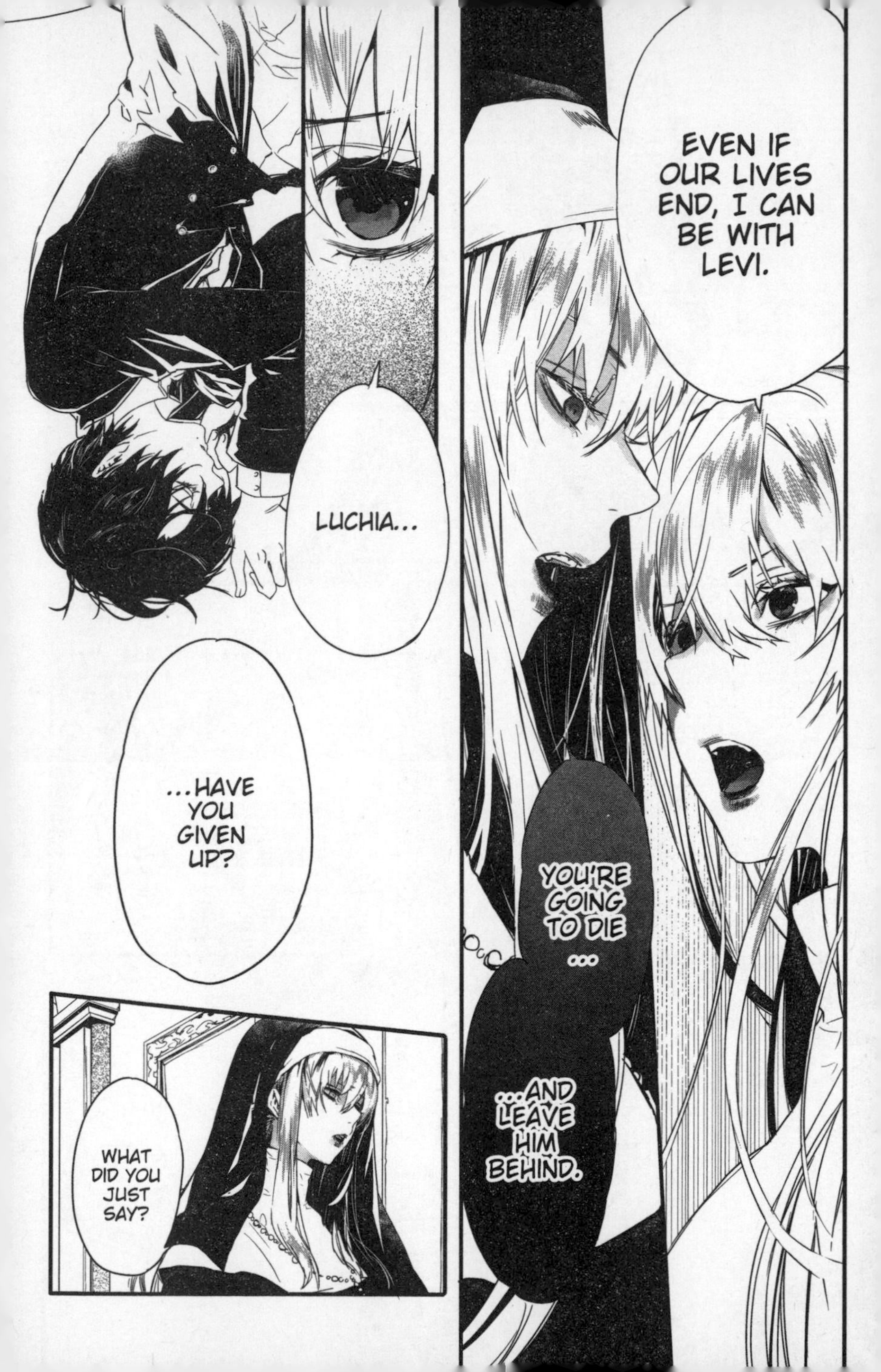
EVEN IF OUR LIVES END, I CAN BE WITH LEVI.
YOU'RE GOING TO DIE ...
...AND LEAVE HIM BEHIND.
LUCHIA...
...HAVE YOU GIVEN UP?
WHAT DID YOU JUST SAY?

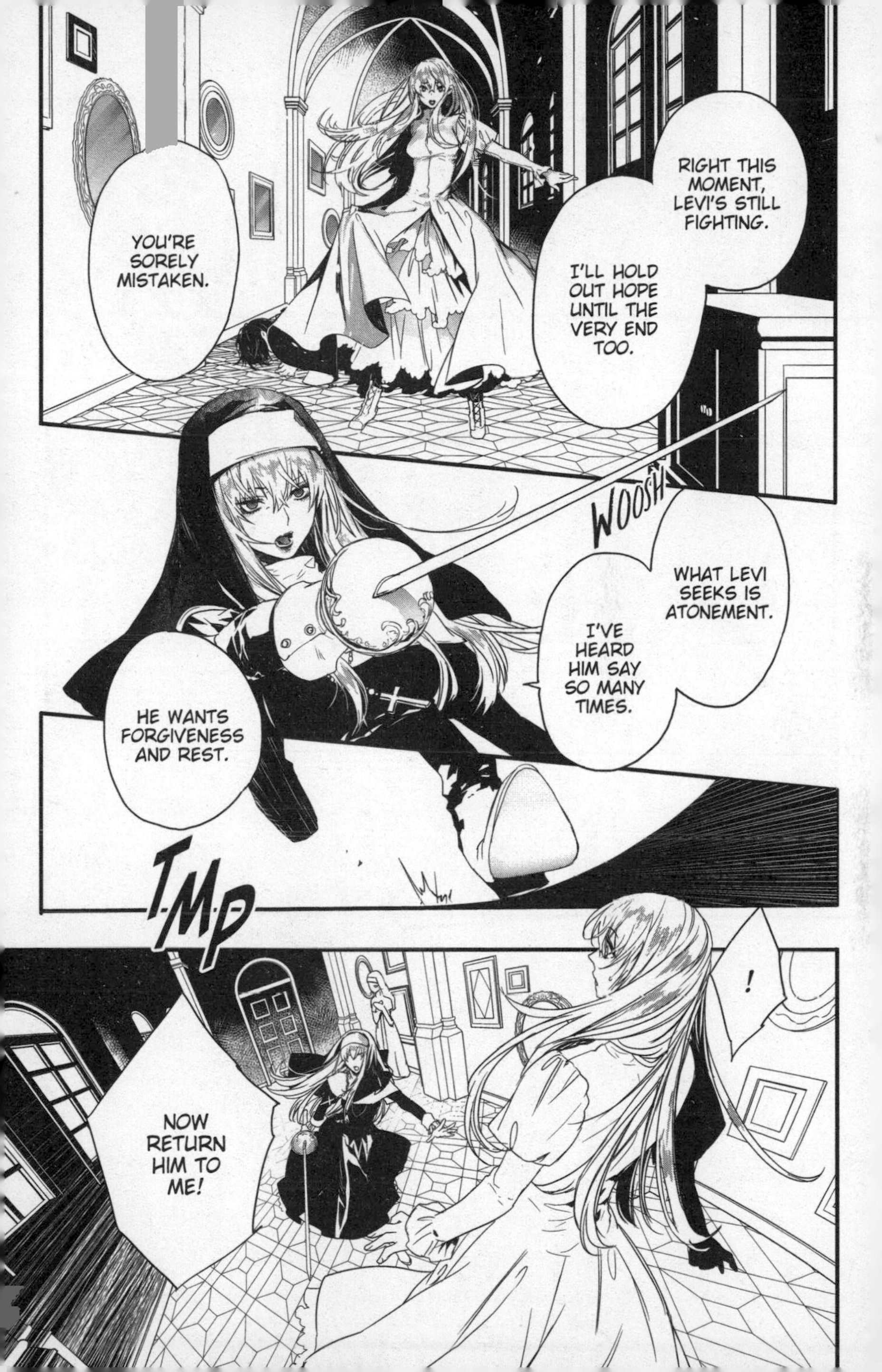
RIGHT THIS MOMENT, LEVI'S STILL FIGHTING.
I'LL HOLD OUT HOPE UNTIL THE VERY END TOO.
YOU'RE SORELY MISTAKEN.
WOOSH
WHAT LEVI SEEKS IS ATONEMENT.
I'VE HEARD HIM SAY SO MANY TIMES.
HE WANTS FORGIVENESS AND REST.
T-M-P
!
NOW RETURN HIM TO ME!

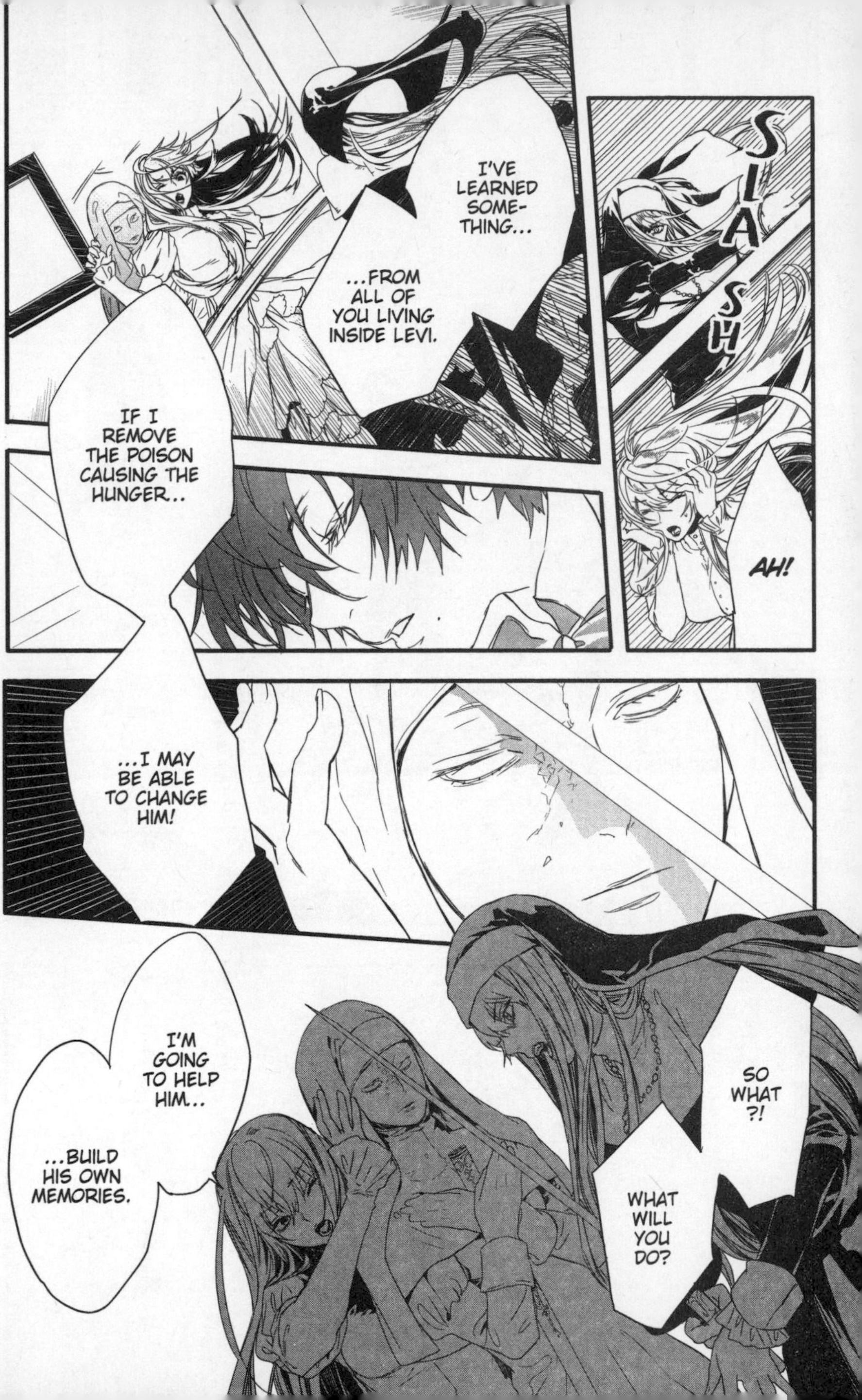
SLASH
AH!
I'VE LEARNED SOME-THING...
...FROM ALL OF YOU LIVING INSIDE LEVI.
IF I REMOVE THE POISON CAUSING THE HUNGER...
...I MAY BE ABLE TO CHANGE HIM!
SO WHAT?!
WHAT WILL YOU DO?
I'M GOING TO HELP HIM...
...BUILD HIS OWN MEMORIES.

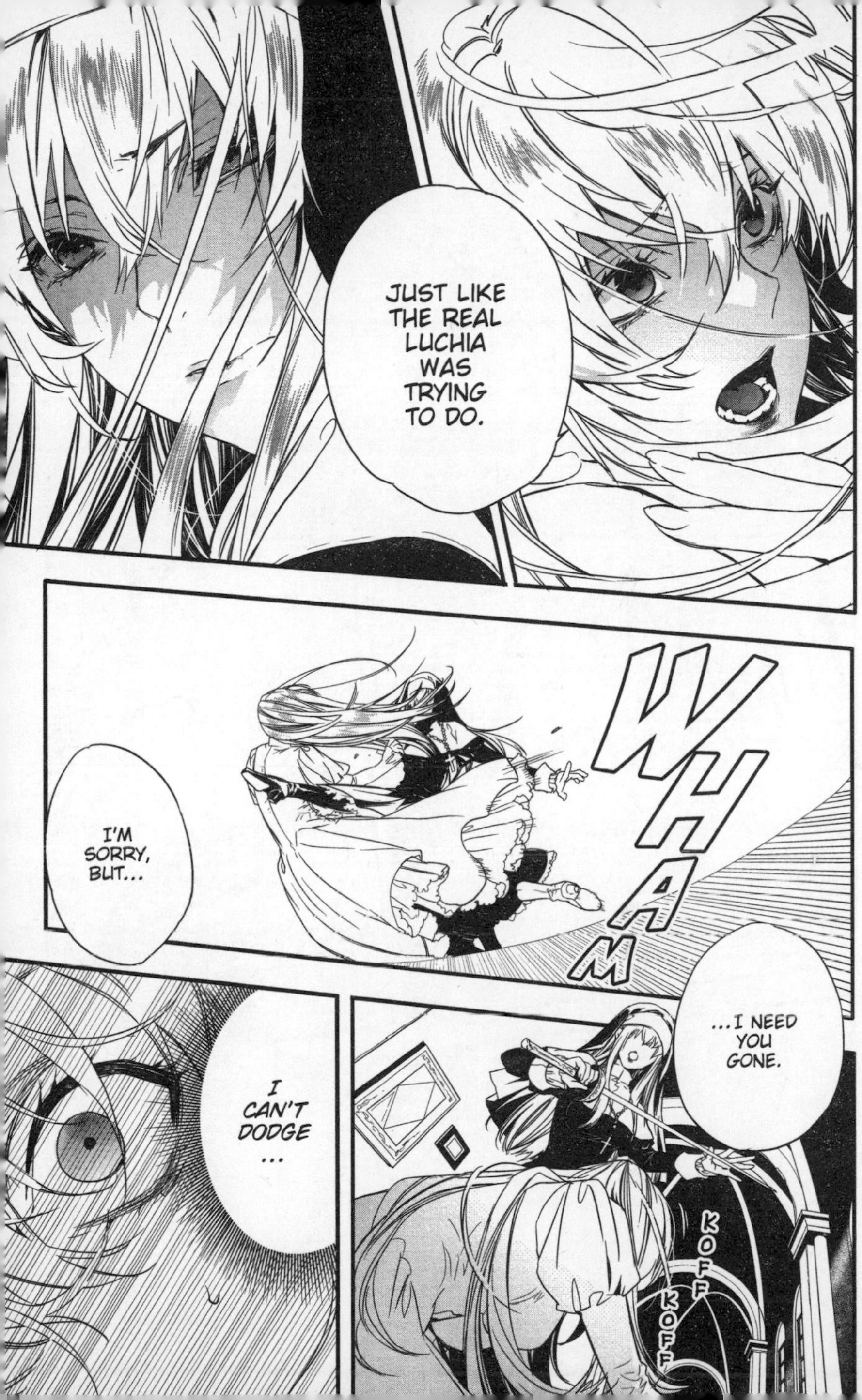
JUST LIKE THE REAL LUCHIA WAS TRYING TO DO.
WHAM
I'M SORRY, BUT...
...I NEED YOU GONE.
KOFF KOFF
I CAN'T DODGE ...

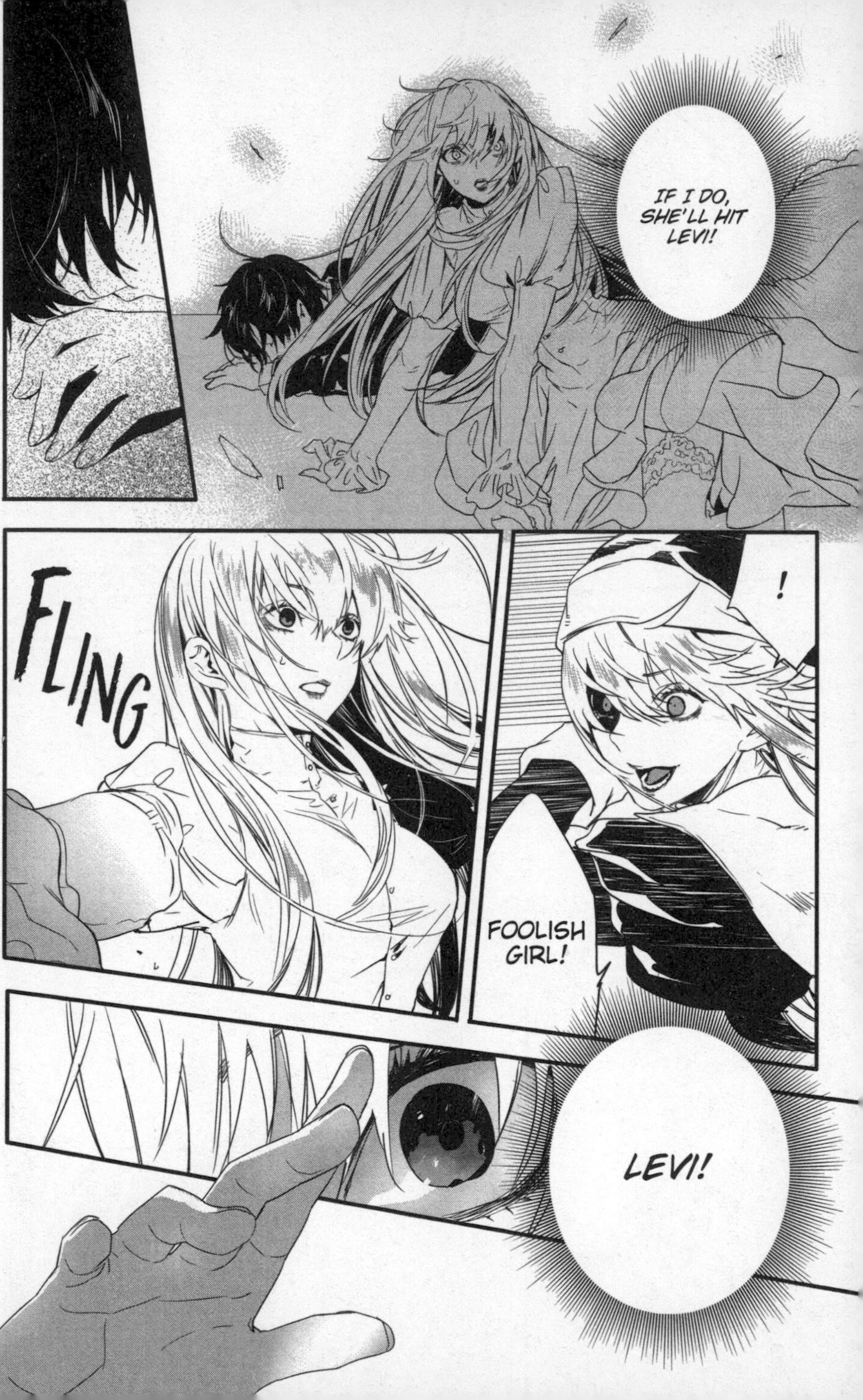
IF I DO, SHE'LL HIT LEVI!
!
FOOLISH GIRL!
FLING
LEVI!

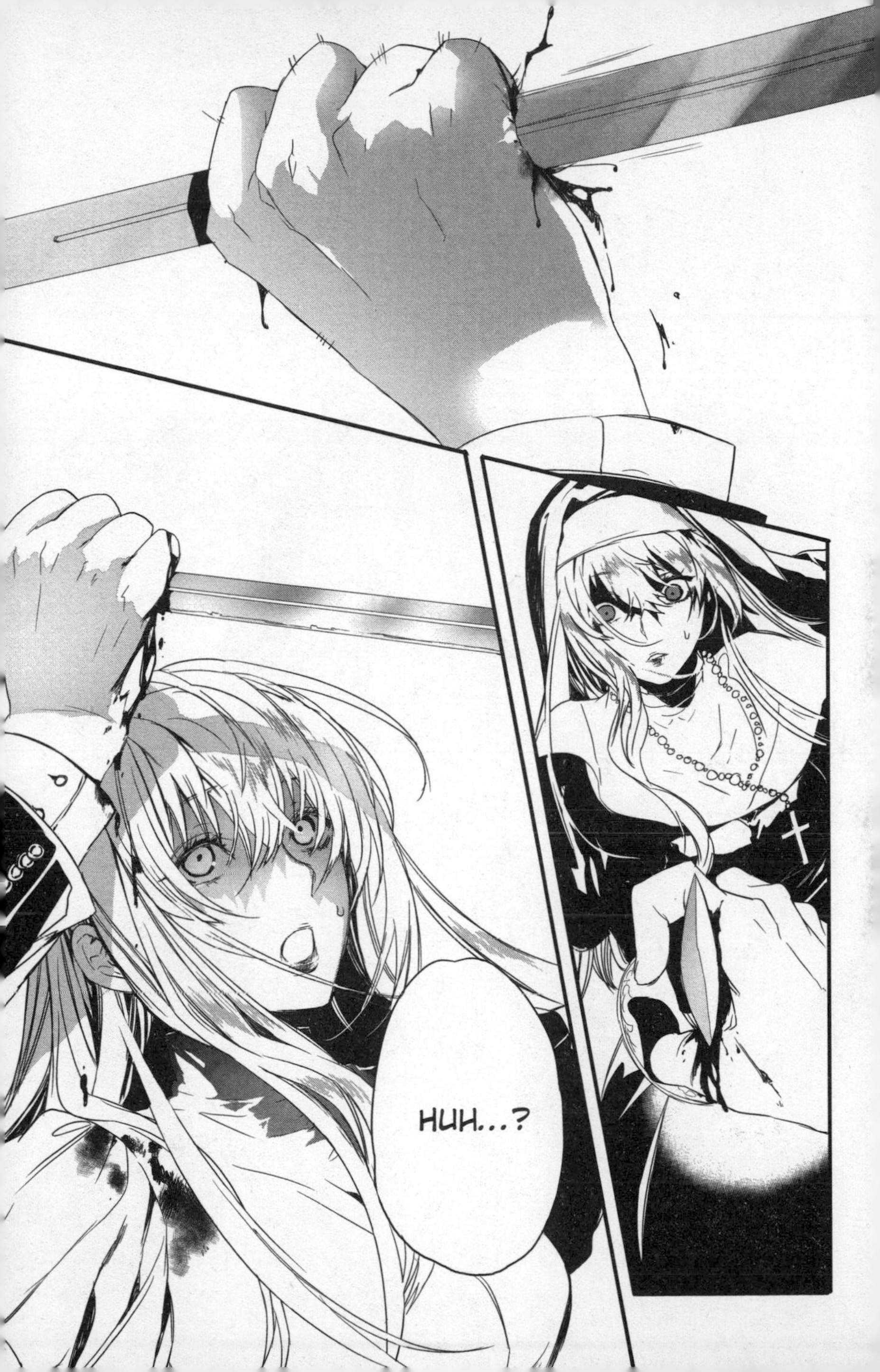
HUH...?

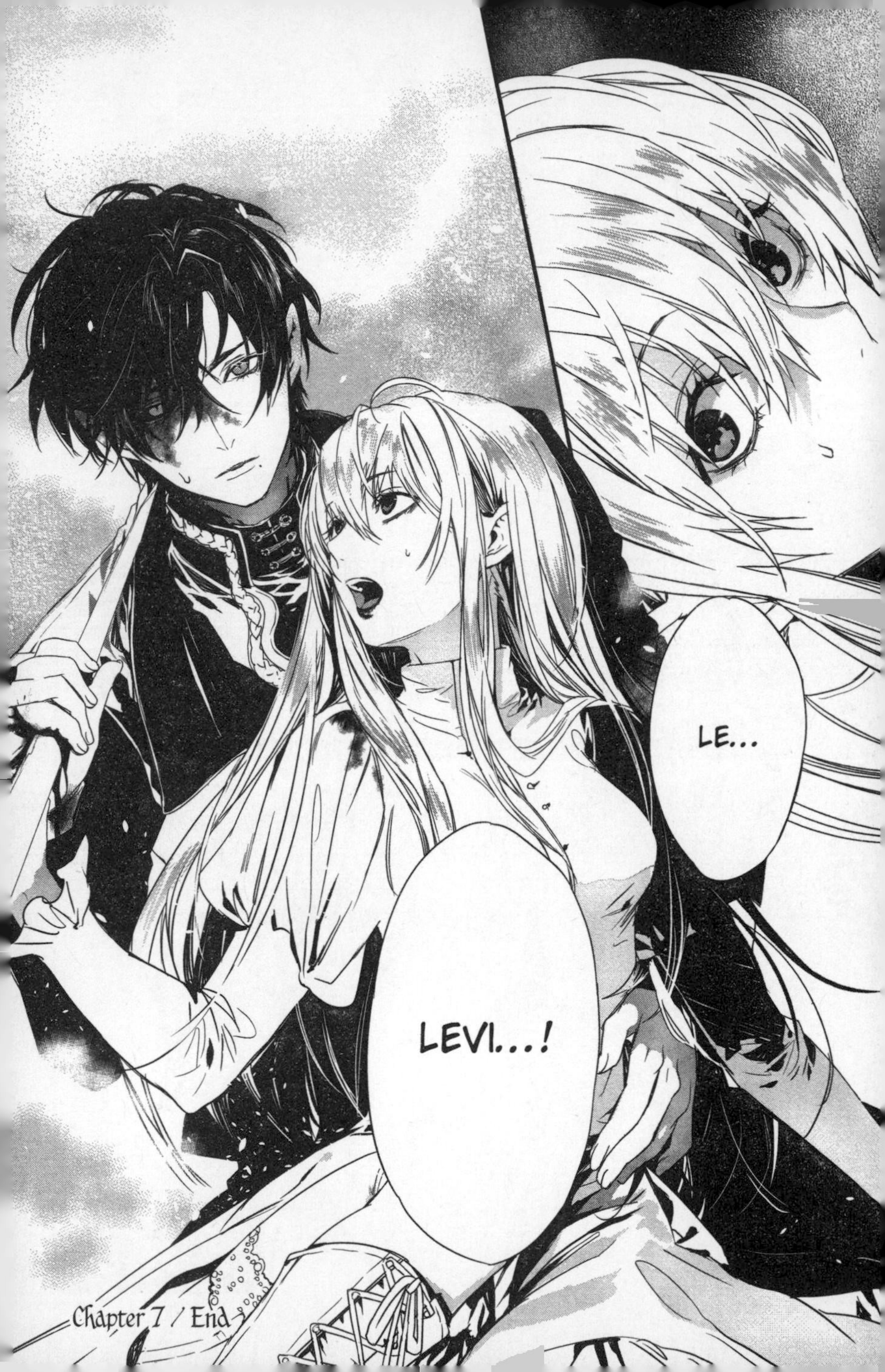
LE...
LEVI...!
Chapter 7 / End

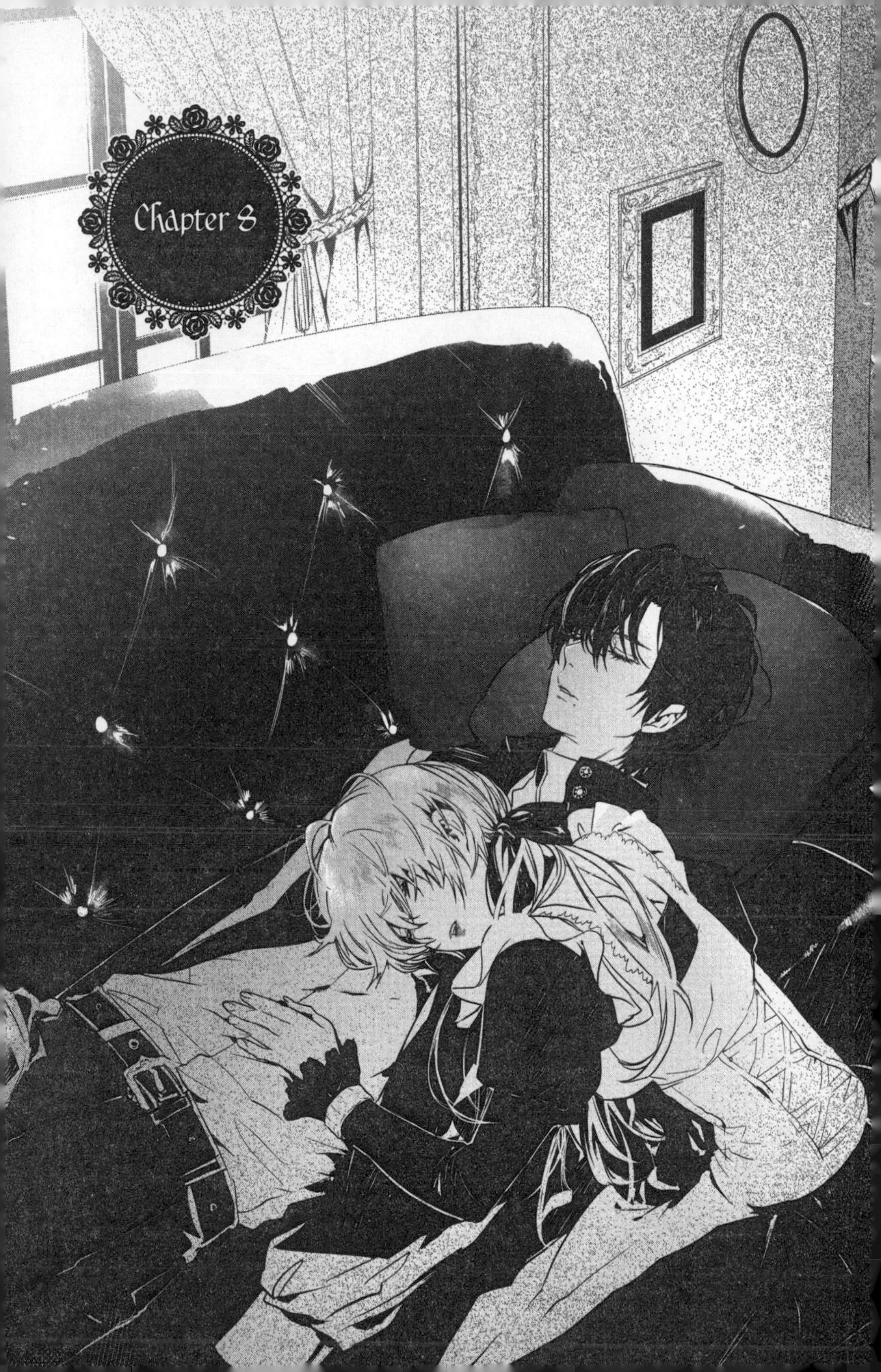
Chapter 8

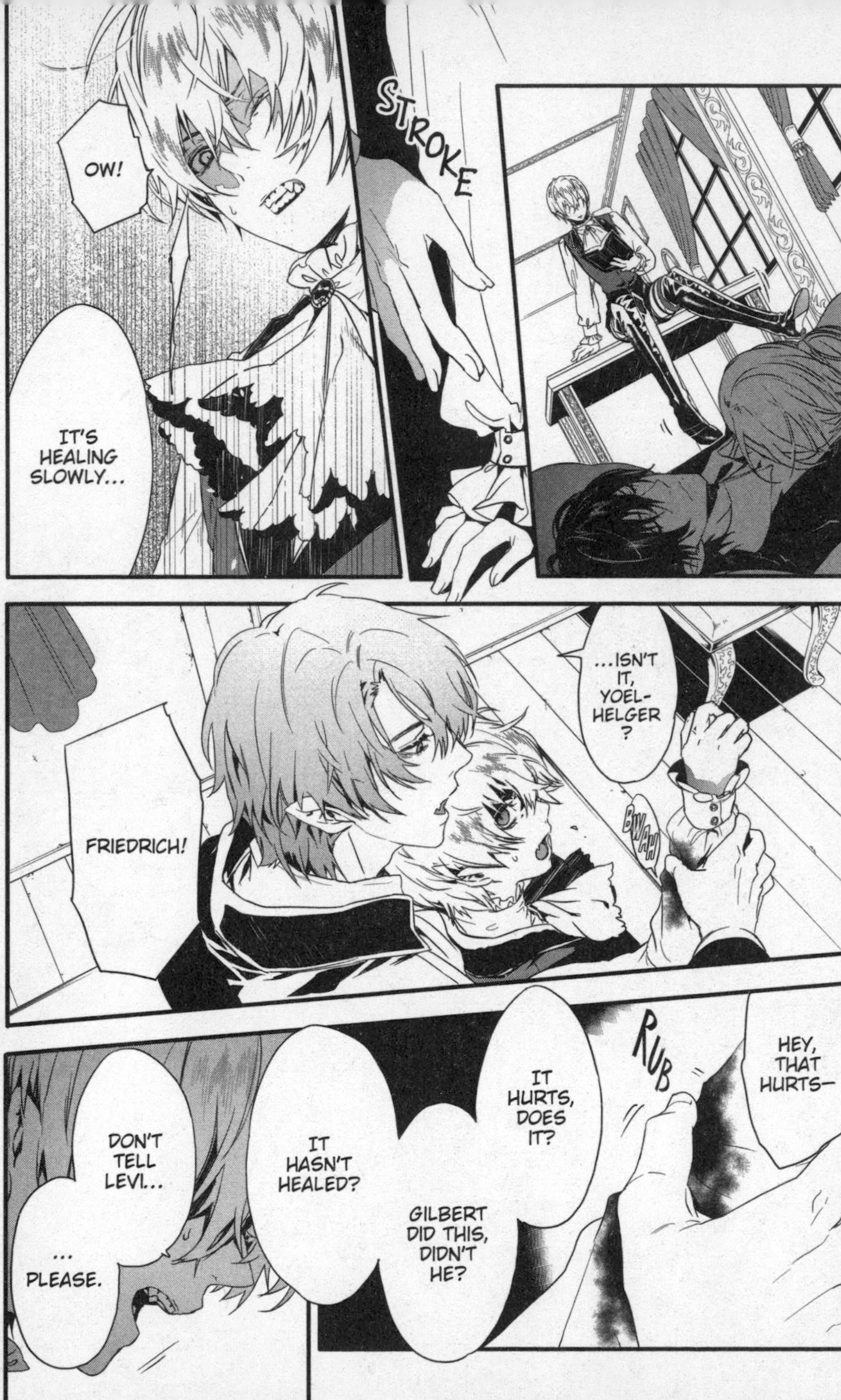
STROKE
OW!
IT'S HEALING SLOWLY...
...ISN'T IT, YOEL-HELGER?
BWAH
FRIEDRICH!
HEY, THAT HURTS—
RUB
IT HURTS, DOES IT?
IT HASN'T HEALED?
GILBERT DID THIS, DIDN'T HE?
DON'T TELL LEVI...
...PLEASE.

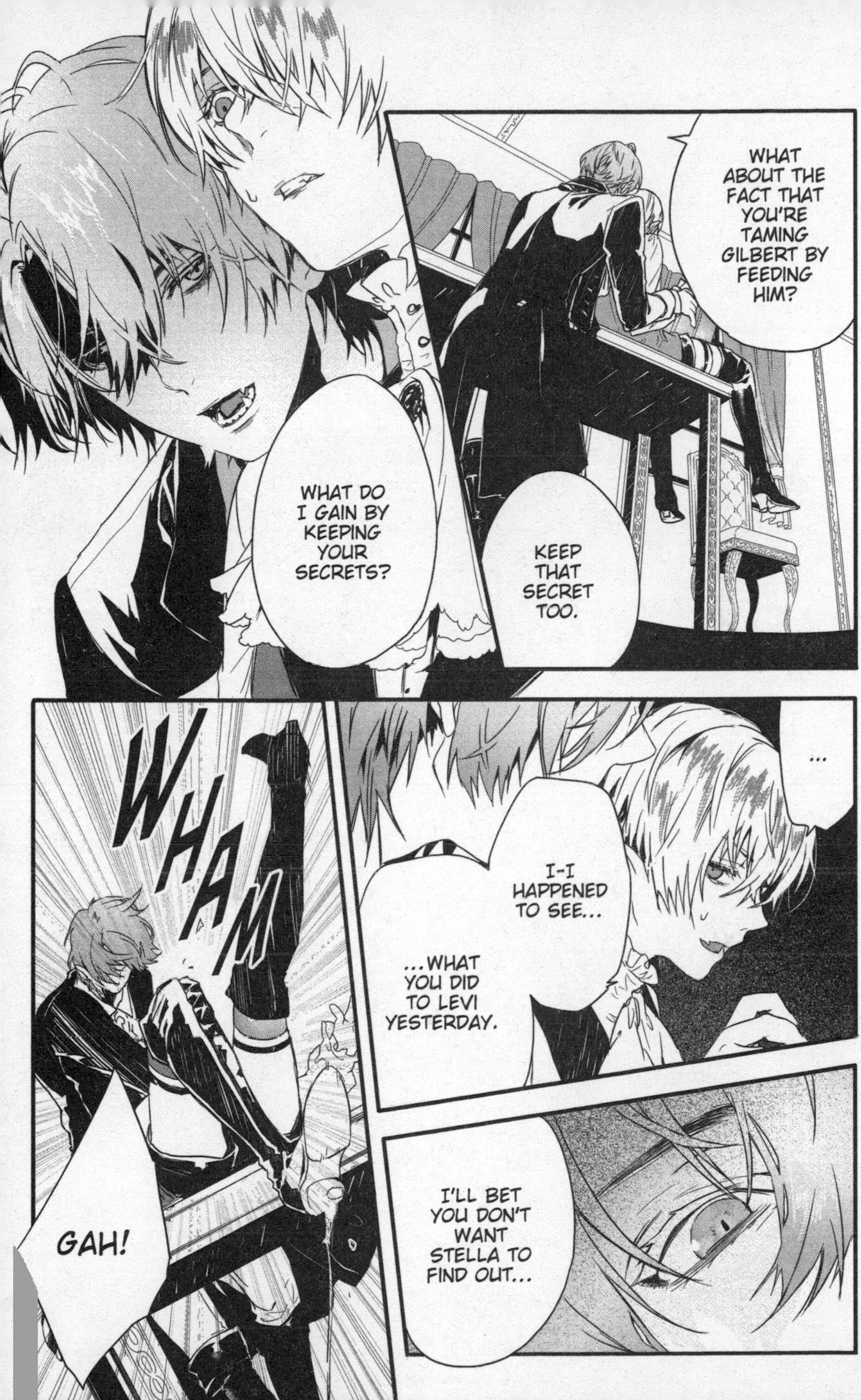
WHAT ABOUT THE FACT THAT YOU'RE TAMING GILBERT BY FEEDING HIM?
KEEP THAT SECRET TOO.
WHAT DO I GAIN BY KEEPING YOUR SECRETS?
...
I-I HAPPENED TO SEE...
...WHAT YOU DID TO LEVI YESTERDAY.
I'LL BET YOU DON'T WANT STELLA TO FIND OUT...
WHAM
GAH!

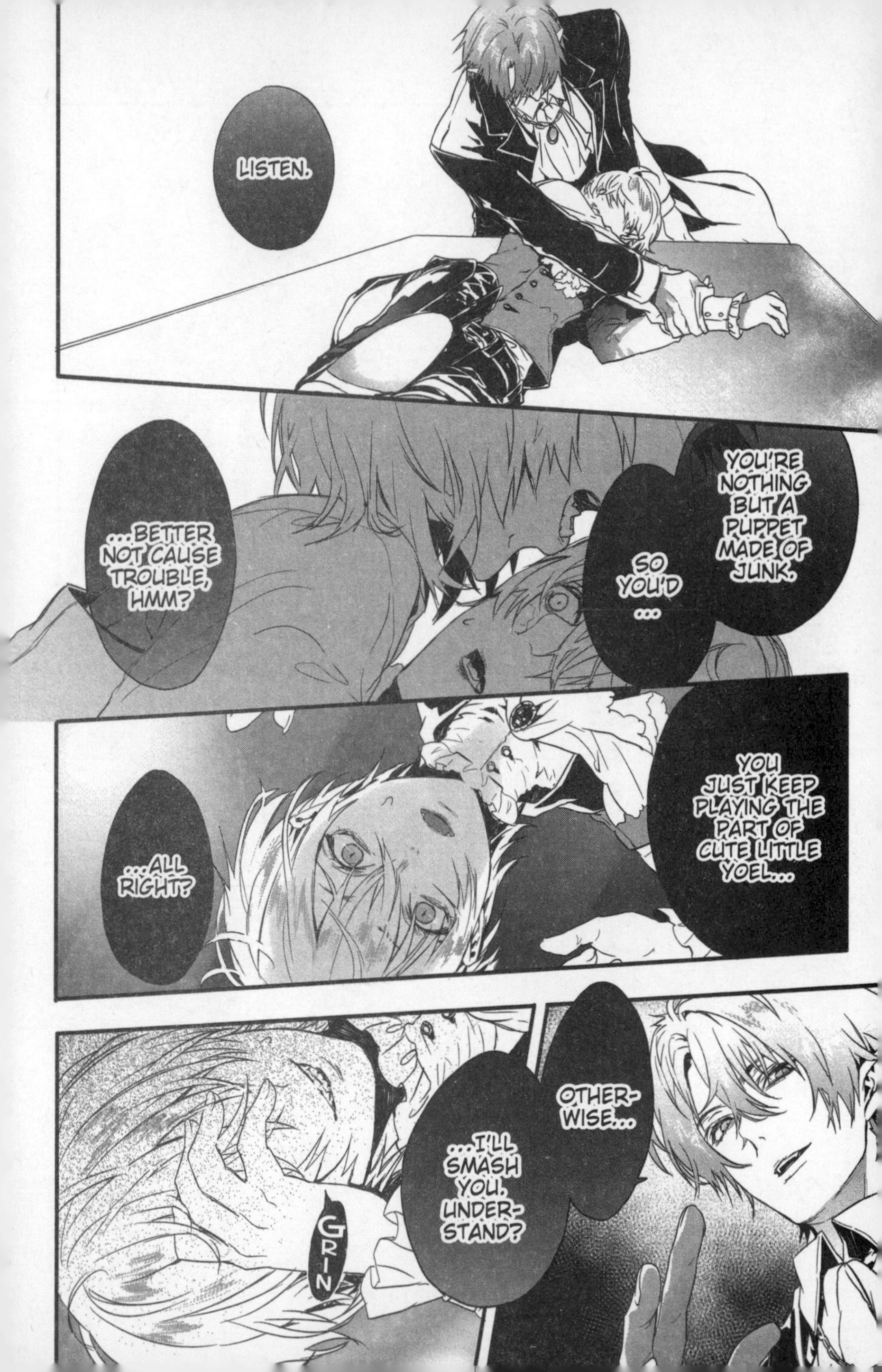
LISTEN.
YOU'RE NOTHING BUT A PUPPET MADE OF JUNK.
SO YOU'D ...
...BETTER NOT CAUSE TROUBLE, HMM?
YOU JUST KEEP PLAYING THE PART OF CUTE LITTLE YOEL...
...ALL RIGHT?
OTHER-WISE...
...I'LL SMASH YOU. UNDER-STAND?
GRIN

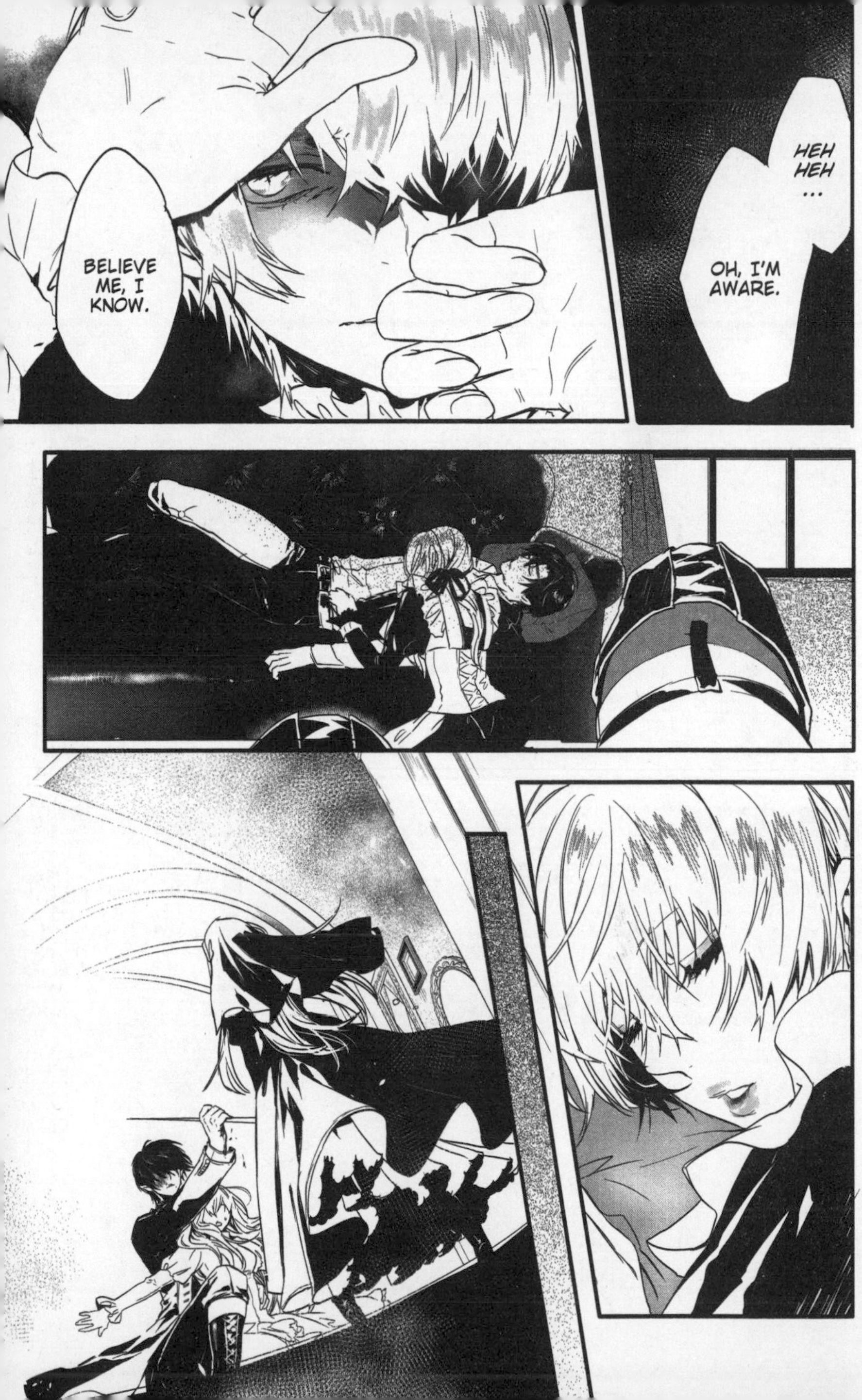
HEH HEH ...
OH, I'M AWARE.
BELIEVE ME, I KNOW.

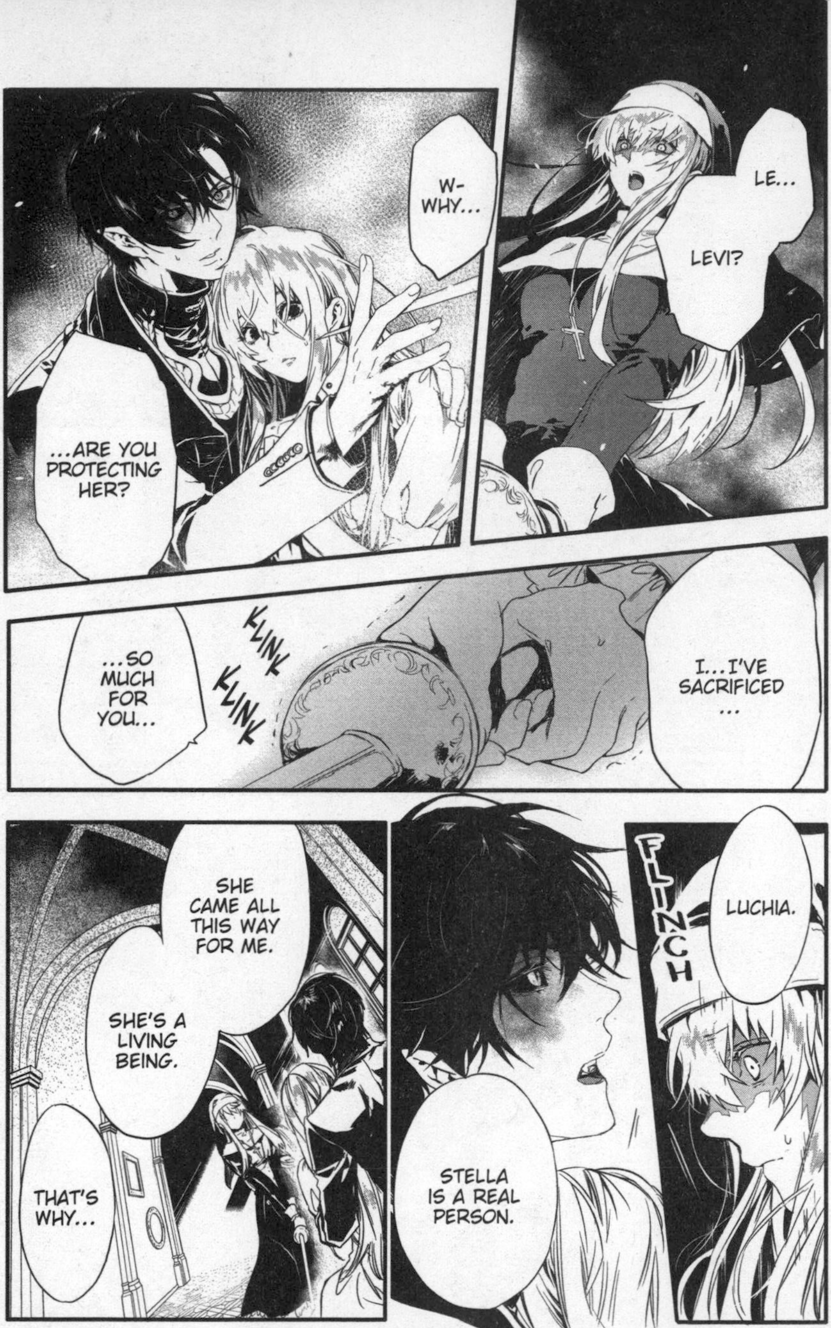
LE...
LEVI?
W-WHY...
...ARE YOU PROTECTING HER?
I...I'VE SACRIFICED ...
KLINK
KLINK
...SO MUCH FOR YOU...
FLINCH
LUCHIA.
STELLA IS A REAL PERSON.
SHE CAME ALL THIS WAY FOR ME.
SHE'S A LIVING BEING.
THAT'S WHY...

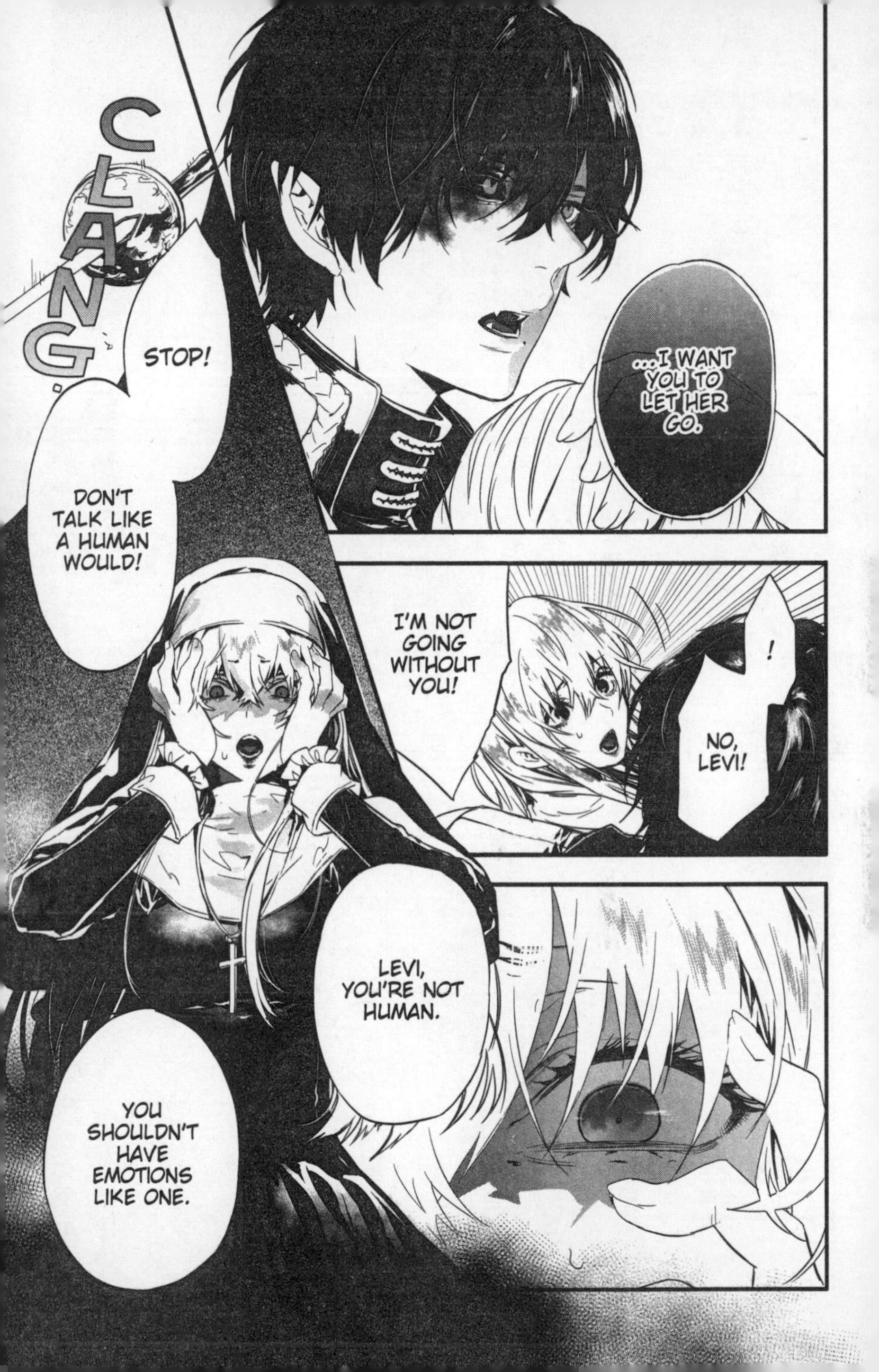
...I WANT YOU TO LET HER GO.
CLANG
STOP!
DON'T TALK LIKE A HUMAN WOULD!
!
NO, LEVI!
I'M NOT GOING WITHOUT YOU!
LEVI, YOU'RE NOT HUMAN.
YOU SHOULDN'T HAVE EMOTIONS LIKE ONE.

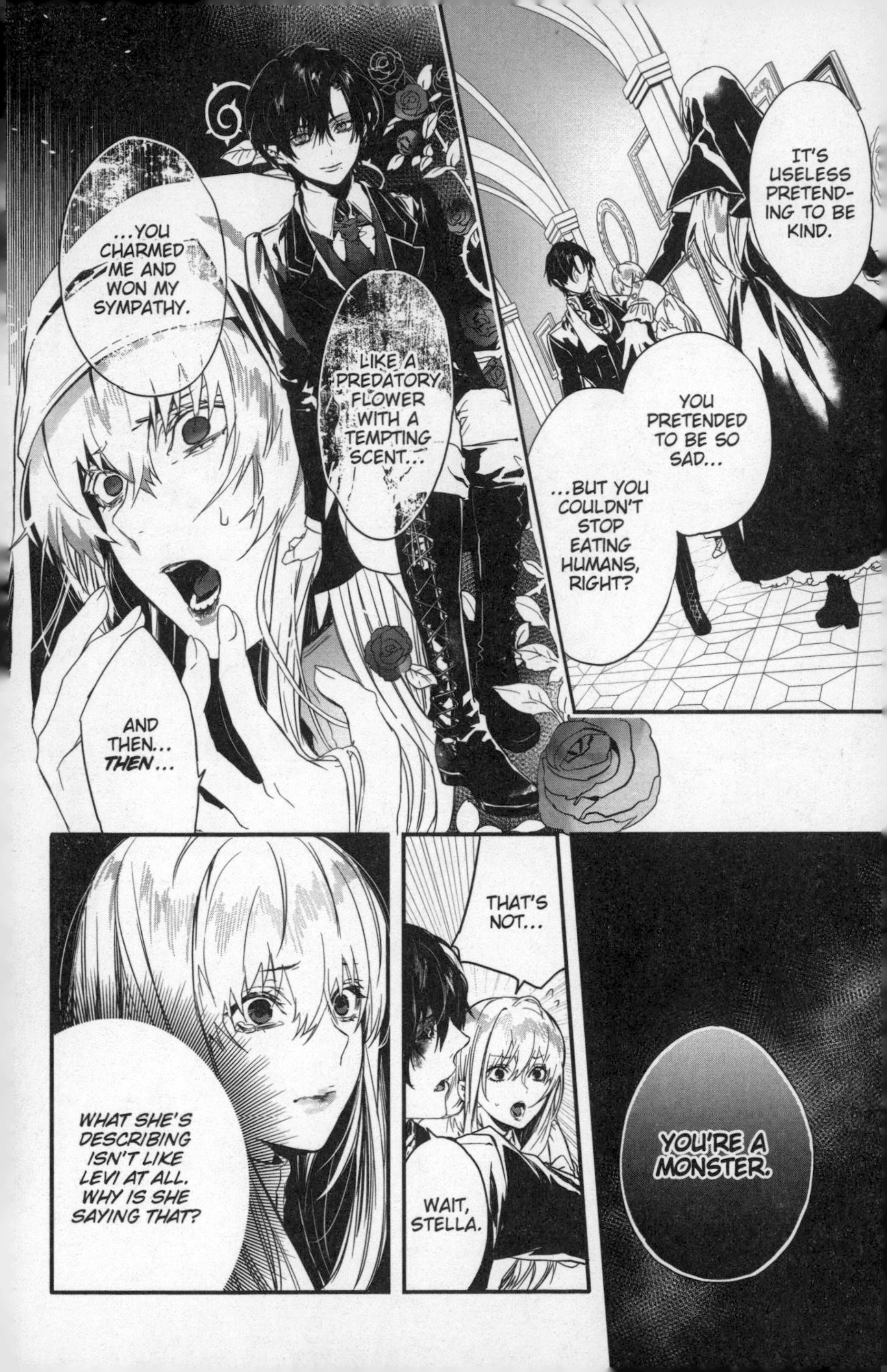
IT'S USELESS PRETENDING TO BE KIND.
YOU PRETENDED TO BE SO SAD...
...BUT YOU COULDN'T STOP EATING HUMANS, RIGHT?
...YOU CHARMED ME AND WON MY SYMPATHY.
LIKE A PREDATORY FLOWER WITH A TEMPTING SCENT...
AND THEN... *THEN*...
YOU'RE A MONSTER.
THAT'S NOT...
WAIT, STELLA.
WHAT SHE'S DESCRIBING ISN'T LIKE LEVI AT ALL. WHY IS SHE SAYING THAT?

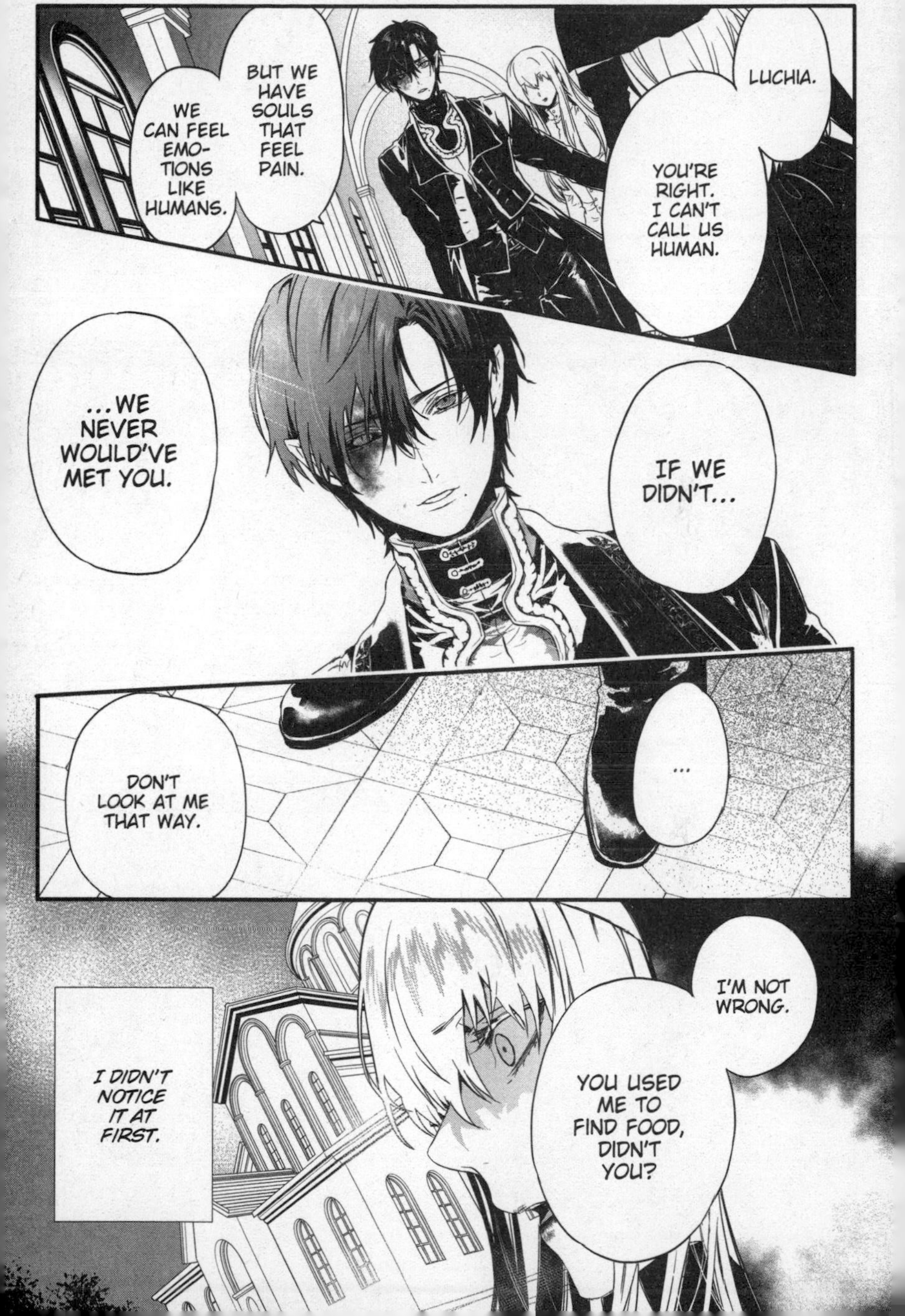
LUCHIA.
YOU'RE RIGHT. I CAN'T CALL US HUMAN.
BUT WE HAVE SOULS THAT FEEL PAIN.
WE CAN FEEL EMO-TIONS LIKE HUMANS.
IF WE DIDN'T...
...WE NEVER WOULD'VE MET YOU.
...
DON'T LOOK AT ME THAT WAY.
I'M NOT WRONG.
YOU USED ME TO FIND FOOD, DIDN'T YOU?
I DIDN'T NOTICE IT AT FIRST.

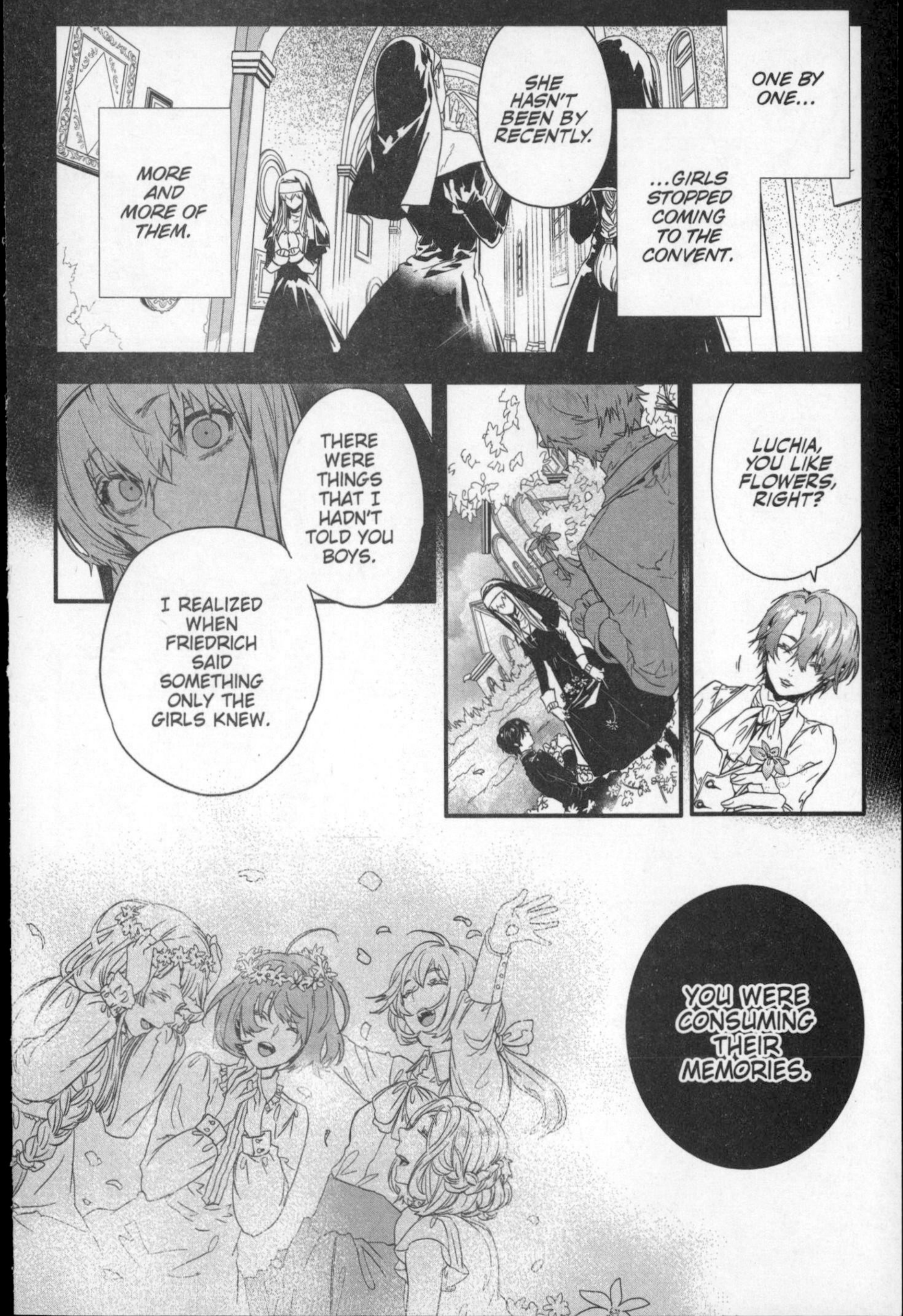
ONE BY ONE...
...GIRLS STOPPED COMING TO THE CONVENT.
SHE HASN'T BEEN BY RECENTLY.
MORE AND MORE OF THEM.
LUCHIA, YOU LIKE FLOWERS, RIGHT?
THERE WERE THINGS THAT I HADN'T TOLD YOU BOYS.
I REALIZED WHEN FRIEDRICH SAID SOMETHING ONLY THE GIRLS KNEW.
YOU WERE CONSUMING THEIR MEMORIES.

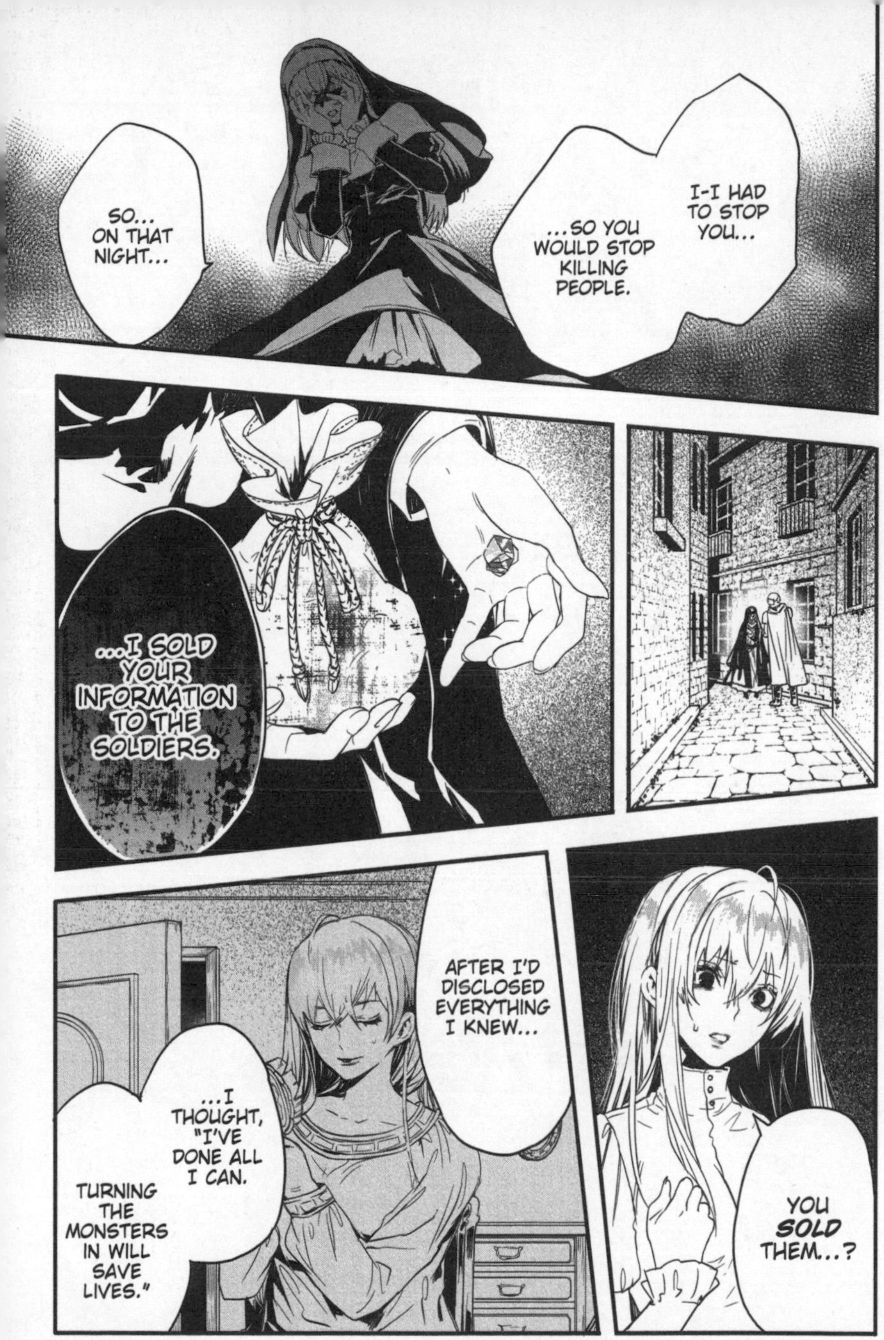
I-I HAD TO STOP YOU...
...SO YOU WOULD STOP KILLING PEOPLE.
SO... ON THAT NIGHT...
...I SOLD YOUR INFORMATION TO THE SOLDIERS.
YOU *SOLD* THEM...?
AFTER I'D DISCLOSED EVERYTHING I KNEW...
...I THOUGHT, "I'VE DONE ALL I CAN.
TURNING THE MONSTERS IN WILL SAVE LIVES."

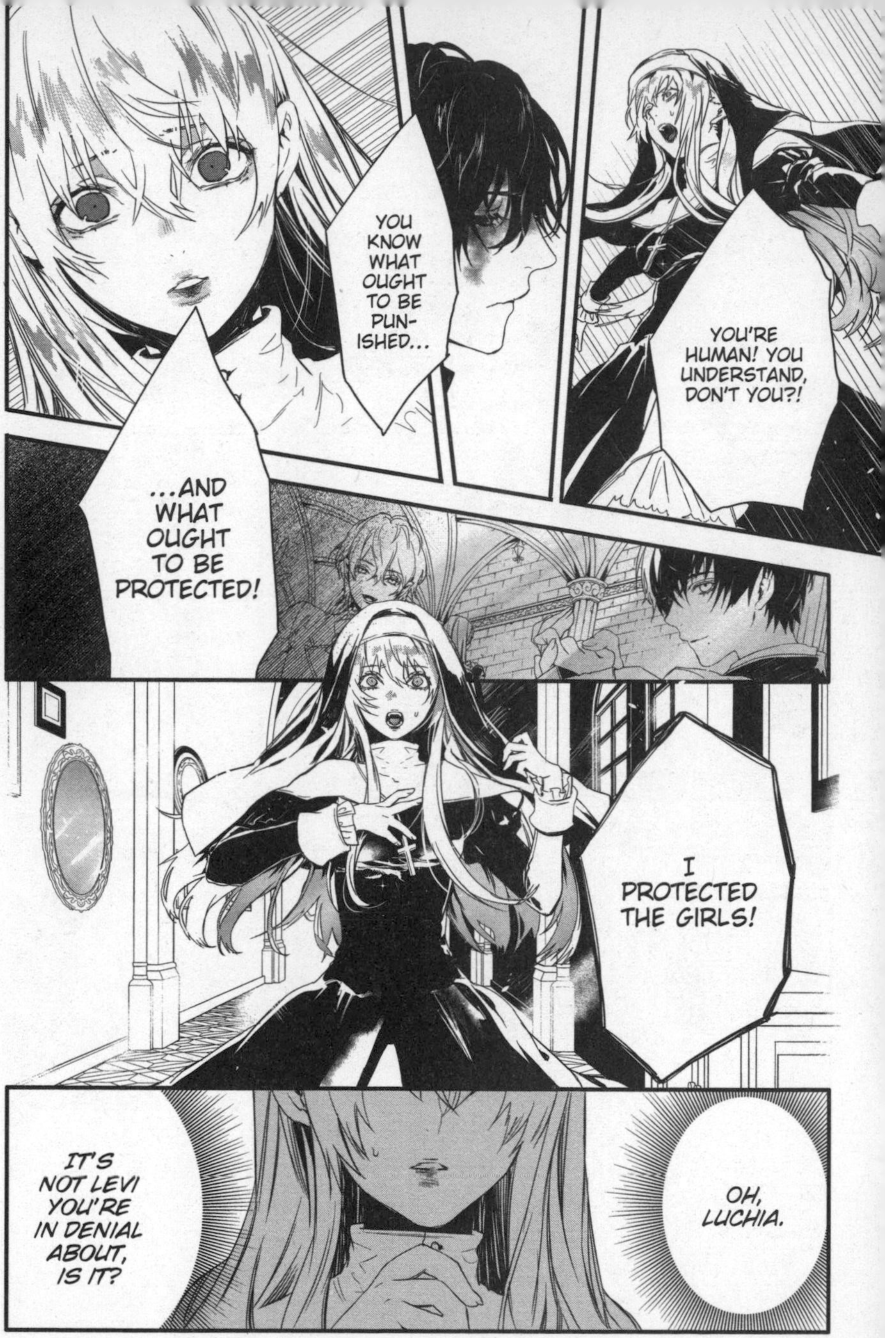
YOU'RE HUMAN! YOU UNDERSTAND, DON'T YOU?!
YOU KNOW WHAT OUGHT TO BE PUN-ISHED...
...AND WHAT OUGHT TO BE PROTECTED!
I PROTECTED THE GIRLS!
OH, LUCHIA.
IT'S NOT LEVI YOU'RE IN DENIAL ABOUT, IS IT?

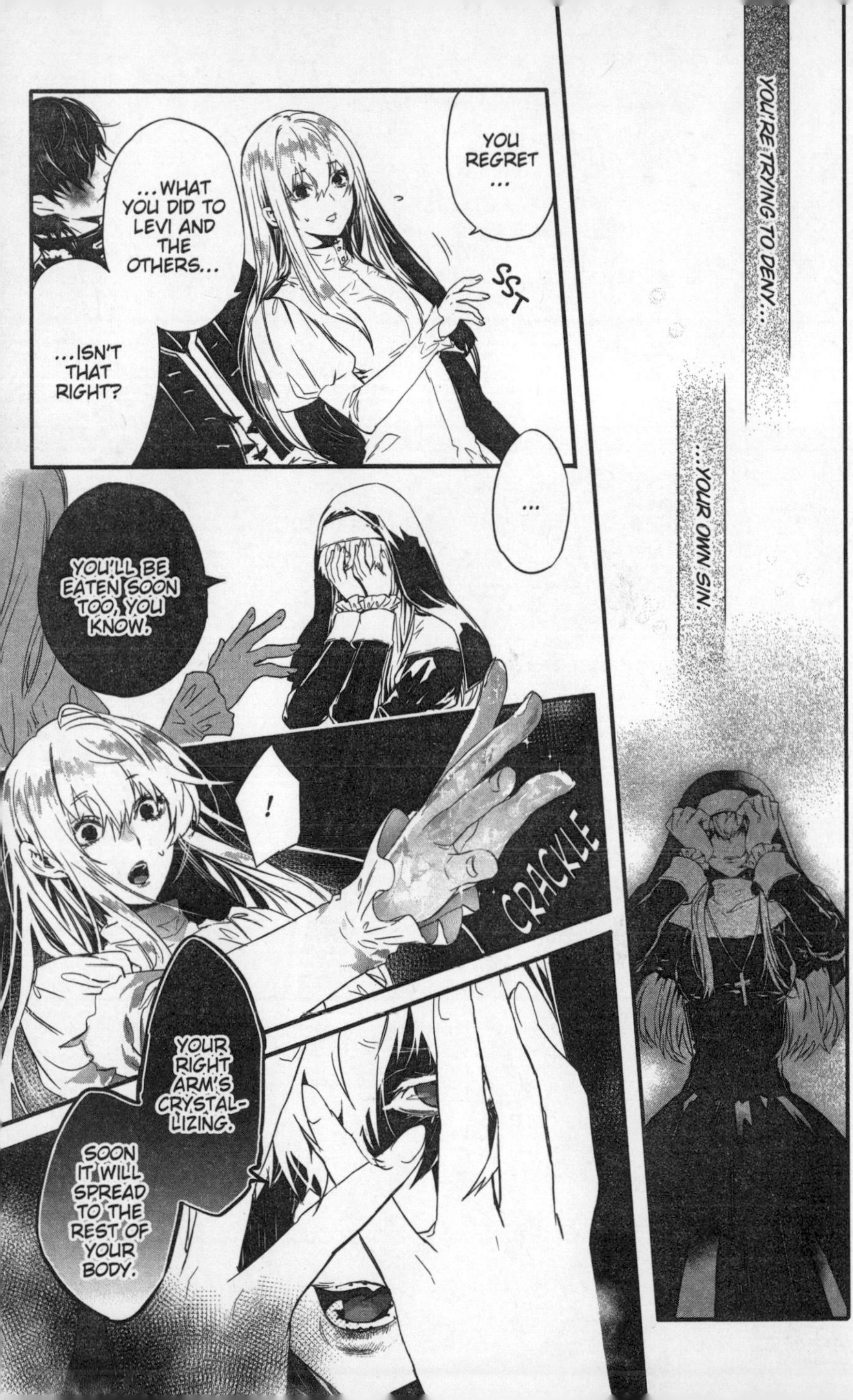
YOU'RE TRYING TO DENY...
...YOUR OWN SIN.
YOU REGRET...
...WHAT YOU DID TO LEVI AND THE OTHERS...
SST
...ISN'T THAT RIGHT?
...
YOU'LL BE EATEN SOON TOO, YOU KNOW.
!
CRACKLE
YOUR RIGHT ARM'S CRYSTAL-LIZING.
SOON IT WILL SPREAD TO THE REST OF YOUR BODY.

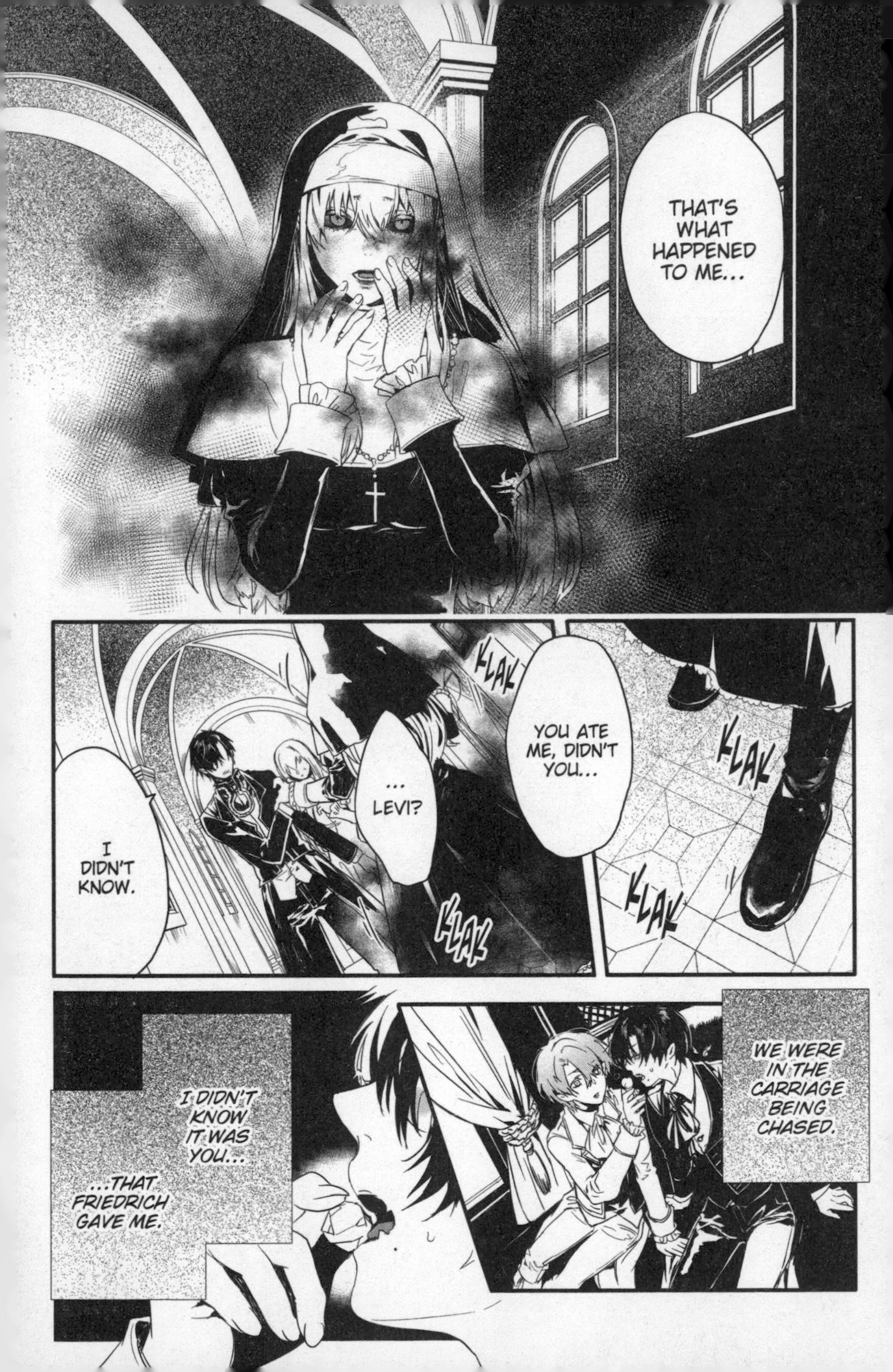
THAT'S WHAT HAPPENED TO ME...
KLAK
YOU ATE ME, DIDN'T YOU...
KLAK
KLAK
...LEVI?
I DIDN'T KNOW.
KLAK
WE WERE IN THE CARRIAGE BEING CHASED.
I DIDN'T KNOW IT WAS YOU...
...THAT FRIEDRICH GAVE ME.

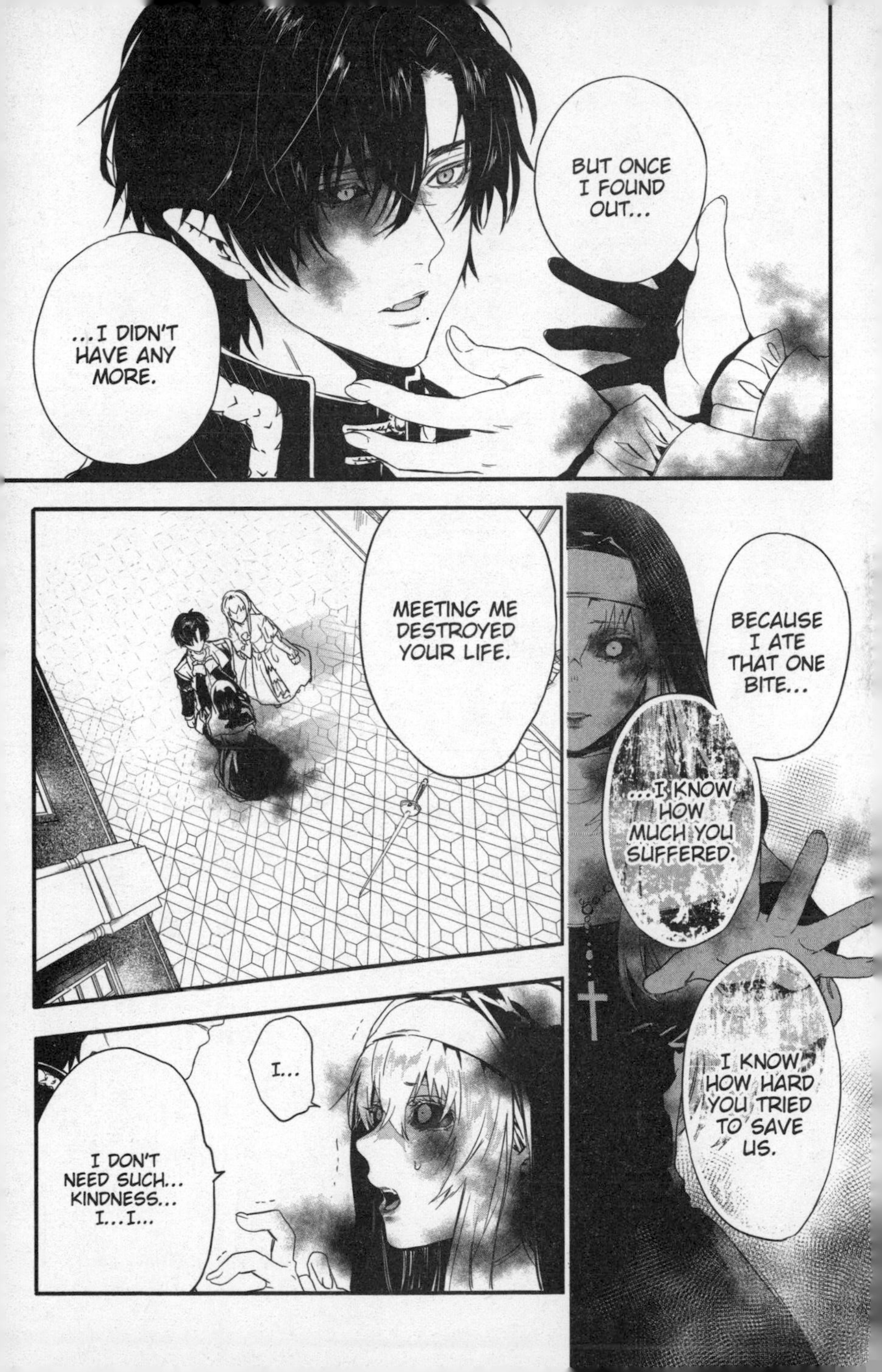
BUT ONCE I FOUND OUT...
...I DIDN'T HAVE ANY MORE.
BECAUSE I ATE THAT ONE BITE...
...I KNOW HOW MUCH YOU SUFFERED.
I KNOW HOW HARD YOU TRIED TO SAVE US.
MEETING ME DESTROYED YOUR LIFE.
I...
I DON'T NEED SUCH... KINDNESS... I...I...

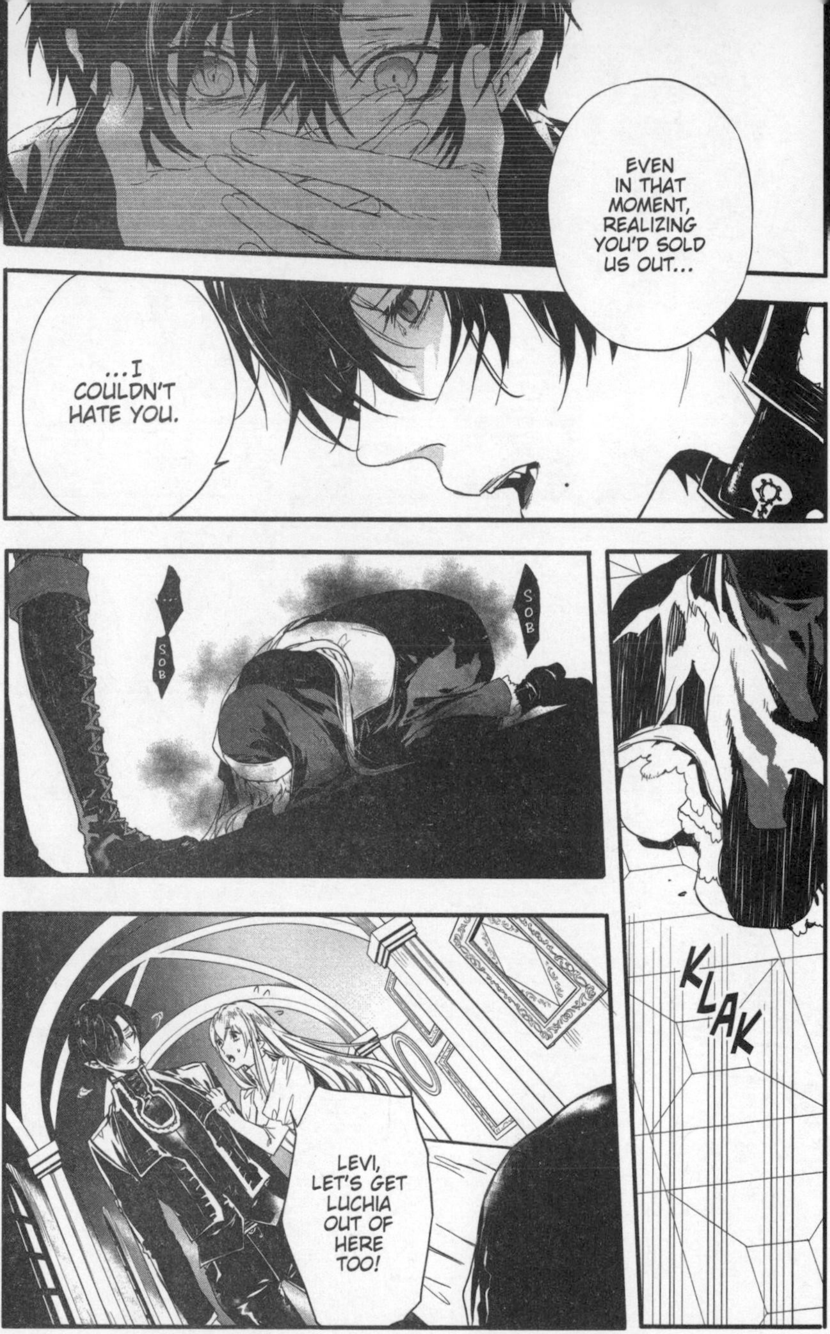
EVEN IN THAT MOMENT, REALIZING YOU'D SOLD US OUT...
...I COULDN'T HATE YOU.
KLAK
SOB
SOB
LEVI, LET'S GET LUCHIA OUT OF HERE TOO!

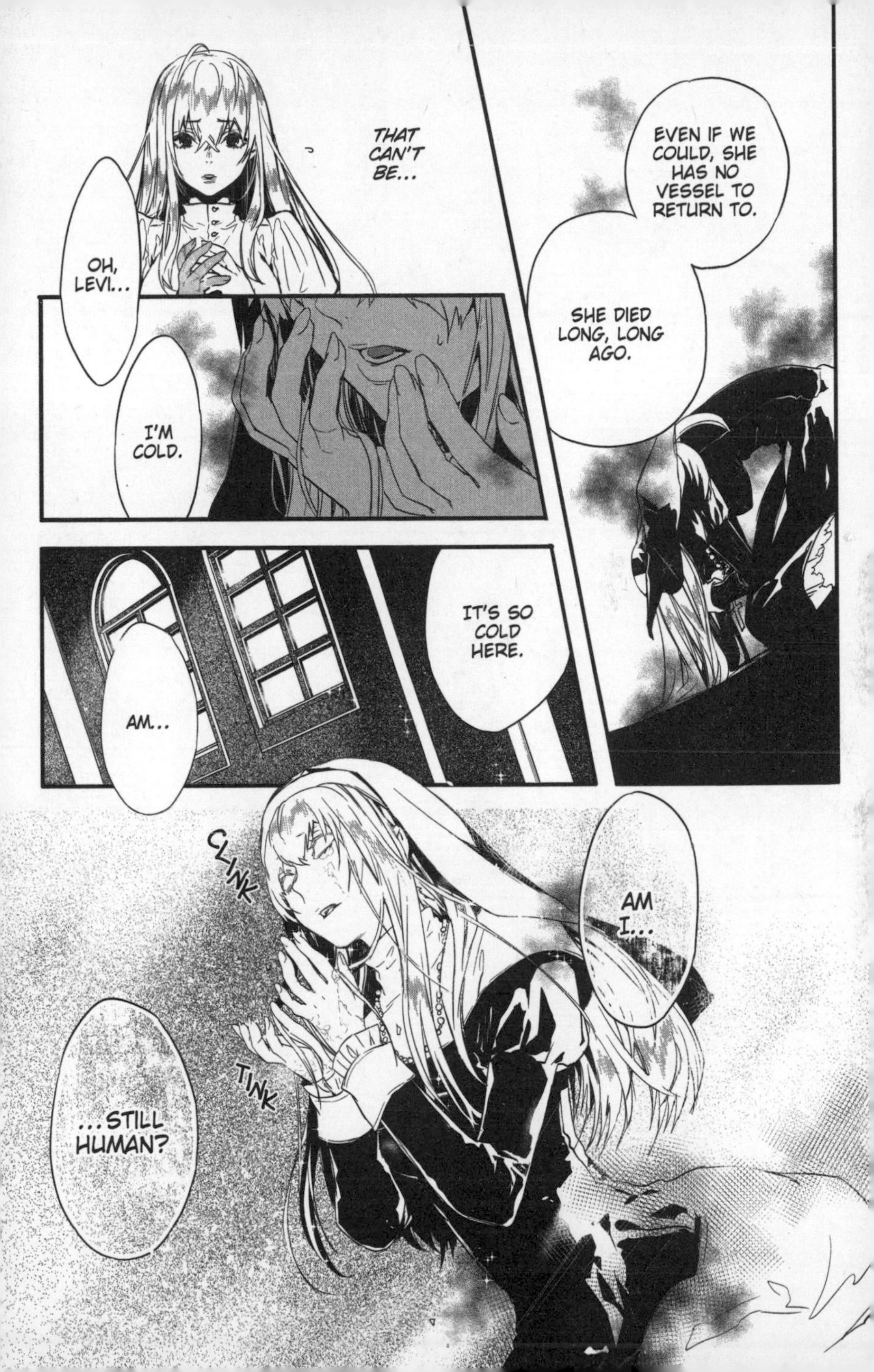
EVEN IF WE COULD, SHE HAS NO VESSEL TO RETURN TO.
SHE DIED LONG, LONG AGO.
THAT CAN'T BE...
OH, LEVI...
I'M COLD.
IT'S SO COLD HERE.
AM...
AM I...
CLINK
TINK
...STILL HUMAN?

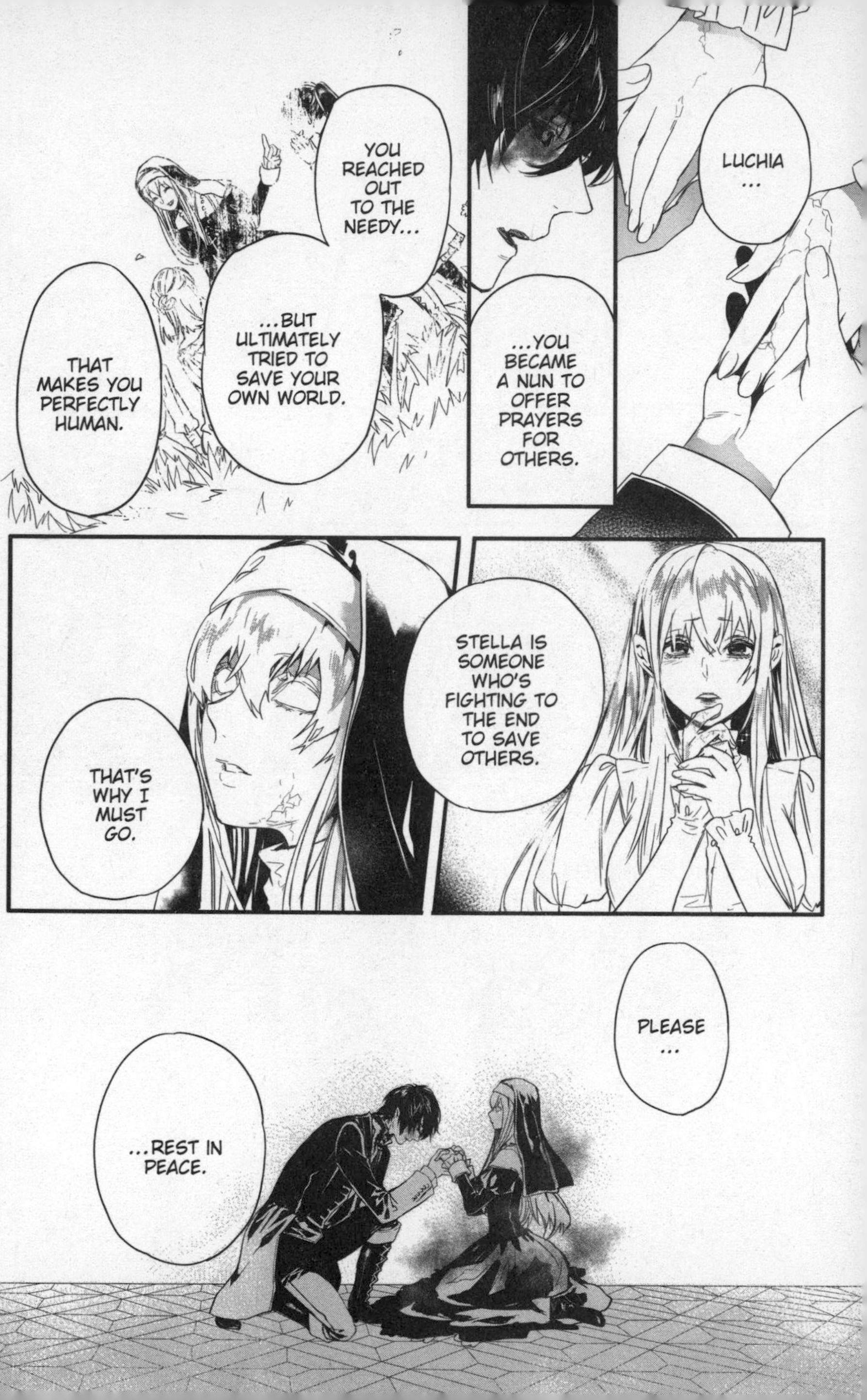
LUCHIA...
...YOU BECAME A NUN TO OFFER PRAYERS FOR OTHERS.
YOU REACHED OUT TO THE NEEDY...
...BUT ULTIMATELY TRIED TO SAVE YOUR OWN WORLD.
THAT MAKES YOU PERFECTLY HUMAN.
STELLA IS SOMEONE WHO'S FIGHTING TO THE END TO SAVE OTHERS.
THAT'S WHY I MUST GO.
PLEASE...
...REST IN PEACE.

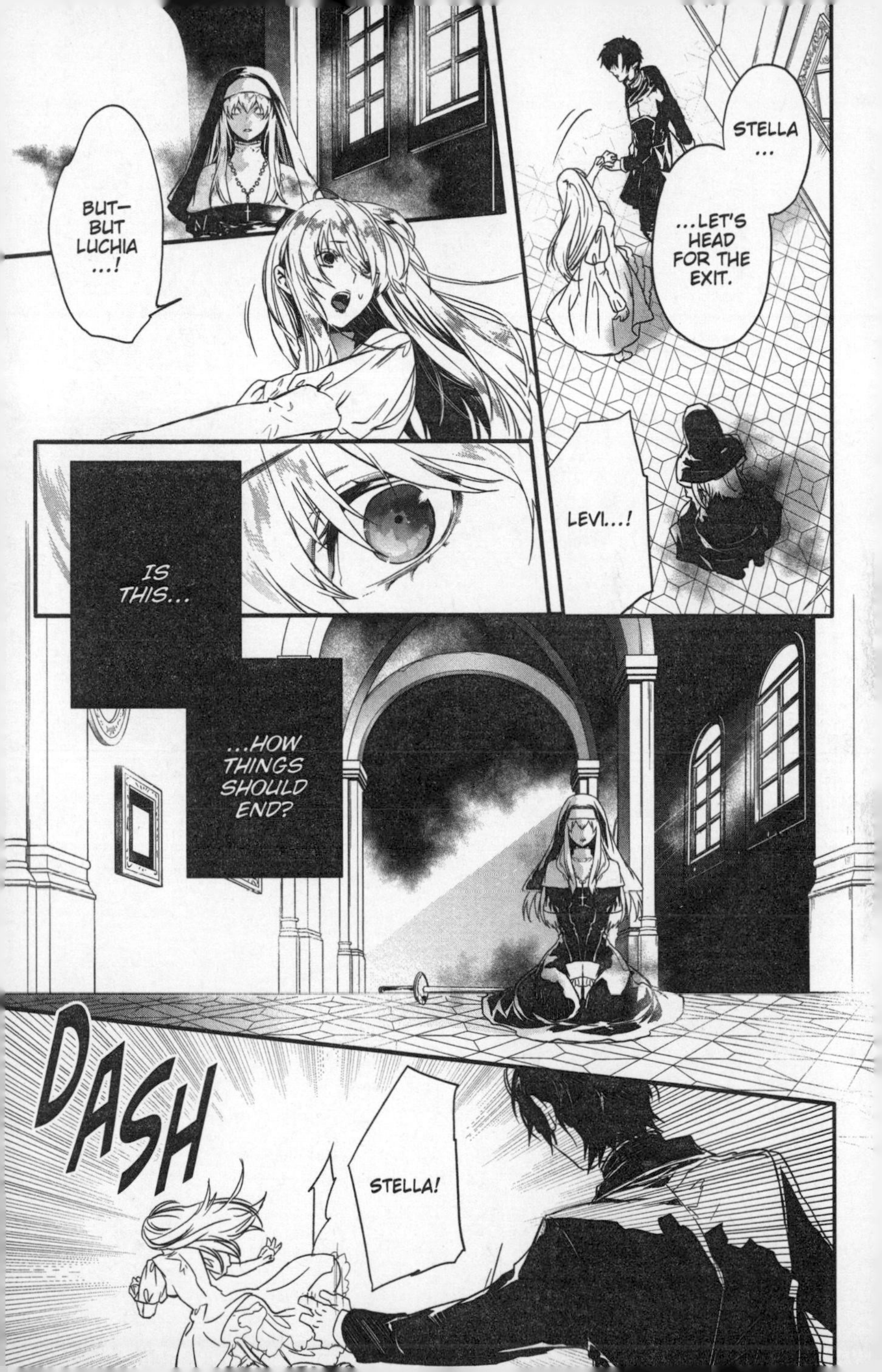
STELLA...
...LET'S HEAD FOR THE EXIT.
LEVI...!
BUT— BUT LUCHIA...!
IS THIS...
...HOW THINGS SHOULD END?
STELLA!
DASH

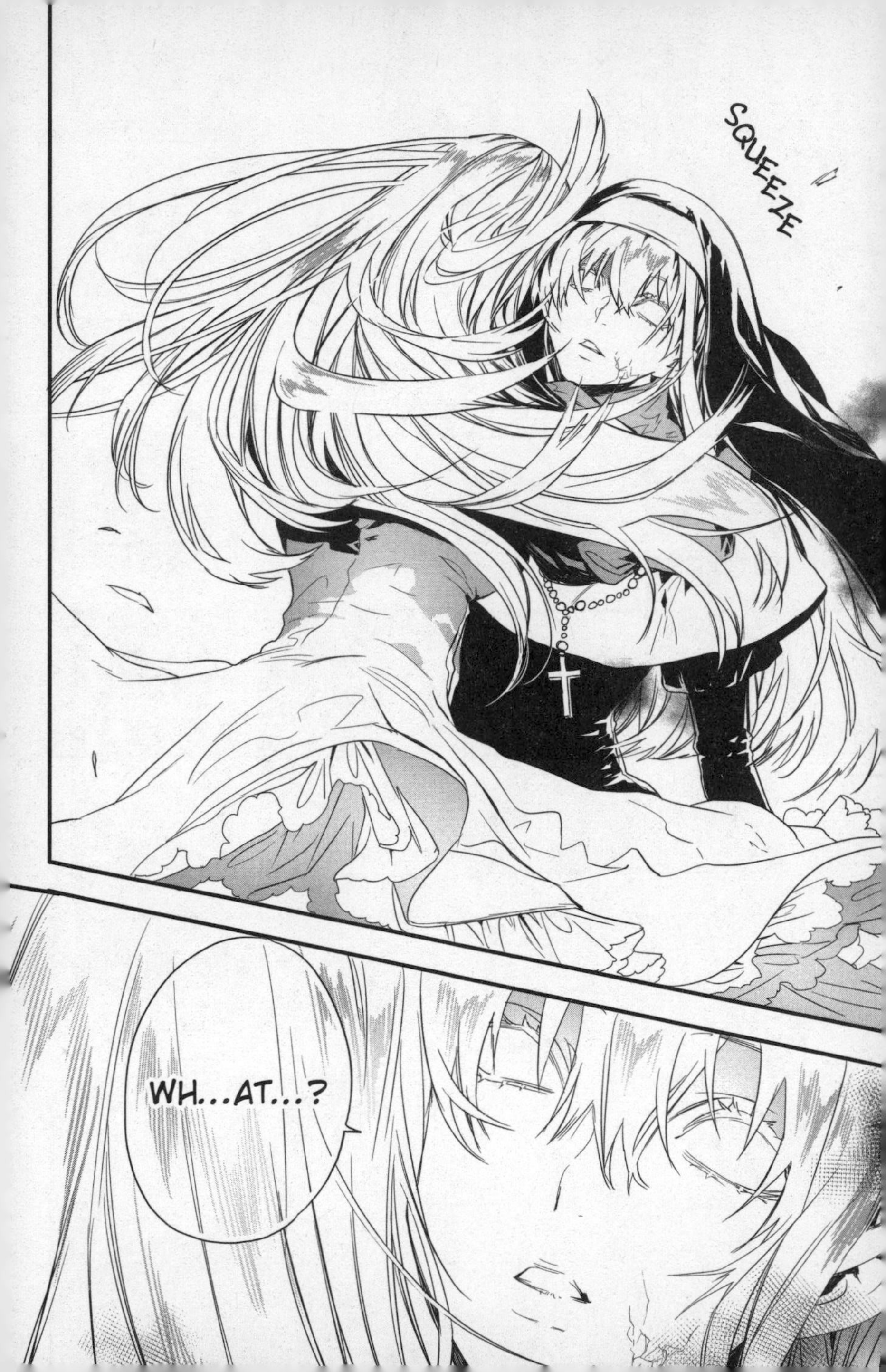
SQUEEZE
WH...AT...?

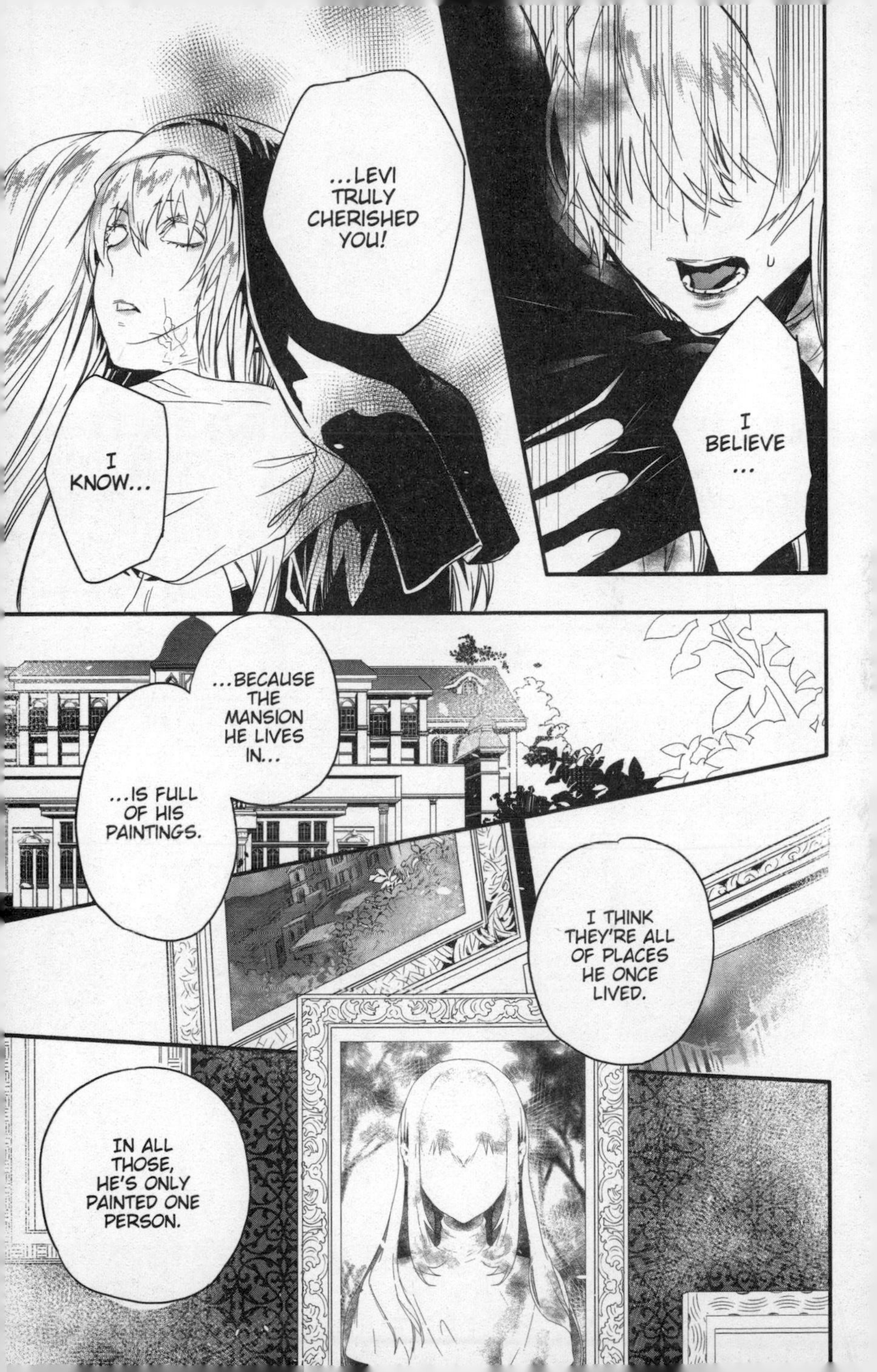
I BELIEVE ...
...LEVI TRULY CHERISHED YOU!
I KNOW...
...BECAUSE THE MANSION HE LIVES IN...
...IS FULL OF HIS PAINTINGS.
I THINK THEY'RE ALL OF PLACES HE ONCE LIVED.
IN ALL THOSE, HE'S ONLY PAINTED ONE PERSON.

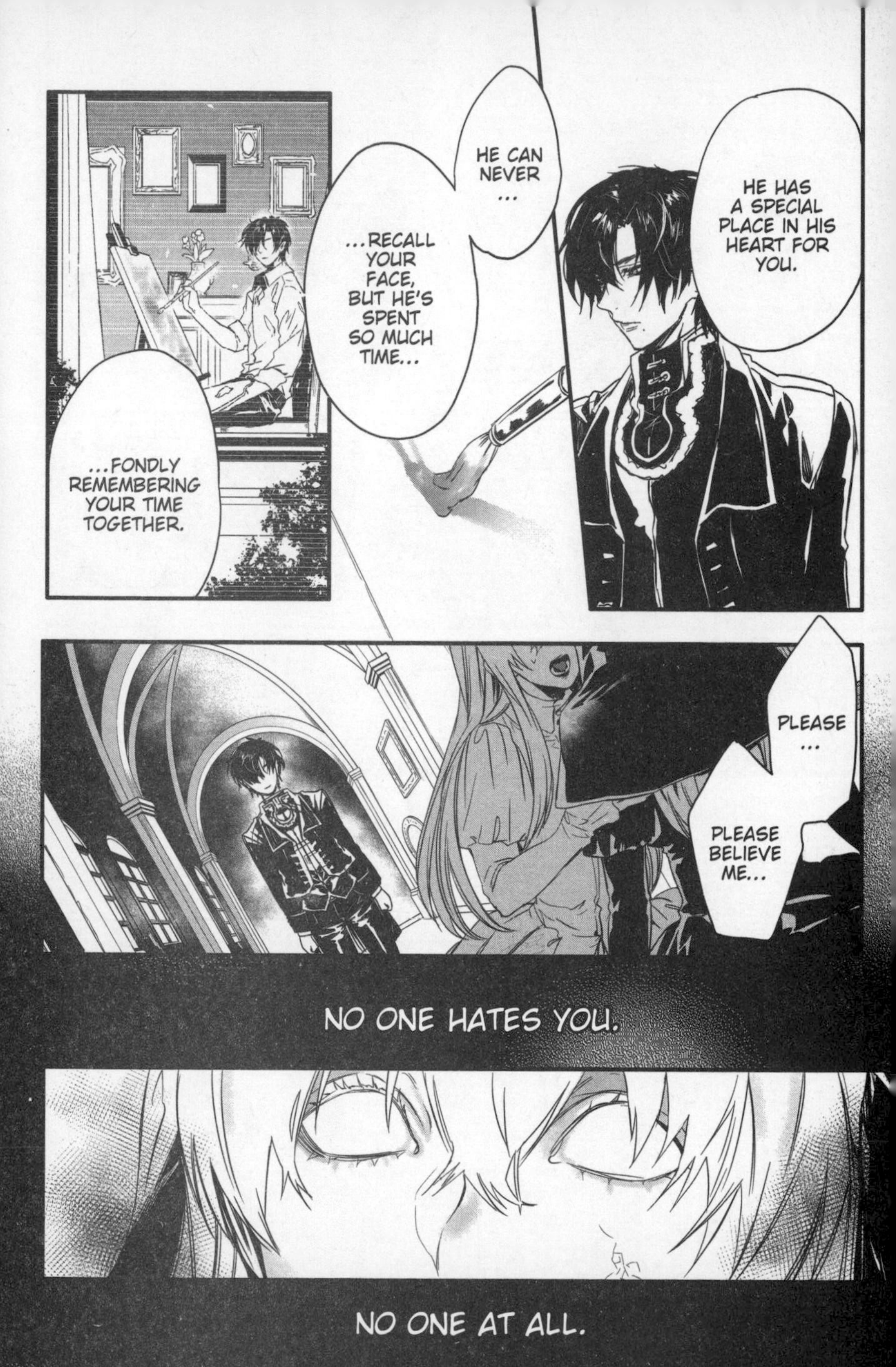
HE HAS A SPECIAL PLACE IN HIS HEART FOR YOU.
HE CAN NEVER ...
...RECALL YOUR FACE, BUT HE'S SPENT SO MUCH TIME...
...FONDLY REMEMBERING YOUR TIME TOGETHER.
PLEASE ...
PLEASE BELIEVE ME...
NO ONE HATES YOU.
NO ONE AT ALL.

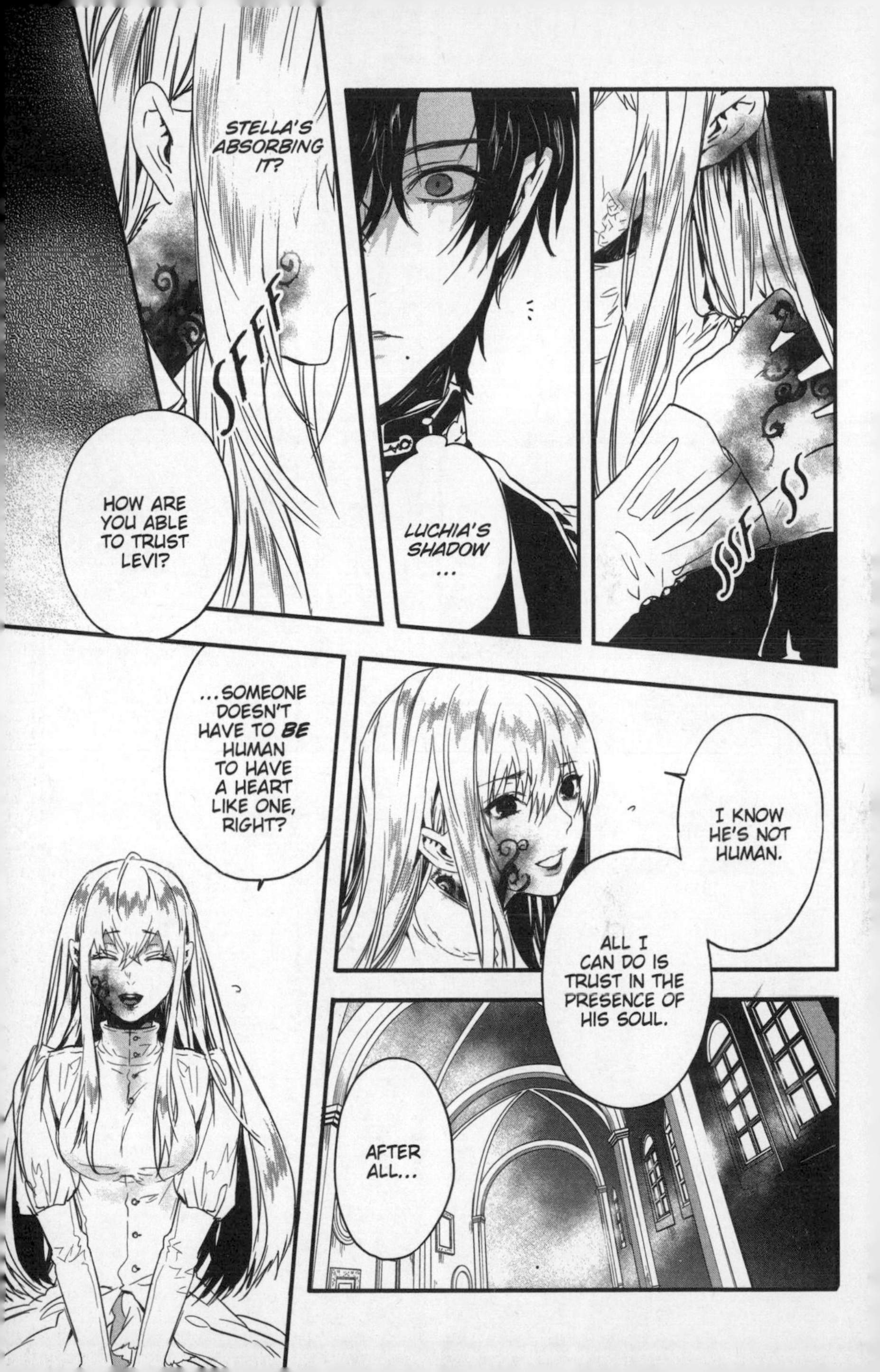
SSF
SS
LUCHIA'S SHADOW ...
STELLA'S ABSORBING IT?
SFFF
HOW ARE YOU ABLE TO TRUST LEVI?
I KNOW HE'S NOT HUMAN.
ALL I CAN DO IS TRUST IN THE PRESENCE OF HIS SOUL.
AFTER ALL...
...SOMEONE DOESN'T HAVE TO *BE* HUMAN TO HAVE A HEART LIKE ONE, RIGHT?

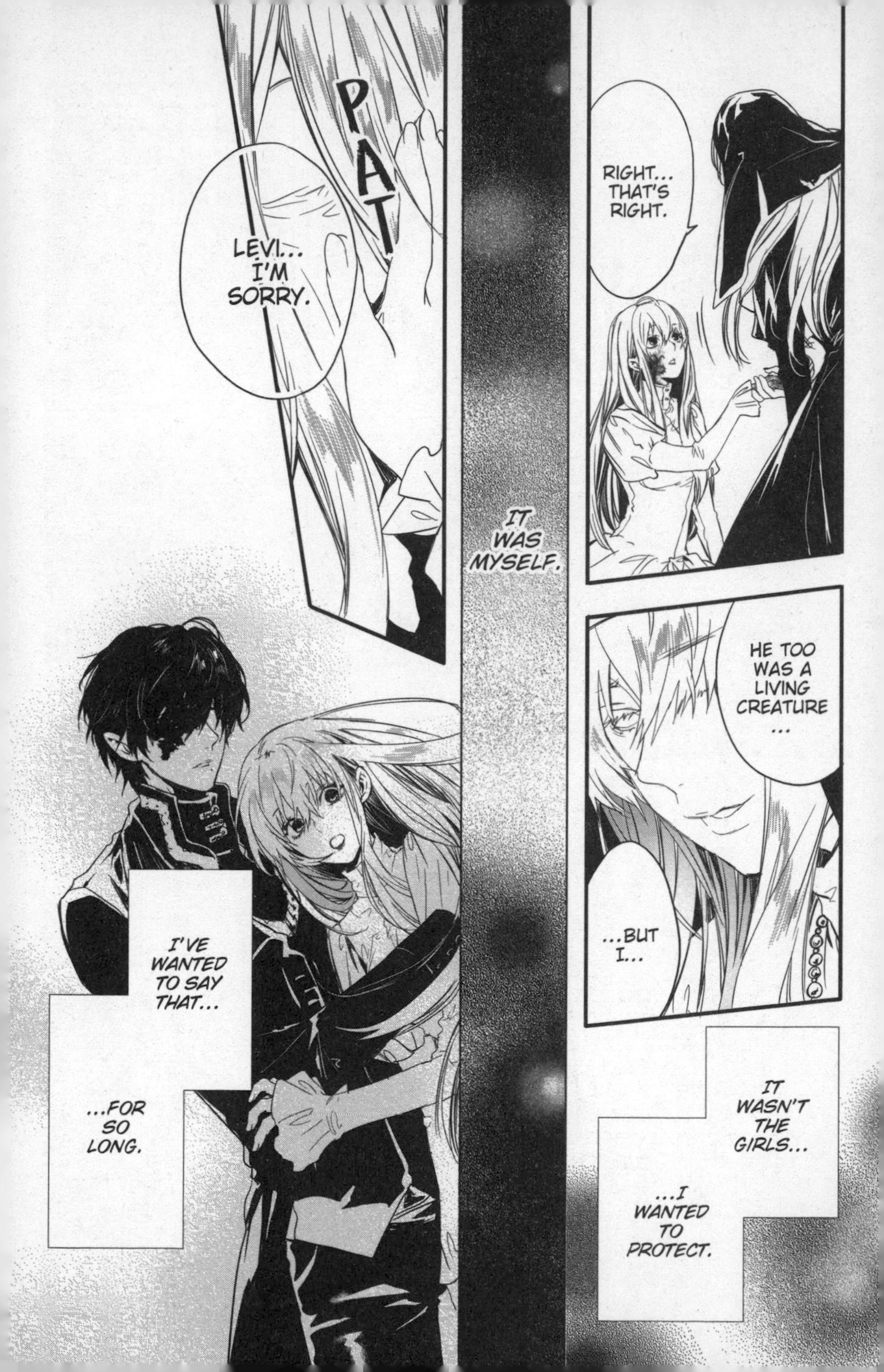
RIGHT... THAT'S RIGHT.
HE TOO WAS A LIVING CREATURE ...
...BUT I...
IT WASN'T THE GIRLS...
...I WANTED TO PROTECT.
IT WAS MYSELF.
PAT
LEVI... I'M SORRY.
I'VE WANTED TO SAY THAT...
...FOR SO LONG.

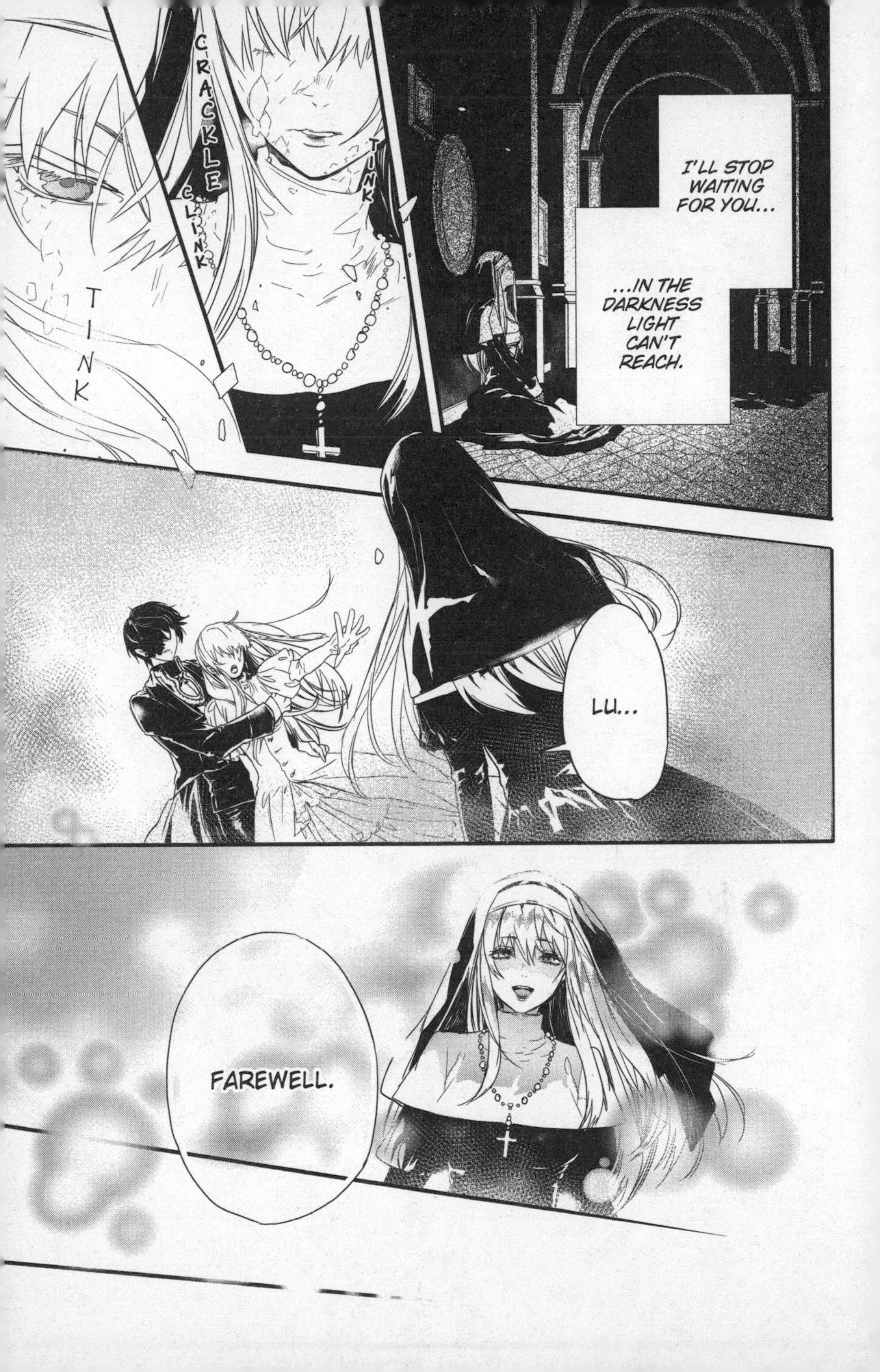
I'LL STOP WAITING FOR YOU...
...IN THE DARKNESS LIGHT CAN'T REACH.
TINK
CRACKLE
CLINK
TINK
LU...
FAREWELL.

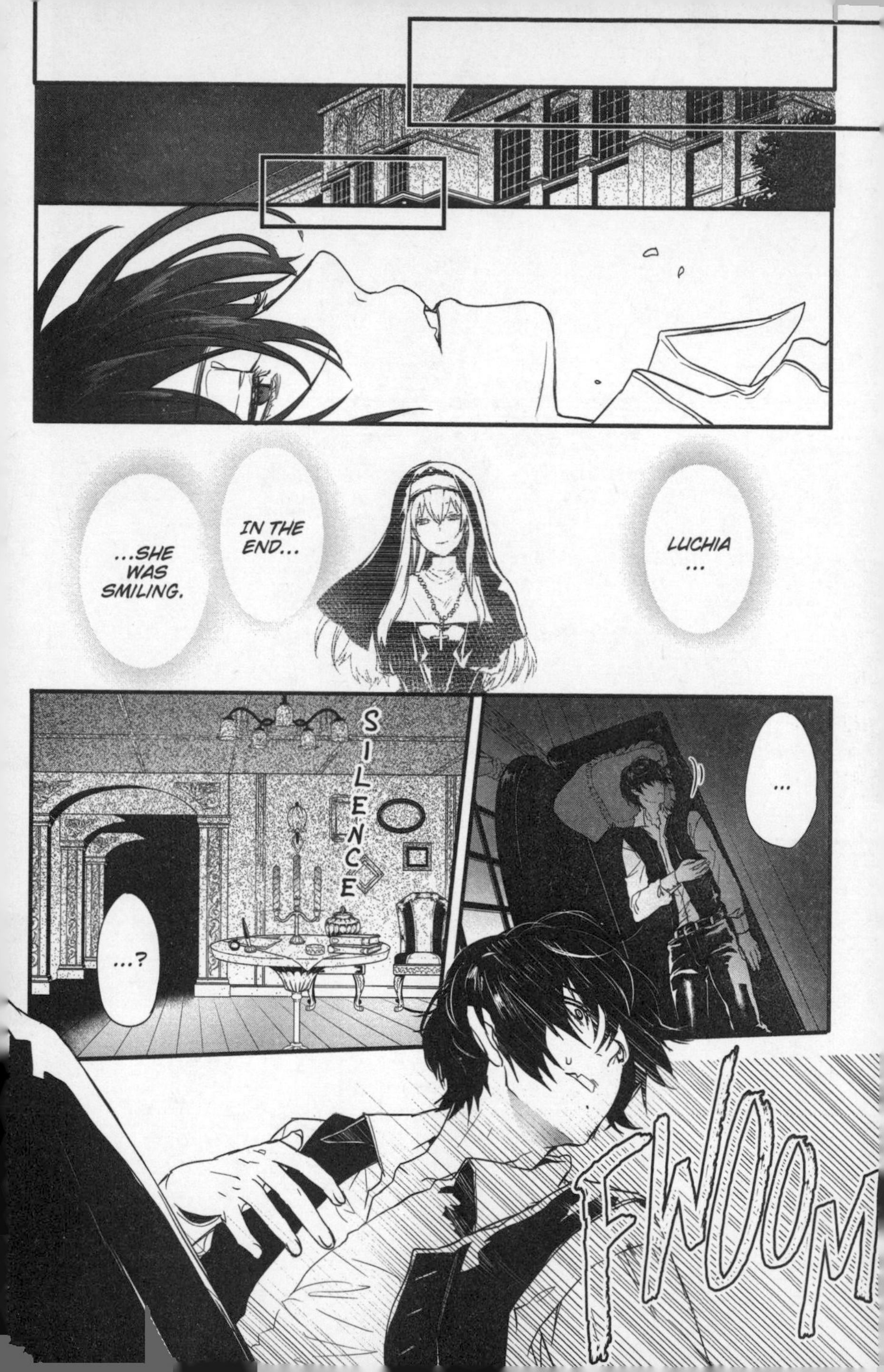
LUCHIA ...
IN THE END...
...SHE WAS SMILING.
...
SILENCE
...?
FWOOM

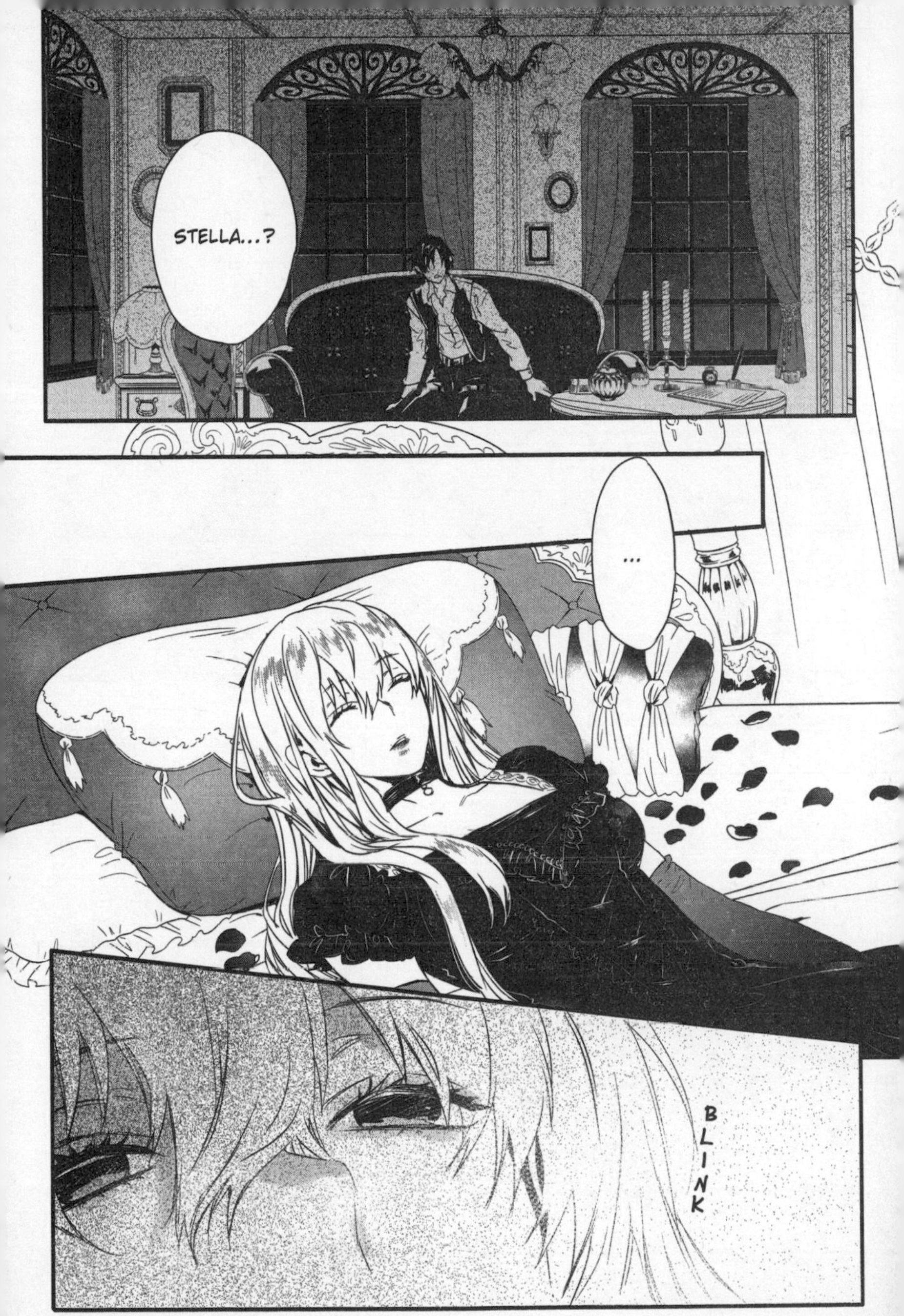
STELLA...?
...
BLINK

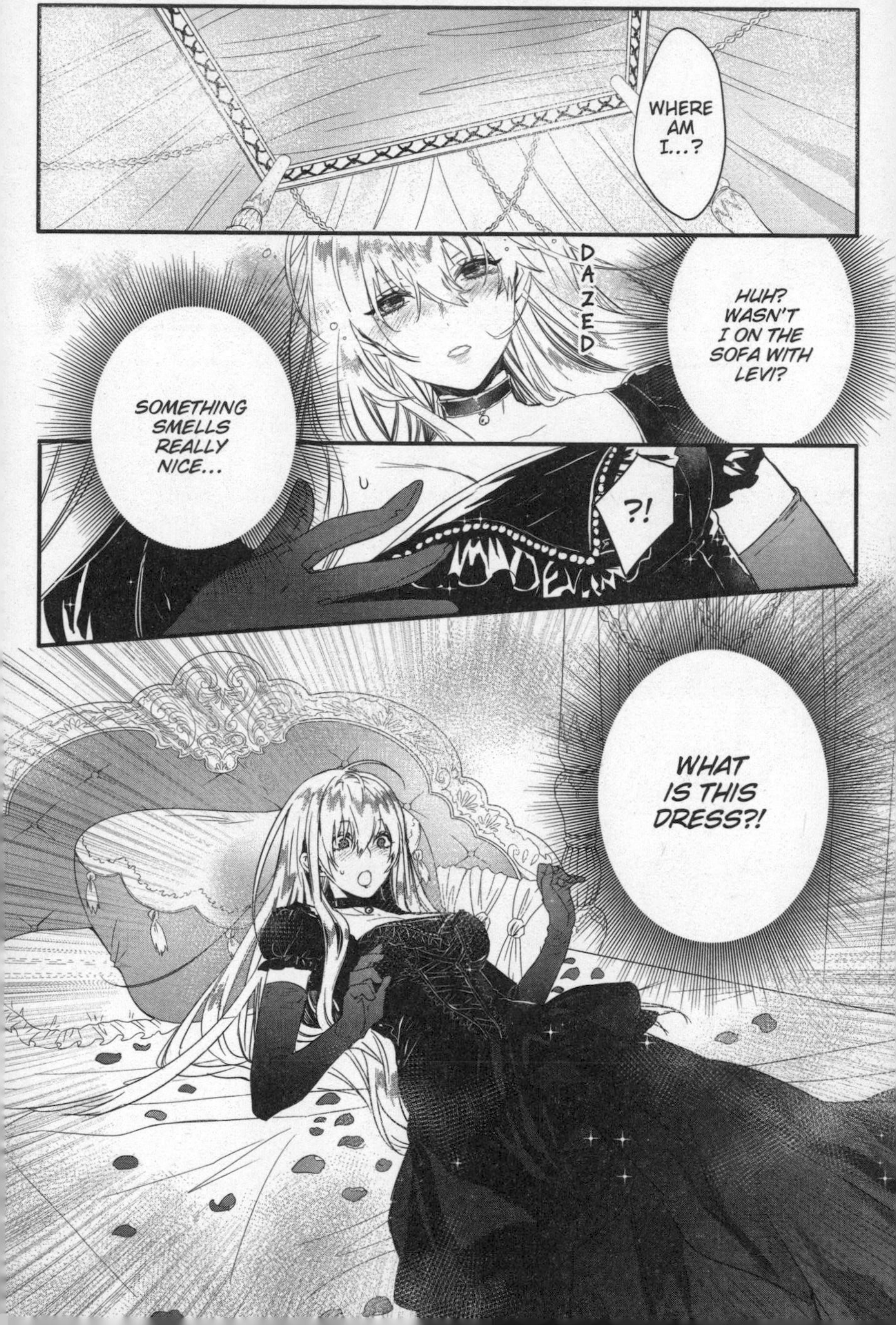
WHERE AM I...?
DAZED
HUH? WASN'T I ON THE SOFA WITH LEVI?
SOMETHING SMELLS REALLY NICE...
?!
WHAT IS THIS DRESS?!

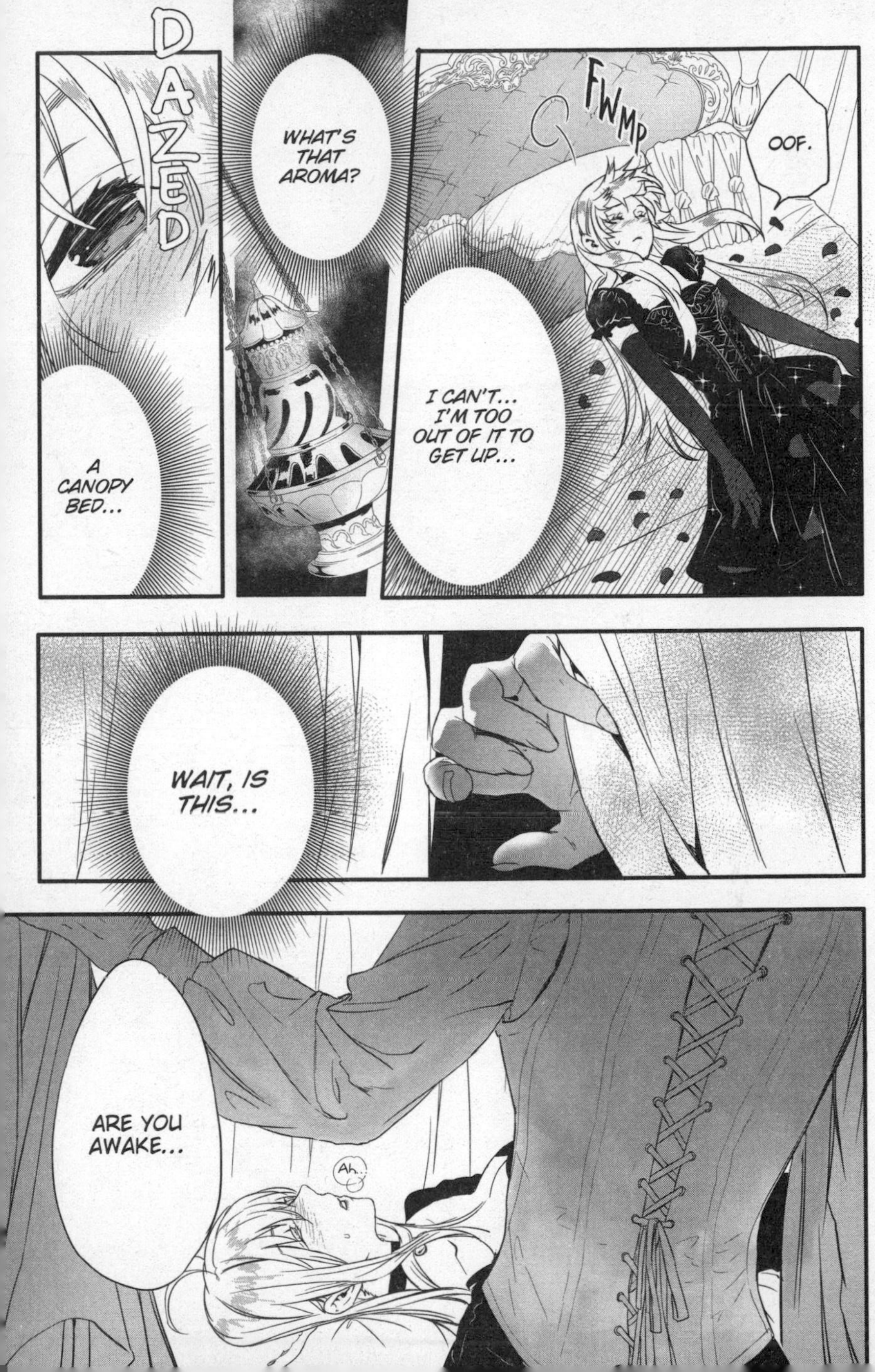
OOF.
FWMP
I CAN'T... I'M TOO OUT OF IT TO GET UP...
WHAT'S THAT AROMA?
DAZED
A CANOPY BED...
WAIT, IS THIS...
ARE YOU AWAKE...
Ah...

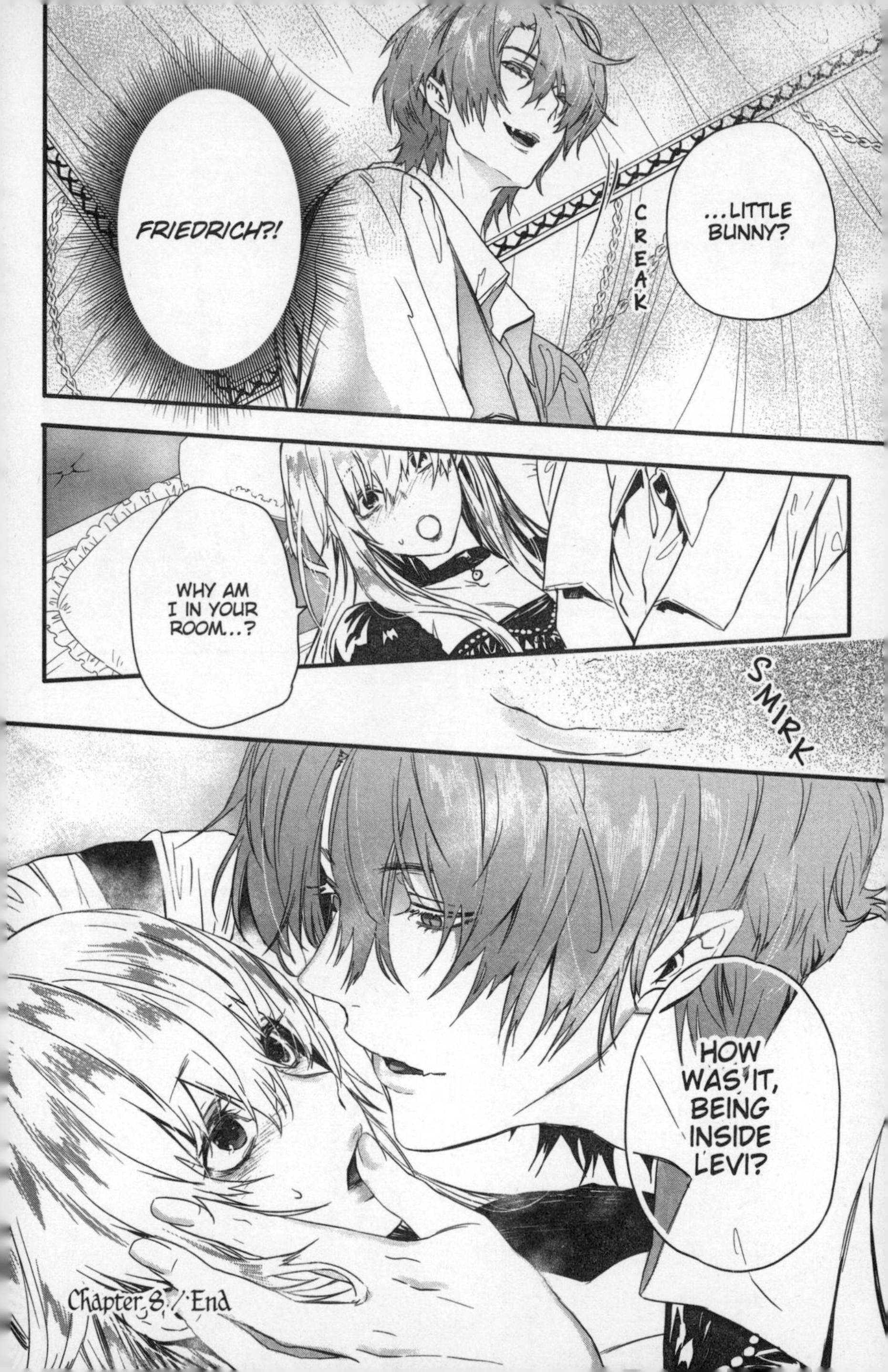
...LITTLE BUNNY?
CREAK
FRIEDRICH?!
WHY AM I IN YOUR ROOM...?
SMIRK
HOW WAS IT, BEING INSIDE LEVI?
Chapter 8 / End

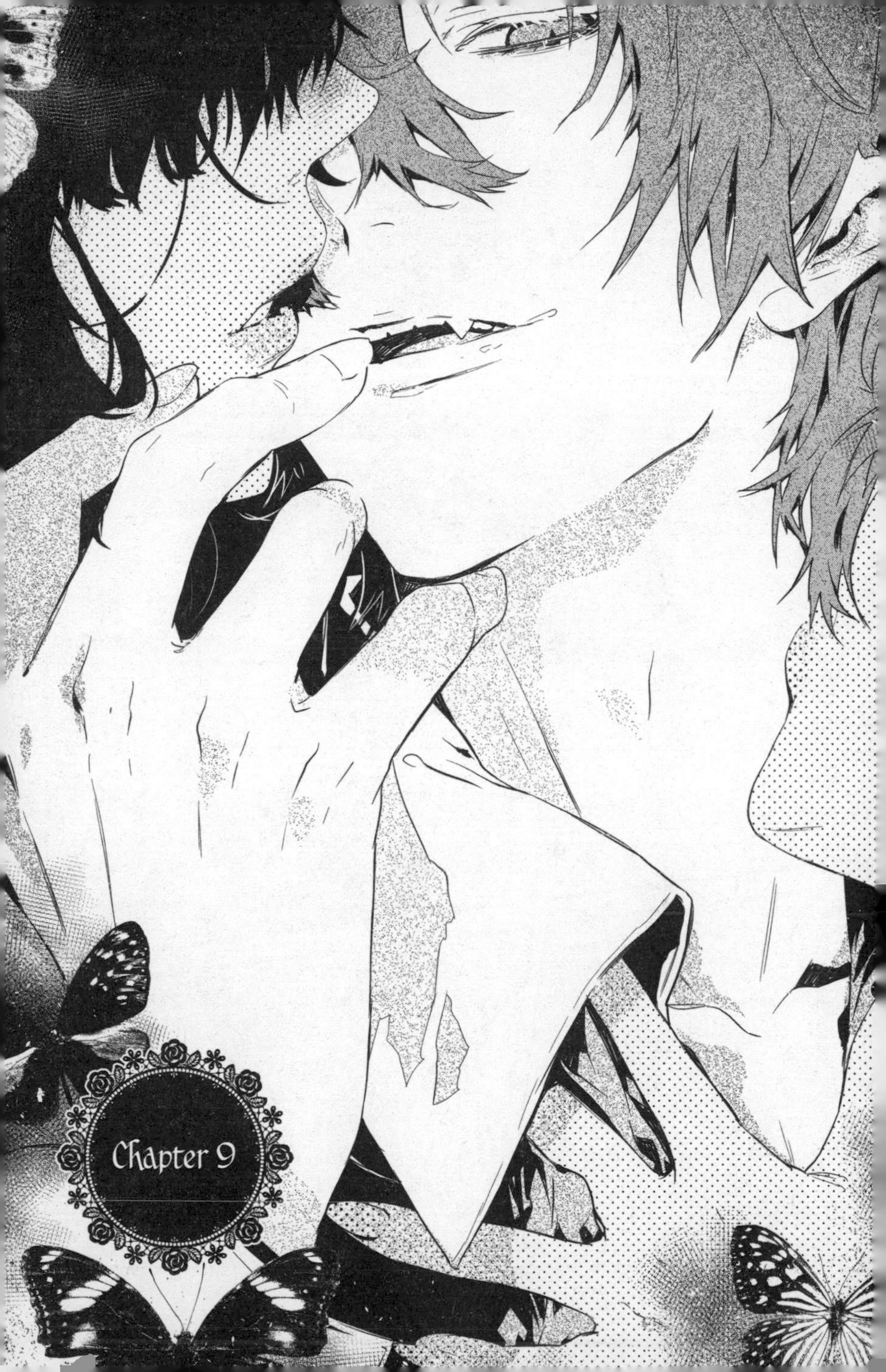
Chapter 9

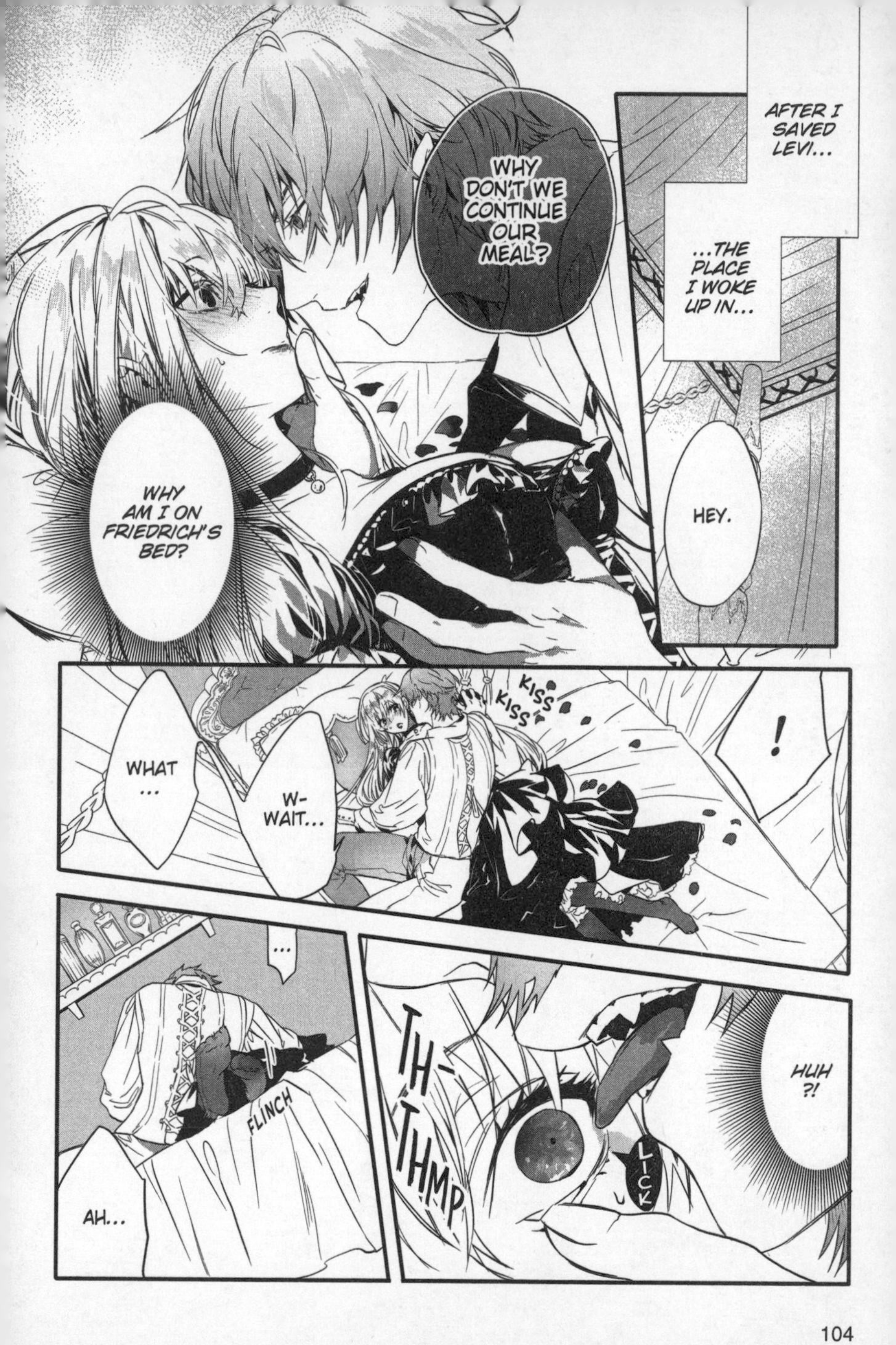
AFTER I SAVED LEVI...
...THE PLACE I WOKE UP IN...
HEY.
WHY DON'T WE CONTINUE OUR MEAL?
WHY AM I ON FRIEDRICH'S BED?
!
KISS KISS
W-WAIT...
WHAT...
HUH?!
LICK
TH-THMP
...
FLINCH
AH...

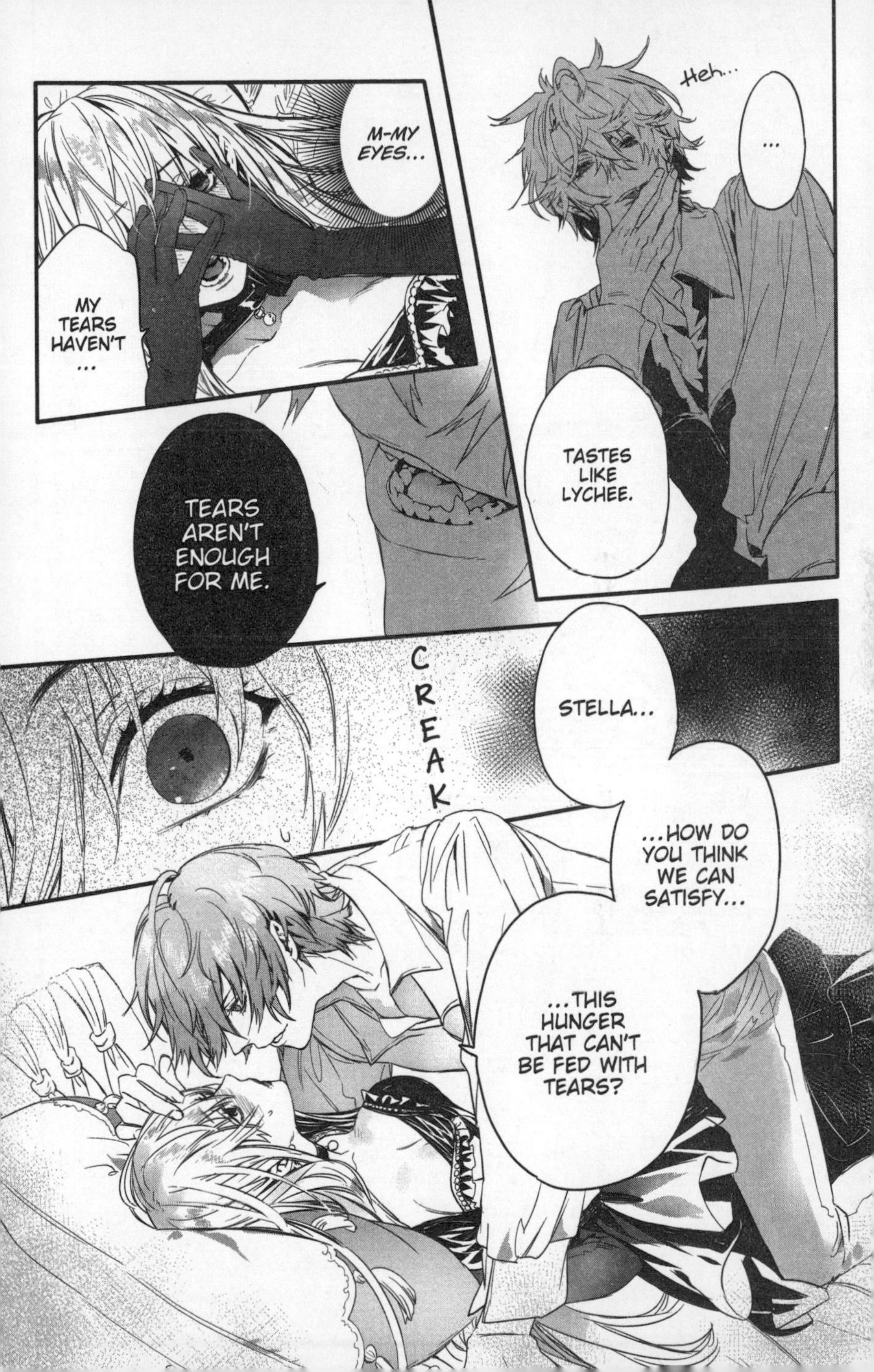
Heh...
...
TASTES LIKE LYCHEE.
M-MY EYES...
MY TEARS HAVEN'T ...
TEARS AREN'T ENOUGH FOR ME.
CREAK
STELLA...
...HOW DO YOU THINK WE CAN SATISFY...
...THIS HUNGER THAT CAN'T BE FED WITH TEARS?

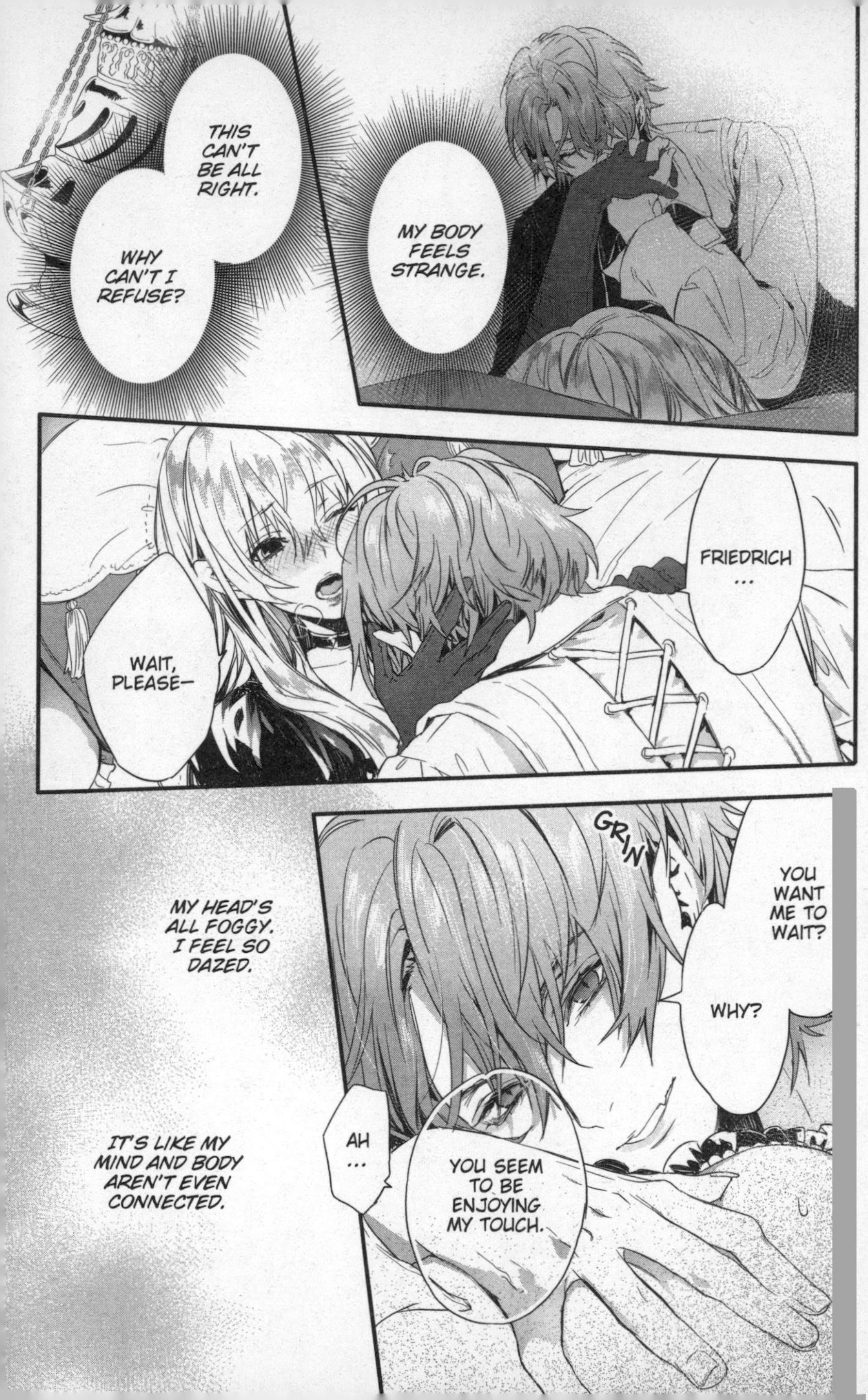
MY BODY FEELS STRANGE.
THIS CAN'T BE ALL RIGHT.
WHY CAN'T I REFUSE?
FRIEDRICH...
WAIT, PLEASE—
GRIN
YOU WANT ME TO WAIT?
WHY?
MY HEAD'S ALL FOGGY. I FEEL SO DAZED.
YOU SEEM TO BE ENJOYING MY TOUCH.
AH...
IT'S LIKE MY MIND AND BODY AREN'T EVEN CONNECTED.

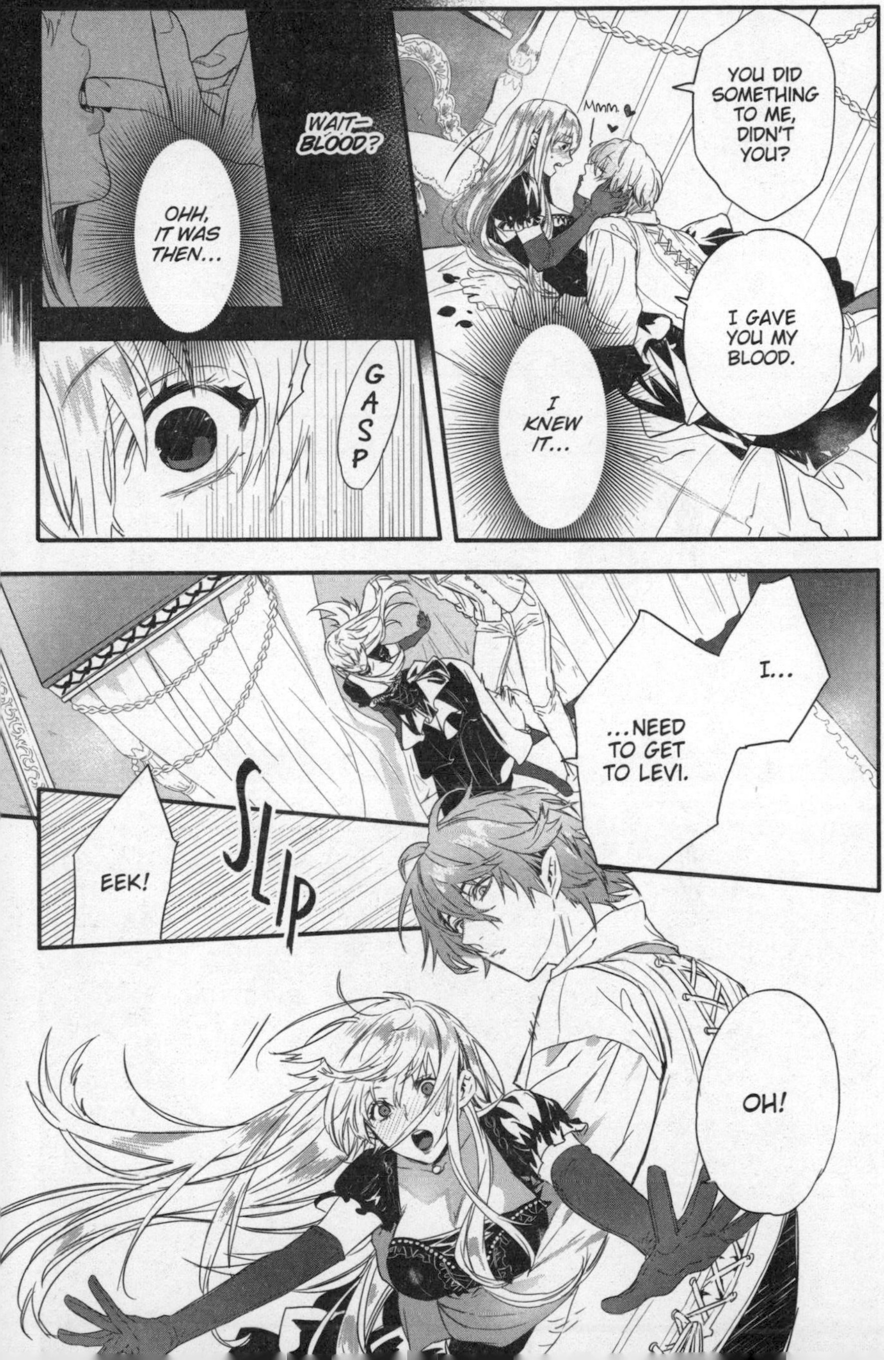
YOU DID SOMETHING TO ME, DIDN'T YOU?
Mmm.
I GAVE YOU MY BLOOD.
I KNEW IT...
WAIT— BLOOD?
OHH, IT WAS THEN...
GASP
I...
...NEED TO GET TO LEVI.
SLIP
EEK!
OH!

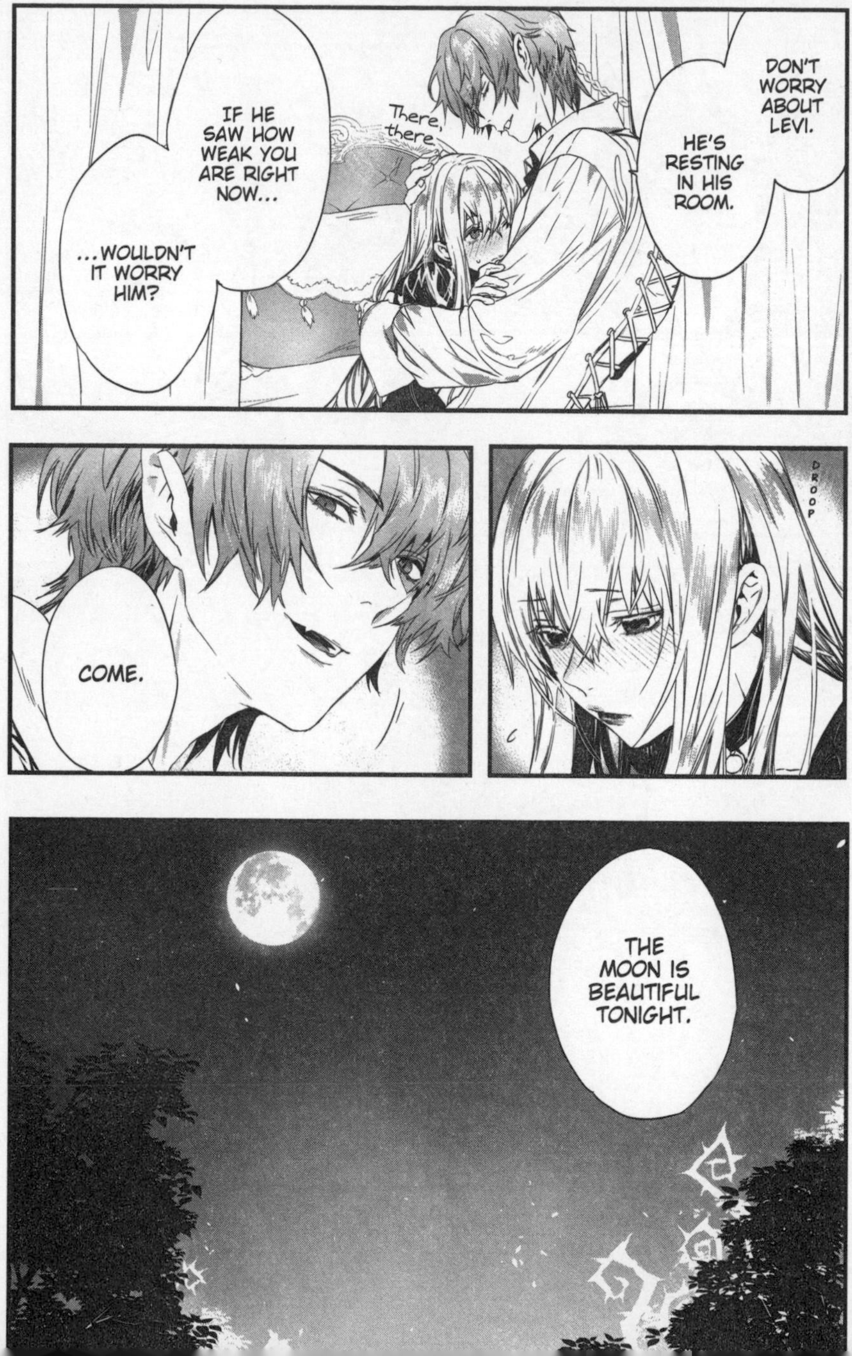
DON'T WORRY ABOUT LEVI.
HE'S RESTING IN HIS ROOM.
There, there.
IF HE SAW HOW WEAK YOU ARE RIGHT NOW...
...WOULDN'T IT WORRY HIM?
DROOP
COME.
THE MOON IS BEAUTIFUL TONIGHT.

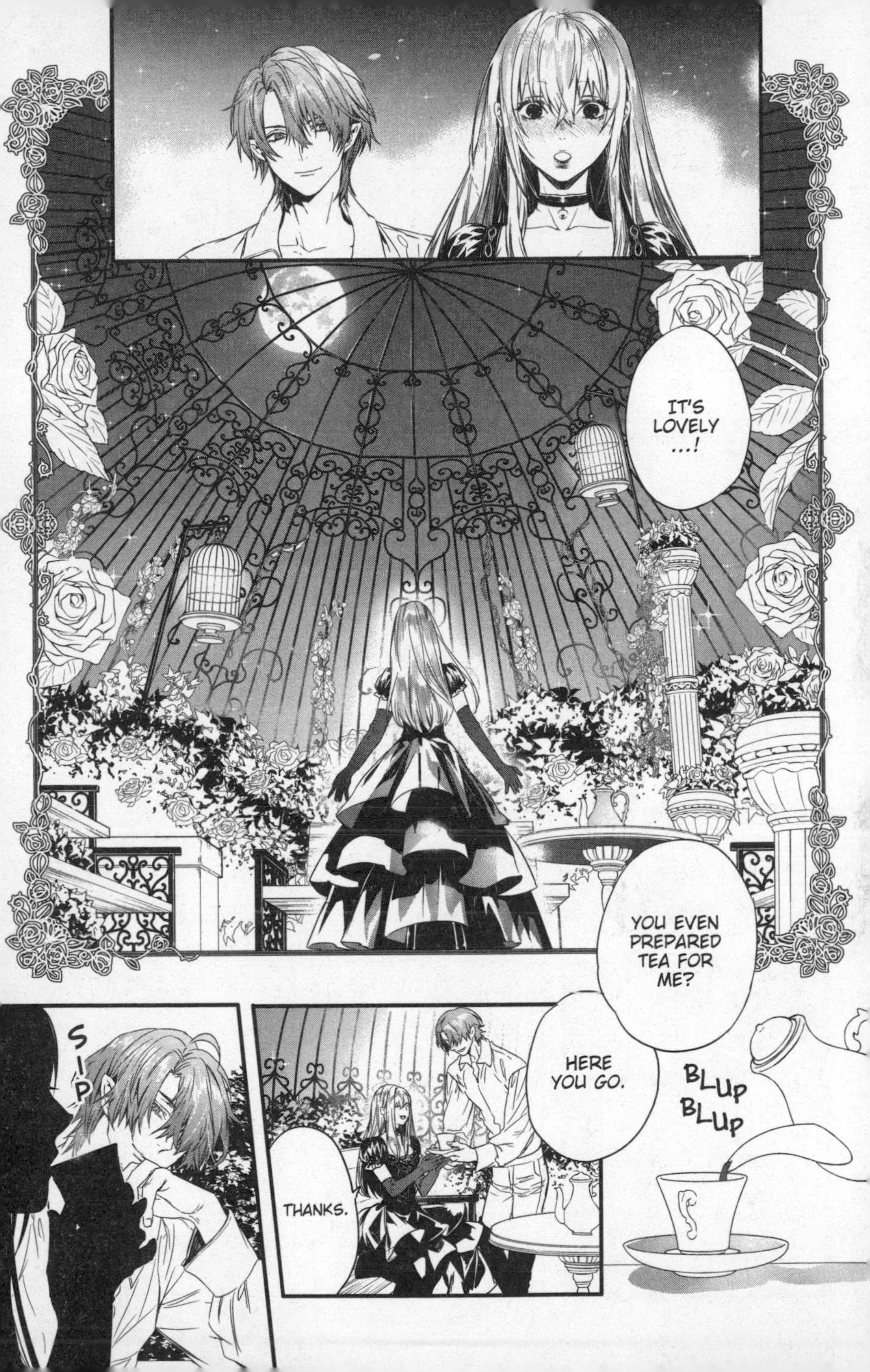
IT'S LOVELY ...!
YOU EVEN PREPARED TEA FOR ME?
BLUP BLUP
HERE YOU GO.
THANKS.
SIP

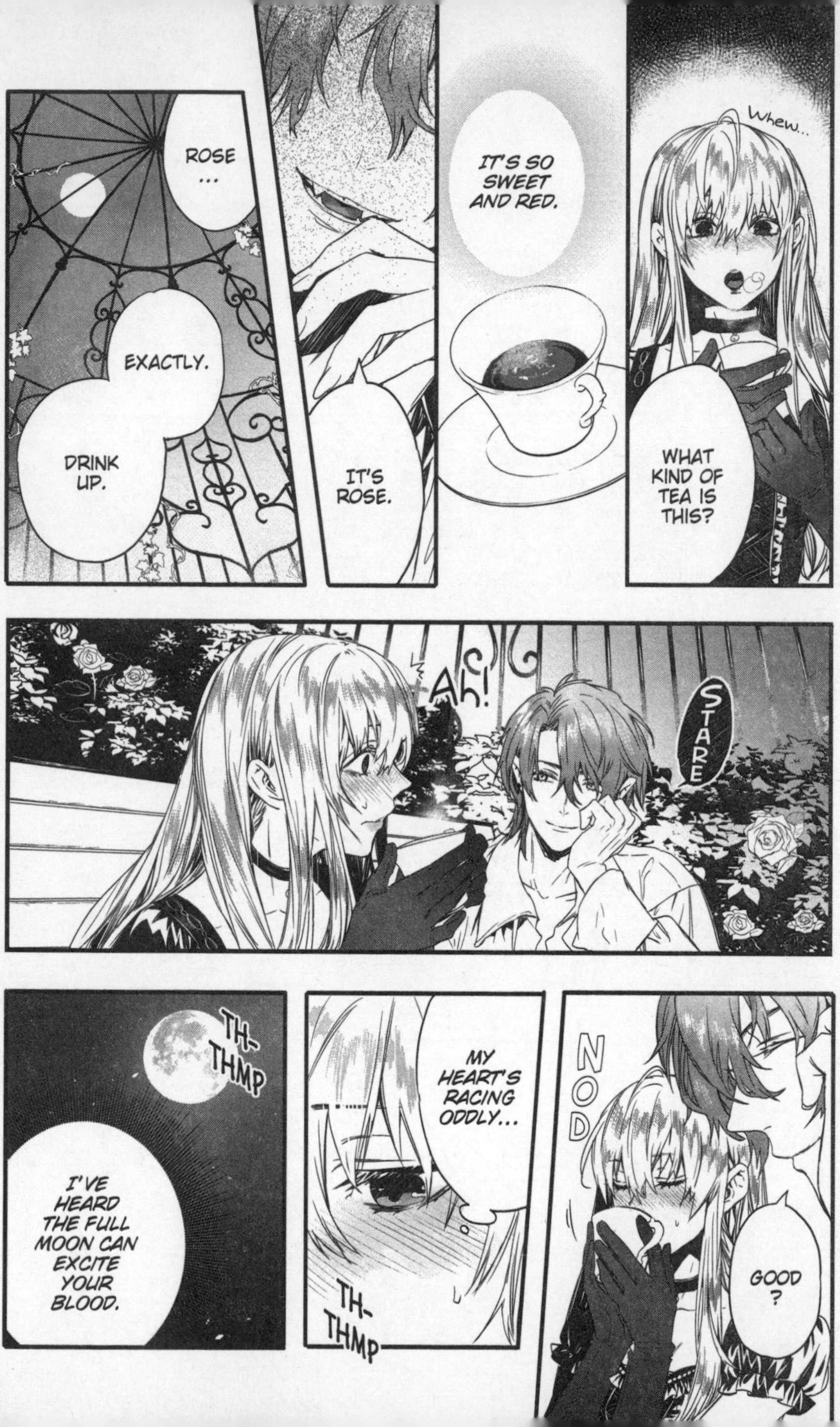
Whew...
WHAT KIND OF TEA IS THIS?
IT'S SO SWEET AND RED.
IT'S ROSE.
ROSE ...
EXACTLY.
DRINK UP.
STARE
Ah!
NOD
GOOD ?
MY HEART'S RACING ODDLY...
TH-THMP
TH-THMP
I'VE HEARD THE FULL MOON CAN EXCITE YOUR BLOOD.

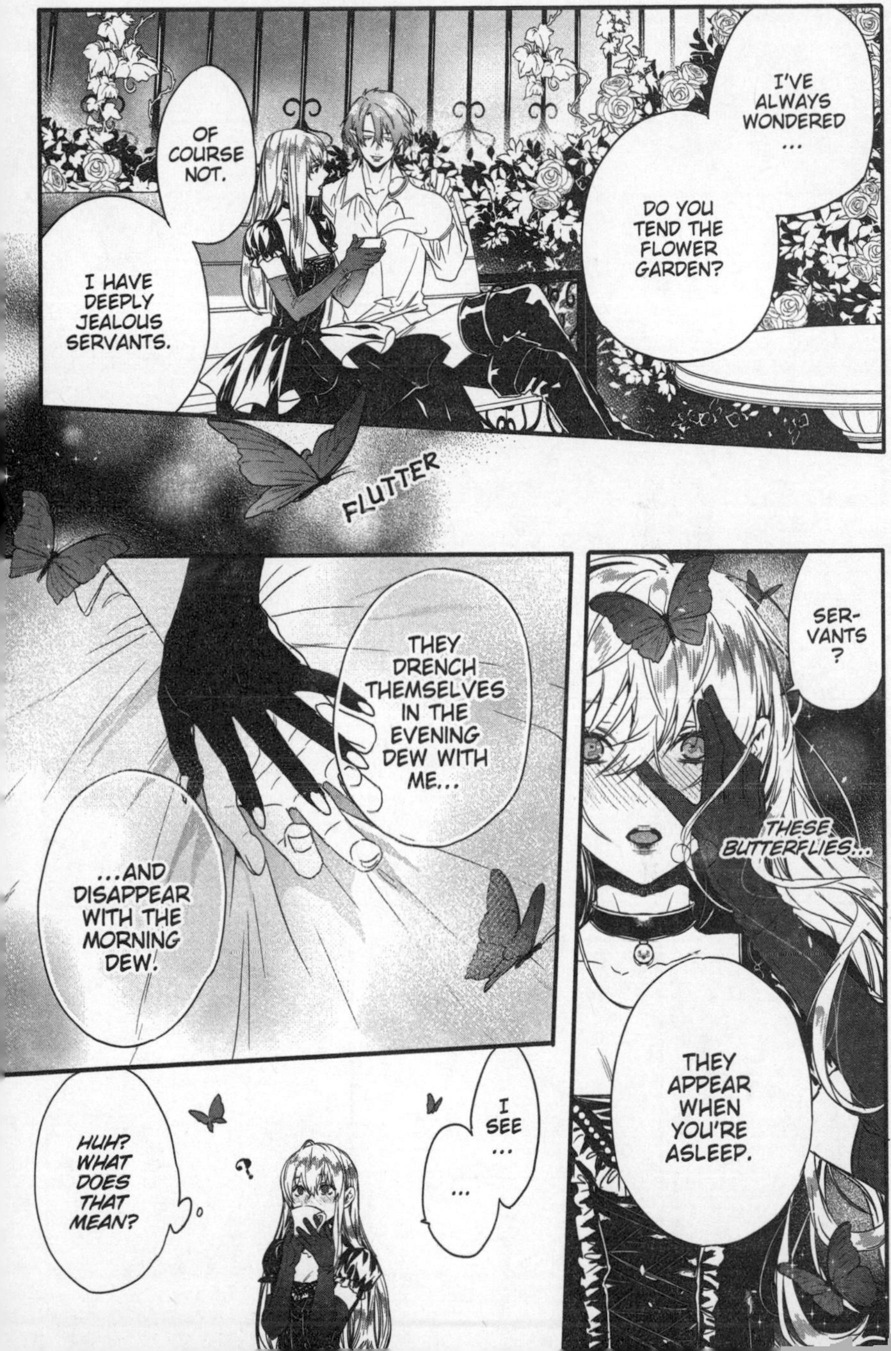
I'VE ALWAYS WONDERED ...
DO YOU TEND THE FLOWER GARDEN?
OF COURSE NOT.
I HAVE DEEPLY JEALOUS SERVANTS.
FLUTTER
SER-VANTS?
THESE BUTTERFLIES...
THEY APPEAR WHEN YOU'RE ASLEEP.
THEY DRENCH THEMSELVES IN THE EVENING DEW WITH ME...
...AND DISAPPEAR WITH THE MORNING DEW.
I SEE ...
...
HUH? WHAT DOES THAT MEAN?

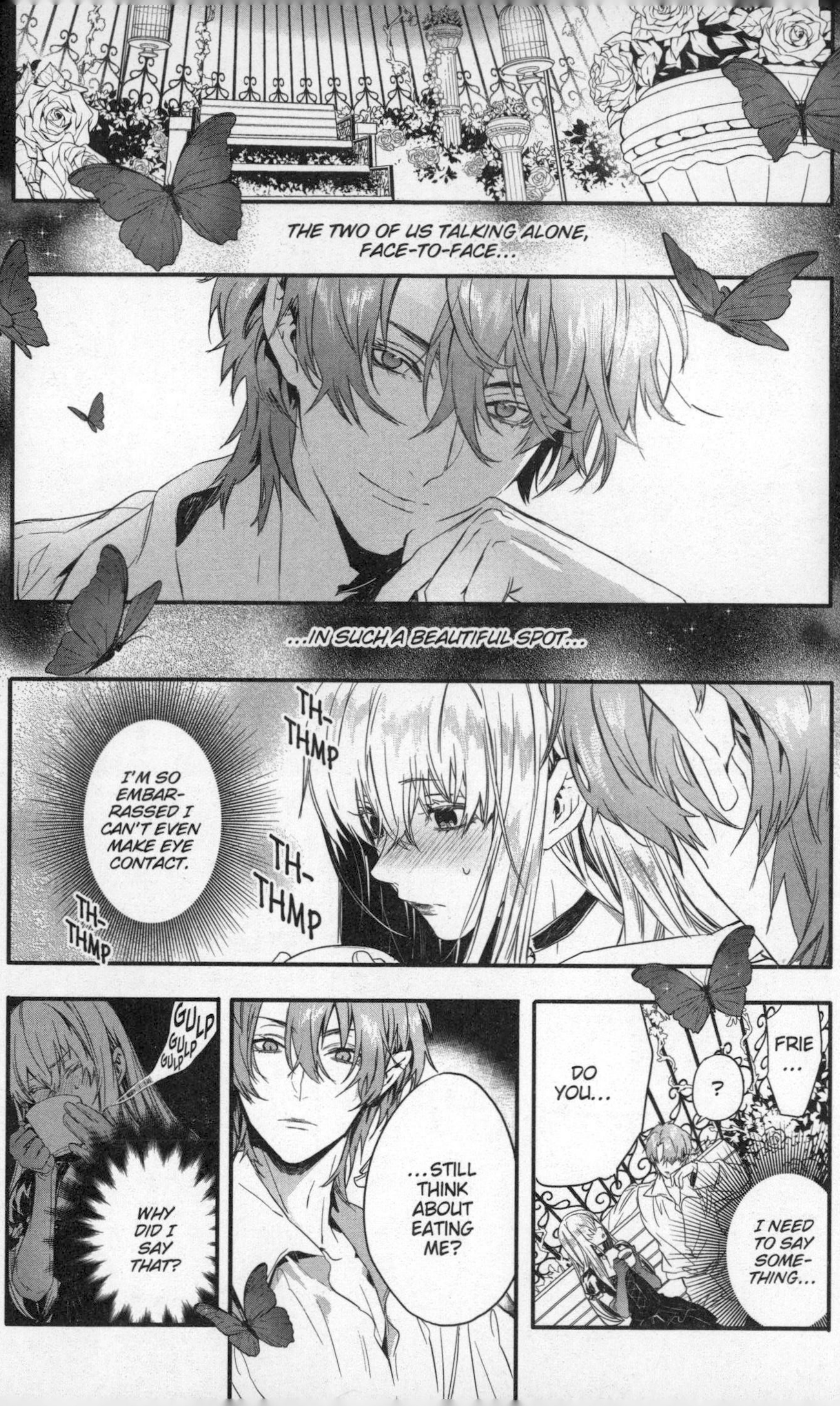
THE TWO OF US TALKING ALONE, FACE-TO-FACE...
...IN SUCH A BEAUTIFUL SPOT...
TH-THMP
I'M SO EMBARRASSED I CAN'T EVEN MAKE EYE CONTACT.
TH-THMP
TH-THMP
FRIE...
?
DO YOU...
I NEED TO SAY SOMETHING...
...STILL THINK ABOUT EATING ME?
GULP GULP GULP
WHY DID I SAY THAT?

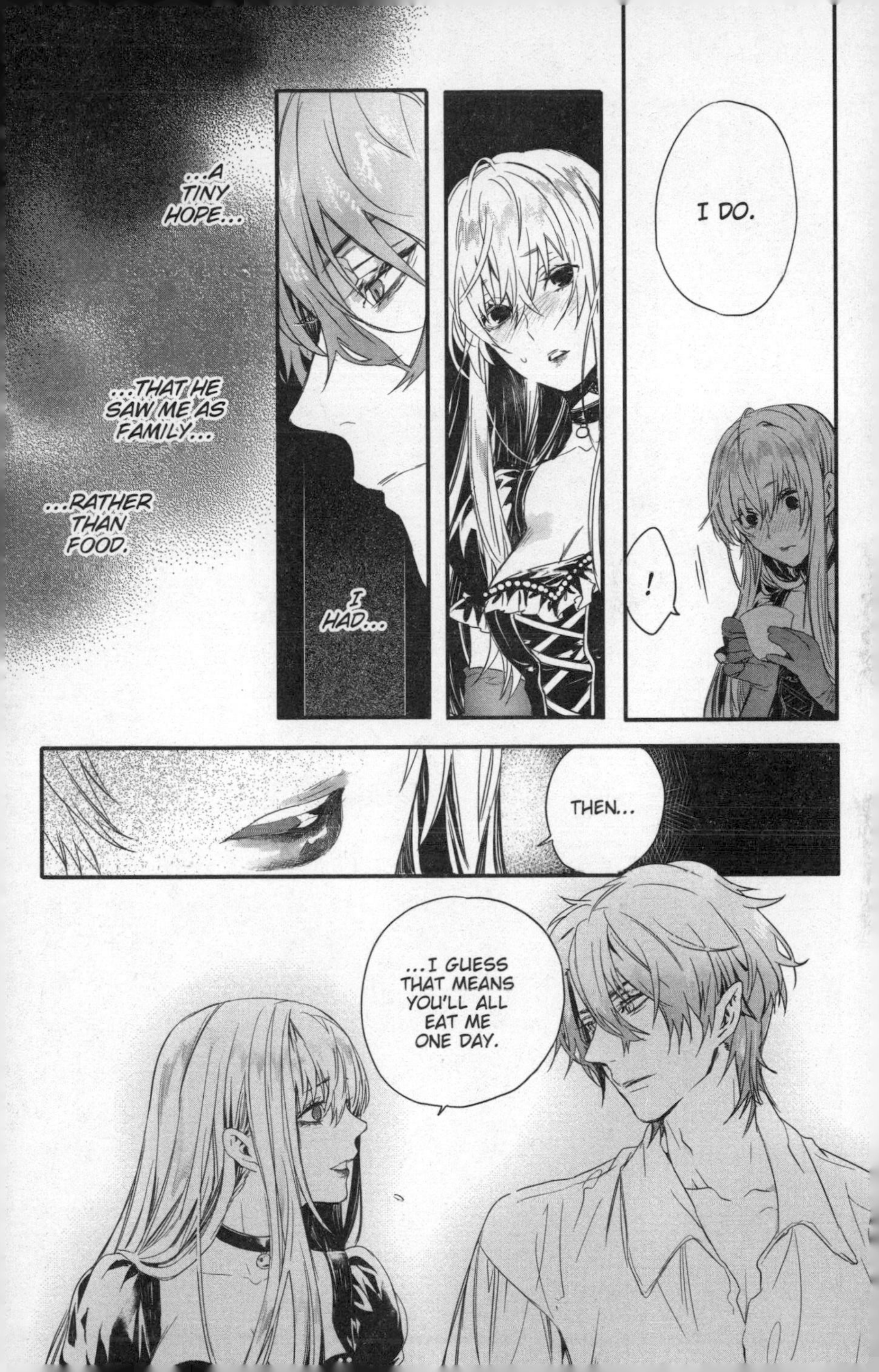
I DO.
!
I HAD...
...A TINY HOPE...
...THAT HE SAW ME AS FAMILY...
...RATHER THAN FOOD.
THEN...
...I GUESS THAT MEANS YOU'LL ALL EAT ME ONE DAY.

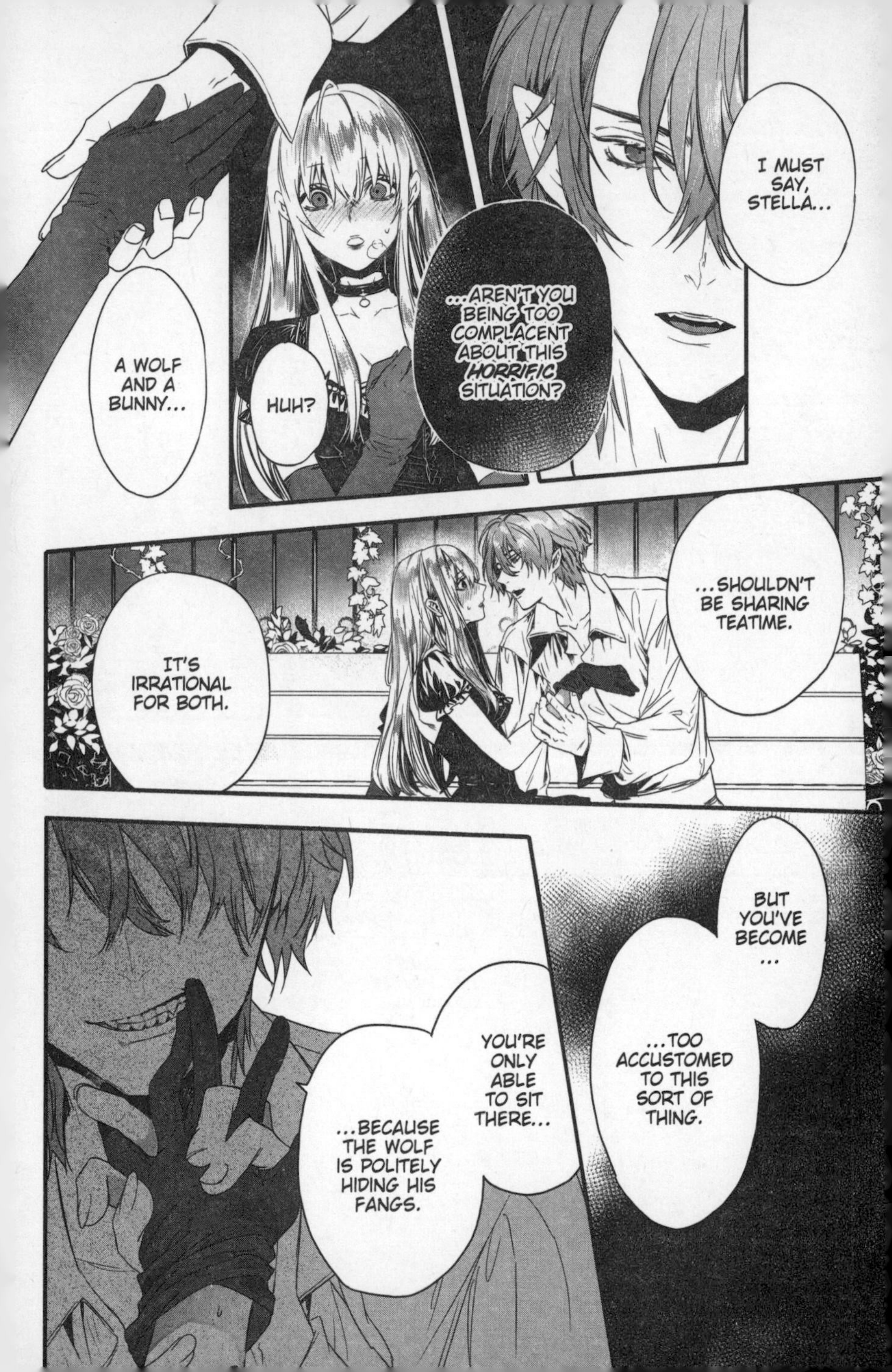
I MUST SAY, STELLA...
...AREN'T YOU BEING TOO COMPLACENT ABOUT THIS *HORRIFIC* SITUATION?
HUH?
A WOLF AND A BUNNY...
...SHOULDN'T BE SHARING TEATIME.
IT'S IRRATIONAL FOR BOTH.
BUT YOU'VE BECOME ...
...TOO ACCUSTOMED TO THIS SORT OF THING.
YOU'RE ONLY ABLE TO SIT THERE...
...BECAUSE THE WOLF IS POLITELY HIDING HIS FANGS.

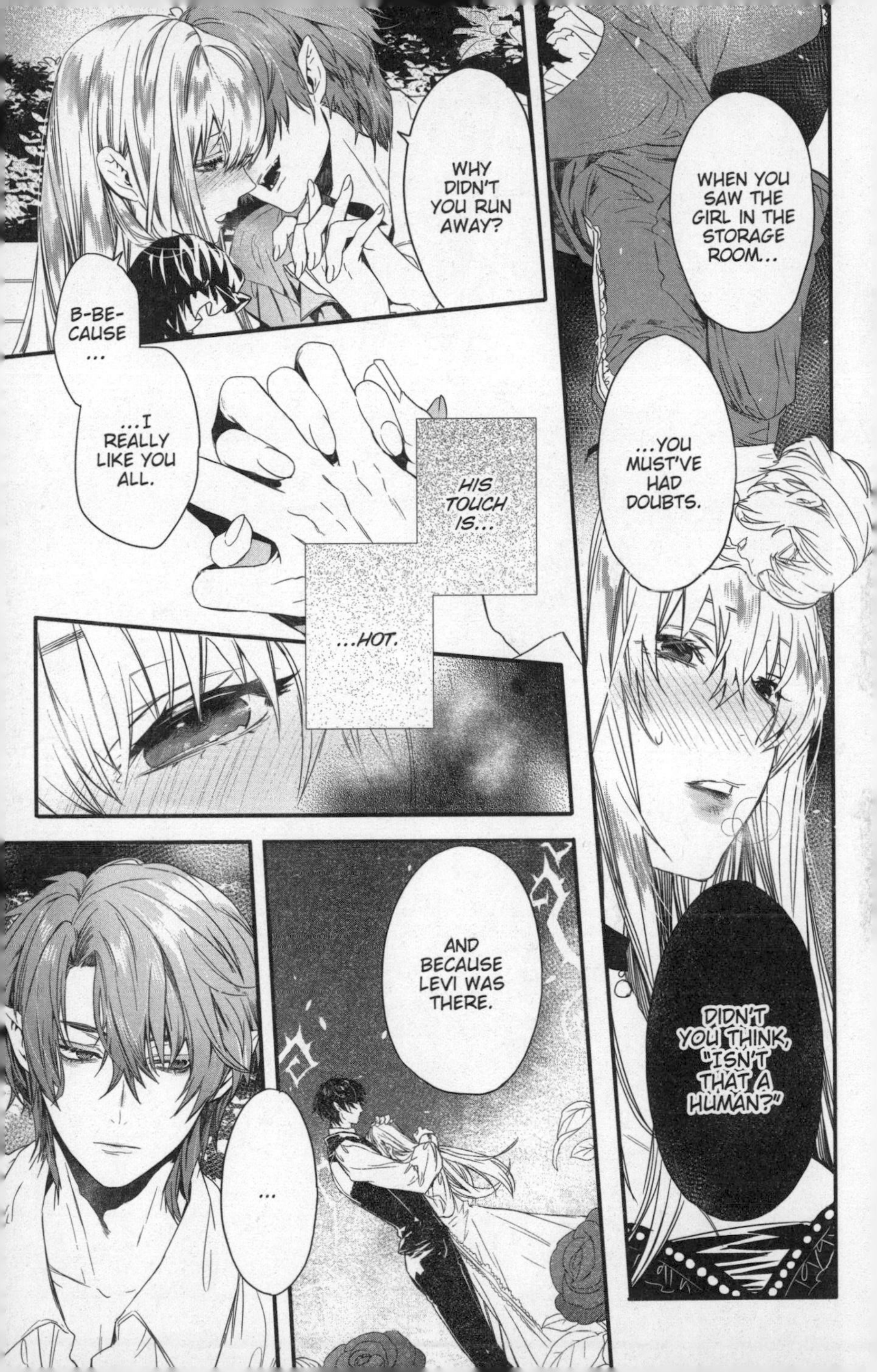
WHEN YOU SAW THE GIRL IN THE STORAGE ROOM...
...YOU MUST'VE HAD DOUBTS.
DIDN'T YOU THINK, "ISN'T THAT A HUMAN?"
WHY DIDN'T YOU RUN AWAY?
B-BE-CAUSE...
...I REALLY LIKE YOU ALL.
HIS TOUCH IS...
...HOT.
AND BECAUSE LEVI WAS THERE.
...

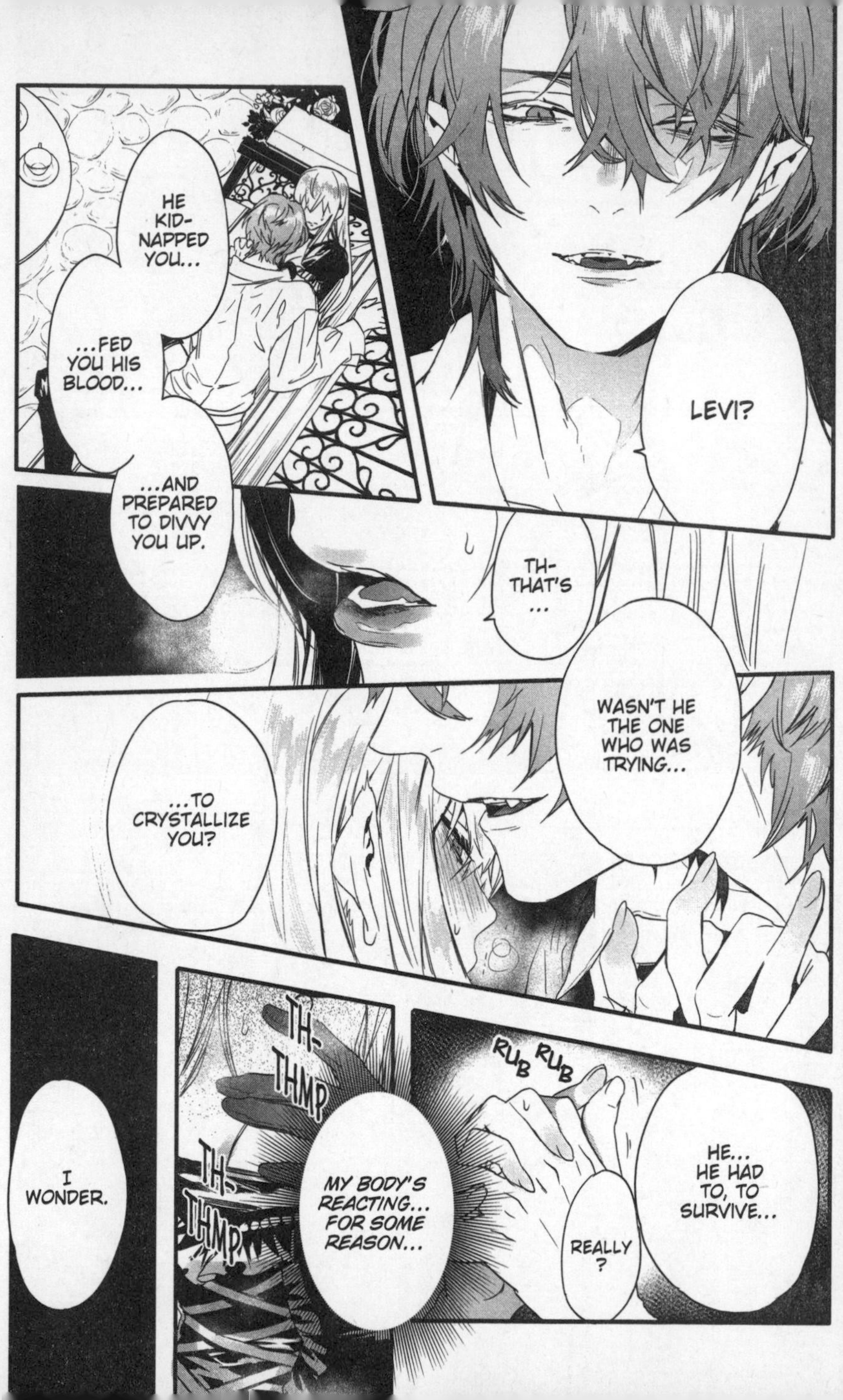
LEVI?
HE KID-NAPPED YOU...
...FED YOU HIS BLOOD...
...AND PREPARED TO DIVVY YOU UP.
TH-THAT'S...
WASN'T HE THE ONE WHO WAS TRYING...
...TO CRYSTALLIZE YOU?
RUB RUB
HE... HE HAD TO, TO SURVIVE...
REALLY?
TH-THMP
MY BODY'S REACTING... FOR SOME REASON...
TH-THMP
I WONDER.

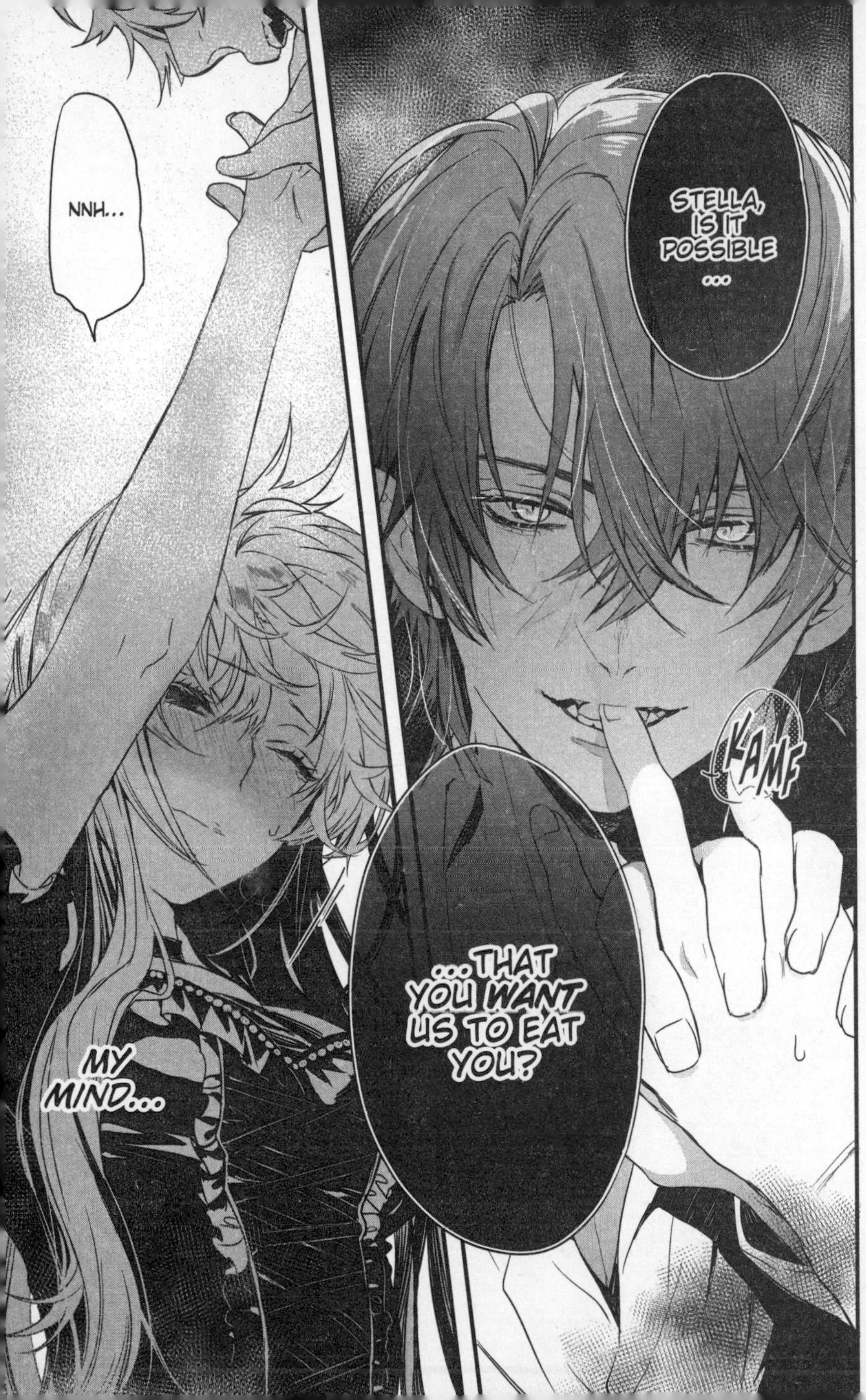
STELLA, IS IT POSSIBLE ...
...THAT YOU WANT US TO EAT YOU?
KAMF
NNH...
MY MIND...

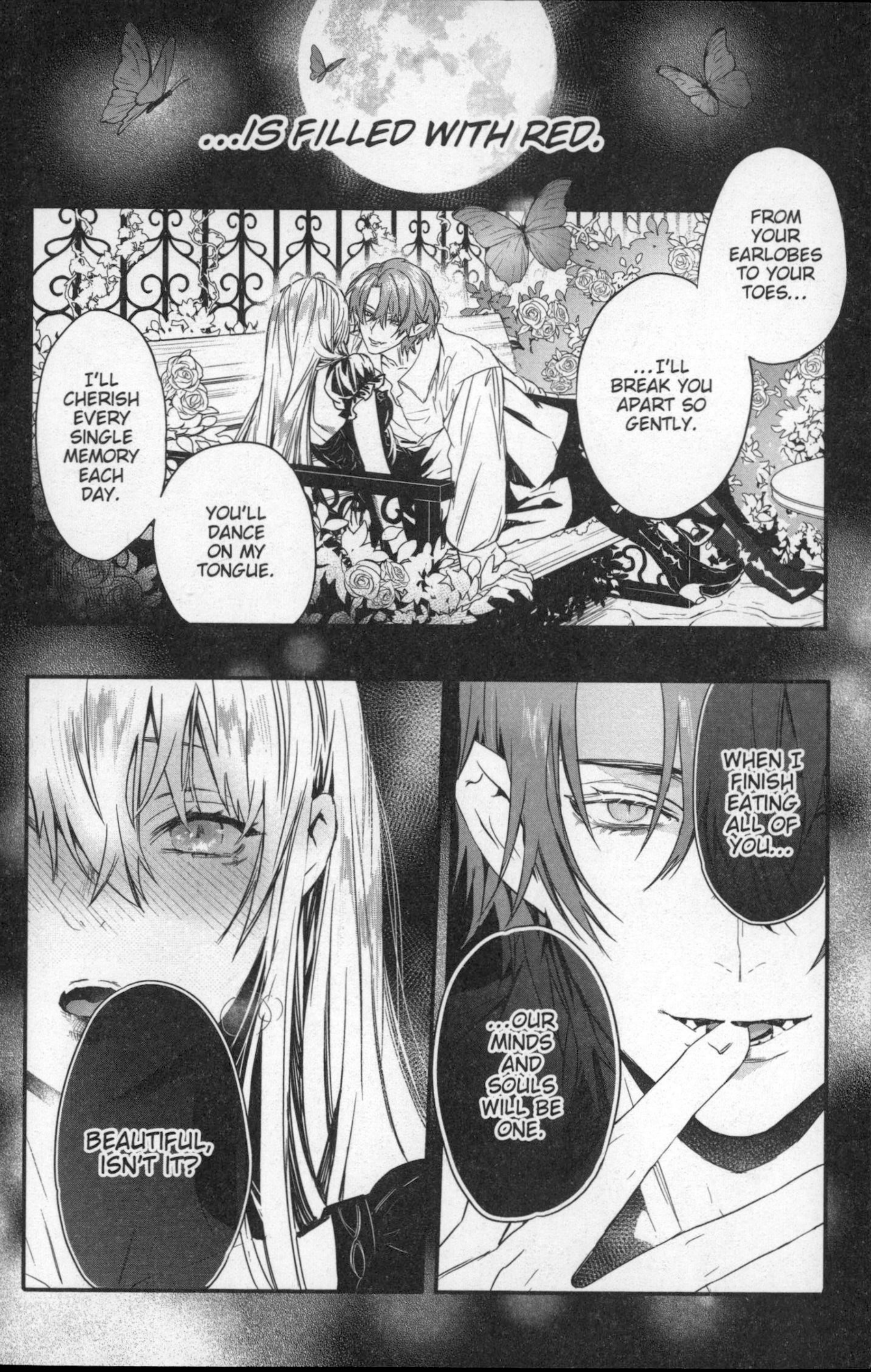
...IS FILLED WITH RED.
FROM YOUR EARLOBES TO YOUR TOES...
...I'LL BREAK YOU APART SO GENTLY.
YOU'LL DANCE ON MY TONGUE.
I'LL CHERISH EVERY SINGLE MEMORY EACH DAY.
WHEN I FINISH EATING ALL OF YOU...
...OUR MINDS AND SOULS WILL BE ONE.
BEAUTIFUL, ISN'T IT?

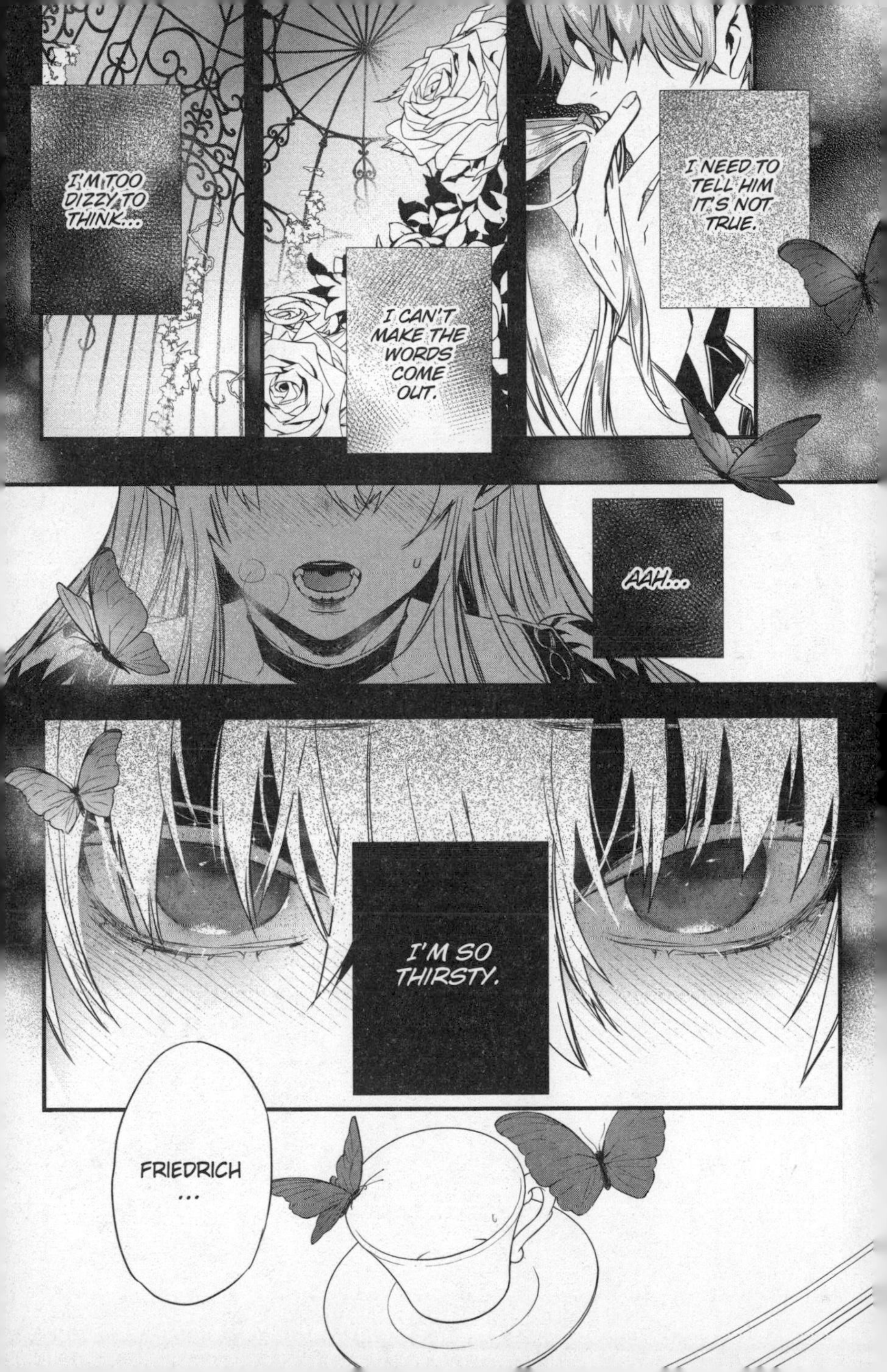
I NEED TO TELL HIM IT'S NOT TRUE.
I CAN'T MAKE THE WORDS COME OUT.
I'M TOO DIZZY TO THINK...
AAH...
I'M SO THIRSTY.
FRIEDRICH ...

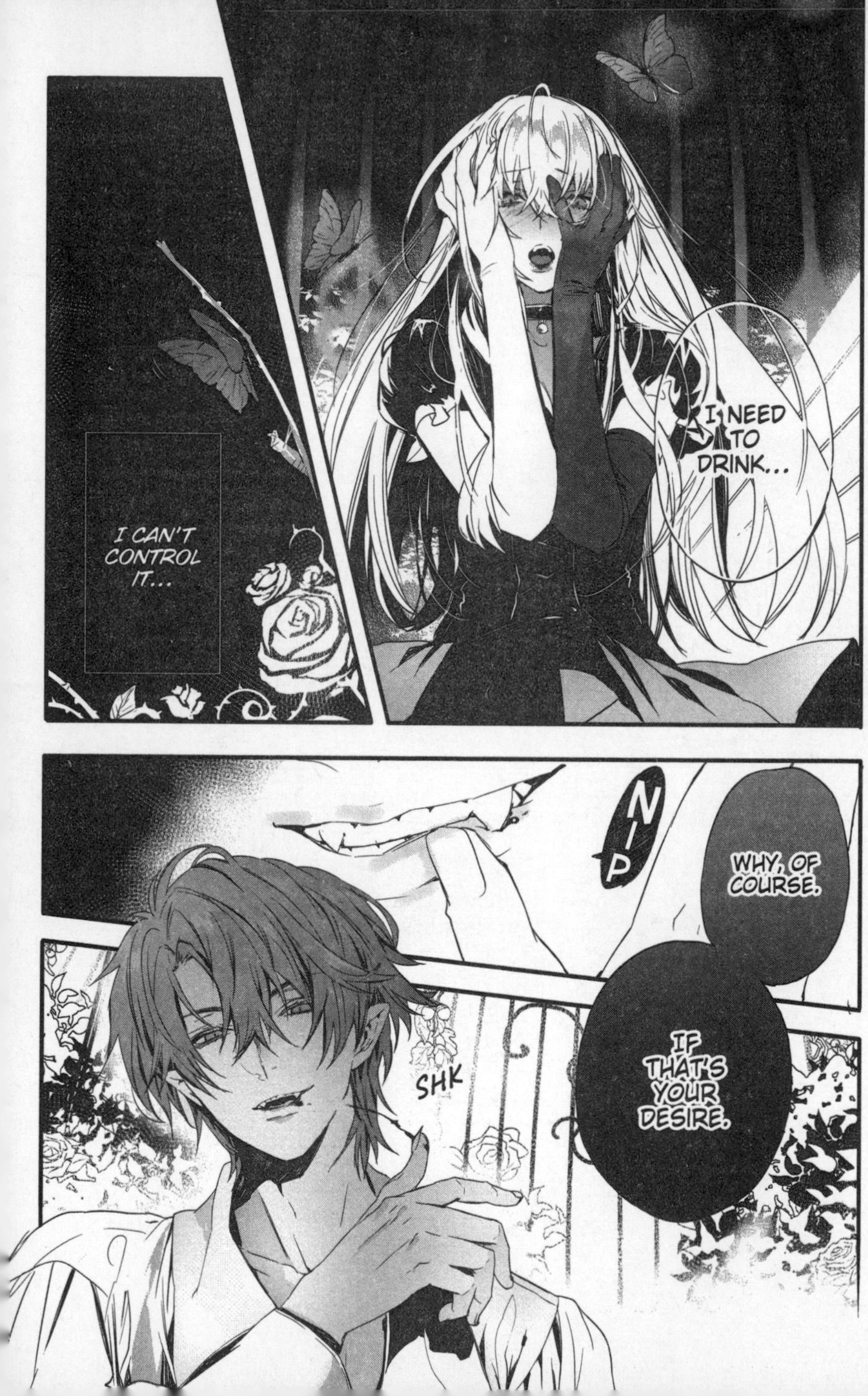
I NEED TO DRINK...
I CAN'T CONTROL IT...
NIP
WHY, OF COURSE.
IF THAT'S YOUR DESIRE.
SHK

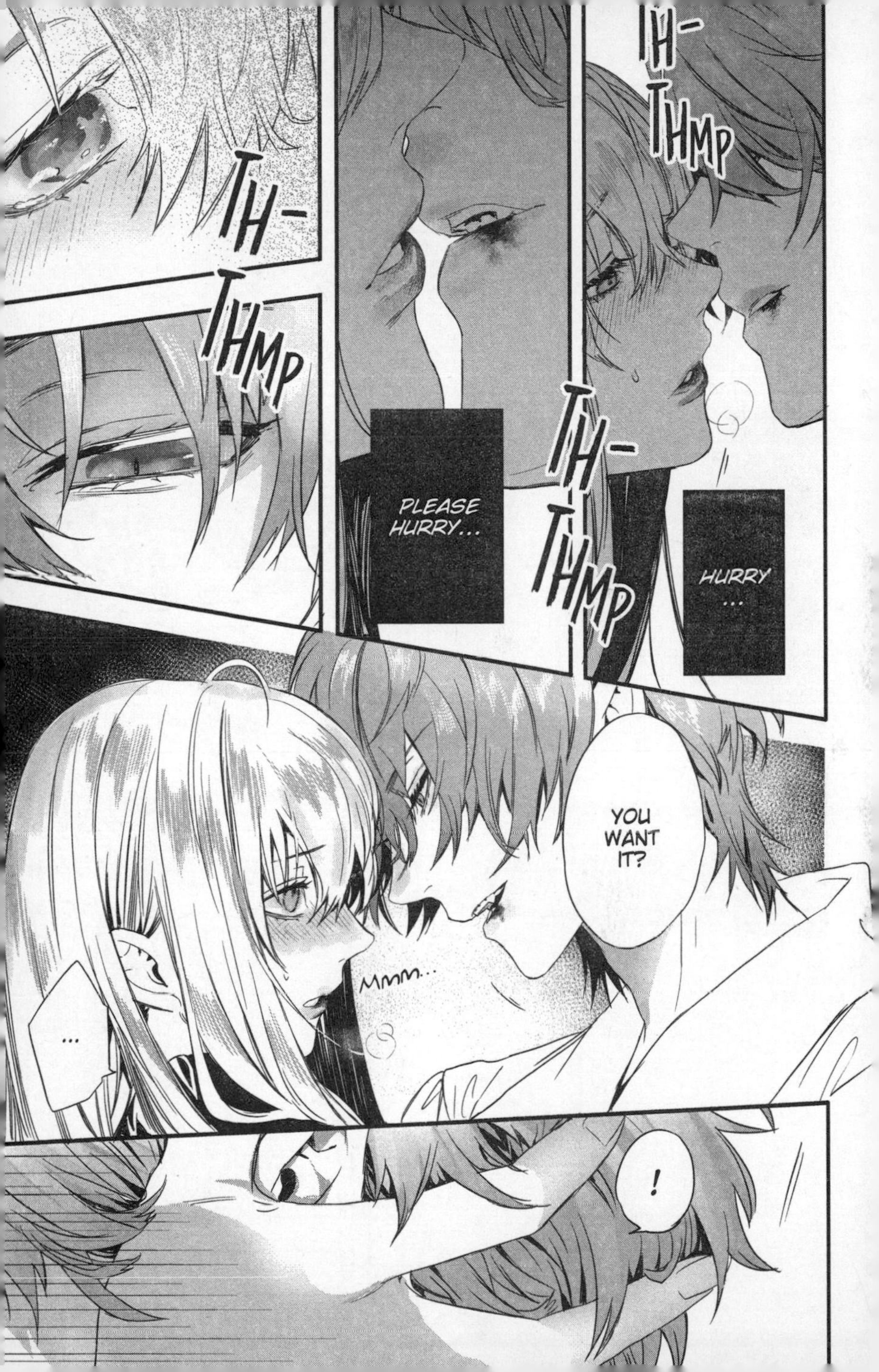
TH- THMP
TH- THMP
HURRY …
PLEASE HURRY…
TH- THMP
YOU WANT IT?
MMM…
…
!

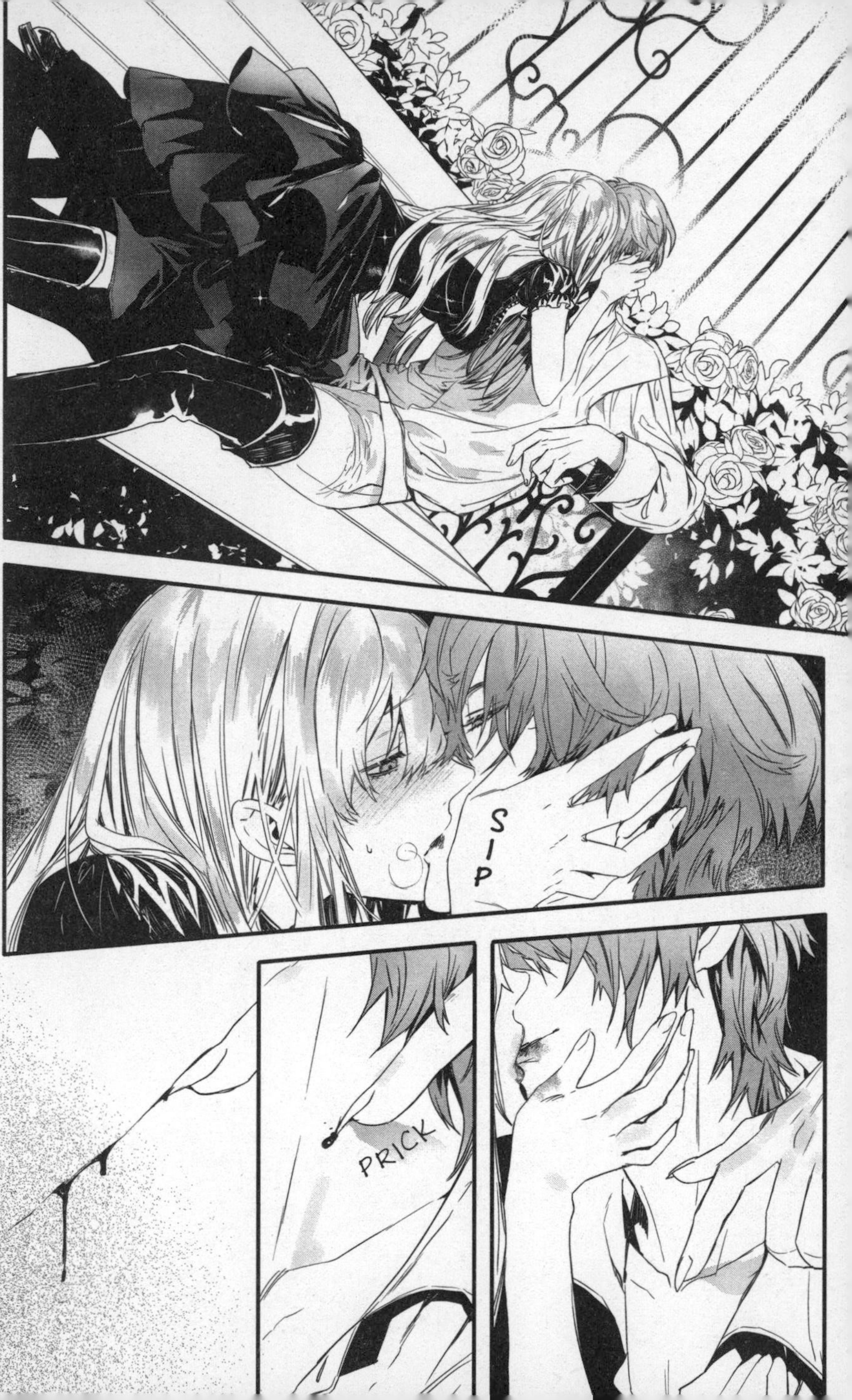
SIP
PRICK

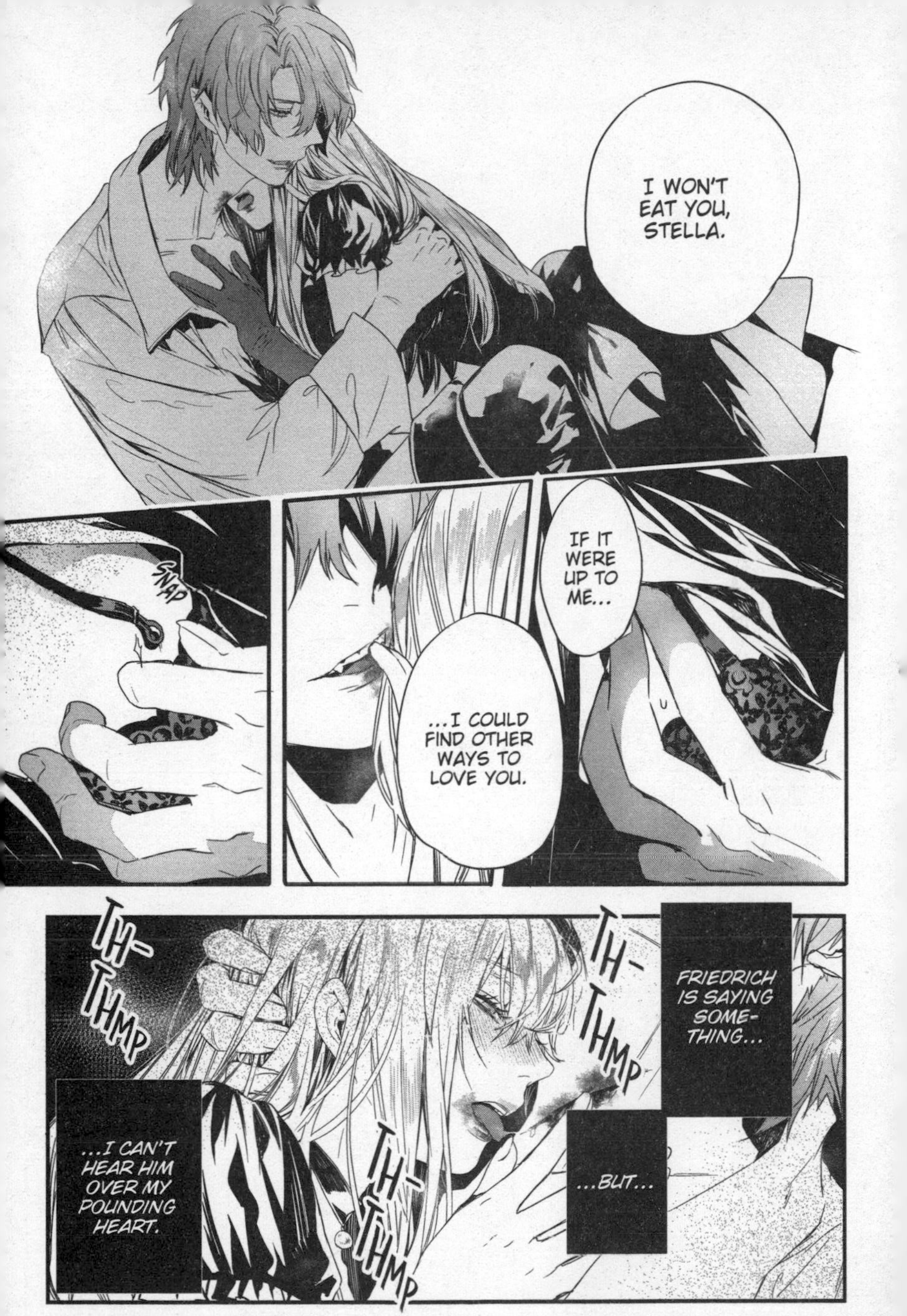
I WON'T EAT YOU, STELLA.
IF IT WERE UP TO ME...
...I COULD FIND OTHER WAYS TO LOVE YOU.
SNAP
FRIEDRICH IS SAYING SOME-THING...
TH-THMP
...BUT...
TH-THMP
...I CAN'T HEAR HIM OVER MY POUNDING HEART.
TH-THMP

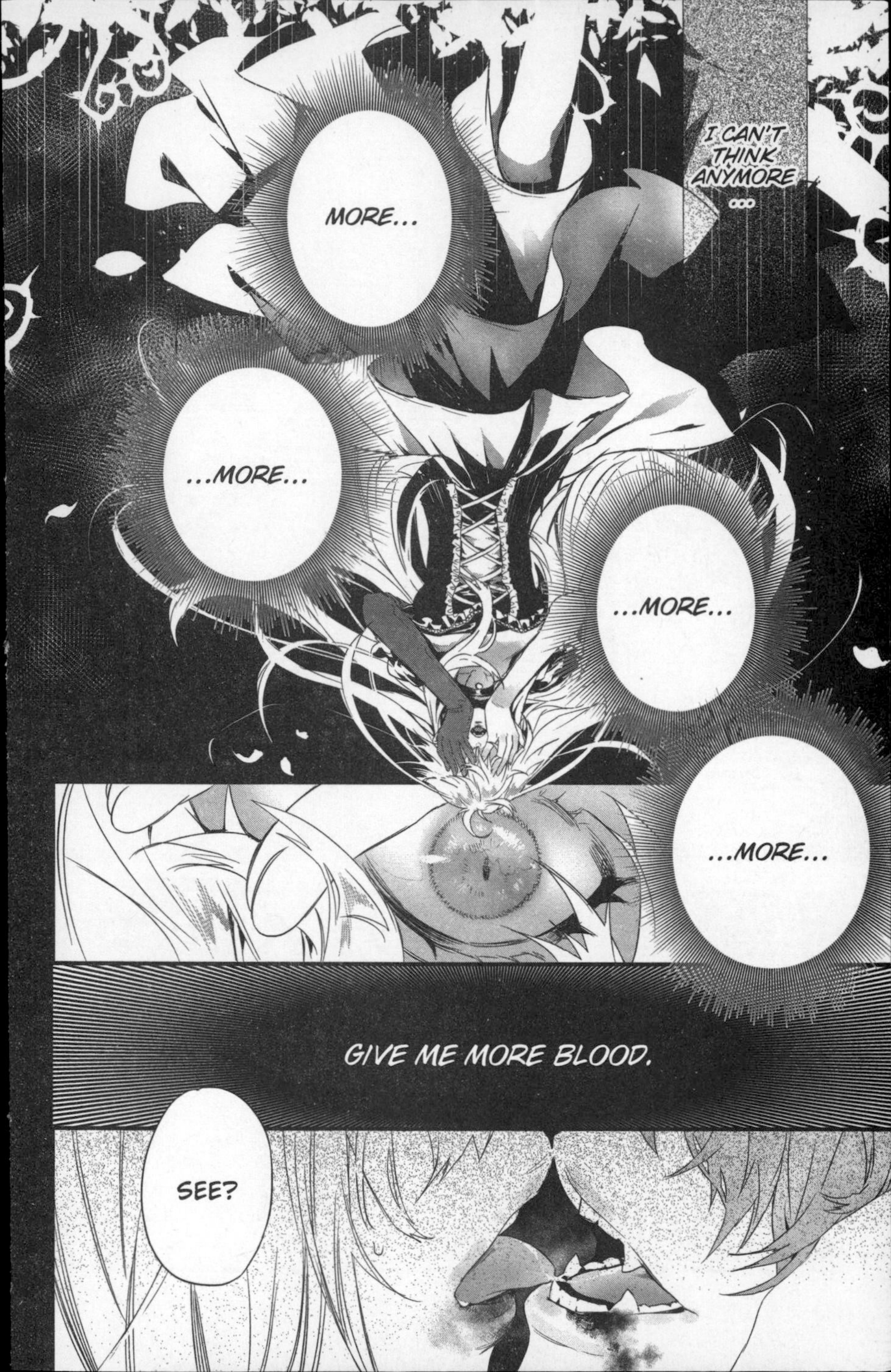

I CAN'T THINK ANYMORE...
MORE...
...MORE...
...MORE...
...MORE...
GIVE ME MORE BLOOD.
SEE?

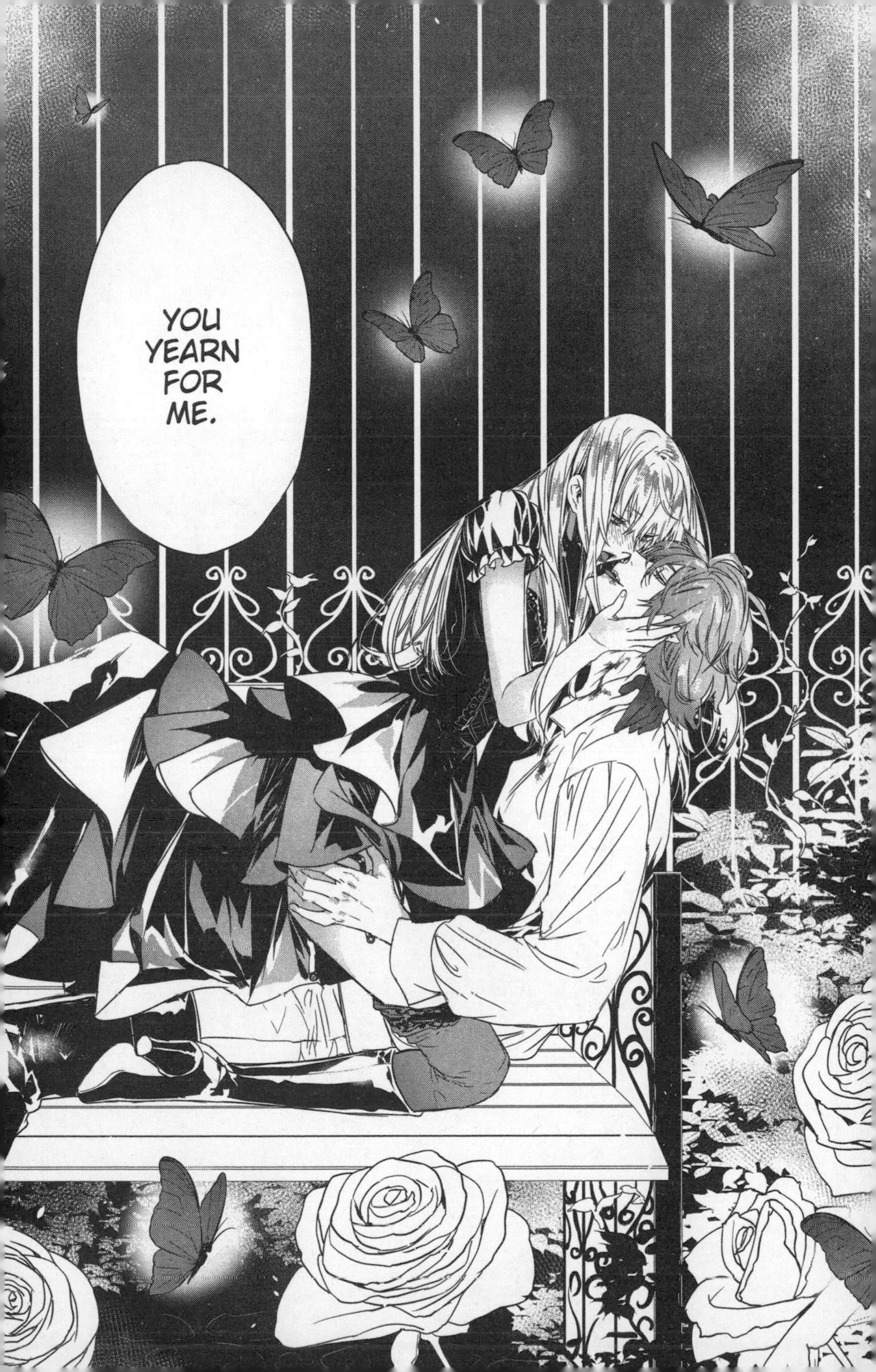
YOU YEARN FOR ME.

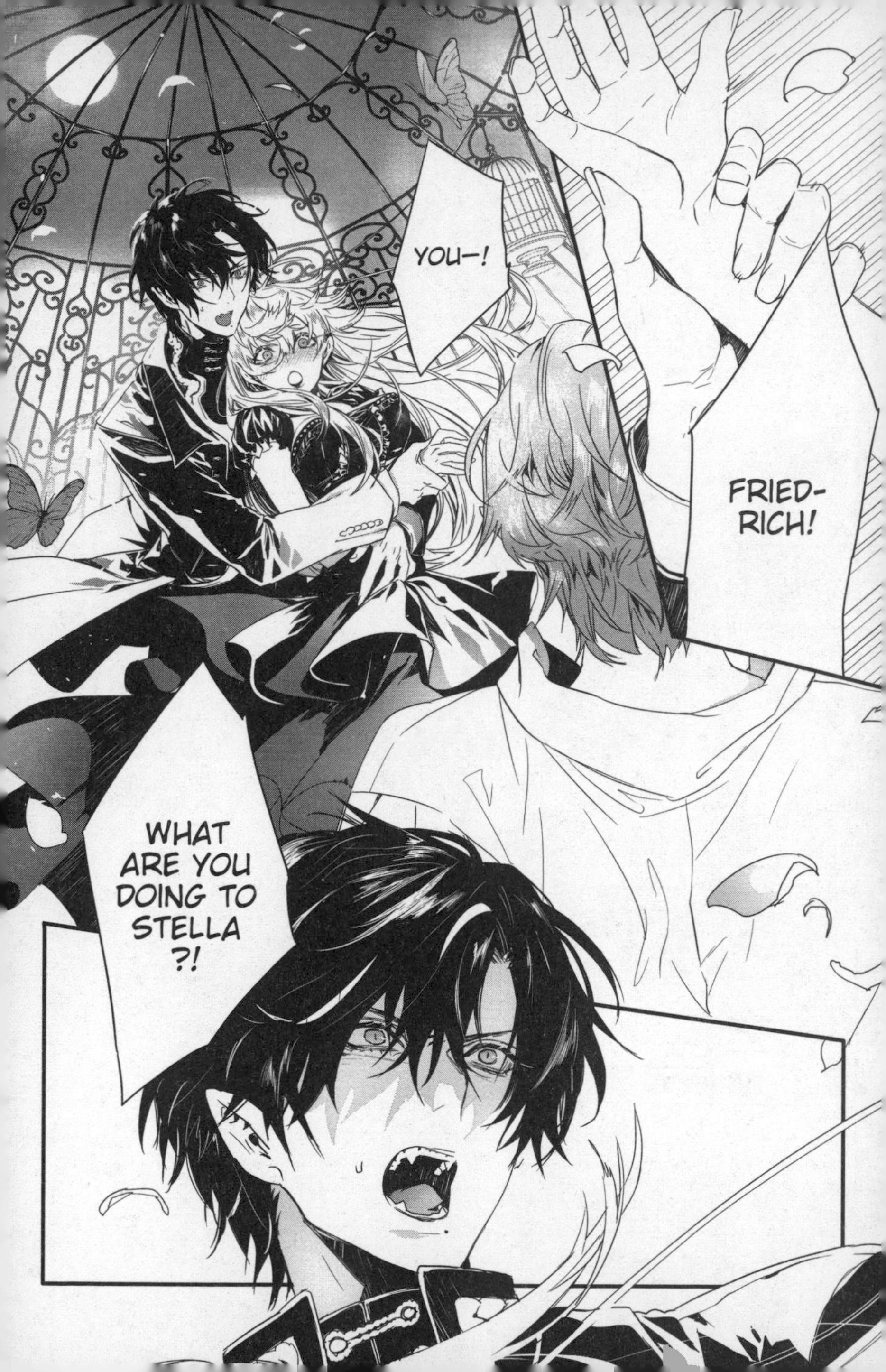
YOU—!
FRIED-RICH!
WHAT ARE YOU DOING TO STELLA ?!

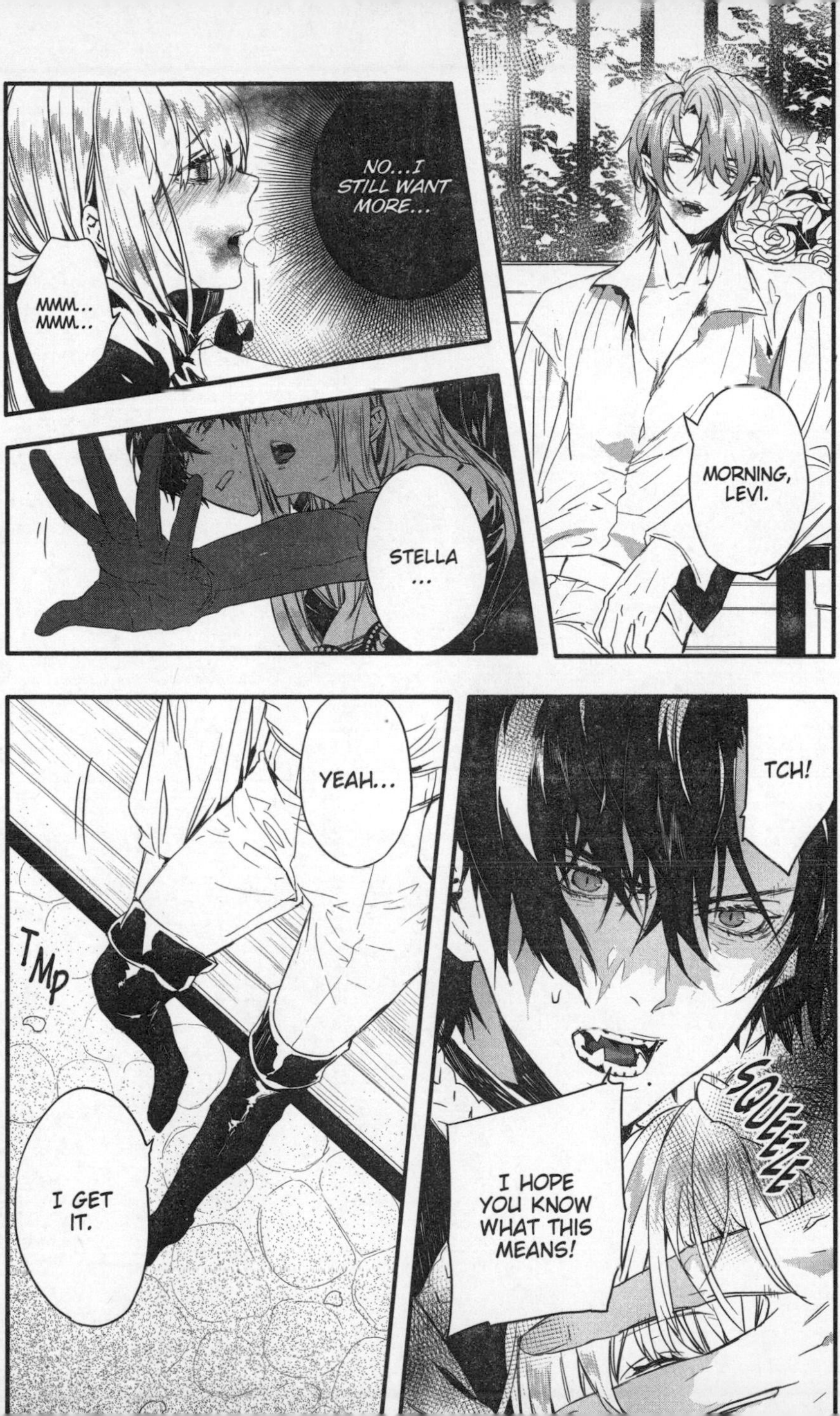
MORNING, LEVI.
NO...I STILL WANT MORE...
MMM... MMM...
STELLA ...
TCH!
SQUEEZE
I HOPE YOU KNOW WHAT THIS MEANS!
YEAH...
TMp
I GET IT.

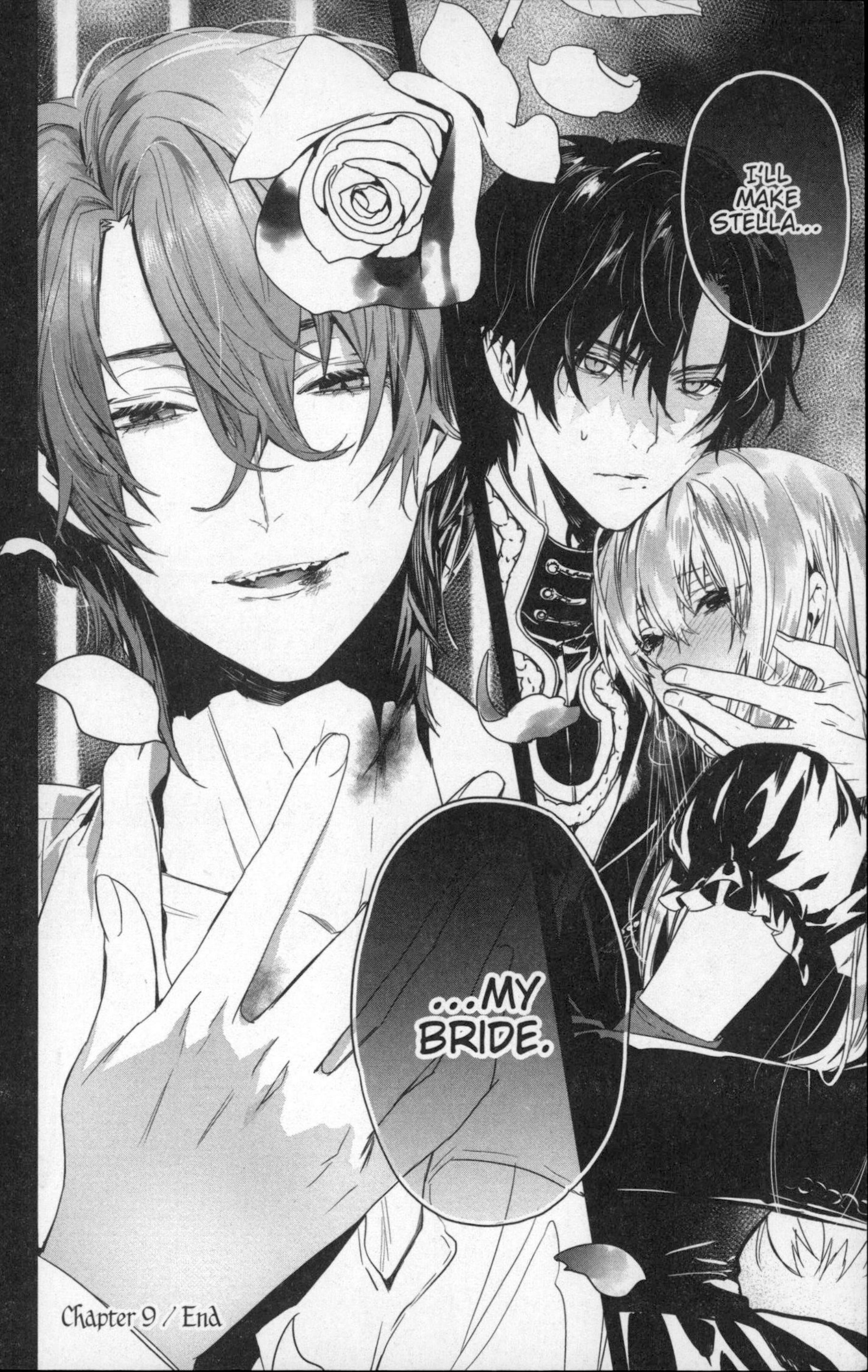
I'LL MAKE STELLA...
...MY BRIDE.

Chapter 9 / End

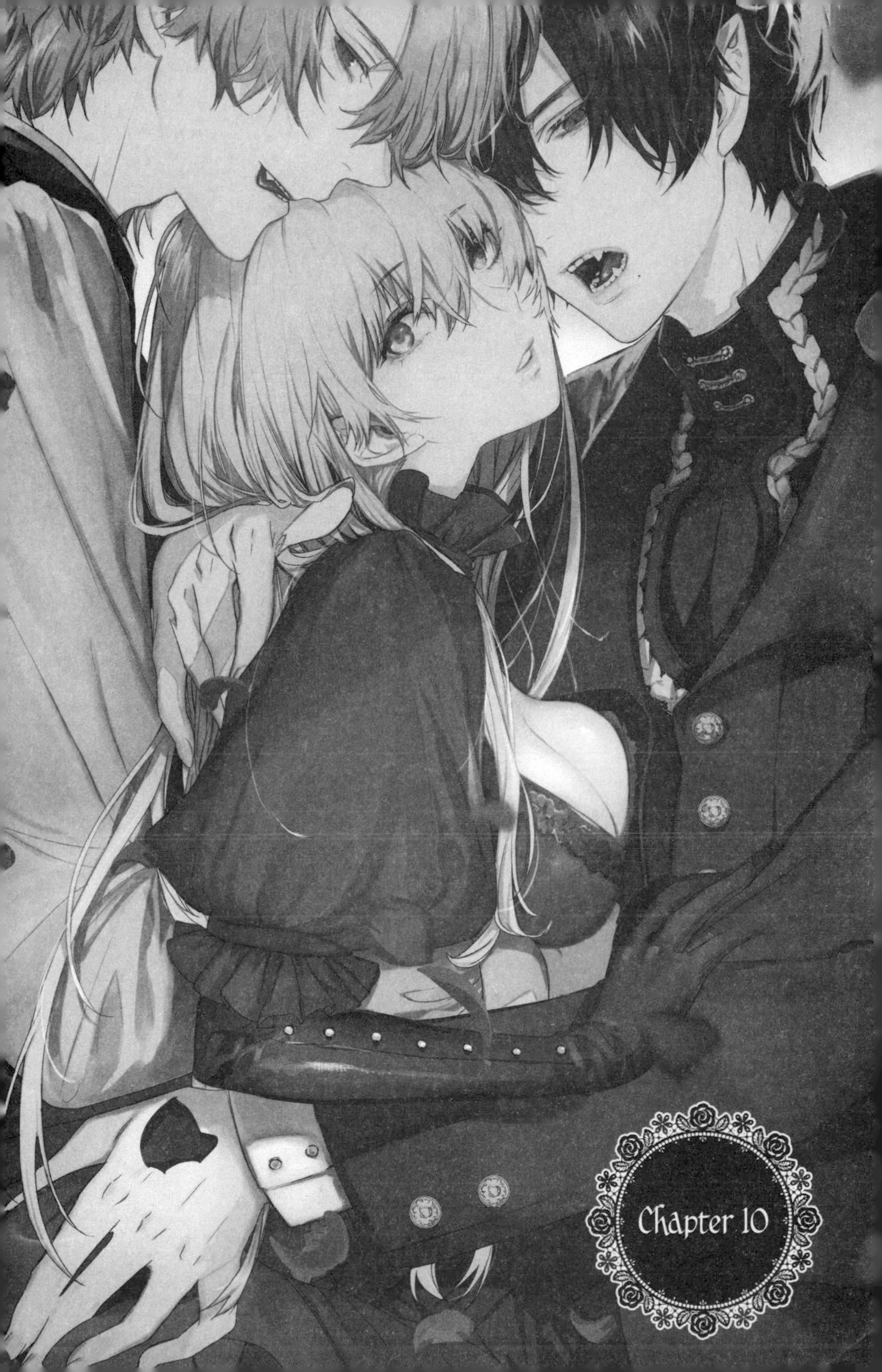
Chapter 10

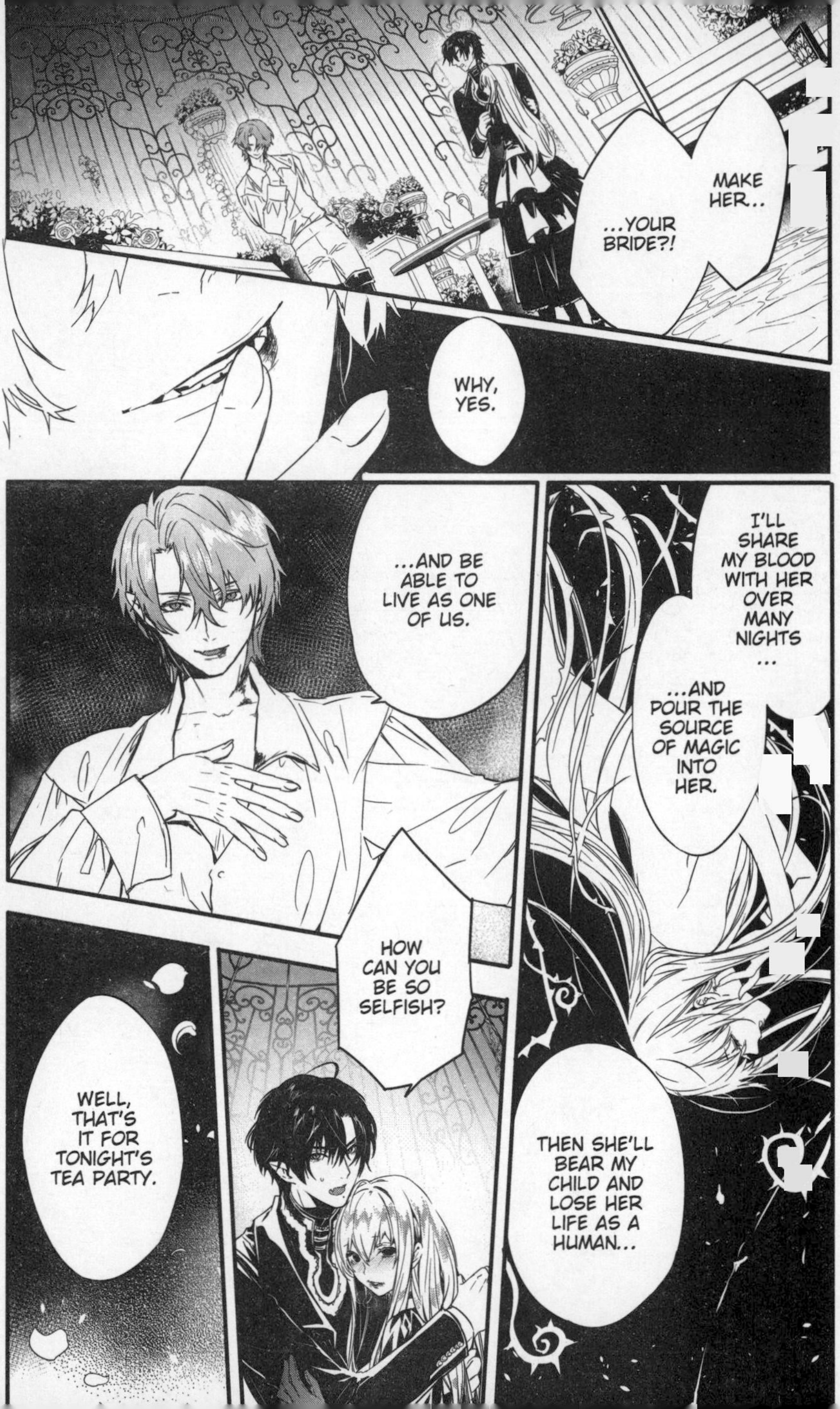
MAKE HER...
...YOUR BRIDE?!
WHY, YES.
I'LL SHARE MY BLOOD WITH HER OVER MANY NIGHTS...
...AND POUR THE SOURCE OF MAGIC INTO HER.
THEN SHE'LL BEAR MY CHILD AND LOSE HER LIFE AS A HUMAN...
...AND BE ABLE TO LIVE AS ONE OF US.
HOW CAN YOU BE SO SELFISH?
WELL, THAT'S IT FOR TONIGHT'S TEA PARTY.

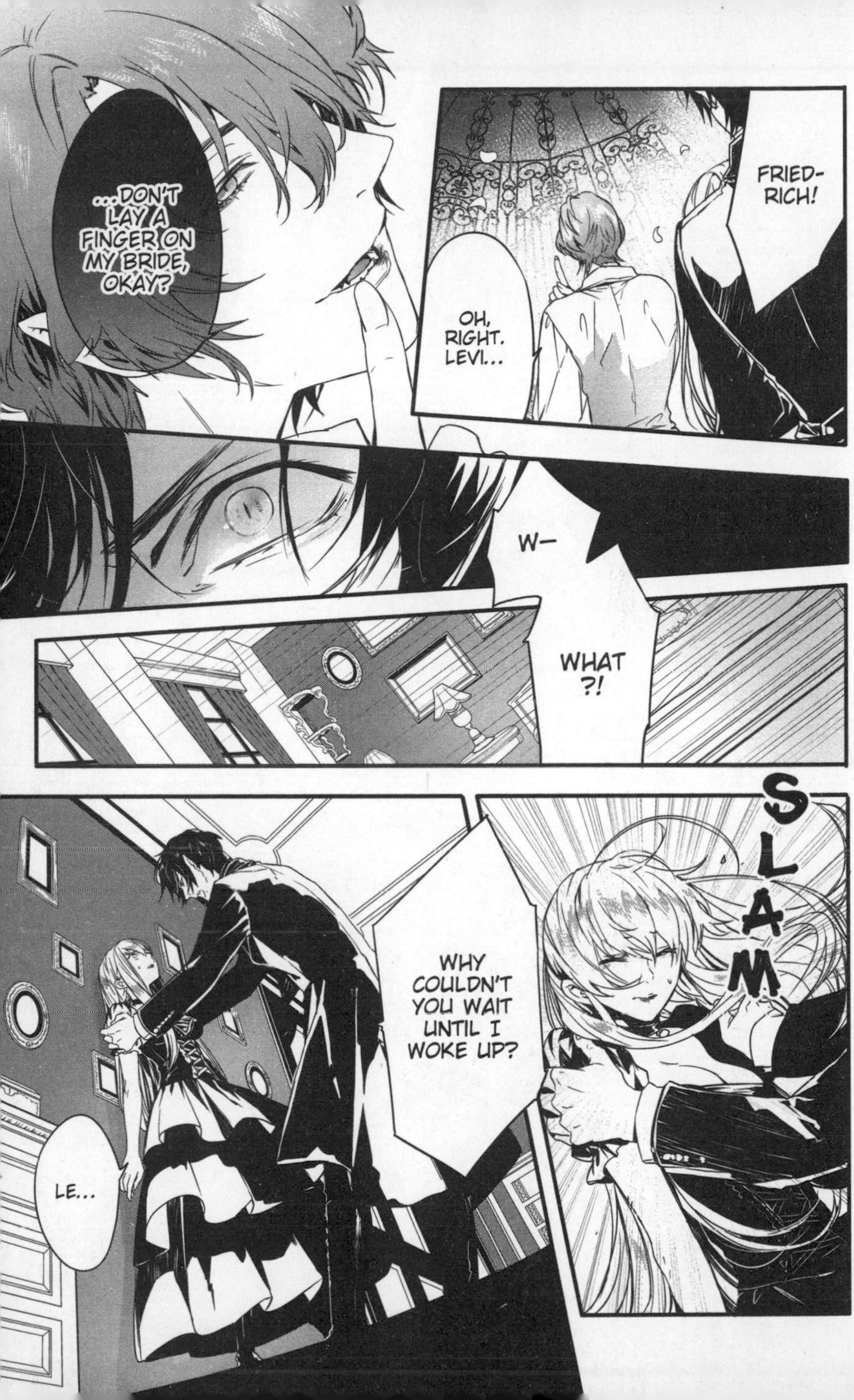
FRIED-RICH!
OH, RIGHT. LEVI...
...DON'T LAY A FINGER ON MY BRIDE, OKAY?
W—
WHAT ?!
SLAM
WHY COULDN'T YOU WAIT UNTIL I WOKE UP?
LE...

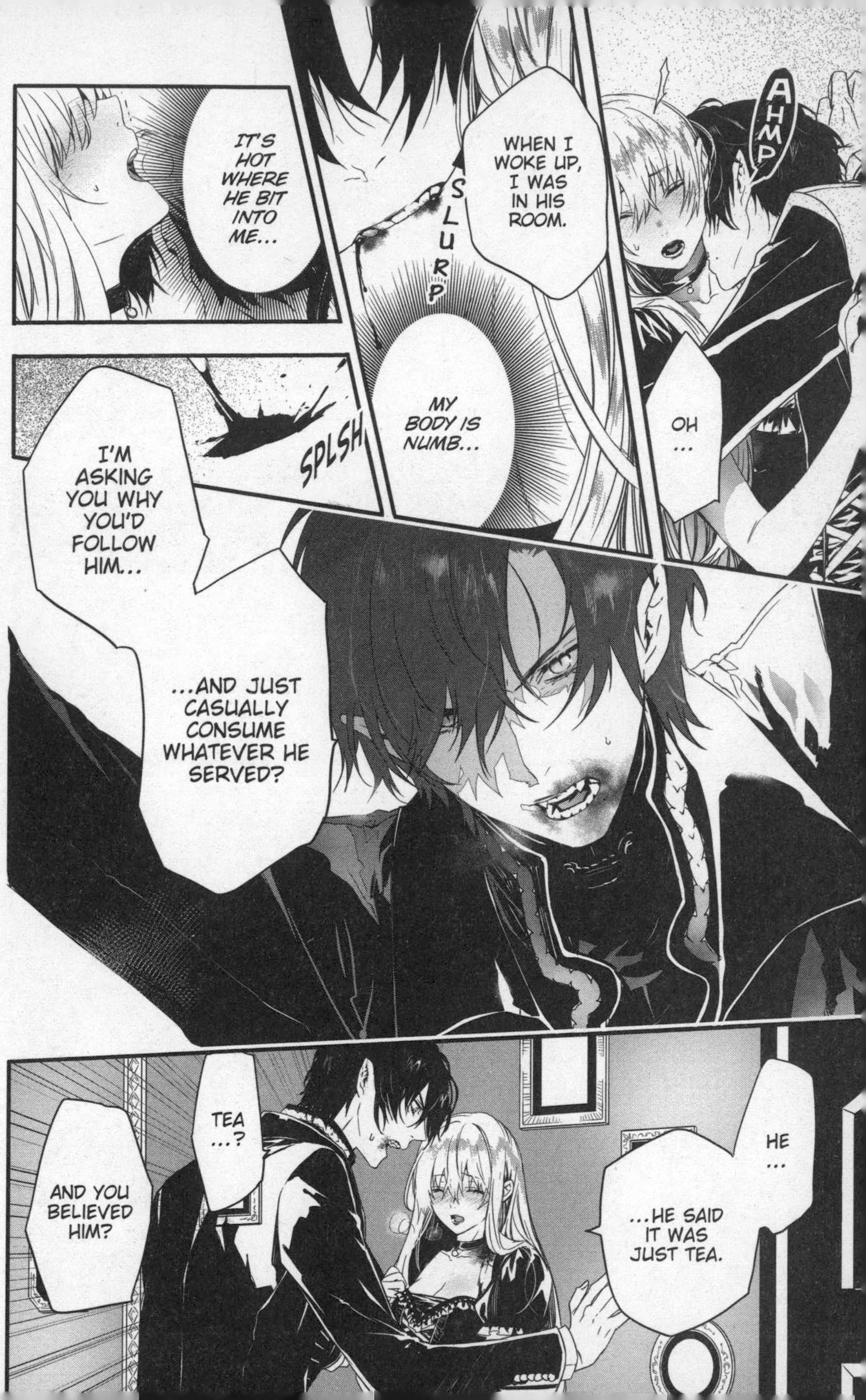
AHMP
OH ...
WHEN I WOKE UP, I WAS IN HIS ROOM.
SLURP
MY BODY IS NUMB...
IT'S HOT WHERE HE BIT INTO ME...
SPLSH
I'M ASKING YOU WHY YOU'D FOLLOW HIM...
...AND JUST CASUALLY CONSUME WHATEVER HE SERVED?
HE ...
...HE SAID IT WAS JUST TEA.
TEA ...?
AND YOU BELIEVED HIM?

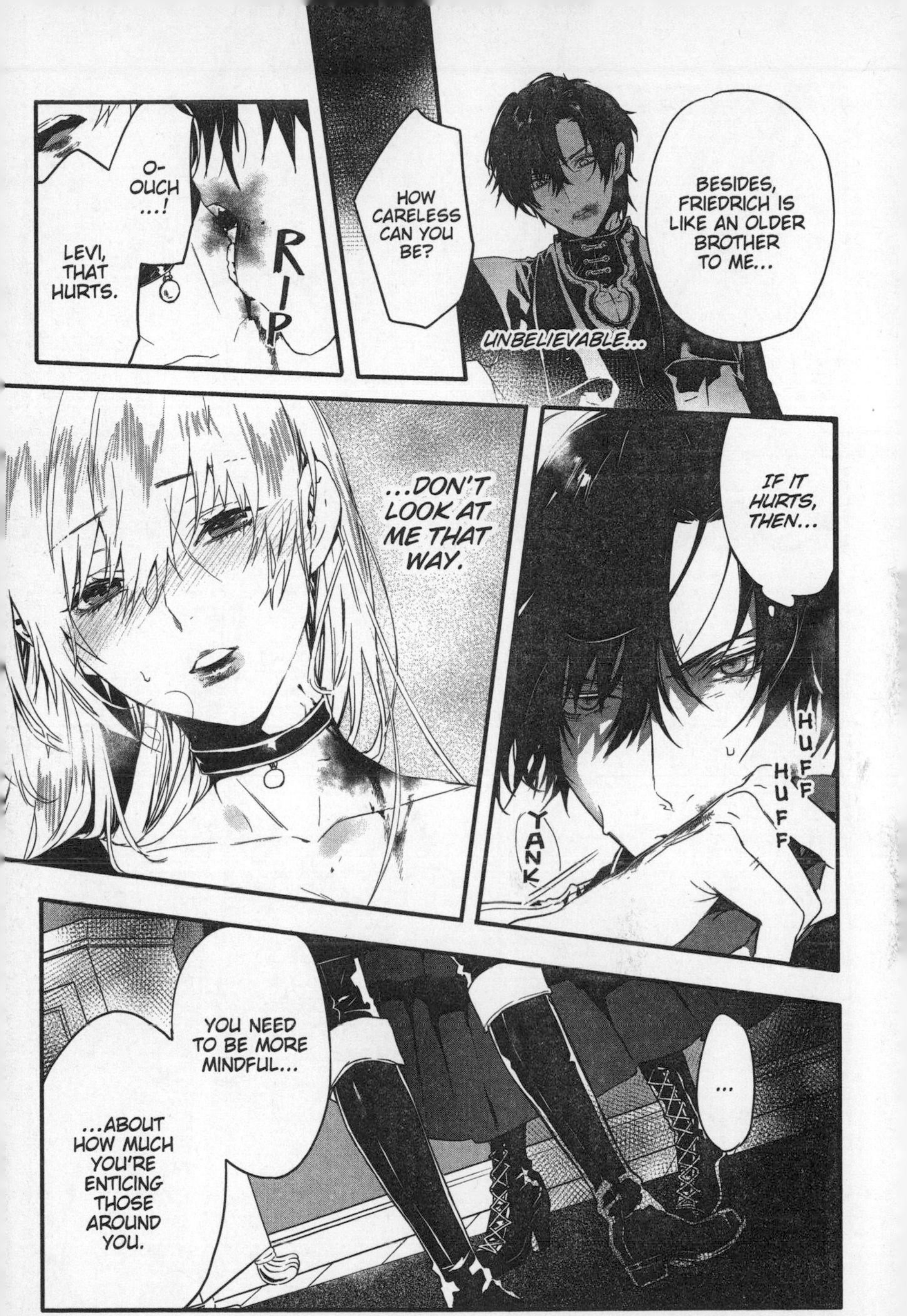
BESIDES, FRIEDRICH IS LIKE AN OLDER BROTHER TO ME...
HOW CARELESS CAN YOU BE?
UNBELIEVABLE...
O-OUCH ...!
RIP
LEVI, THAT HURTS.
IF IT HURTS, THEN...
HUFF HUFF
HUFF HUFF
YANK
...DON'T LOOK AT ME THAT WAY.
...
YOU NEED TO BE MORE MINDFUL...
...ABOUT HOW MUCH YOU'RE ENTICING THOSE AROUND YOU.

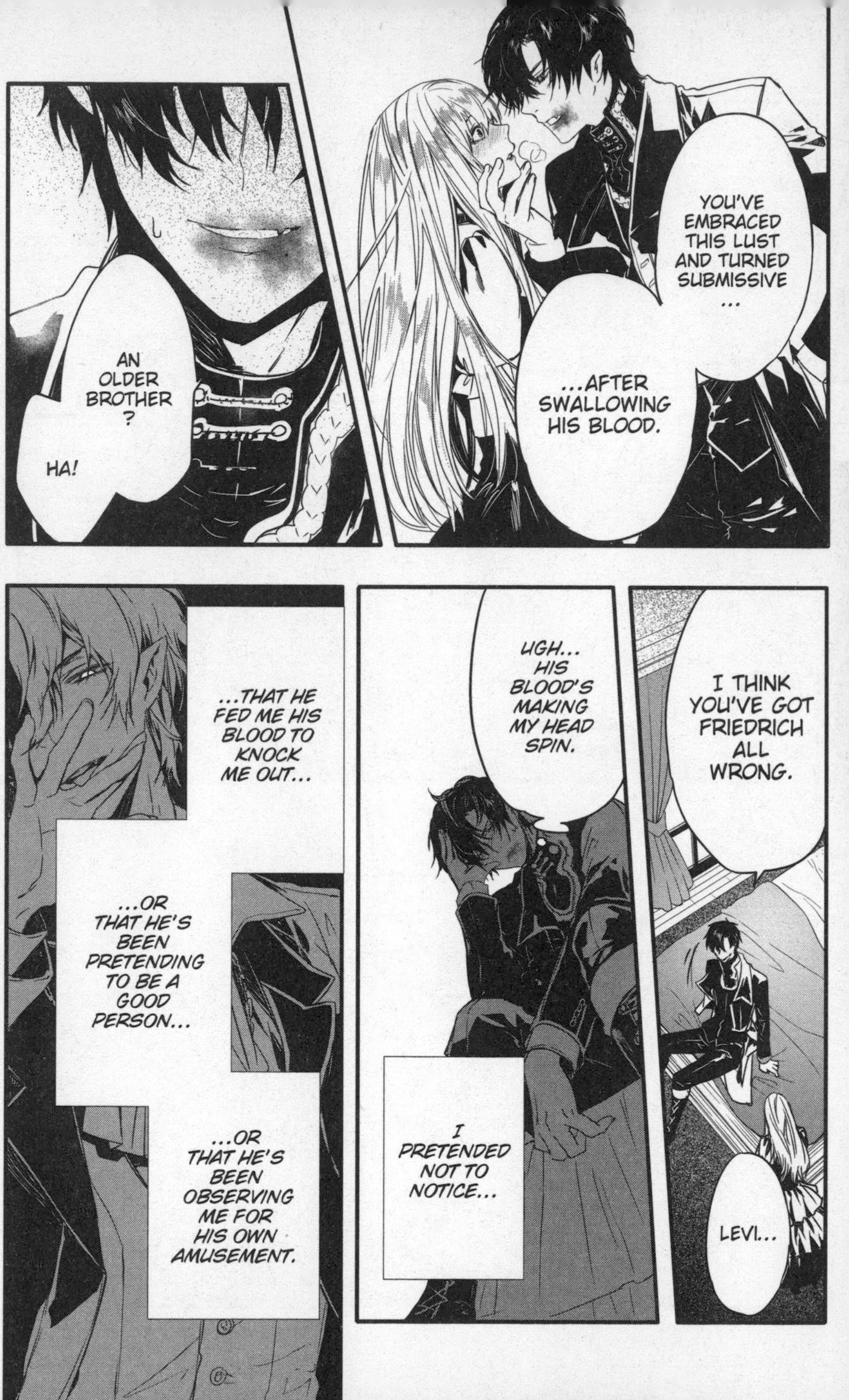
YOU'VE EMBRACED THIS LUST AND TURNED SUBMISSIVE ...
...AFTER SWALLOWING HIS BLOOD.
AN OLDER BROTHER?
HA!
I THINK YOU'VE GOT FRIEDRICH ALL WRONG.
LEVI...
UGH... HIS BLOOD'S MAKING MY HEAD SPIN.
I PRETENDED NOT TO NOTICE...
...THAT HE FED ME HIS BLOOD TO KNOCK ME OUT...
...OR THAT HE'S BEEN PRETENDING TO BE A GOOD PERSON...
...OR THAT HE'S BEEN OBSERVING ME FOR HIS OWN AMUSEMENT.

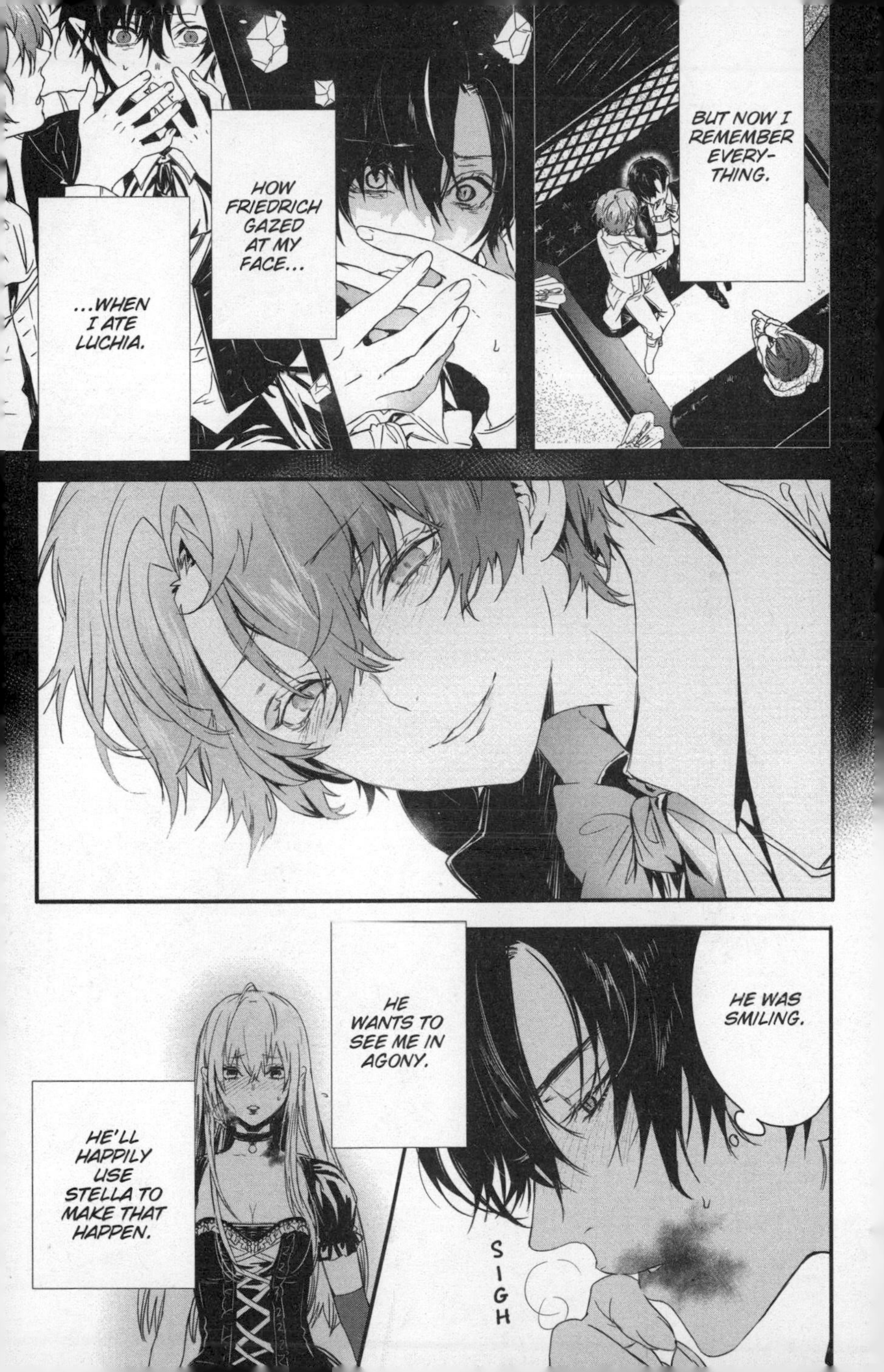
BUT NOW I REMEMBER EVERY-THING.
HOW FRIEDRICH GAZED AT MY FACE...
...WHEN I ATE LUCHIA.
HE WAS SMILING.
HE WANTS TO SEE ME IN AGONY.
HE'LL HAPPILY USE STELLA TO MAKE THAT HAPPEN.
SIGH

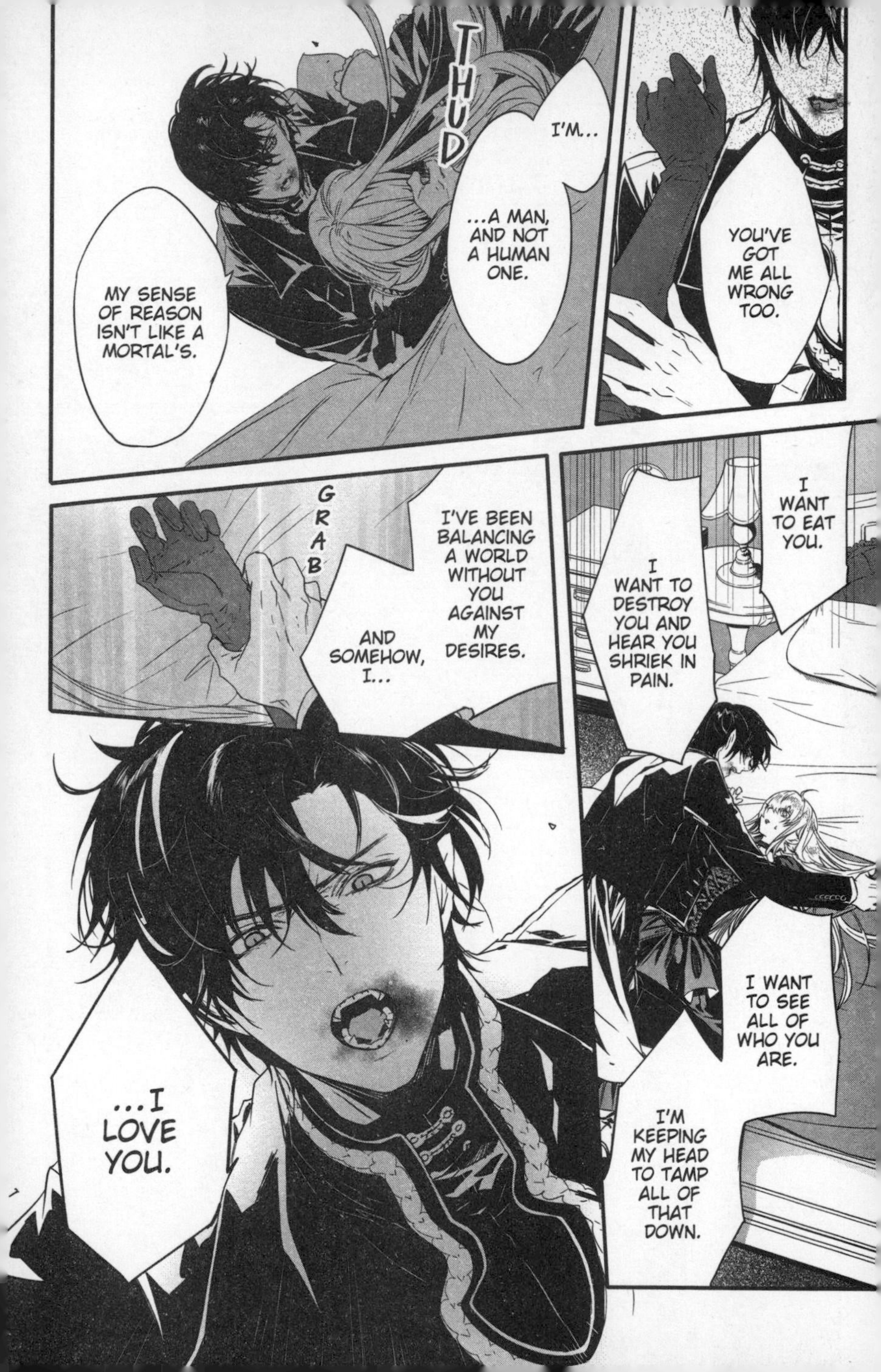
YOU'VE GOT ME ALL WRONG TOO.
THUD
I'M...
...A MAN, AND NOT A HUMAN ONE.
MY SENSE OF REASON ISN'T LIKE A MORTAL'S.
I WANT TO EAT YOU.
I WANT TO DESTROY YOU AND HEAR YOU SHRIEK IN PAIN.
I WANT TO SEE ALL OF WHO YOU ARE.
I'M KEEPING MY HEAD TO TAMP ALL OF THAT DOWN.
GRAB
I'VE BEEN BALANCING A WORLD WITHOUT YOU AGAINST MY DESIRES.
AND SOMEHOW, I...
...I LOVE YOU.

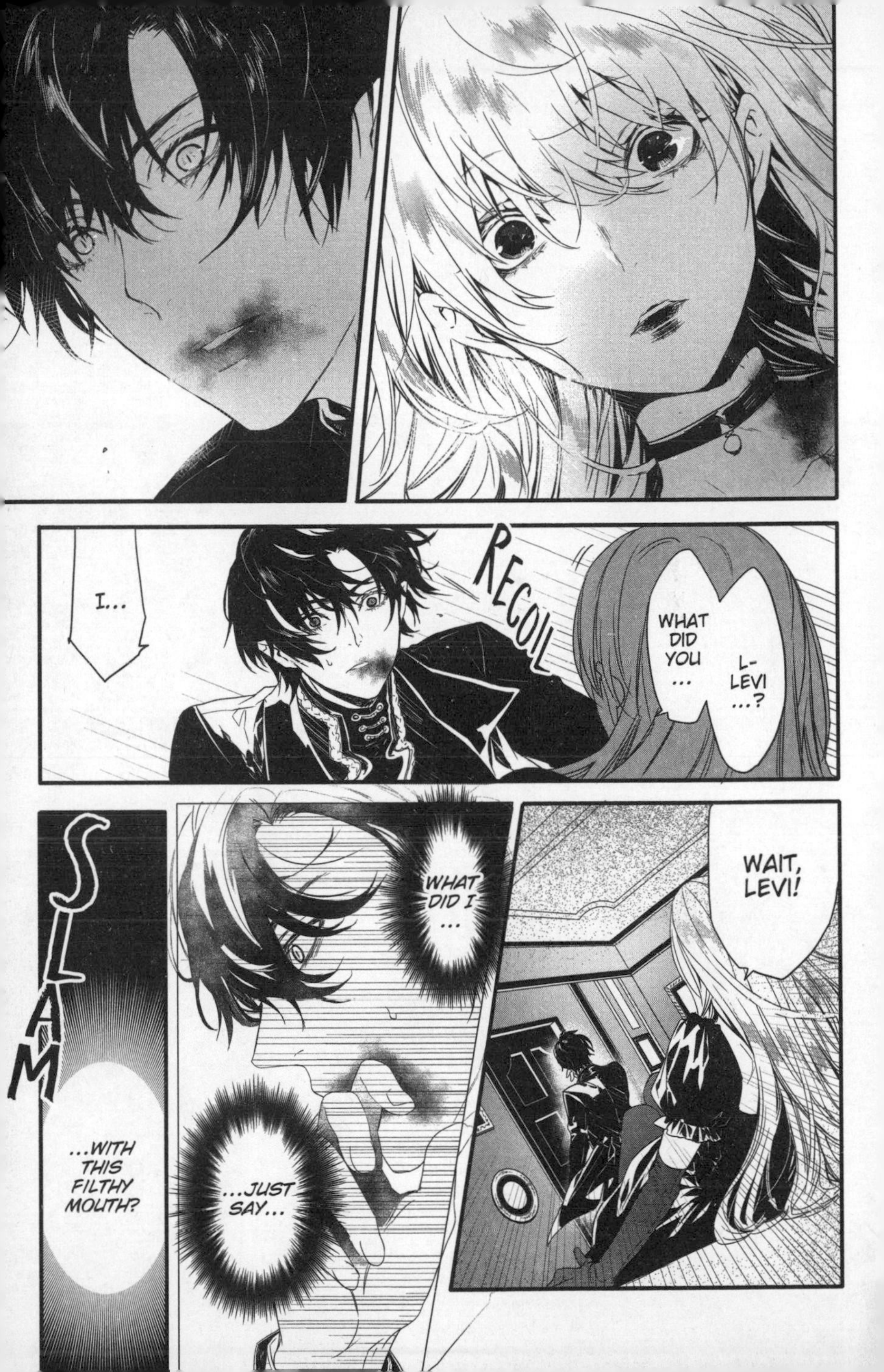
L-LEVI ...?
WHAT DID YOU ...
RECOIL
I...
WAIT, LEVI!
WHAT DID I ...
...JUST SAY...
...WITH THIS FILTHY MOUTH?
SLAM

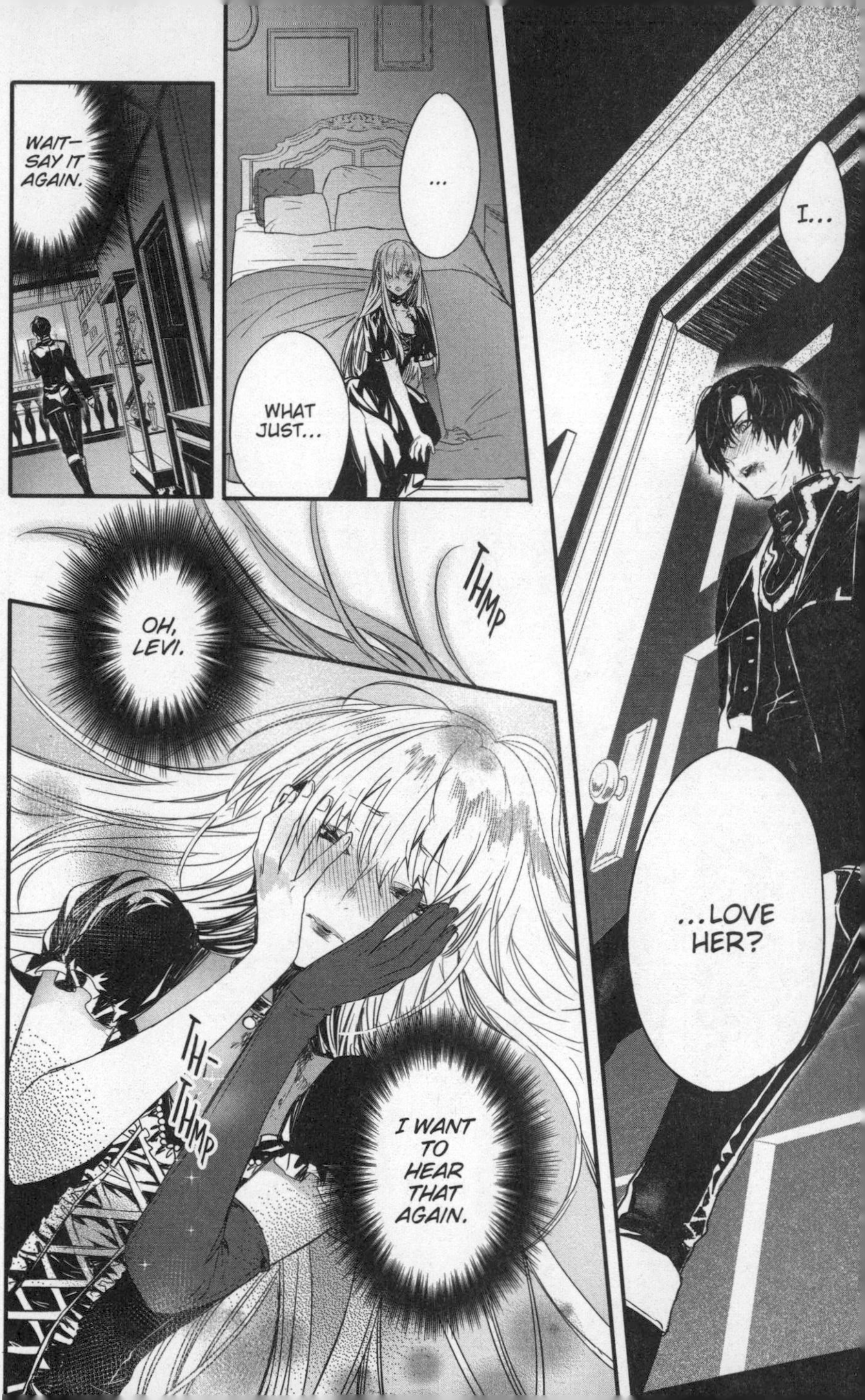
I...
...LOVE HER?
...
WHAT JUST...
WAIT—SAY IT AGAIN.
THMP
OH, LEVI.
I WANT TO HEAR THAT AGAIN.
TH-THMP

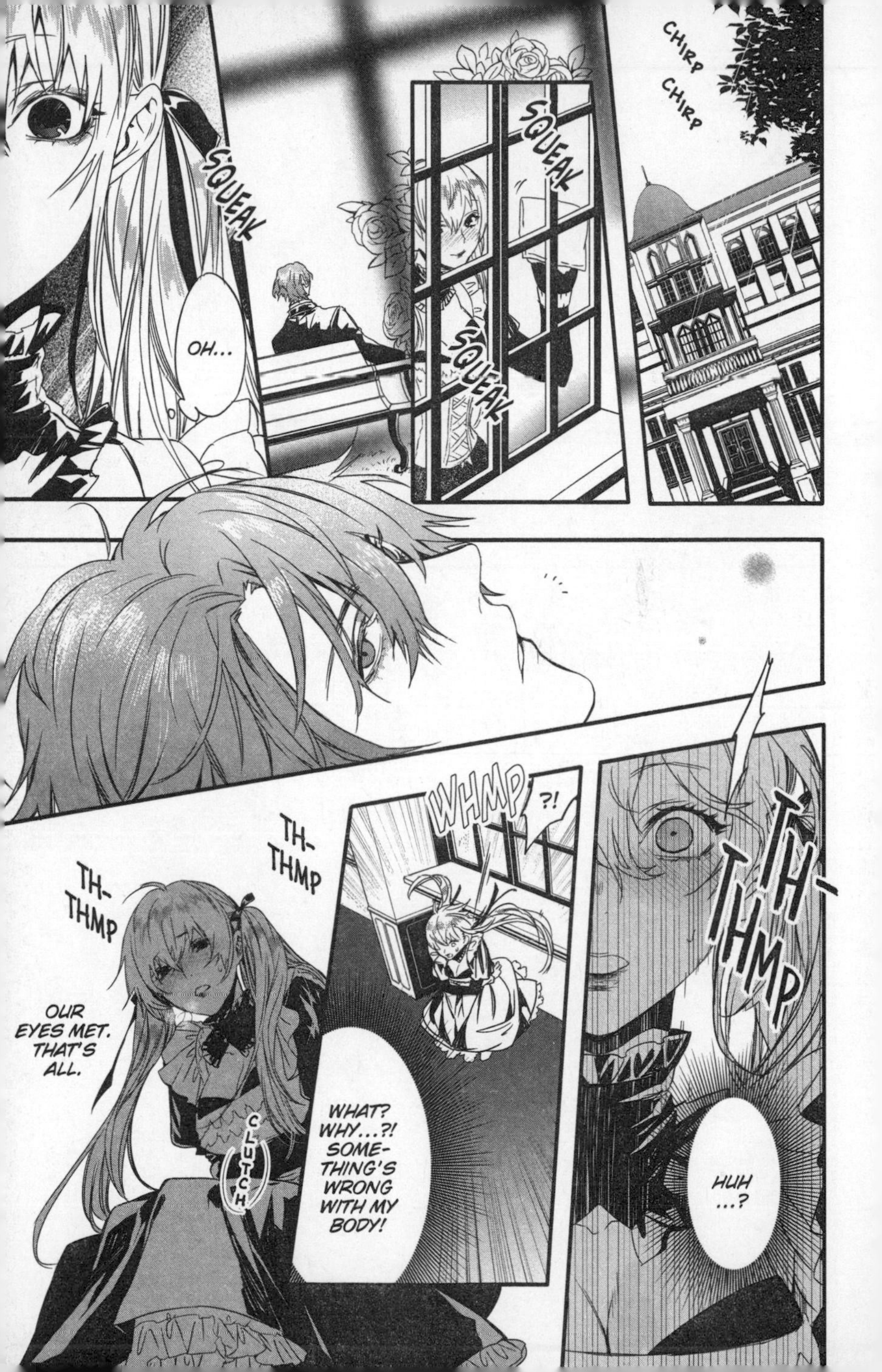
CHIRP
CHIRP
SQUEAK
SQUEAK
SQUEAK
OH...
TH-THMP
HUH ...?
WHMP
?!
WHAT? WHY...?! SOME-THING'S WRONG WITH MY BODY!
TH-THMP
TH-THMP
OUR EYES MET. THAT'S ALL.
CLUTCH

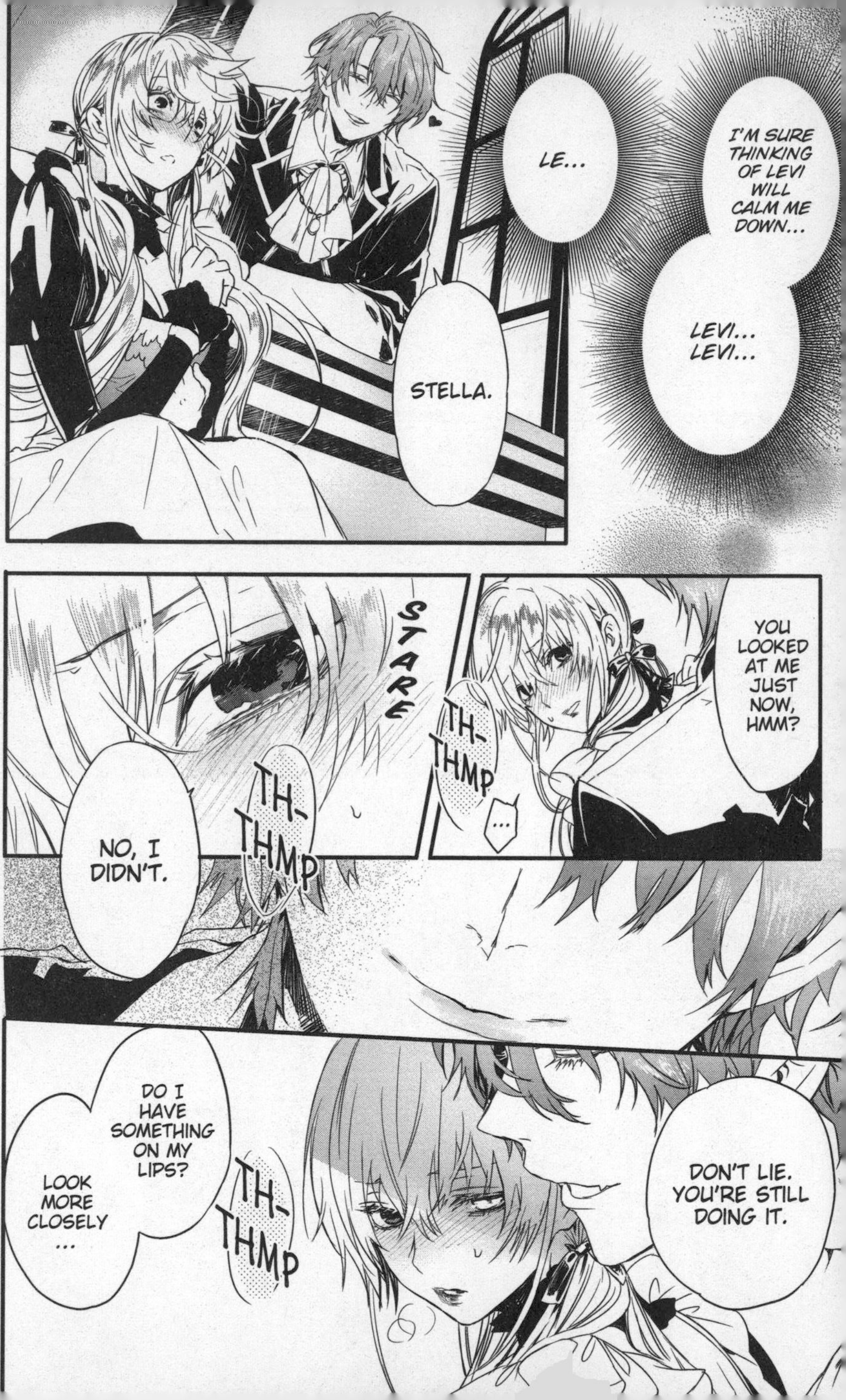
I'M SURE THINKING OF LEVI WILL CALM ME DOWN...
LEVI... LEVI...
LE...
STELLA.
YOU LOOKED AT ME JUST NOW, HMM?
TH-THMP
...
STARE
TH-THMP
NO, I DIDN'T.
DON'T LIE. YOU'RE STILL DOING IT.
TH-THMP
DO I HAVE SOMETHING ON MY LIPS?
LOOK MORE CLOSELY...

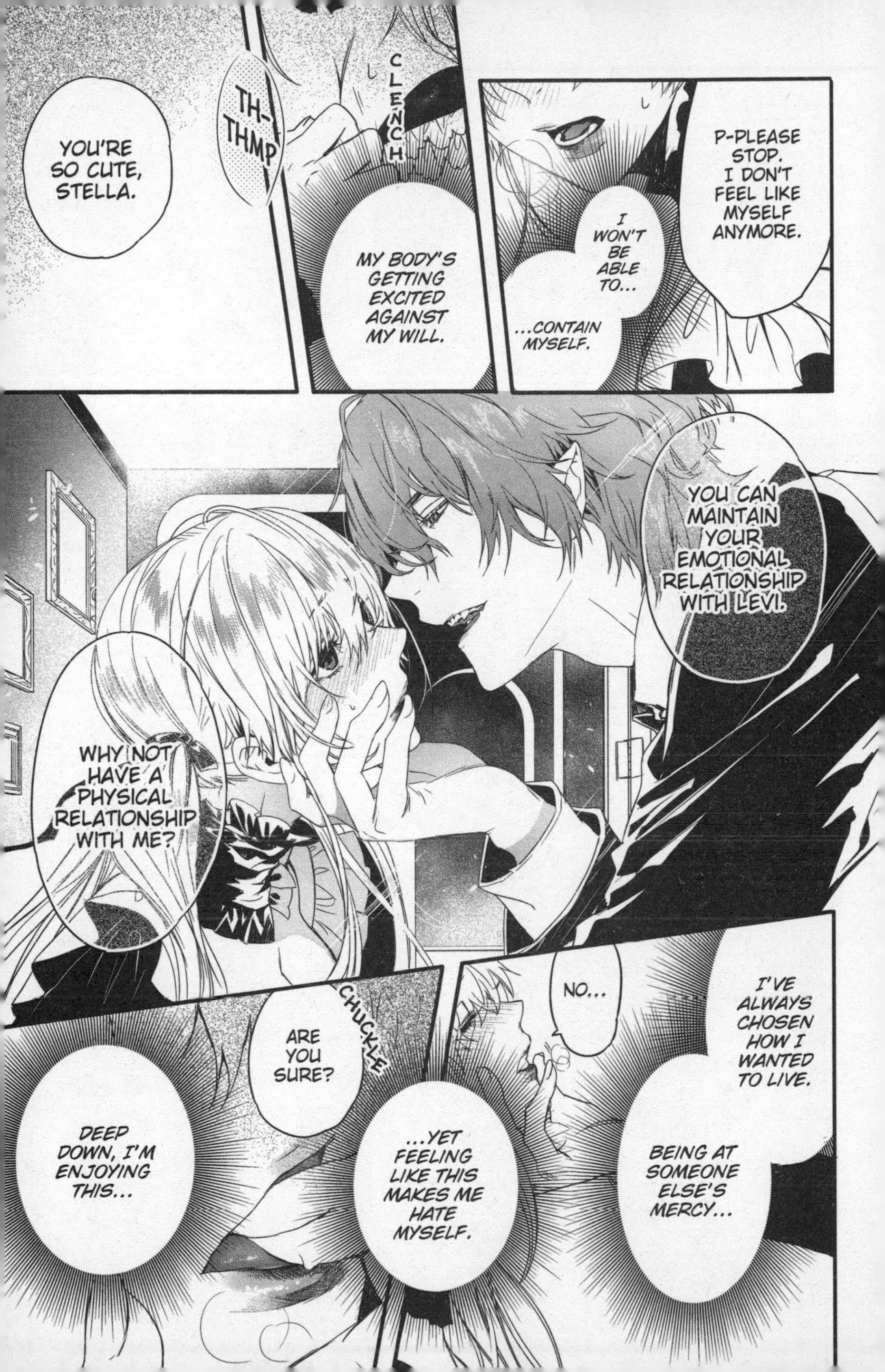
P-PLEASE STOP. I DON'T FEEL LIKE MYSELF ANYMORE.
I WON'T BE ABLE TO...
...CONTAIN MYSELF.
CLENCH
MY BODY'S GETTING EXCITED AGAINST MY WILL.
TH-THMP
YOU'RE SO CUTE, STELLA.
YOU CAN MAINTAIN YOUR EMOTIONAL RELATIONSHIP WITH LEVI.
WHY NOT HAVE A PHYSICAL RELATIONSHIP WITH ME?
I'VE ALWAYS CHOSEN HOW I WANTED TO LIVE.
NO...
BEING AT SOMEONE ELSE'S MERCY...
...YET FEELING LIKE THIS MAKES ME HATE MYSELF.
CHUCKLE
ARE YOU SURE?
DEEP DOWN, I'M ENJOYING THIS...

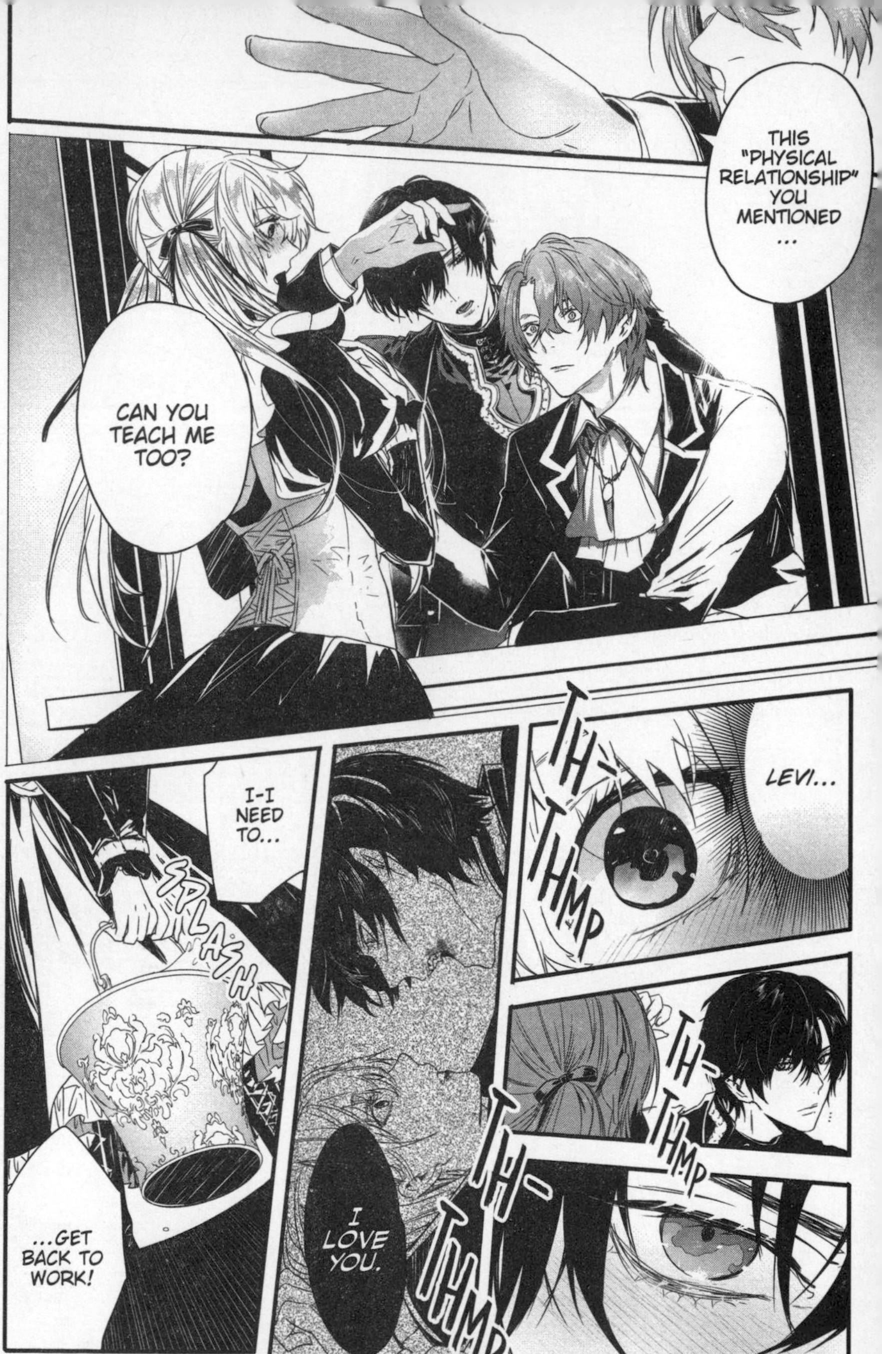
THIS "PHYSICAL RELATIONSHIP" YOU MENTIONED...
CAN YOU TEACH ME TOO?
LEVI...
TH-THMP
TH-THMP
TH-THMP
I LOVE YOU.
I-I NEED TO...
SPLASH
...GET BACK TO WORK!

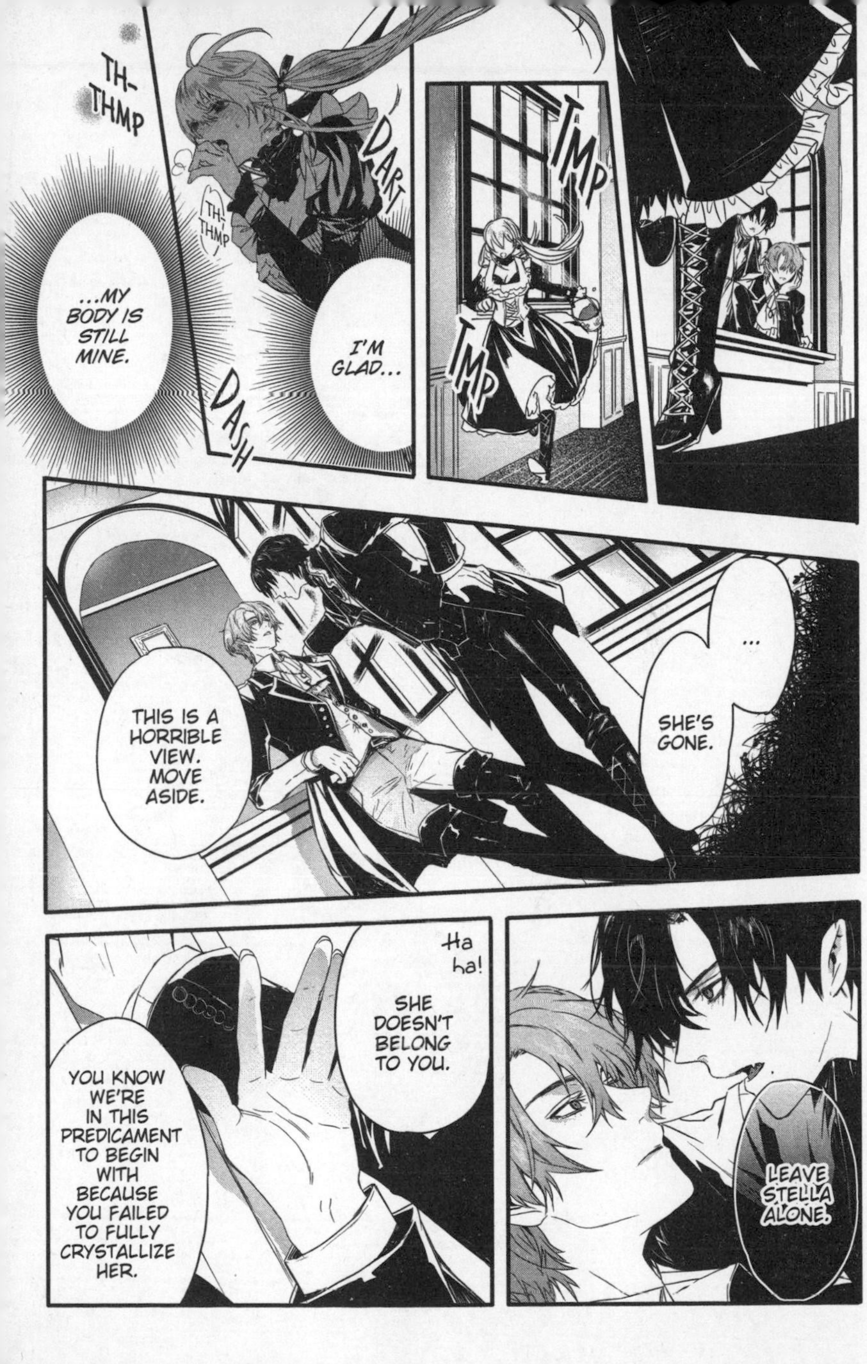
TMP
TMP
DART
TH-THMP
I'M GLAD...
TH-THMP
...MY BODY IS STILL MINE.
DASH
...
SHE'S GONE.
THIS IS A HORRIBLE VIEW. MOVE ASIDE.
LEAVE STELLA ALONE.
Ha ha!
SHE DOESN'T BELONG TO YOU.
YOU KNOW WE'RE IN THIS PREDICAMENT TO BEGIN WITH BECAUSE YOU FAILED TO FULLY CRYSTALLIZE HER.

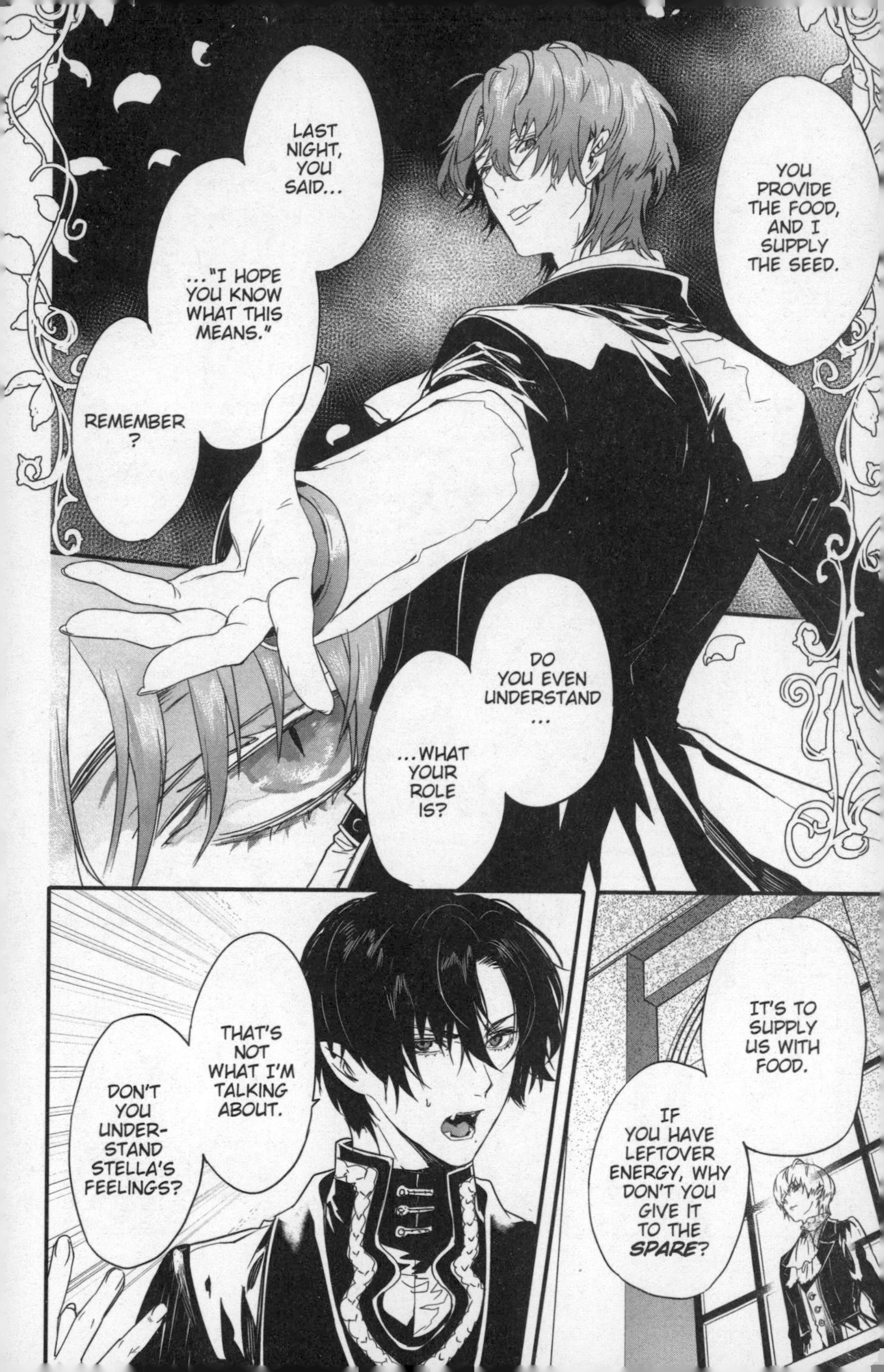
YOU PROVIDE THE FOOD, AND I SUPPLY THE SEED.
LAST NIGHT, YOU SAID...
..."I HOPE YOU KNOW WHAT THIS MEANS."
REMEMBER?
DO YOU EVEN UNDERSTAND...
...WHAT YOUR ROLE IS?
IT'S TO SUPPLY US WITH FOOD.
IF YOU HAVE LEFTOVER ENERGY, WHY DON'T YOU GIVE IT TO THE *SPARE*?
THAT'S NOT WHAT I'M TALKING ABOUT.
DON'T YOU UNDER-STAND STELLA'S FEELINGS?

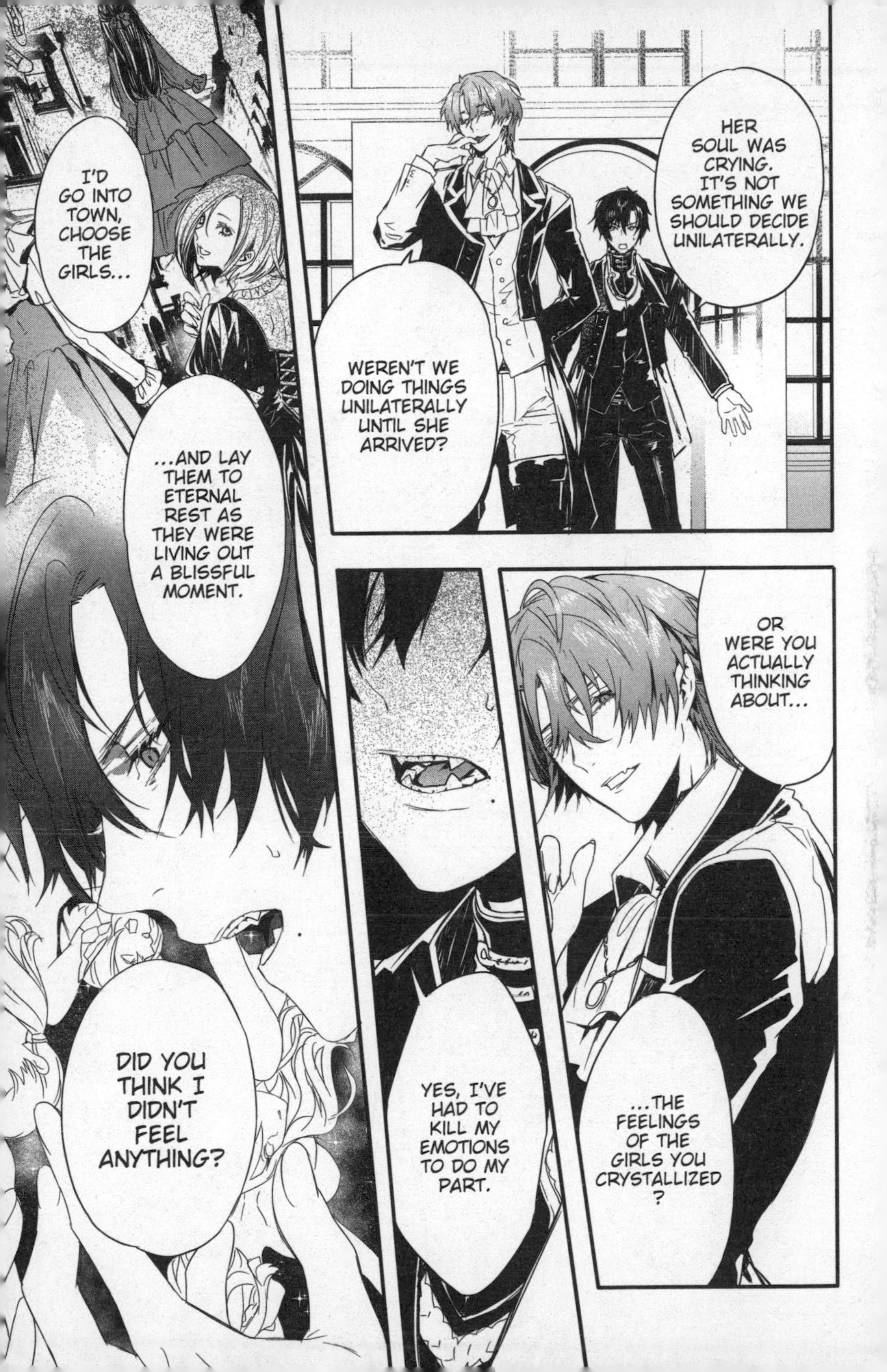
HER SOUL WAS CRYING. IT'S NOT SOMETHING WE SHOULD DECIDE UNILATERALLY.
WEREN'T WE DOING THINGS UNILATERALLY UNTIL SHE ARRIVED?
OR WERE YOU ACTUALLY THINKING ABOUT...
...THE FEELINGS OF THE GIRLS YOU CRYSTALLIZED?
YES, I'VE HAD TO KILL MY EMOTIONS TO DO MY PART.
I'D GO INTO TOWN, CHOOSE THE GIRLS...
...AND LAY THEM TO ETERNAL REST AS THEY WERE LIVING OUT A BLISSFUL MOMENT.
DID YOU THINK I DIDN'T FEEL ANYTHING?

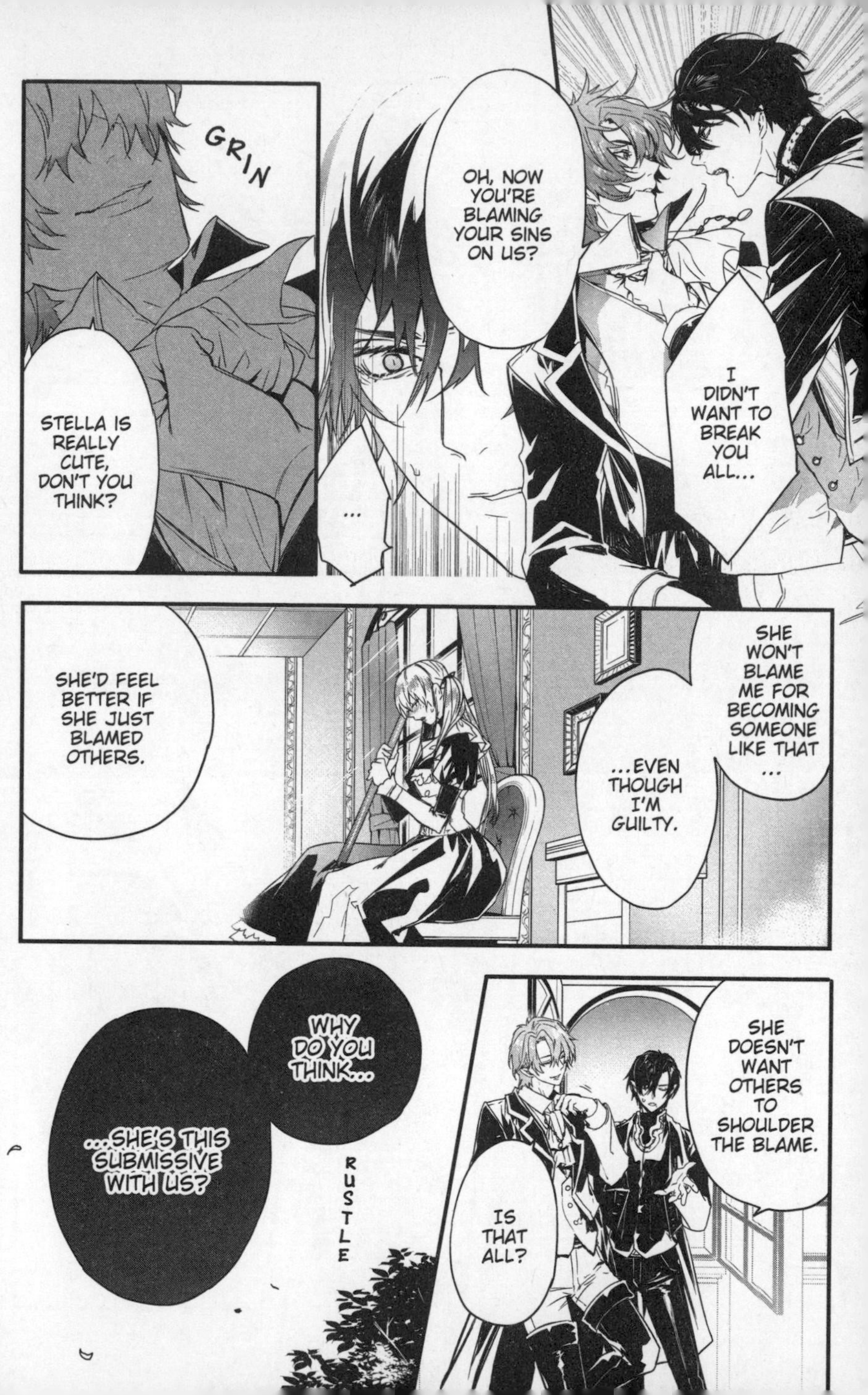
I DIDN'T WANT TO BREAK YOU ALL...
OH, NOW YOU'RE BLAMING YOUR SINS ON US?
...
GRIN
STELLA IS REALLY CUTE, DON'T YOU THINK?
SHE WON'T BLAME ME FOR BECOMING SOMEONE LIKE THAT...
...EVEN THOUGH I'M GUILTY.
SHE'D FEEL BETTER IF SHE JUST BLAMED OTHERS.
SHE DOESN'T WANT OTHERS TO SHOULDER THE BLAME.
IS THAT ALL?
RUSTLE
WHY DO YOU THINK...
...SHE'S THIS SUBMISSIVE WITH US?

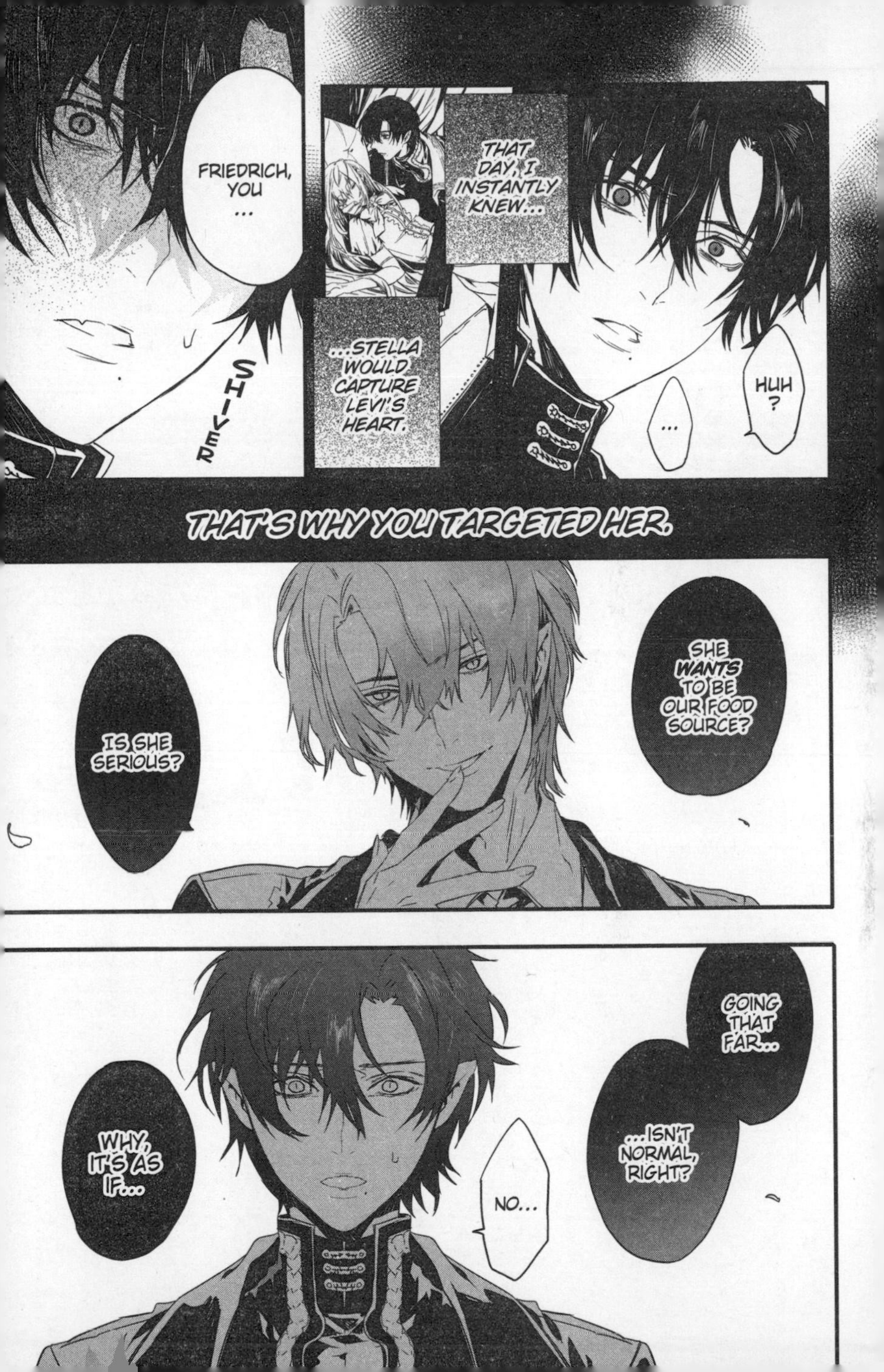
HUH?
...
THAT DAY, I INSTANTLY KNEW...
...STELLA WOULD CAPTURE LEVI'S HEART.
FRIEDRICH, YOU ...
SHIVER
THAT'S WHY YOU TARGETED HER.
SHE WANTS TO BE OUR FOOD SOURCE?
IS SHE SERIOUS?
GOING THAT FAR...
...ISN'T NORMAL, RIGHT?
NO...
WHY, IT'S AS IF...

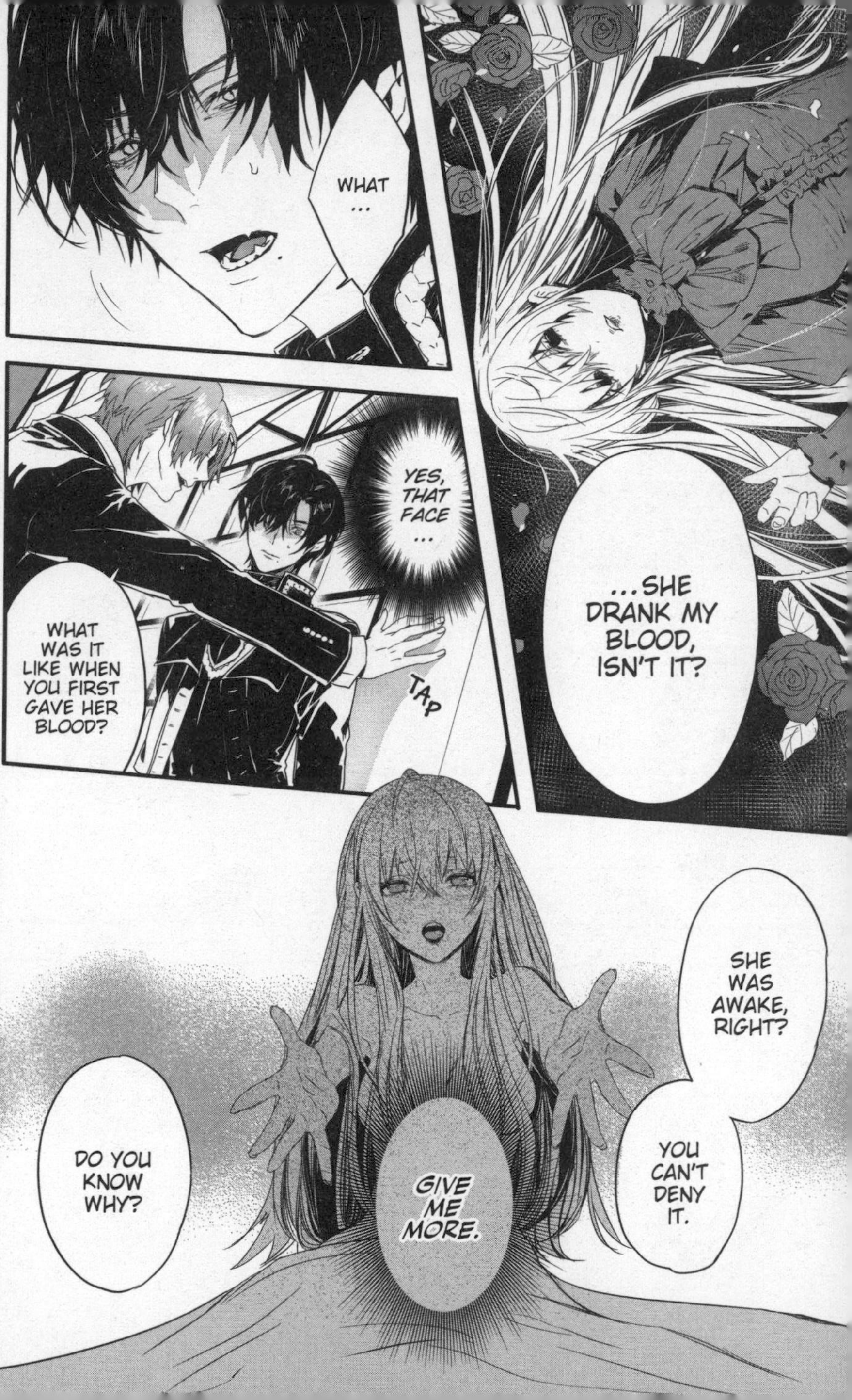
...SHE DRANK MY BLOOD, ISN'T IT?
WHAT ...
YES, THAT FACE ...
WHAT WAS IT LIKE WHEN YOU FIRST GAVE HER BLOOD?
TAP
SHE WAS AWAKE, RIGHT?
YOU CAN'T DENY IT.
GIVE ME MORE.
DO YOU KNOW WHY?

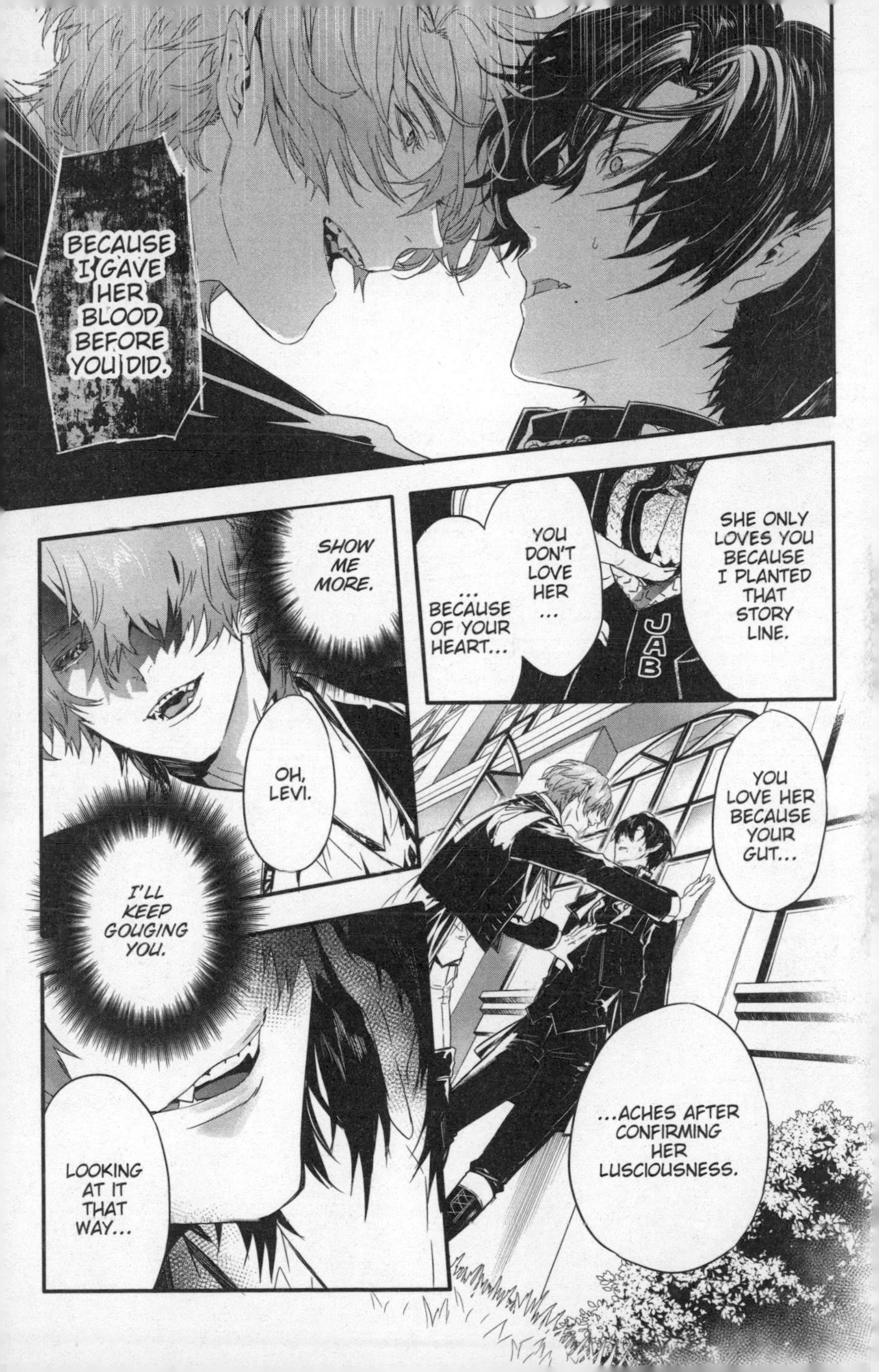
BECAUSE I GAVE HER BLOOD BEFORE YOU DID.
SHE ONLY LOVES YOU BECAUSE I PLANTED THAT STORY LINE.
YOU DON'T LOVE HER...
...BECAUSE OF YOUR HEART...
JAB
SHOW ME MORE.
OH, LEVI.
YOU LOVE HER BECAUSE YOUR GUT...
...ACHES AFTER CONFIRMING HER LUSCIOUSNESS.
I'LL KEEP GOUGING YOU.
LOOKING AT IT THAT WAY...

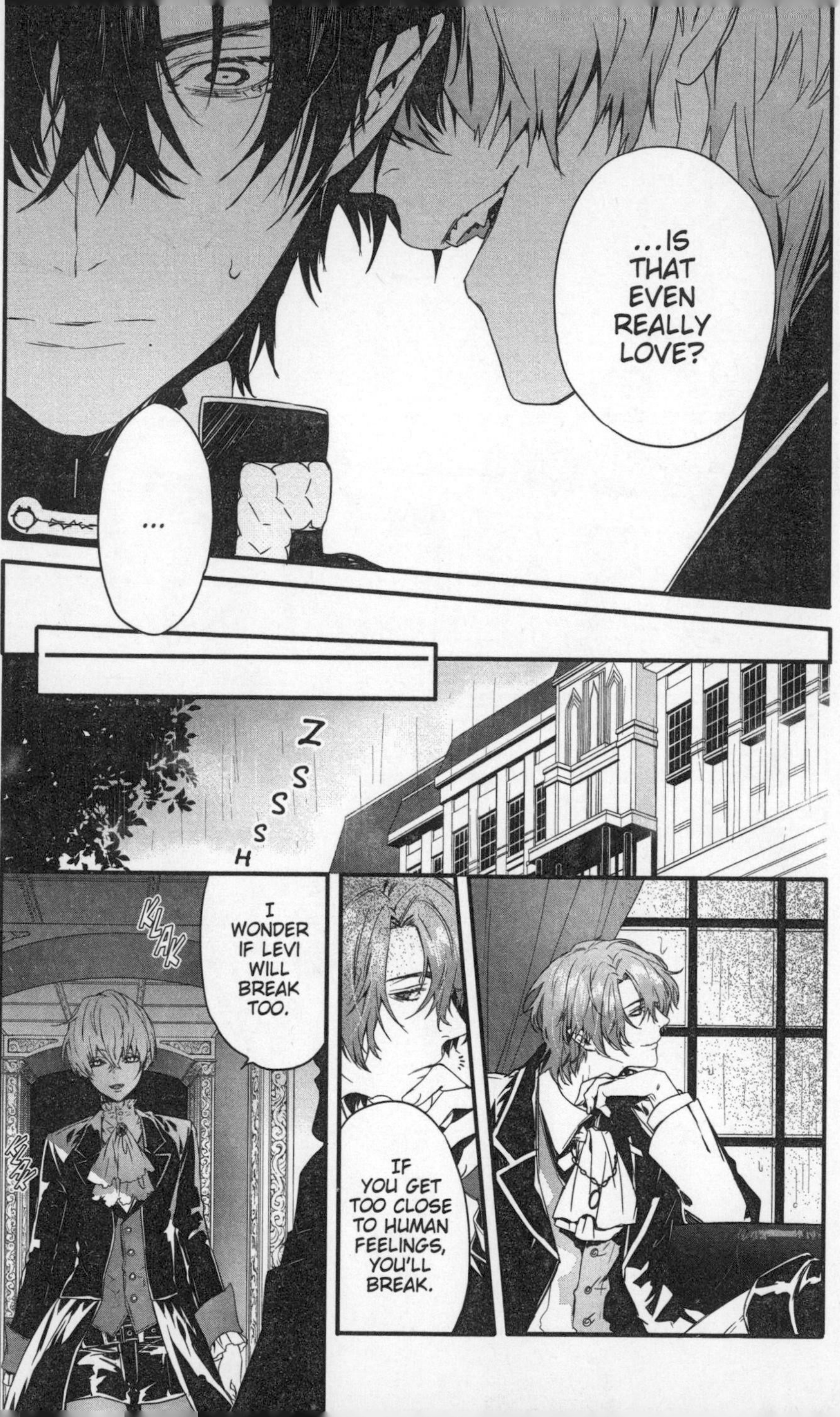
...IS THAT EVEN REALLY LOVE?
...
ZSSSH
IF YOU GET TOO CLOSE TO HUMAN FEELINGS, YOU'LL BREAK.
I WONDER IF LEVI WILL BREAK TOO.
KLAK
KLAK

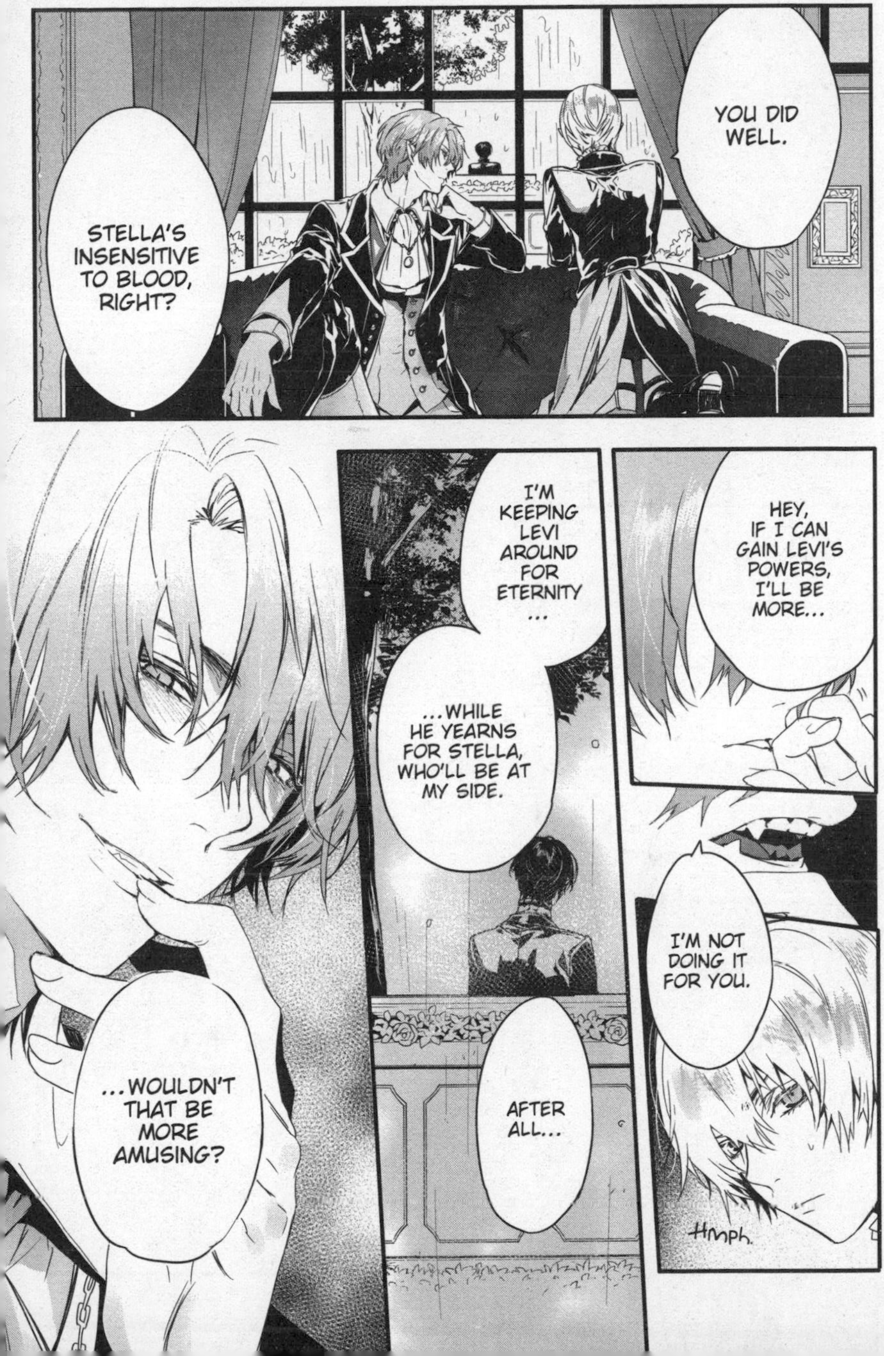
YOU DID WELL.
STELLA'S INSENSITIVE TO BLOOD, RIGHT?
HEY, IF I CAN GAIN LEVI'S POWERS, I'LL BE MORE...
I'M NOT DOING IT FOR YOU.
Hmph.
I'M KEEPING LEVI AROUND FOR ETERNITY...
...WHILE HE YEARNS FOR STELLA, WHO'LL BE AT MY SIDE.
AFTER ALL...
...WOULDN'T THAT BE MORE AMUSING?

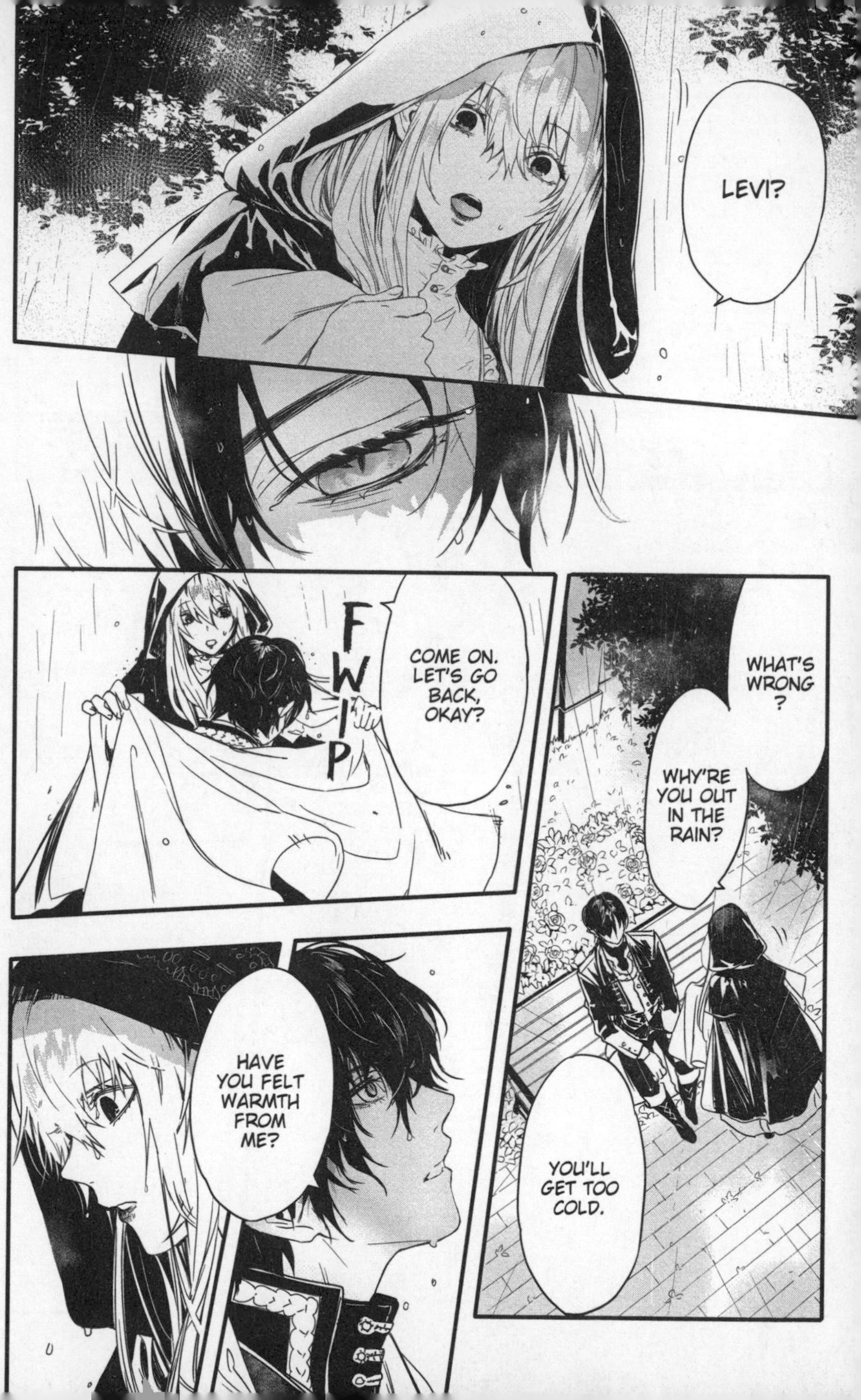
LEVI?
WHAT'S WRONG?
WHY'RE YOU OUT IN THE RAIN?
YOU'LL GET TOO COLD.
FWIP
COME ON. LET'S GO BACK, OKAY?
HAVE YOU FELT WARMTH FROM ME?

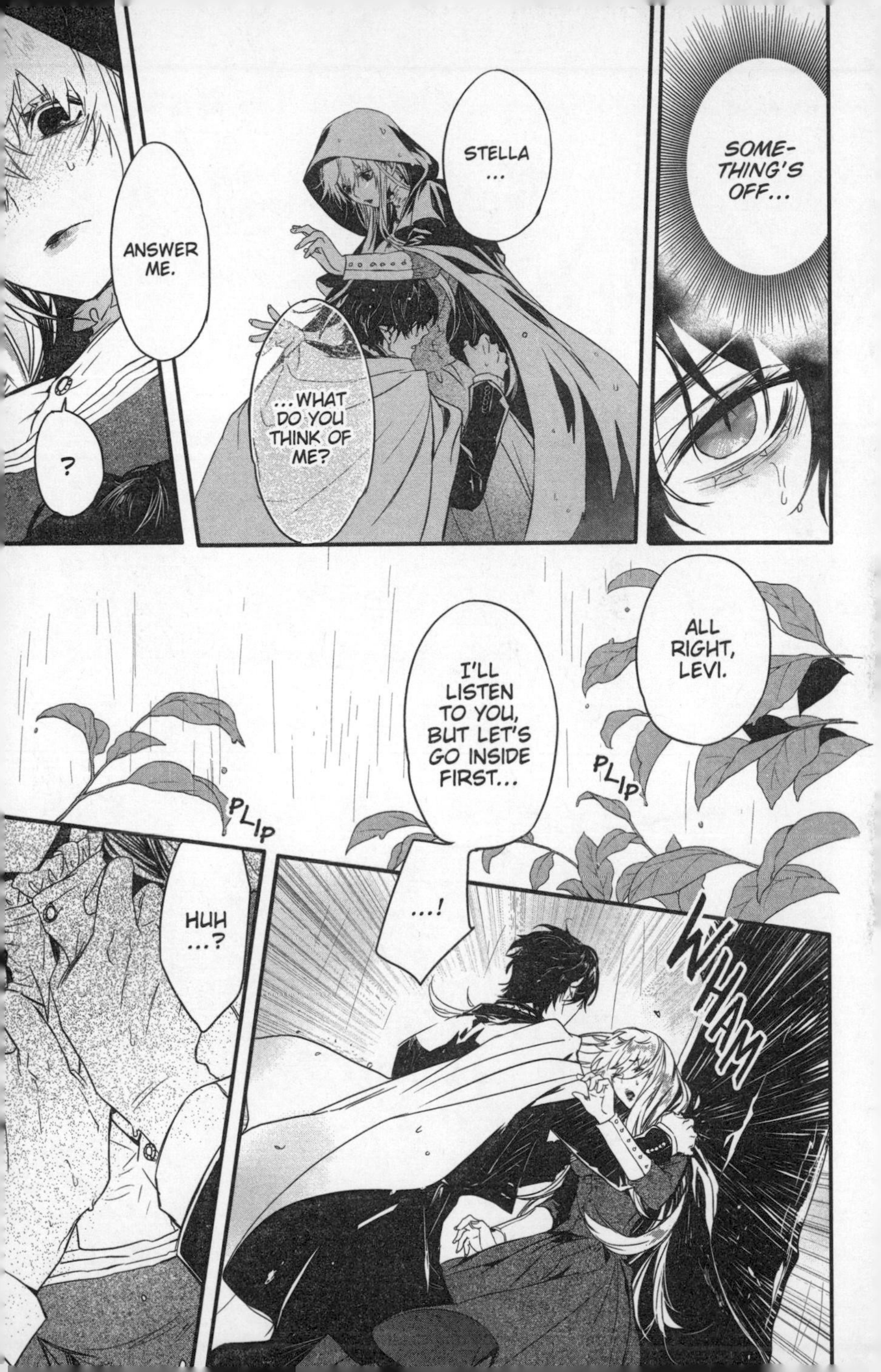
SOME-THING'S OFF...
STELLA ...
...WHAT DO YOU THINK OF ME?
ANSWER ME.
?
ALL RIGHT, LEVI.
I'LL LISTEN TO YOU, BUT LET'S GO INSIDE FIRST...
PLIP
PLIP
WHAM
...!
HUH ...?

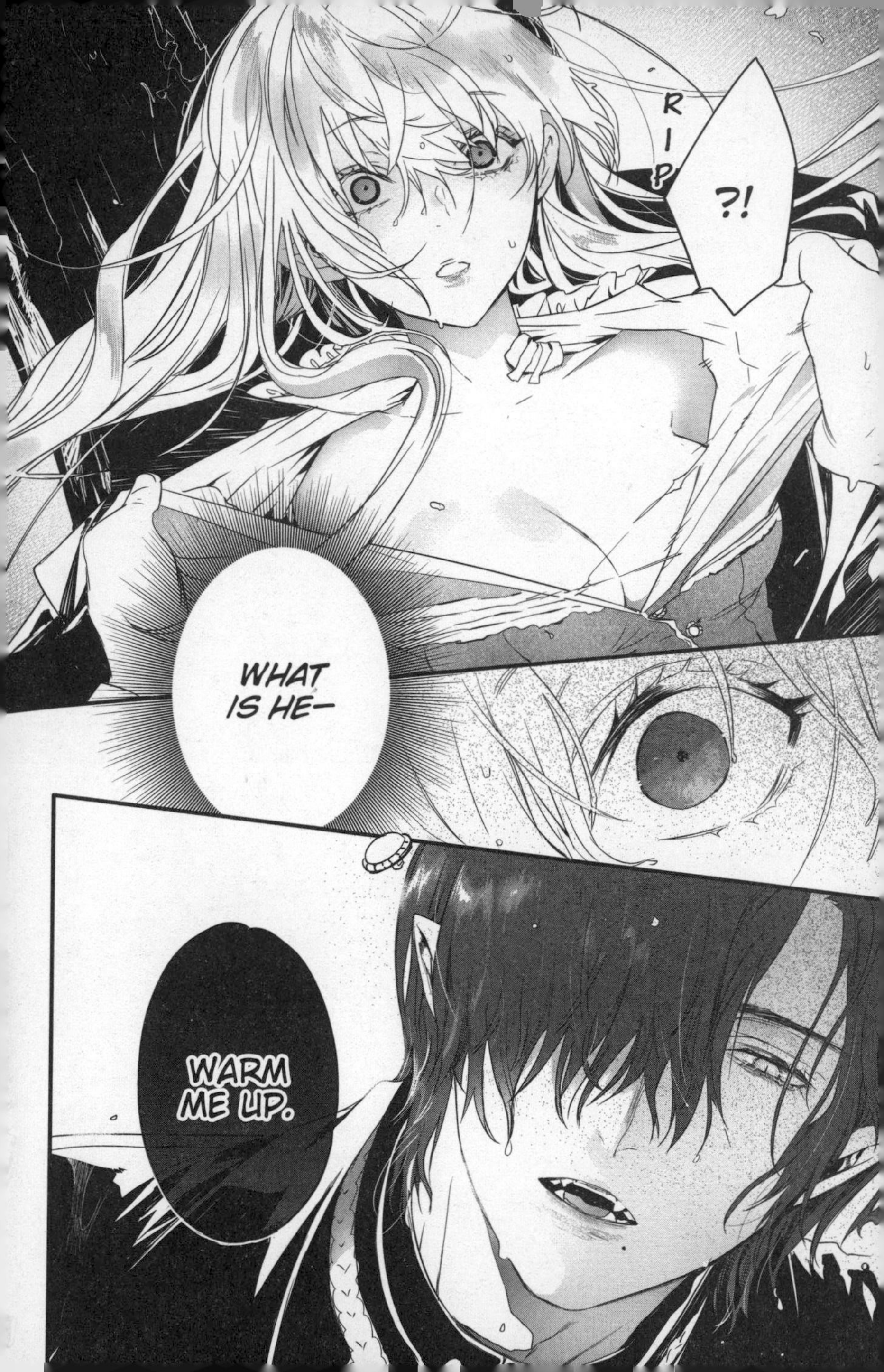
RIP
?!
WHAT IS HE—
WARM ME UP.

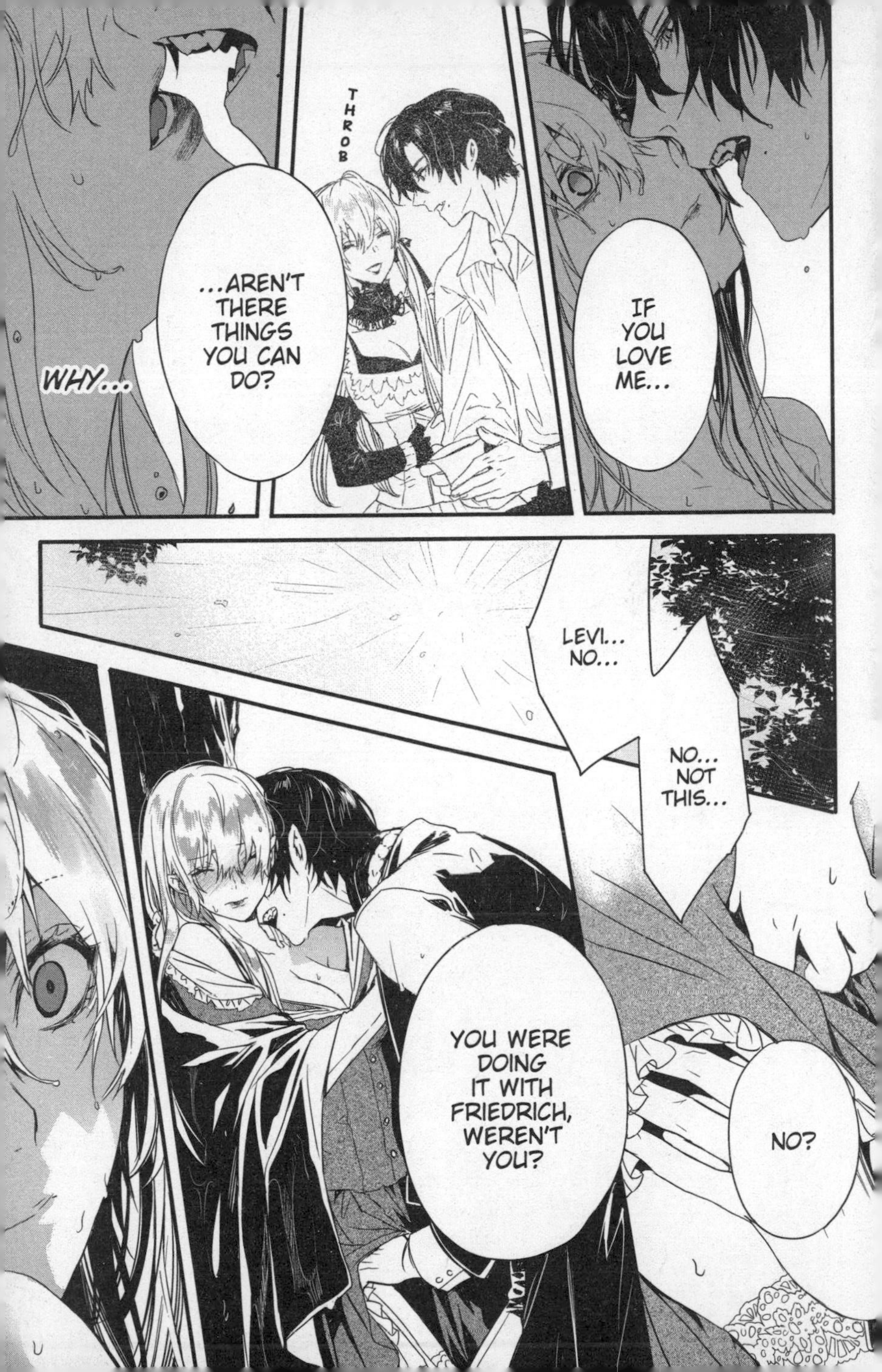
IF YOU LOVE ME...
THROB
...AREN'T THERE THINGS YOU CAN DO?
WHY...
LEVI... NO...
NO... NOT THIS...
NO?
YOU WERE DOING IT WITH FRIEDRICH, WEREN'T YOU?

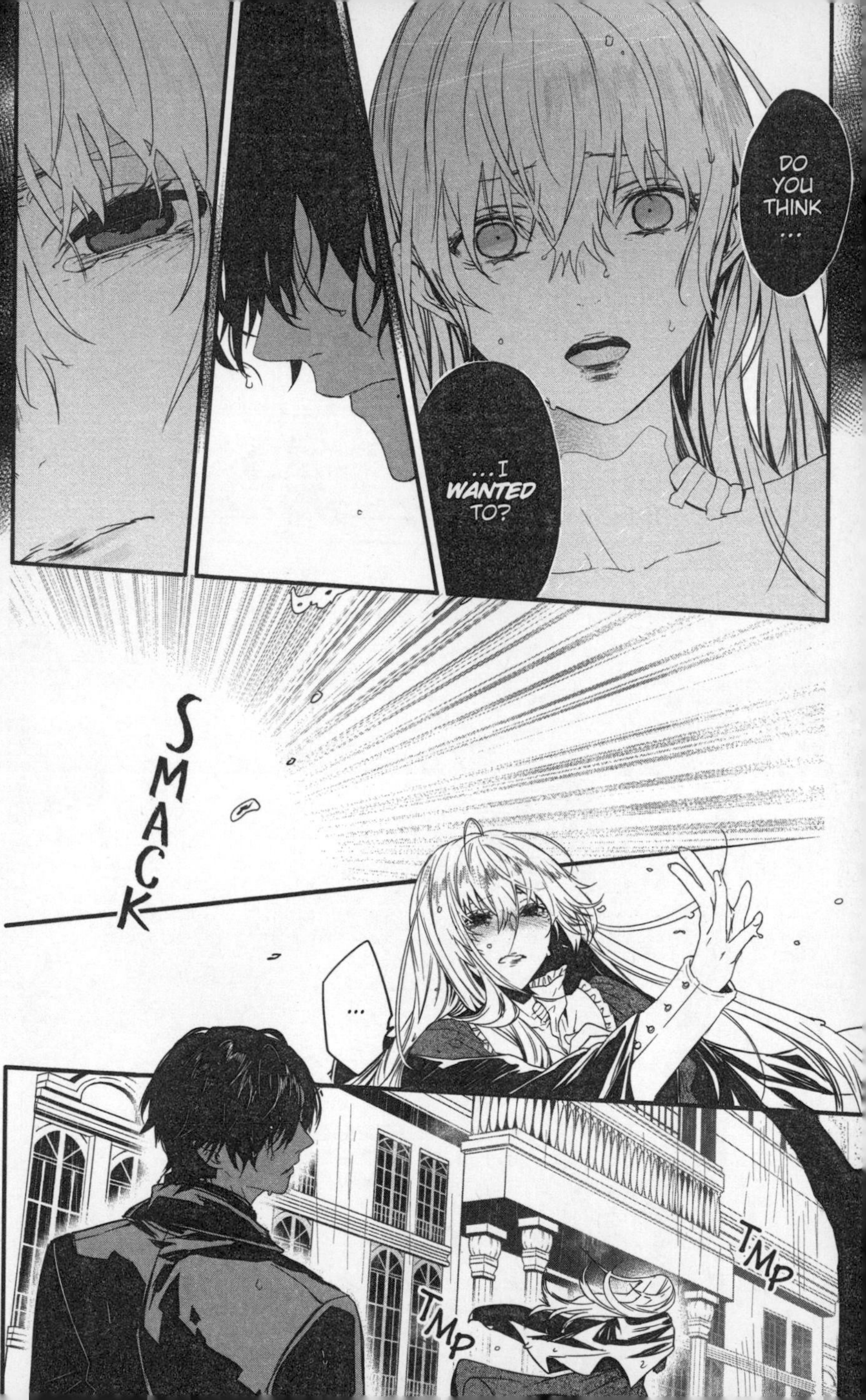
DO YOU THINK ...
...I WANTED TO?
SMACK
...
TMP
TMP

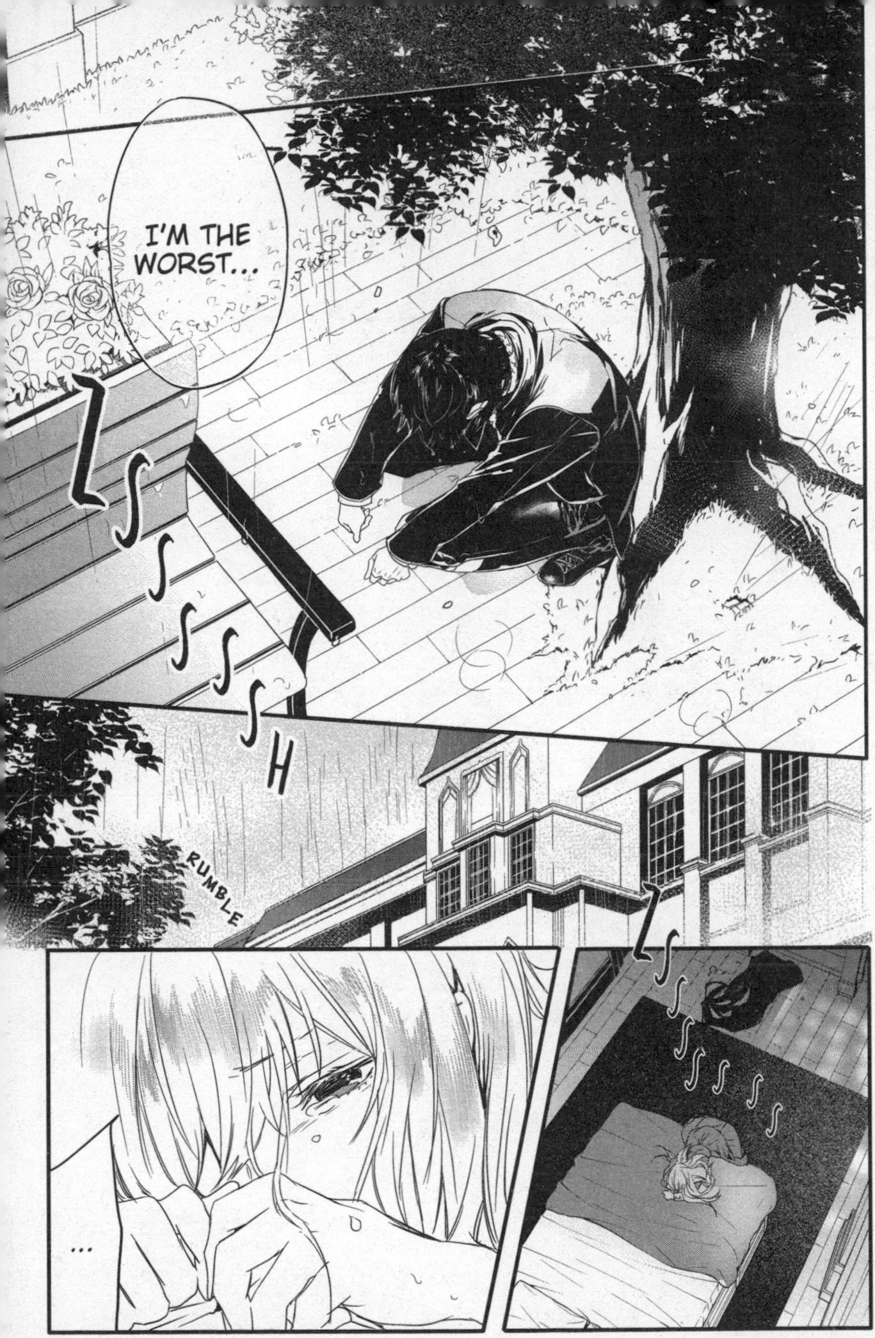
I'M THE WORST...
ZSSSSSH
RUMBLE
...
ZSSSSSS

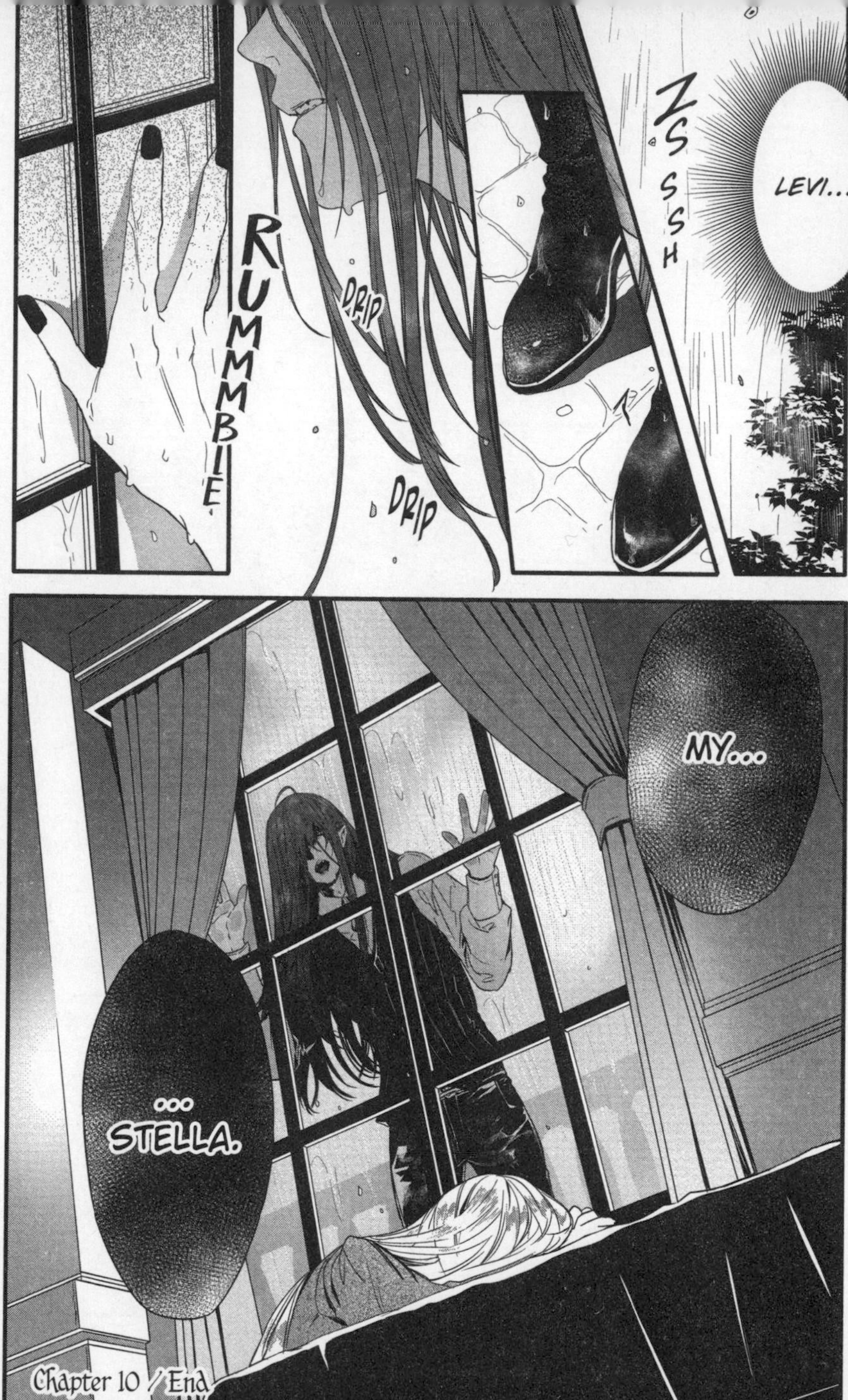
LEVI...
ZSSSH
DRIP
DRIP
RUMMMBLE
MY...
...STELLA.
Chapter 10 / End

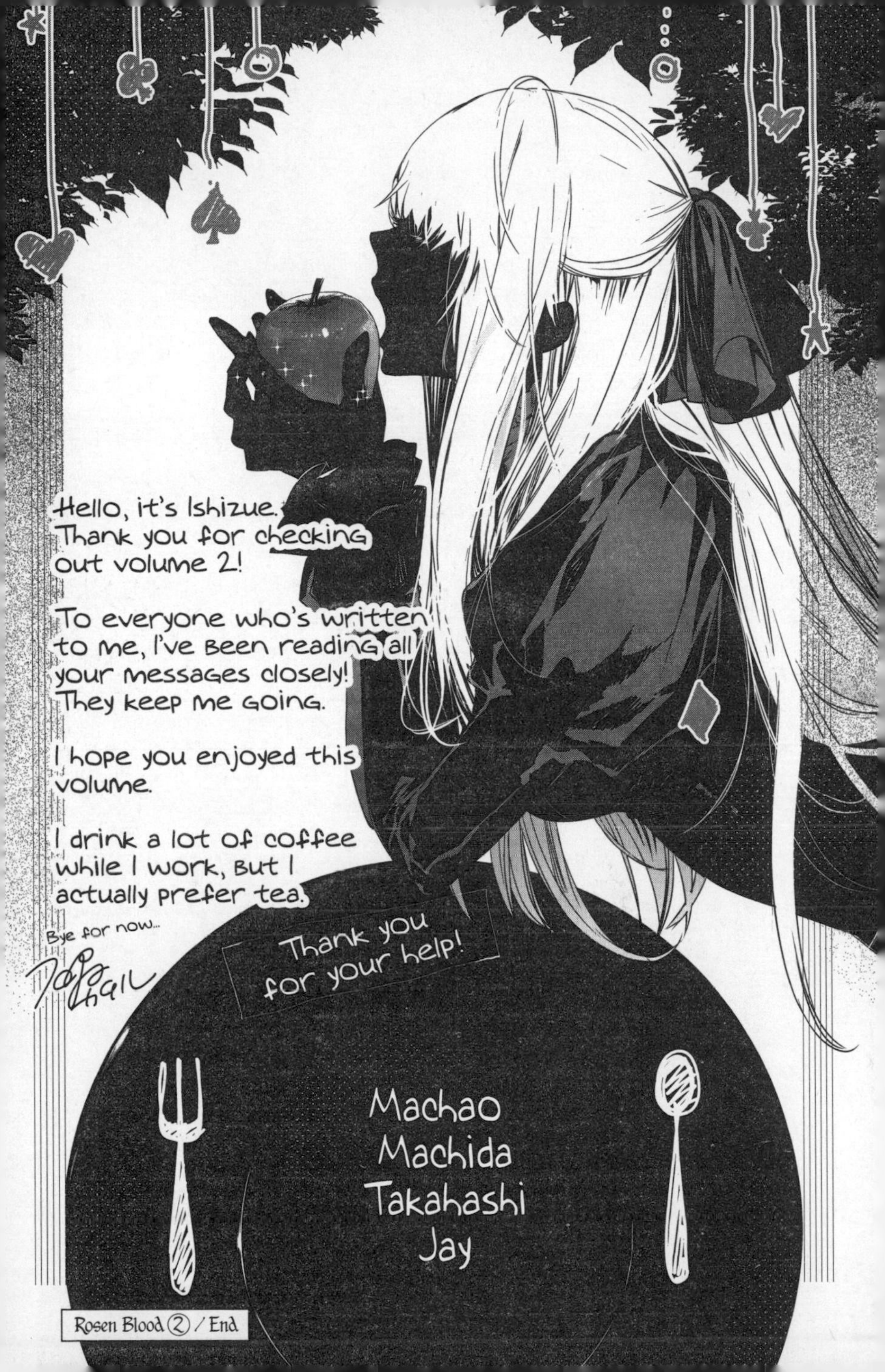
Hello, it's Ishizue.
Thank you for checking out volume 2!
To everyone who's written to me, I've been reading all your messages closely! They keep me going.
I hope you enjoyed this volume.
I drink a lot of coffee while I work, but I actually prefer tea.
Bye for now...
Thank you for your help!
Machao
Machida
Takahashi
Jay
Rosen Blood ② / End

KACHIRU ISHIZUE

Born on October 12 in Yamanashi
Prefecture, Kachiru Ishizue
is a Libra with blood type O.
She is the author of *Kuutei Kaiko
Toshi* (Airborne Nostalgia City)
and also works as an illustrator.
Rosen Blood is her first
work published in English.
Her Twitter handle is @kachiru_i.

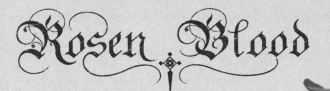

Rosen Blood

VOLUME 2

SHOJO BEAT EDITION

STORY AND ART BY

KACHIRU ISHIZUE

English Adaptation ❖ **Ysabet Reinhardt MacFarlane**
Translation ❖ **JN Productions**
Touch-Up Art & Lettering ❖ **Joanna Estep**
Design ❖ **Alice Lewis**
Editor ❖ **Jennifer Sherman**

First published in Japan in 2019 by Akita Publishing Co., Ltd., Tokyo
English translation rights arranged with Akita Publishing Co., Ltd.
through Tuttle-Mori Agency, Inc., Tokyo

Printed in the U.S.A.

Published by VIZ Media, LLC
P.O. Box 77010
San Francisco, CA 94107

10 9 8 7 6 5 4 3 2 1
First printing, March 2022

ratings.viz.com RATED T+ OLDER TEEN

PARENTAL ADVISORY
ROSEN BLOOD is rated T+ for Older Teen and is recommended for ages 16 and up. This volume contains violence and suggestive themes.

VIZ MEDIA
viz.com

Shojo Beat
shojobeat.com

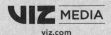

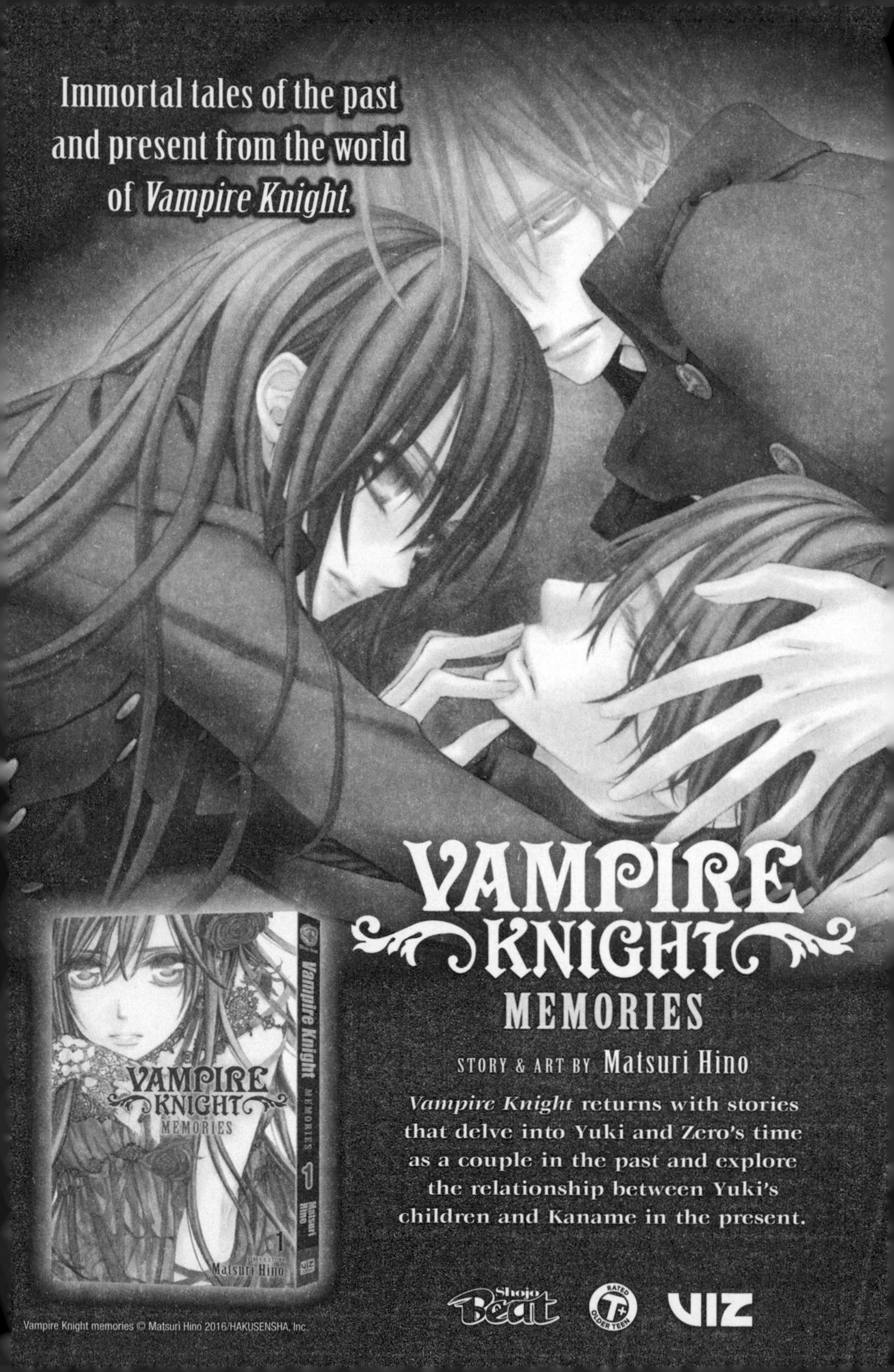
Immortal tales of the past and present from the world of *Vampire Knight.*
VAMPIRE KNIGHT
MEMORIES
STORY & ART BY Matsuri Hino
Vampire Knight returns with stories that delve into Yuki and Zero's time as a couple in the past and explore the relationship between Yuki's children and Kaname in the present.
Vampire Knight MEMORIES 1 Matsuri Hino
Shojo Beat
RATED T+ OLDER TEEN
VIZ
Vampire Knight memories © Matsuri Hino 2016/HAKUSENSHA, Inc.

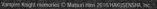

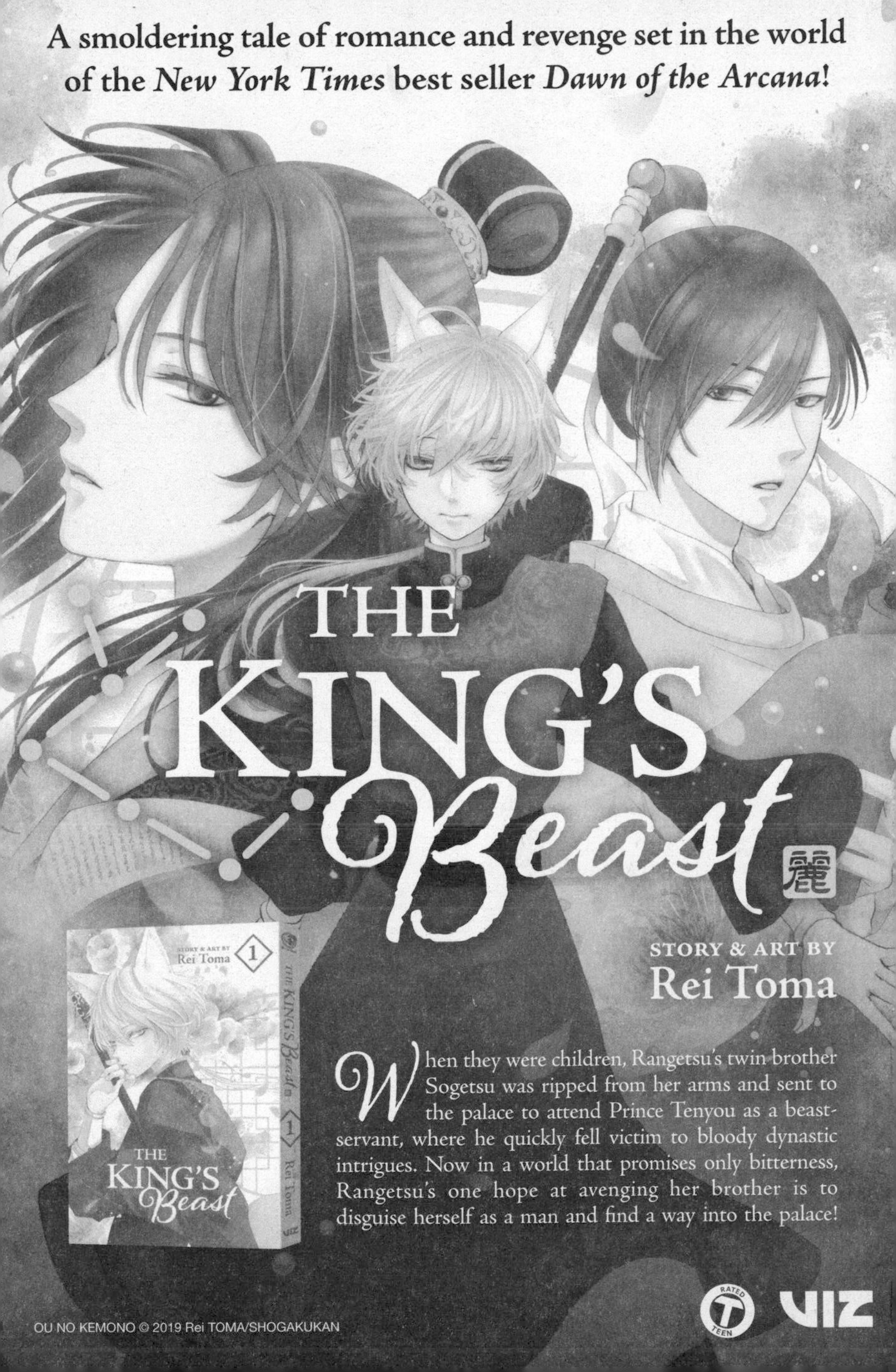
A smoldering tale of romance and revenge set in the world of the *New York Times* best seller *Dawn of the Arcana*!
THE KING'S Beast
STORY & ART BY Rei Toma
1
THE KING'S Beast
When they were children, Rangetsu's twin brother Sogetsu was ripped from her arms and sent to the palace to attend Prince Tenyou as a beast-servant, where he quickly fell victim to bloody dynastic intrigues. Now in a world that promises only bitterness, Rangetsu's one hope at avenging her brother is to disguise herself as a man and find a way into the palace!
RATED T TEEN
VIZ
OU NO KEMONO © 2019 Rei TOMA/SHOGAKUKAN

"**Bloody**" **Mary**, a vampire with a death wish, has spent the past 400 years chasing down a modern-day exorcist named Maria who is thought to have inherited "The Blood of Maria" and is the only one who can kill Mary. To Mary's dismay, Maria doesn't know how to kill vampires. Desperate to die, Mary agrees to become Maria's bodyguard until Maria can find a way to kill him.

Story and Art by
akaza samamiya

The Water Dragon's Bride

Story & Art by
Rei Toma

In the blink of an eye, a modern-day girl
named Asahi is whisked away from her
warm and happy home and stranded in a
strange and mysterious world where she
meets a water dragon god!

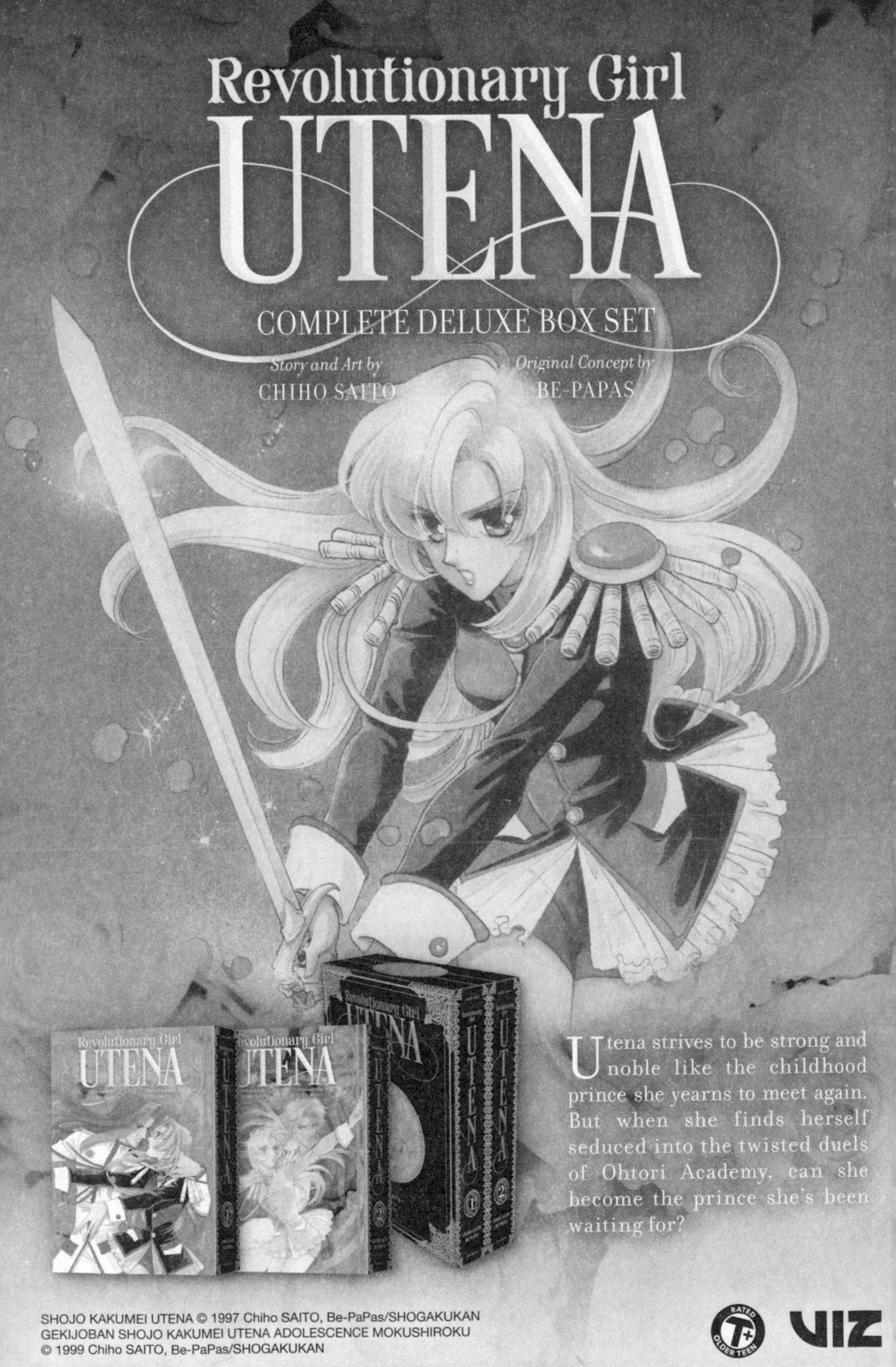
Revolutionary Girl
UTENA
COMPLETE DELUXE BOX SET
Story and Art by
CHIHO SAITO
Original Concept by
BE-PAPAS
Utena strives to be strong and noble like the childhood prince she yearns to meet again. But when she finds herself seduced into the twisted duels of Ohtori Academy, can she become the prince she's been waiting for?
SHOJO KAKUMEI UTENA © 1997 Chiho SAITO, Be-PaPas/SHOGAKUKAN
GEKIJOBAN SHOJO KAKUMEI UTENA ADOLESCENCE MOKUSHIROKU
© 1999 Chiho SAITO, Be-PaPas/SHOGAKUKAN
RATED T+ OLDER TEEN
VIZ

STOP!

You may be reading the wrong way!

In keeping with the original Japanese comic format, this book reads from right to left—so word balloons, action, and sound effects are reversed to preserve the orientation of the original artwork.

Check out the diagram shown here to get the hang of things, and then turn to the other side of the book to get started!

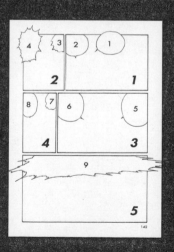